The Johns Hopkins University Studies in
Historical and Political Science
122nd Series (2004)

George Calvert

Cecil Calvert

Charles Calvert

English and Catholic

The Lords Baltimore in the Seventeenth Century

John D. Krugler

The Johns Hopkins University Press

Baltimore and London

© 2004 The Johns Hopkins University Press
All rights reserved. Published 2004
Printed in the United States of America on acid-free paper
9 8 7 6 5 4 3 2 1

The Johns Hopkins University Press
2715 North Charles Street
Baltimore, Maryland 21218-4363
www.press.jhu.edu

Library of Congress Cataloging-in-Publication Data

Krugler, John D., 1940–
  English and Catholic: the Lords Baltimore in the seventeenth century
/ John D. Krugler.
     p. cm.
  Includes bibliographical references and index.
  ISBN 0-8018-7963-9 (hardcover : acid-free paper)
  1. Calvert family. 2. Colonial administrators—Maryland—Biography. 3.
Businessmen—Maryland—Biography. 4. Landowners—Maryland—Biog-
raphy. 5. Catholics—Maryland—Biography. 6. Colonial administrators—
Great Britain—Biography. 7. Catholics—Great Britain—Biography. 8.
Church and state—Great Britain—History—17th century. 9. Church and
state—Maryland—History—17th century. 10. Maryland—History—Colo-
nial period, ca. 1600–1775. I. Title.
  F184.K78 2004
  975.2′02′0922—dc22   2003027316

A catalog record for this book is available from the British Library.

Frontispiece: George Calvert by Daniel Mytens the elder, a painter at the
court of James I. Copy made by Willem Wirtz during Maryland's
Tercentenary and owned by Historic St. Mary's City. The Enoch Pratt Free
Library currently owns the original. Cecil Calvert by Gerard Soest, court
painter to King Charles II, c. 1670. Copy made by Willem Wirtz during
Maryland's Tercentenary from an earlier copy made by Florence Mckubin
and owned by Historic St. Mary's City. The Enoch Pratt Free Library currently owns the original. Charles Calvert, attributed to Peter Lely. Copy
made by Ada Cole Chase during Maryland's Tercentenary and owned by
Historic St. Mary's City. Dr. and Mrs. T. Morris Murray owned the original in 1934. Images courtesy of Historic St. Mary's City.

For Dee,
my companion and soul mate

Contents

Preface

Religion and politics, church and state, uniformity and dissent: commingling them in the sixteenth and seventeenth centuries created a maze that the English had difficulty traversing. Consider the example of Tobie Mathew. In 1608 he was incarcerated in the Fleet. He petitioned the king's Privy Council for his release. A recent convert to Roman Catholicism, Mathew believed that the archbishop of Canterbury had imprisoned him solely for a matter of conscience. The prisoner steadfastly maintained that his altered "opinion of Religion" was of no consequence to the government because it did not affect his "loyal and obedient harte to the king and the state." Mathew's statement defied accepted wisdom. The practice of religious uniformity—one state, one religion—made diversity of opinion on religion dangerous. The penal laws that followed the English Reformation attempted to force English Catholics to choose between their church and their nation. After extended negotiations, Mathew gained his freedom. The price? The government banished the unrepentant recusant from his homeland. Mathew, who was the son of the Protestant archbishop of York, became a Catholic priest. Curiously, the king later knighted him for loyal service. A tangled web indeed.

The story that follows considers another case of lives divided between allegiance to church and to state. This saga follows Mathew's classmate and friend George Calvert, the first baron of Baltimore, and his family. Beyond their successes and failures as English colonial entrepreneurs, it tells of conflicted and divided loyalties that confronted individuals attempting to live as both English and Catholic.

Pursuit of worldly fortune led the peripatetic elder Calvert to London, to European capitals, to Ireland, to Newfoundland, and finally to the banks of the Chesapeake Bay. He was, among other things, a Yorkshireman, a courtier during the reign of James I, a politician and diplomat, a sometime Catholic, a sometime conforming Protestant, an owner of extensive land, a capitalist, and a colonizer. He conceived the family's colonial enterprises and experienced the tribulations of colonization firsthand, but he died before the Maryland charter received its final approval. That left implementation of his objectives to his eldest son, Cecil, the second Lord Baltimore. Cecil's son Charles, the third Lord Baltimore, eventually inherited a prosperous colony but lost it when a rebellion stripped him of his proprietary power.

Expanding their king's dominions to North America in the seventeenth century provided the English with the opportunity to reshape the existing relationship between the state and the church, institutions that both enhanced and restricted human freedom. Colonies such as Virginia replicated, to the extent possible in the crude conditions of the New World, the model employed at home: a church established by law that required inhabitants to conform to its polity. Other English colonies, such as Massachusetts, rejected the Church of England model and created a new relationship based on a congregational polity. This model, which left the spiritual and the temporal intimately intertwined, afforded new liberties to those who qualified but denied the liberties to many. One colony, Maryland, broke the mold completely and fashioned a new and radically different model for church-state relations. That colony became part of an escalating struggle in seventeenth-century England and English America to liberate the human mind from governmentally imposed restraints affecting religion and politics.

What did the Calverts' commitment to living as Catholics in Protestant England mean, not only for individual goals, but for some of the larger political and religious questions that the English faced? The discrepancy between traditional interpretations and the historical record led me to this reconsideration of the Catholic Lords Baltimore and their responses to the tensions that existed for those who lived as both English nationals and Roman Catholics in the seventeenth century. What circumstances and ideas motivated this Catholic family to risk their lives and their fortunes in the uncertain business of colonization? How did they implement their radical ideas? This study invites readers to think anew about the Catholic Lords Baltimore and their accomplishments in seventeenth-century England and North America.

This book came into being not solely from the exertions of the author. Indeed, I am overwhelmed as I reflect on the number of colleagues, relatives, and friends who contributed to the completion of this study. I regret that the debts incurred in researching and writing cannot be adequately acknowledged in the allotted space. Many cannot even be called by name. These include the librarians and archivists in Maryland and the United Kingdom who assisted in the research and permitted me to copy their documents. I am especially grateful to the staffs at the British Library, the Public Record Office, the Maryland Historical Society, and the Maryland Hall of Records, among others. Reference librarians at the University of Illinois and Marquette University (exemplified by my colleague Dr. John Jentz) assisted by acquiring needed documents, books, and articles. Dozens of research assistants at Marquette contributed to gathering data, checking sources, and compiling bibliographies. Support from my department chairs and graduate deans advanced this study in ways that are not always evident in the text. I would be remiss not to acknowledge the assistance of the many secretaries and administrative assistants who provided the behind-the-scenes assistance that all too often goes unrecognized. I also am indebted to the journals (and their editors) that have published earlier versions of my work. I appreciate being able to use portions of those articles.

On an individual level, the assistance of a number of persons and institutions must be acknowledged. Graduate Dean Thaddeus Burch, S.J., and the Marquette Committee on Research financially supported this book in its various manifestations. Thanks also to the Bradley Institute for Democracy and Public Values for its research support. Erik McDermott, S.J., as he closed out his academic career at Georgetown University, gave me his extensive collection of notes on early Maryland. Not possessing George Calvert's familiarity with foreign languages, I sought help from my colleagues Professors John Patrick Donnelly, S.J., Julius R. Ruff, James Krysiek (now at Mount St. Mary's College), and German Carrillo, who graciously translated documents from Latin, French, and Spanish. Other colleagues, Professors Ronald E. Zupko and Athan G. Theoharis and Dr. John Berens (now of the University of Wisconsin—Oshkosh), read earlier versions of this work. Psychology professor Stephan Franzoi assisted with aspects of social-behavior theory.

Professors David F. Healy, who rekindled my interest in history at Illinois College, and Raymond Phineas Stearns, who served as my graduate mentor at the University of Illinois, deserve special recognition for their confidence in my work. Professor Thomas E. Hachey, now of Boston College but a longtime colleague, provided valuable support.

My colleagues at Historic St. Mary's City, Dr. Henry M. Miller, Dr. Martin Sullivan, Dorsey Bodeman, and Silas Hurry, contributed in a variety of ways. I am especially grateful to the Historic St. Mary's Commission for permission to reprint its portraits of the Catholic Lords Baltimore.

A number of people contributed endless hours reading the manuscript as it went through its various emendations. Professor David F. Krugler at the University of Wisconsin—Platteville read the first draft and offered excellent counsel. Dr. Timothy Riordan at Historic St. Mary's City read an early version and saved me from numerous errors. Marjorie Hutchinson of Menomonee Falls, Wisconsin, generously proofread two versions of the manuscript and contributed to making the final product eminently more readable. The grande dame of Chesapeake studies, Dr. Lois Carr, read the manuscript for The Johns Hopkins University Press and provided excellent advice that greatly strengthened the final version. This is a book she easily could have written: I am grateful that she left some space for me. My colleague Professor John Pustejovsky read parts of the manuscript and offered sage observations for improving the text. At the Press, many contributed to translating an overly long manuscript into a book. I especially acknowledge history editor Bob Brugger and copy editor Lois Crum. Collectively, they did their best to save me from errors of fact and confusions in the text. Final responsibility for what I have written rests solely with me.

No one knows the solitary life of the scholar better than a spouse. Dee lived the project longer than either of us wish to recount. Without her support, especially during the past six years, this book would not have been possible. I dedicate the study to her, but also to Fred Krugler; to David Krugler, who is not only my son but also a trusted colleague, Amy Lewis; to Katie, Mike, Megan, and Kayla Pospisil; and to the memories of Raymond Phineas Stearns, Donald M. Parkinson, Roy and Florine Olson, Brett Michael Pospisil, and Marge Krugler.

A Note on Spelling and Dates

The seventeenth-century quotations have been left as they were printed or written, except that I have silently converted certain sixteenth- and seventeenth-century conventions to modern ones. For example, *v* is converted to *u*, and *i* converted to *j*. In addition, I have expanded abbreviated words to make the quotations more readable. I have made no effort to bring the rich variation in spelling (the bane of spell-checker programs) into conformity with modern usage. Dates are for the most part in the old-style calendar that the English used until 1722. The new year began on March 25 (Maryland's founding day in 1634). Thus, letters written between January 1 and March 25 are dated as, for example, March 6, 1620/21. Letters from diplomats and other foreign observers in England as well as Catholic priests are either in the new-style calendar or double dated, for example, March 6/16, 1621, or March 6, 1620/21.

English and Catholic

"A man is not English who gives first allegiance elsewhere"

Reconciling National and Religious Loyalties in an Age of Uniformity

In early modern England, the state assumed that secular and religious loyalties were indistinguishable. To be English in the sixteenth and seventeenth centuries meant regular worship in the Church of England. To be English and Catholic raised a troubling question regarding civic loyalty: did those who failed to conform in religion forfeit their claims as English nationals? George Calvert and his heirs felt and responded to the tensions that existed for those who lived as both English nationals and Roman Catholics. Could English Catholics successfully pursue their material interests in an inhospitable Protestant world and maintain their loyalty to the state while offering their spiritual allegiance to the pope, a foreign prince? The state, through its elaborate set of penal laws, said no; the Calverts, with some interesting twists and turns, said yes. In the face of rabid anti-Catholicism, endemic in English culture, they confronted a parallel issue: could English Catholics and Protestants live together and prosper? Experience, not only in England but in other European cultures as well, suggested no; the Calverts said yes. English penal laws made reconciling temporal obligations and religious allegiance difficult but, as the English Catholic Calverts demonstrated, not impossible.

The independent Church of England resulted from Henry VIII's personal quarrel with the Roman Catholic Church in the 1530s. Severing ties with the Catholic hierarchy fragmented religious institutions and created new issues about loyalty for civil authorities. Much of the debate on these issues centered on English Catholics. As Church of England bishop John Hooper accurately characterized the situation in 1546: "Our king has destroyed the pope, but not popery."[1]

The presence of a substantial number of English Catholics who no longer shared a common religious commitment with their monarch aroused intense anxiety. The new arrangement compelled English magistrates, clerics, and intellectuals to determine the proper role of civil government in religious matters. To ensure stability, religious leaders conceded the dominant role to the state. Religious uniformity became received doctrine and made religion the handmaiden of the state. The monarch and Parliament served as protectors of the "true religion." The entente came with a price, however. It made religious decisions public; it denied individuals the right to choose how they worshiped; and it allowed civil authorities to dominate the human conscience.

Successive English governments committed to the belief that all subjects must accept a common form of worship and doctrine. The country vacillated between Protestantism and Catholicism until the religious settlement of 1559 and its subsequent revisions compelled subjects to worship in the Protestant state church. Through a series of laws that became increasingly severe, the government attempted to proscribe the new Church's enemies—Roman Catholics and dissenting radical Protestants (aka Puritans). These laws destroyed the Catholic Church in England and wreaked havoc in the Catholic community. Most Catholics eventually conformed to the state church. However, those Catholics who survived and kept the faith alive demonstrated remarkable adroitness at avoiding the full impact of the penal laws. As a result, the laws, hampered by the government's inconsistent enforcement, did little to erase Protestant uneasiness regarding Catholic loyalty to the state. Protestants assumed that Catholics gave their highest allegiance to Rome, thereby forfeiting their status as English subjects.

This belief that Catholics could not be loyal members of the body politic not only created anxiety among Protestants, but it agitated Catholics as well. Some, such as George and Cecil Calvert, responded to a heartfelt desire to demonstrate their national loyalties. By their actions, they manifested their intentions to work for the best interests of the English nation. This, in turn, created some practical issues that they had to confront: How would allegiance to Catholicism after 1624 affect the implementation of their economic, political, and religious agendas? What strategies could they adopt that would enable them to succeed without running afoul of the penal laws? Most English Catholics knew that calling undue attention to themselves and their projects heightened anti-Catholic sentiments and led to calls for stricter enforcement of the penal laws. Founding colonies in America was hardly an inconspicuous undertaking. Not only did Catholics feel the tensions between national loyalty and religious allegiance with an intensity that Protestants did not, but their efforts to resolve them also entailed greater risks.

One interpretation that long prevailed in Maryland historiography held that the Catholic Lords Baltimore responded to a set of repressive laws that drove them to found a colony for their persecuted coreligionists in English America. This view failed to explain in any full sense the forces that motivated them. Certain terms associated with this interpretation—*conservative Catholics*, *martyrs*, *feudal lords*, and *pilgrims*—reflected a misleading perspective: the Catholic as victim. They emphasized Catholic suffering and Catholics' need to flee England. As one priest put it, Catholics were "persecuted, proscribed, and hunted to death for their religion." There was no question that Catholic persecution was real, but did it encompass the experiences of all English Catholics?[2]

This interpretation misrepresented and undervalued the Calverts' accomplishments on a number of counts. First, the Catholic Calverts never acted like victims. Second, it failed to reconcile their religious objectives with the economic and personal motives that pushed these Catholic entrepreneurs. Third, "the Catholic as victim" view overlooked the success of the Catholic Calverts in securing a potentially lucrative grant to thousands of acres in the Chesapeake region from an oppressive government. Fourth, it did not consider George Calvert's rampant nationalism. Fifth, it did not explain the disinterest of English Catholics in relocating to America. Finally, and perhaps most important, the traditional historical view never came to grips with the Calverts' Catholicism.

Another dominant interpretation stood in marked contrast to the "Catholic as victim" perspective. It presented the Lords Baltimore as colonial entrepreneurs who acted solely or primarily for economic gain. This interpretation also misrepresented or undervalued the Calverts' accomplishments. Although it overcame some of the deficiencies of the Maryland-as-a-religious-refuge thesis, it failed to explain why the Calverts persisted as Catholics after 1624. Treating economic objectives and religious motives separately did not capture what the

Calverts accomplished. Neither did acknowledging that both profoundly influenced the Calverts. A fuller understanding of Calvert behavior can be achieved by showing the enigmatic relationship between religious and economic factors.

This study relies on terms such as *nationalism, privatization, secularization, volunteerism, pluralism, practical visionaries, capitalists, pragmatic,* and *reckless innovators,* which flow from a contrasting perspective and present a different image: the Catholic as victor. It was not easy, but some English Catholics beat the system and flourished. Families like the Calverts, who willingly risked practicing their faith openly while pursuing public goals, helped to keep the Catholic religion alive in England and in America. Rather than seeing the Catholic Calverts as running from something negative (government persecution), this study sees them as moving toward something positive (founding viable English colonial enterprises). These terms better explicate why they did what they did, why they succeeded, and why they failed. They explain the most intriguing element of their saga: why this Catholic family's colonial enterprises became part of one of the great movements of the sixteenth and seventeenth centuries, the struggle to free the human conscience, especially in matters of religion, from the dictates of civil governments that demanded religious uniformity.

This account begins with the concept of uniformity and the pernicious penal legislation, the elaborate set of laws designed to force English Catholics to conform to the state church and thereby confirm their loyalty to the nation. These laws complicated George Calvert's life. If his life illustrates some of the disruptive and contentious characteristics of the English Reformation, it also calls attention to one of the ways Catholics responded to the threats. His childhood provided him with two examples for countering these laws. One, that of his stepmother, modeled tenacious loyalty to the ancient faith. The other, that of his father, modeled conformity to the state church. George Calvert followed the example of his father in 1592 and conformed to the state religion.

In many respects, George Calvert the conformist seems an unlikely reformer, an improbable advocate of freedom of conscience. It was not a role he sought. Rather, three factors, above others, brought him face-to-face with the issue of potentially conflicting loyalties. One was religious in nature. Although born a Roman Catholic, for most of his life Calvert conformed to the state religion; eventually he reasserted his allegiance to the Catholic faith. For him, reconciling religious and secular allegiances was more than an intellectual exercise; it was part of his very being.

Another factor, which he initially separated from the first, was secular. Building a career at court (1603–25) also defined Calvert's life. His cautious nature, his language skills, his administrative abilities, his lack of financial independence, and his willingness to work within the idiosyncratic structure of court politics suited him well for advancement. His experiences as a courtier brought him into constant contact with issues involving religious allegiance. For more than five years, he negotiated the king's major foreign policy objectives and administered the government from London. But in 1624 the world he had so carefully crafted collapsed. His continued support of the Spanish match, the ill-fated effort to marry James's heir to a Spanish princess, made him odious and forced his resignation as secretary of state.

However unhappy the circumstances of that resignation in February 1625, he retired a rich man with an Irish title, baron of Baltimore, and extensive land holdings in England, Ireland, and America. More important, he left on good terms with his many friends in the government. His departure from the Privy Council in March provided an opportunity to pursue his colonial enterprises. Equally significant, Calvert realized during the crisis that led to his resignation that he could resolve a long-standing personal religious controversy. He converted to his childhood religion and, for the remainder of his life, lived openly as a Catholic.

The third factor, his intention to profit from his colonial enterprises, brought the first two together. An interest in extending the empire and increasing his own wealth further defined his life. As early as the mid–sixteenth century, some Englishmen saw the unlimited possibilities and risked life and capital to take advantage of overseas expansion. George Calvert joined a select company of venturers who saw an opportunity to gain wealth, enhance their status, and enlarge the king's dominions. As a conforming courtier, he had invested in overseas enterprises such as the Virginia and East India companies for very practical reasons. The profits of office and his influence allowed him to purchase, or secure through grants, land in Yorkshire, Newfoundland, and Ireland. After 1625 the now Catholic first Lord Baltimore acted *boldly* and *confidently* in pursuing his colonial interests. He resourcefully combined English nationalism and Catholicism with his desire to exploit the New World's potential.

Juxtaposing two seemingly contradictory objectives—English and Catholic—necessitated a dose of caution as well. Nothing makes sense without seeing that the Calverts acted to secure their religious freedom and the right of their coreligionists to worship without fear of the penal laws. However, this created a paradox: they needed to pursue that (Catholic) goal without seeming too Catholic. The brilliance of their vision, to say nothing of its execution, enabled them to achieve both objectives. Simply put, presenting them as victims who fled England in the face of persecution drained much of the vitality from the story. The "Catholic as victim" view failed to recognize that, despite the peaks and valleys, the story of the Catholic Lords Baltimore is not only one of Catholic survival in seventeenth-century England and America, but also one of triumph.

Their colonial enterprises allowed the Calverts to join another select group of English subjects: the handful of Catholics and dissenting Protestants who struggled to liberate the human mind and soul from governmentally imposed restraints. The first two Catholic Lords Baltimore established colonies in English North America that promised liberty of conscience to the Christians who joined with them. They envisioned a prosperous and peaceful community that would provide them with wealth, status, and freedom from the onerous penal laws that restricted Catholic worship in England. They acted on the belief that they could not affirm liberty of conscience for themselves and other Catholics without extending that liberty to all who came to their colonies. To accomplish this end, they severed the traditional relationship between secular and religious institutions. The Calverts threw out the dominant doctrine of religious uniformity. Liberty of conscience was one of the means by which they intended to achieve their colonial objectives.[3]

Another means by which the Calverts sought to satisfy their ambitions was the manorial system. Their use of contradictory elements—profiting from a capitalist enterprise that entailed embracing vestiges of a dying feudal age—demonstrated the brilliance of their plans. In the Calvert vision, the manor deftly brought together their economic and religious goals. The Calverts knew the manorial system intimately and recognized that manors had ensured Catholic survival, especially in the North of England. This institution, with its potential for social control, and liberty of conscience, with its potential to reduce factionalism, would serve as agents for creating the peaceful society they desired.

Entrepreneurs George and Cecil Calvert were practical visionaries. Those who championed liberty of conscience for idealistic or philosophical reasons usually fell short of their goals. Not so with these pragmatic English Catholics. Religious decisions made in England compelled them to be recklessly innovative as they conceived their colonial enterprises in Newfoundland and in Maryland. In an era characterized by religious strife and warfare, they believed that they could build prosperous colonial societies only if religion remained a private matter. Well in advance of those English radicals who founded a colony in Rhode Island or those who led the English nation into civil war in the 1640s, the Calverts envisioned a pluralistic society where religious beliefs were private and outside the guardianship or interference of civil authorities. They created a form of "religious *laissez-faire*" that allowed individuals to determine their own religious commitments.[4]

George and Cecil Calvert assumed that they could find ways to bridge the gap between English and Catholic. To accomplish this they had to overcome Protestant views that hardly flattered Catholics. Not only did Protestants perceive the religion as filled with gross ignorance and superstition; they saw the pope as a foreign prince whose assertion of the right to excommunicate and depose rulers struck boldly at English nationalism. As one English bishop put it: the "pope amongst Catholics is as powerful a governor as any temporal prince." Thus, allegiance to one negated faithfulness to the other. By their actions, first in Newfoundland and then in Maryland, the Calverts would demonstrate that English and Catholic were not mutually exclusive loyalties and that Catholics could act in the best interests of the English nation. Here they acted courageously, *almost* as if their Catholicism was not a factor in what they did to enhance the empire and their own well-being. Pride in England was not the exclusive domain of Protestants. Charles's government generously granted land along the Chesapeake to these Catholic Calverts because they implemented English goals.[5]

The first Lord Baltimore's death in April 1632, shortly before the Maryland charter received final approval, meant that his young and inexperienced son Cecil had to manage the enterprise. Untested as a leader, in some ways he became the most remarkable of the three Catholic Lords Baltimore. The young lord benefited from his father's experiences in Avalon and shared his father's ambitions. He, too, sought a place where he could enjoy the privileges that came as proprietor of his own domain, where he and those who ventured with him could prosper, and where he and his coreligionists could worship without the threat of the vexatious penal laws. Cecil Calvert's actions conformed to a position later articulated by William Penn: "Though I desire to extend religious freedom, yet I want some recompense for my trouble."[6]

Like his father, Cecil understood that most men acted on the basis of their material interests, and he proposed to satisfy them. The "Maryland designe" coupled liberty of conscience in religious matters with the opportunity to pursue worldly goals unimpeded by religious restraints. This, he reasoned, would ensure the cooperation and loyalty of both Protestants and Catholics who now had a material stake in the enterprise and a reason to work for its success. The formula was simple. He distributed land to those (lords of the manors) who invested most substantially in the enterprise, in order to gain their loyalty. He privatized religious practices. His government would not support religious institutions, nor would the proprietor force Marylanders to worship. In Maryland, religion conveyed neither privilege nor liability. The uncertainty that loomed large was whether the religiously diverse English immigrants who sailed under his banner could accept the innovations.[7]

Although the vision was straightforward, its implementation was complex. With religious issues arising at every juncture, could this Catholic family and their coreligionists surmount the English penal legislation, overcome traditional Protestant hostilities, and prosper? What the second Lord Baltimore sought was too novel, too drastic, to have unfolded without wrinkles. Events in the first twenty-seven years, from 1634 to 1661, severely tested his skills, resources, and patience. Time and time again, the Virginians or his colonists challenged the basic vision. Not even his coreligionists fully grasped the "Maryland designe" and the constraints under which the proprietor labored as an English Catholic.

Twice, once in the 1640s and once in the 1650s, his adversaries—the Virginians, disgruntled Marylanders, and parliamentary representatives—invaded his colony and stripped him of his proprietary rights. Both incidents might seem to reinforce the "Catholic as victim" perspective, since both assaults featured strong anti-Catholic sentiments. Persecution of Catholics, however, cannot explain the remarkable fact that twice he regained control of his province. The second time, he negotiated with Oliver Cromwell, a man with conflicted views on freedom of conscience and Catholicism. In the end, Baltimore prevailed because the radical Protestant government recognized the legitimacy of the Catholic proprietor's original grant and because Cromwell favored his commitment to freedom of conscience. This Catholic Lord Baltimore never escaped the anti-Catholic sentiments that dominated his culture. He did, however, take advantage of his opportunities to manipulate the system for his and his colony's benefit.

The next twenty-seven years, from 1661 to 1688, proved remarkably tranquil and peaceful in comparison. The Calverts and many other Marylanders prospered. No group succeeded as well as the small Catholic minority. The brick chapel built at St. Mary's reflected more than Catholic prosperity: it made a public statement that would have been inconceivable in 1634. The irony is that in the Calverts' success lay the seeds of their failure.

Ultimately, any consideration of the Catholic Lords Baltimore has to recognize that they failed to sustain their bold experiment with freedom of conscience and lost the colony. Why they failed is critically important to understanding what they attempted. Certainly human frailties played a part. Their success in colonization, to say nothing of their survival as Catholics, depended on the political and managerial skills of the proprietors. The charters for both Newfoundland and Maryland invested great power in the hands of the proprietors, the Lords Baltimore. As heads of state, they were the single most important players in the colonies' successes and failures.

Charles Calvert, the third Lord Baltimore, proved incapable of sustaining the endeavor implemented by his father. Proprietary rule ended when the Protestant Association overthrew his government in 1688–89. The English government did not restore the Calvert proprietorship until 1715, when the fourth Lord Baltimore converted to the state church. Had the Calverts finally fallen victim to government persecution, or should their fall be attributed to other forces?

Unlike his father, Charles served both as resident governor (beginning in 1661) and as resident proprietor after his father's death in November 1675. Did this Catholic Lord Baltimore have the requisite skills to preserve what he inherited from his father? He was wealthy, he worshiped openly as a Catholic, and he was arrogant. Like his father, he had to face the anti-Catholic passions that imbued his culture. However, the issues that had resonated so loudly for his father and his grandfather seemed remote to him. He seemed oblivious to the growing anti-Catholicism in the colony and to the isolation felt by those outside his immediate circle of family and friends. Departing from his father's practice, he failed to incorporate discordant elements into his increasingly small ruling clique. After the overthrow of his government in 1689, he had to observe events in Maryland from his exile in England.

The Calverts' decision to maintain allegiance to Roman Catholicism is central to understanding what they attempted. English Catholicism both restricted and amplified opportunities for those who professed the faith. The restrictions—the penal laws and virulent anti-Catholicism—demoralized and effectively crippled many English Catholics. Not so with this family, and not so with other elite English Catholic families. When George Calvert converted to Catholicism in late 1624, he saw a vitality within the small Catholic community that appealed to him. He also perceived that success lay not in fighting the system but in working through it. Few Catholics enjoyed the advantages George Calvert did as a former government official. Those Catholics who lacked influence did indeed fall victim to the repressive efforts to enforce religious uniformity. The Calverts, however, call attention to another part of the story. Some Catholics in England and America vigorously pursued their interests and succeeded.[8]

The Calverts do not fit the mold of a typical Catholic family (if such an entity existed). Nevertheless, the manner in which they achieved their goals is important for understanding the Catholic experience in general. The continued existence of Catholicism was not so much corporate as it was familial. Each family had to cut its own path. The Calverts demonstrated that some English Catholics could function within a culture that all too frequently proclaimed its hostility to their religion. They accepted their situation for what it was and made the most of it.

The founding of Maryland, the only successful overseas plantation by English Catholics in the seventeenth century, was a singular experience in English colonization. As English Catholics, Calvert and his family brought a unique perspective to colonization and encountered a unique set of problems that complicated their efforts. Their affiliation with Catholicism did not necessarily define them as conservative. Nor did it compel them to risk their worldly interests to create a religious haven, to implement Catholic thinking or utopian concepts, or to seek martyrdom. Their Catholic connection led them to build a community on a vision of religious and political allegiance that was radically different from that of other English colonial entrepreneurs. In their effort to succeed, they offered religious liberty to the religiously diverse planters who ventured to their colony. In return, they expected loyalty to themselves as proprietors.

The Calvert vision of a prospering society based on freedom of conscience transcended traditional thinking. The eventual defeat of the "Maryland designe" after almost six decades of struggle does not at all lessen its historical significance. By spurning the concept of religious uniformity, the Catholic Lords Baltimore became involved in an adventure to free the human conscience from the dictates of the civil government. The Calverts' bold experiment was a refreshing oasis in an age when the state advocated coercion and persecution to achieve religious uniformity and secure political allegiance. It also stood as a stark testimonial to a family's ability to prosper as English Catholics.

CHAPTER ONE

"There should be a correspondence betwixt the Church and the State"

Uniformity, the Penal Legislation, and the Early Stuarts

Substantial theological differences separated English Catholics and Protestants. However, they stood as one when it came to uniformity and the magistrate's obligation to protect the true religion. Public tensions between them usually came down to questions of political loyalty. Could a man or a woman serve two masters, a pope in Rome and a king at home, and be loyal to both? Could a society countenance subjects whose religious commitment differed from that of the monarch? In post-Reformation England, the usual answer was no. The deeply rooted concept of religious uniformity meant that there was little willingness to tolerate contrary religious beliefs in England. The English, in common with many other Christian Europeans, maintained that civil peace and political stability depended on the monarch's charge to protect the true faith (however defined). They further believed that the subject's religion must conform to that of the ruling monarch. These tenets inexorably bound church and state in a tangled web. A threat against one constituted a threat against the other.

Henry VIII, "defender of the faith," affirmed this role for the English monarch when he severed the traditional relationship with the Catholic Church. At his urging, Parliament recognized him as "the only supreme head in earth of the Church of England" and acknowledged his extensive powers over religious institutions. The law recognized his "full power and authority" to combat all errors and heresies, to foster the "increase of virtue in Christ's religion," and to conserve the peace, unity, and tranquility of the realm.[1]

During the reign of Henry's Catholic daughter Mary, Parliament repealed the 1544 act and returned England to the Roman fold. In 1559, to accommodate Mary's Protestant half-sister Elizabeth, another parliament passed legislation that replicated much of the 1544 act. The new bill recognized Elizabeth as "the only supreme governor of this realm," with authority over all spiritual and temporal matters. To avoid diversities of opinions touching "true religion," a convocation of the clergy quickly acknowledged the queen's authority, given "to all godly princes in holy scriptures by God," to govern the clergy in those matters committed to their charge by God. Further, the convocation empowered her to restrain stubborn subjects and evildoers in religious matters with temporal power.[2]

Ecclesiastical leaders welcomed the magistrate's responsibility "to promote the glory of God, and to advance the Kingdom of Christ." John Jewel, a leading established church theorist, summarized the monarch's role: "For princes are nursing fathers of the church, and keepers of both tables," that is, the two parts of the Ten Commandments that delineated religious and secular obligations. He asserted that "God willed governments to exist" in order "to maintain and preserve religion and piety." In a similar vein, Henry Bullinger argued that the care of religion belonged to the magistrate, whose duty was to advance religion. He carefully qualified this by stating that the offices of magistrates and ministers must not be confounded. For example, the king does not baptize or administer the Lord's Supper, nor does the priest give judgment against a murderer. The queen and her subjects accepted religious uniformity as the standard. In return for preserving the true faith (however defined), the Church promoted obedience to temporal authority.[3]

Thus, Elizabethans rejected the notion that subjects could be loyal members of the state if their faith (worship practices) differed from that of the chief magistrate. Political allegiance and religious practices must be in step. Religious diversity only intensified the competition for loyalty owed the state and due the Church. The contending parties, with few exceptions, did not advocate that all religious doctrines had a fundamental right to coexist with theirs. Rather, each sought to establish the supremacy of its own true faith. Even among the groups that decried the established religion's supremacy, there existed no particular quarrel with the concepts of religious uniformity and the magistrate's duty to enforce the true faith.

Although the demise of the concept of religious uniformity seems inevitable with hindsight, sixteenth- and seventeenth-century English civil and religious leaders were not ready to abandon it and made every effort to ensure its continuance. Nowhere was the commitment to religious uniformity more evident than in Elizabeth's policies toward dissident Protestants and recalcitrant Catholics. The Church lacked the power to compel individuals to worship according to its dictates. Its partner, the secular state, did—and used its power to invade the religious domain and force outward compliance to the Church of England.

Beginning in 1559, England's parliaments passed laws that required its subjects to worship in the Ecclesia Anglicana. Richard Hooker stated the basic assumption: "There is not any man a member of the *Church of England*, but the same man is also a member of the *Commonwealth*, nor any man a member of the *Commonwealth*, which is not also of the *Church of England*." The broadly based national church created by the Elizabethan religious settlement embraced some of the theology of the more radical Protestant reformers while also maintaining much of the polity of the Catholic Church. Elizabeth and her successors expected their subjects to comply with the laws and be willing to embrace the amalgamated church. Protestantism, conformity to the state church, became essential to the definition of the English state. Catholics, who did not fit into the nation thus defined, saw the laws as spiritual. Jesuit priest William Allen, who organized the invasion of missionary priests from Douai Seminary in France, missed the point when he questioned the benefits of compelling English Catholics to conform and profess outwardly that which they hated in their hearts. The point was, as a later parliamentarian so crudely stated, unless they conformed, "Papists" were "but half subjects under the lockes of Rome."[4]

The presence of English Catholics threatened more than the emerging religious settlement. Most Protestants believed that Catholics gave their first allegiance to the pope, who was not only their spiritual leader but also a temporal power. They perceived Catholics as a potentially subversive force linked to Rome and to Spain, the most powerful Catholic nation. The penal laws defined the legal status of Catholics and forced most of them to conform to the state church for the better security of the realm.

After re-creating the national church, Parliament attempted to induce conformity to it through light fines and occasional imprisonments. The Acts of Supremacy and Conformity constituted the basis for the religious settlement and gave the government a means to intercede in the private lives of individuals. The Act of Conformity, for example, required mandatory church attendance for fifty-two Sundays and twenty-seven feast days each year at a church that conformed to the new polity. The act established procedures for enforcing compliance. The Act of Supremacy contained an oath that called upon all subjects to recognize Elizabeth as the head of the Church. Catholics found themselves caught between contending loyalties. To refuse the oath called into question their allegiance to their temporal leader. To take it called into question their loyalty to their spiritual head. Parliament strengthened the laws with another act in 1563 that imposed penalties on those who appealed to the authority of the pope. The law further required that the oath of supremacy be given to members of the House of Commons, university graduates, and minor governmental officials. Enforcement during the first decade of Elizabeth's reign was unsystematic and unorganized. Not wishing to provoke a conservative backlash to official Protestantism, the government limited enforcement of the 1559 laws to urban areas. Throughout the period under consideration, government enforcement of the laws remained inconsistent.[5]

Members of Parliament responded to the 1569 Northern Rebellion in support of the Catholic Mary Stuart, the papal excommunication of Elizabeth in 1570, and the closer identification of English Catholics with Spain in 1571 with more severe laws. Challenging the papal excommunication, which labeled Elizabeth a heretic, deprived her of "her pretended title" to the kingdom, and released her subjects from all allegiance, Parliament decreed it high treason to question Elizabeth's rightful place as queen or to regard her as a heretic. Another act made it treason to receive and dispense written or printed orders from Rome. Giving aid to a person who did so or bringing into England any crosses, pictures, beads, or other "vain and superstitious things from the Bishop of the See of Rome" incurred severe penalties. A third law forbade dissenters, including Catholics, to leave the country for the purpose of evading the penalties of the penal laws or to be trained as missionaries. The law also stated that anyone traveling abroad had to secure a license and that those already overseas had six months to return and conform to the Church of England. Failure to comply could lead to permanent forfeiture of their lands and goods. Both sides had drawn their lines. The pope decreed that English Catholics who recognized Elizabeth's claim to the throne risked excommunication. Parliament decreed that if they followed orders from Rome, they committed treason.[6]

Under the leadership of Father Allen, the Catholic Church initiated a missionary effort in 1580. Priests disguised as merchants, soldiers, and courtiers flocked into England in alarming numbers. Parliament retaliated with new legislation in 1581. One act was intended to impede the efforts of the priests to reconcile English men and women to Rome. It raised the shilling fine for nonattendance at Church of England services to £20 a month, "a vast sum (especially as exacted by lunary months, consisting of twenty-eight days, and so making thirteen months in the year,) enough to shatter the containment of a rich man's estate." The law also imposed the penalty of high treason on proselytizing priests. Plots against the queen's life led to new legislation in 1585 that aimed to curtail the covert activities of priests. This act made it a felony for anyone to knowingly relieve, comfort, aid, or board a priest.[7]

The execution of Mary Stuart in 1587 and the fortuitous destruction of the Spanish Armada in the next year marked the high point of militant Catholic opposition. In the aftermath of these events, government activity against Catholics slackened but did not end. Ever suspicious, the government continued its vigil, and in 1593 Parliament passed the last of the Elizabethan penal laws. It restricted Catholics to within five miles of their permanent place of abode. To travel beyond that point required a license from the government.[8]

The Elizabethan religious settlement and its alterations disrupted the lives of English Catholics. What did these government-induced conversions mean? The Acts of Supremacy and Conformity in 1559 and the penal laws that followed left many people confused. They vacillated between their convictions and the need to obey the laws. As a result, religious loyalties during this period cannot be viewed as an either-or proposition, that is, either Protestant or Catholic. To do so obscures the nuances that were so much a part of the legacy of the Elizabethan religious settlement. Many English people, George Calvert included, were neither exclusively Catholic nor exclusively Protestant.

The Roman Catholic umbrella in England covered a wide spectrum of commitments. Everyday language encumbered understanding. For example, some contemporaries questioned the legitimacy of using the term *Catholic* to describe those who leaned toward Rome. King James thought those who adhered to the Roman Church were "falsely called Catholics"; instead, he considered them "truly Papists." Moreover, the English created a number of pejorative terms to describe their contemporaries who had Roman loyalties. In 1596 Thomas Wright listed *church Papists, schismatics, half-Catholics, Catholic-like Protestants, external Protestants,* and *external Catholics* among the unflattering terms applied by the English to his coreligionists. Equally negative were the terms *equivocators* and *hermaphrodite Christians*, which Isaac Bargrave used in his sermon to the 1624 Parliament. These labels indicated the considerable confusion within both Catholic and Protestant circles when it came to understanding the Catholic response to mandatory attendance at Church of England services.[9]

Contemporaries rarely clarified what they meant when they applied these derisive appellations. This analysis identifies four categories of Catholics or Papists: public Catholics or recusants, church Papists, schismatics, and crypto-Catholics. *Public Catholics or recusants* took great pride in their fidelity to the ancient faith. Their conspicuous display of religion, most notable by their refusal to attend Church of England services, sometimes incurred incarceration and fines. They accepted the financial burdens imposed upon them by the penal legislation as a show of faith. In 1600 Andrew Willet wished "with all my heart" that all the Papists in England were recusants. That way, he believed, the government might take better heed of them. He feared that there were "many close Papists in England," who temporized while waiting for the hour to reestablish their church. At the other extreme were the "close Catholics" or *crypto-Catholics*. These individuals, who practiced their religion without attracting suspicion for nonattendance, remained an unknown but feared quantity in England.[10]

Between the poles stood the *church Papists* and the *schismatics*. One unsympathetic contemporary described a church Papist as "one that parts religion between his conscience and his purse, and comes to church not to serve God, but the king. The fear of the Law makes him wear the mark of the Gospel, which he useth, not as a means to save his soul, but his charges. He loves Popery well, but is loth to lose by it." To avoid punishment, church Papists attended services in the state church on an occasional basis. The *schismatic* was, according to Jesuit John Gerard, "a Catholic by conviction but conforming externally to the state religion" to the point of taking communion. Contemporaries used the term to belittle those who failed to live up to the clerical standard of Catholic behavior. The two terms were not synonymous. Church Papists, who avoided the full impact of the laws by periodical participation in the established church worship, were Catholics. Schismatics denied or ignored their Catholic convictions, conformed to the laws, and lived as Protestants.[11]

The Elizabethan penal laws had worked. Without its hierarchy, the Catholic Church no longer functioned as it had before 1558. In the absence of effective leadership among laity and clergy, the number of open Catholics steadily decreased from a majority in 1558 to less than one in ten by 1603. Disruptive as the laws were, however, they did not destroy the Catholic community. Those who remained relied on itinerant missionary priests for their religious needs and on their status and the goodwill of their neighbors for protection. Having survived everything the English government could throw at them, English Catholics optimistically anticipated a dynastic change.

James VI of Scotland, Elizabeth's cousin and successor, had ample opportunity to deal with religious strife and conflicting loyalties. His mother, Mary, Queen of Scots, was Catholic, but he had been reared a Presbyterian. Although many at Elizabeth's court doubted his political skills, he had experienced some success as king of the unruly and religiously divisive Scots. His new kingdom offered even greater challenges. Issues relating to religious allegiance absorbed both the new king and his new subjects between 1603 and 1625. Members of the established Church expected him to use his temporal authority to achieve the much desired uniformity in worship. His English Catholic subjects, long disgruntled with their queen, applauded the new king as if he were the "greatest Catholike in the world."[12]

Dynastic change, however, did little to alter government actions toward Catholics or Protestant perceptions of them. The concept of uniformity remained unchallenged. James I found his position as the supreme governor of the Church of England compatible with his sense of authority. A statement made by the master of Sidney College in Cambridge resonated with him. "There are two Kingdomes in this world, a temporall and a spiritual or mysticall, eache needing [the] other." The king took his role of defender of the faith seriously. As king of Scotland, he had lectured in *The Trew Law of Free Monarchies* that it was the duty of kings to maintain the religion professed within their countries as established by their laws and to punish those who tried to alter or disturb profession of the established religion. James reassured the clergy of the Church of England at their 1604 convocation that he would have "one Doctrine and one discipline, one Religion in substance, and in ceremonie."[13]

This commitment left little room for Catholics to maneuver. Hopeful that the king might act on his own, Catholics petitioned for toleration or liberty of conscience. His visceral reaction indicated that even if he could, he was a long way from granting any formal concessions. John Manningham noted the king's reaction to one petition: If "40,000 of them in armes should present such a petition, himself would rather die in the field than condescend to be false to God." True to form, he modified this statement with a pledge not take extreme measures if Catholics remained dutiful subjects. These actions confirmed the Venetian secretary's assessment that the best Catholics could hope for was freedom from "persecution for their religious acts in private."[14]

King James's commitment to uniformity did not lead him to persecution of contrary religious beliefs. On the contrary, he professed his abhorrence at the idea of shedding blood over a diversity of opinion in religion. No one should die for an error of faith against the first table of the Commandments, but no one should be permitted to commit rebellion against the second table. His willingness to abstain from wielding the sword against Catholics to reduce their numbers came at a price. He admonished "the Papists of the Land" not to mistake his leniency "(because I would be loath to be thought a Persecutor)" and presume that it was lawful to increase their number and strength in England. He further counseled them not to harbor any false hopes regarding the reestablishment of their religion in England. Secretary of State Robert Cecil spoke for his master when he told the Venetian ambassador "that we hold as undesirable in a well-governed monarchy to allow the increase of persons who profess obedience to the will of a foreign sovereign, as the Catholics do." This was the bone James tossed to his Catholic subjects: be peaceable and loyal, do not grow as a community, and your presence will be overlooked.[15]

This paradoxical policy appeared too generous to zealous Protestants. In an age of uniformity, diversity necessitated that each religion assert the supremacy of its own doctrines and the suppression of all others. John Pym had no doubt of this. If the chief magistrate granted favor to Catholics, they would expect toleration. After "toleration they will look for equality, after equality for superiority, and after superiority they will seek the subversion of that religion which is contrary to theirs." He saw the king's moderate policy as the first dreaded step for advancing Catholicism. As the Venetian secretary noted, the king could not ignore these stalwart Protestants. Secure in his Protestantism, he "would certainly be indifferent as to the question of religion," were it not for his fear that "this would breed discord among his people."[16]

Members of Parliament suffered no such scruples against coercing Catholic conformity. At their first opportunity, they passed the entire body of Elizabethan penal laws. Inconsistent enforcement of these laws by James I, however, contributed to a revitalization of the Catholic community in the early seventeenth century. Lax enforcement of the penal laws remained a constant source of friction between the accommodating monarch and his punitive parliaments. Although James understood that he could not repeal the laws, he could limit their effectiveness. But as the king discovered on more than one occasion, pursuing a moderate policy toward Catholics lacked popular support and thereby entailed risks. The question of Catholic loyalty was too tainted by extremists on both sides to be solved rationally. Catholics remained pawns in the battles between king and Parliament over finances, foreign policy, and religious institutions.[17]

If the penal laws presented an obstacle for toleration, so, too, did Catholic behavior. Lay Catholics had little opportunity to influence events in a positive manner. When exiled Catholics returned from the Continent in anticipation that religious toleration might be granted, they aroused Protestant suspicions. When Catholics in London worshiped openly in the chapels of Catholic embassies, they aroused Protestant suspicions. When the government, temporarily at least, suspended the collection of fines imposed by the penal laws and released some Jesuits from incarceration, it aroused Protestant suspicions. Catholics, by their very presence in England, exacerbated long-standing Protestant fears. They could never feel completely comfortable with a status dependent on the goodwill of the king and his ability to resist those who clamored for their demise.

Cecil confided in a letter to Lord Sheffield that neglect "to punish priests and popery" led some to believe that the king had a "hidden purpose to grant toleration." The king soon yielded to popular pressures and resolved to enforce the laws, "which are of great severity and bitterness, affecting property and life," against Catholics. When the Venetian ambassador asked the cause of the extraordinary change, Cecil blamed the Catholics. The king ended his clemency because "priests go openly about the county, the city, and private homes saying Mass." This offended a great many of the king's subjects. The news from Rome that the pope had appointed a congregation of cardinals to deal with the affairs of England worsened the situation. This, said the king's chief servant, has led many to think that the king is about to grant freedom of conscience, which caused an uproar among the bishops and other clergy. The ambassador had previously reported that many desired the total ruin of Catholics, who had been well treated since the king's accession. He worried that lenient treatment was not enough: Unless the existing restraints were eased, Catholics faced the possibility of "absolute destruction."[18]

In November 1605, some disgruntled Catholics put their community in peril when they attempted to destroy the government. The plotters, led by Guy Fawkes, tunneled under the houses of Parliament, brought in gunpowder, and waited for the nation to gather. At the eleventh hour, authorities discovered the infamous Gunpowder Plot and saved the king and the nation. The catastrophic threat from Catholic plotters thwarted, anxious members of Parliament passed a law making November 5 an annual day of obligation for a public "thanksgiving to Almighty God" and devised a new set of penal laws.[19]

The 1606 penal laws were the most disabling since the laws of 1581. The most important, and some ways the most innovative, clause of the new laws, was the oath of allegiance. With this oath, James added an element that, had it worked, would have modified dramatically the existing concepts of conformity, uniformity, and political allegiance. The oath of allegiance, flawed as it was, reflected the king's desire to distinguish between dutiful and disloyal Catholics. In his own mind, he separated the laity from the clergy. He excused lay Catholics because of their "ignorant, doubtful, and implicit kinds of faith" that led them to believe whatever "their teachers please to affirm." He saved his enmity for the Catholic clergy, "factious stirrers of Sedition." James feared the pope's "arrogant and ambitious" assertion of imperial civil power over kings and emperors. He feared priests who accepted a doctrine that allow the pope to dethrone a legitimate ruler.[20]

The new oath contained language that forced Catholics to choose between their temporal allegiance and their spiritual loyalty. Many took it, albeit reluctantly. The first part of the oath presented no problem. The oath taker declared "in my conscience before God and the world," that King James was the legitimate ruler of England. More controversially, the oath challenged papal authority. Catholics taking it denied that the pope had the power to depose kings. Further, the oath required a Catholic to affirm "from my heart that notwithstanding any declaration or sentence of excommunication or deprivation made or granted by the Pope, I will bear faith and true allegiance to his Majesty." Finally, oath takers swore that they abhorred "as impious and heretical" the damnable doctrine that princes whom the pope excommunicated "may be deposed or murdered by their subjects." For anyone other than the nobility, failure to take the oath "duly tendered" meant imprisonment in the common jail without bail until the next court session. A second refusal incurred the "danger and penalty of Praemunire."[21]

The Gunpowder Plot produced a new wave of anti-Catholicism. Shrill voices demanded more effective enforcement of the penal laws. The actions of a few militant plotters in November 1605 caused many Catholics to feel the sting of the government's wrath, at least temporarily. The Venetian ambassador noted that the tension between strict enforcement of the laws and leniency greatly troubled the king. However, once King James realized that the plotters lacked support among most Catholics, he lost interest. As was so often the case, when the urgency passed, enforcement slackened.[22]

In the aftermath of this crisis, the king returned to his policy that allowed lay Catholics an unofficial toleration based on three conditions: they had to demonstrate their political loyalty, curtail the activities of their priests, and avoid any rapid and conspicuous growth in their numbers. The king, contrary to the desires of many of his advisers and members of Parliament, acted on the assumption that he could distinguish between Catholics who were true subjects and those whom he characterized as false-hearted traitors. Parliament in 1606 provided James with his instrument for making the distinction, the oath of allegiance. He posed this question in *An Apologie for the Oath of Allegiance:* "Had not wee then, and our Parliament great reason, by this Oath to set a marke of distinction between good Subjects and bad?" He answered that Catholics could, by taking the oath, "wipe off that imputation and great slander" that had been laid on all Catholics by the furious enterprise of the Gunpowder Plot. The controversial nature of the oath aside, James garnered support by this means among moderate Catholic clergy and laity.[23]

Was the oath an article of faith or a civil matter? According to papal representatives, the oath must not be taken, because the pope's authority to chastise princes upon just cause "is de fide" and could not "be denied without a notable error." According to the king, the purpose of the oath was to distinguish between the "civilly obedient Papists" and the perverse "disciples of the Powder-Treason." Here James evidenced a philosophical commitment to limited religious toleration that put him ahead of the majority of his subjects. He recognized, in his more enlightened moments, that "God never loves to plant his Church by violence and bloodshed." The king held that natural reason and daily experience demonstrated that religious persecution all too often produced results opposite from what was intended. He believed that "when men are severely persecuted for Religion," the gallantry of their "spirits and wilfulness of their humors," rather than the justness of the cause, led them to take pride in enduring any torments to force them to think otherwise. Only the work of God could alter Catholic minds. Because the government could not force a true conversion, and because the attempt to do so would create martyrs, James willingly overlooked the religious doctrines of his Catholic subjects as long as they remained loyal to him.[24]

The king reiterated that no man had suffered corporal punishment "in any degree or respect for his conscience in matter of religion." This may have been spurious reasoning on his part, as his critics charged, but it formed an important ingredient in his thinking. He believed that the punishments meted out to English Catholics resulted from temporal transgressions, not religious ones. Such thinking allowed him to relax the enforcement of the penal laws and to rely on those Catholics whose loyalty was not in question. In a speech in the Star Chamber in 1616, he summarized his views. What he held for recusants, he held for priests. He reiterated his loathing for hanging a priest only for a religious affair such as saying Mass. The king left priests who refused the oath of allegiance to the law, asserting that it was not persecution "but good justice." Let "the Pope and all the devils in Hell say what they will," it was a civil oath.[25]

Acceptance of the oath did not remove the threat of a more intense enforcement of the penal laws against the Catholics. New rumors, suspicious activities, or overt actions led to calls for greater enforcement. A rumor, supposedly from reliable sources, that four seminarians or Jesuits had recently arrived in England with the intention of killing the king and the prince no doubt led to increased action against Catholics. The government issued a proclamation calling for the due execution of the penal laws against recusants, who were ordered to leave London, and against priests and Jesuits, who were banished from the realm. It also called for administering the oath of allegiance to suspected Catholics. Such proclamations had little practical effect but seemed to satisfy a need to do something.[26]

The effort to add new laws against Catholics ended in 1610. James informed Parliament that he wanted no further enactments, "lest the Jesuits spread abroad the slander that we are persecutors, a charge I have rebutted with my own pen." Nonetheless, expediency sometimes dictated that he succumb to popular pressures. Catholics, the Spanish ambassador noted, were persecuted by the archbishop of Canterbury, the bishop of London, and the king, "in hope to propitiate Parliament into granting subsidies, and that he may have their forfeitures to give his servants." Any overt actions by Rome or its agents exacerbated the fears of the Catholic threat on the part of members of Parliament. Catholic fortunes, to the extent that they were dependent on national or international conditions, were in direct proportion to the monarch's willingness to withstand popular pressures.[27]

With no new laws and a monarch determined to pursue a moderate policy, Catholics saw a gradual improvement in their condition. To some extent, this resulted from the king's reluctance to torment Catholics solely for matters of conscience. More important, foreign policy considerations led him to flirt with the notion to extend a toleration of sorts to his Catholic subjects. Although Catholic fortunes continued to fluctuate, Catholics enjoyed relative peace under James I and his son Charles. During the years (1619–1624) when Calvert served as secretary, the king came close to embracing a full toleration for Catholics. But the reality was that selective enforcement of the penal laws continued throughout the period and that many Catholics conformed out of sheer necessity.

The issue of how the government treated Catholics became inexorably intertwined with the king's goal to bring peace to Europe through an alliance with Spain, the dominant Catholic power on the Continent. James wanted to seal the alliance through what came to be known as the Spanish match, the marriage between the Prince of Wales and the Spanish infanta. In agreeing to the conditions demanded by the Spanish, James did not act against his principles. In the guise of the wisest fool in Christendom, he played a deep game, making "large half-promises": negation of the penal laws, toleration for public worship by the infanta, and permission for her to raise her children as Catholics. Circumstances, his unwillingness to sacrifice the Church of England, his own convictions, and the deep hostility of his people toward Catholicism, however, limited what he could do on his own. He could ease enforcement of the penal laws, but he knew he could never induce Parliament to repeal them.[28]

The king's policies reduced the threat of the penal laws. At the height of the Spanish negotiations in the mid-1620s, the government avoided imposing the penalties against Catholics. The fines collected from recusants again dropped dramatically. The total collected for 1623–24 was the lowest since 1603–4. In preparation for the marriage, James wished "the Catholics of England to taste the royal clemency." Priests, some of whom had previously been incarcerated, moved about freely. Judges received instructions to deal leniently with recusants, who were promised that the penal laws would be suspended within five years. In an ironic twist, this lax enforcement more often than not produced a backlash against Catholics.[29]

Not all subjects understood the king's policies. Diaries, letters, and public documents indicate that they became increasingly restive. James attempted to alleviate their concerns in his opening speech to the 1621 Parliament. Negotiations to marry Charles to the Spanish infanta created great anxiety in Commons. The king warned members not to think his pursuit of the match caused him to grow "cold in Religion" or that he was one man in private and another in public. He urged them to trust his word as king. If the treaty with Spain did not appear to be for the glory of God and the well-being of England, "I will never give my consent to it," he said. Admonishing Catholics not to grow insolent in anticipation of the match, he promised that if they did, and he was informed of it, he would deal with them "as is fit."[30]

In 1622, the king released a number of recusants, thereby offending many subjects. Lord Keeper John Williams expressed the official justification. He acknowledged that the "common people are unable to penetrate the actions of Kings," but he explained anyway. The king, he asserted, though he "is no favorer of Popery," thought this action proper "because he could not hope to mediate successfully for distressed Protestants in France, Germany, &c. while he was rigorous with Papists in England." As was so often the case, the government based its policy toward Catholics on external concerns that might or might not be understood by the general public.[31]

This was a vicious circle. Leniency only exacerbated Protestants' fears and increased their calls for more rigid enforcement of the laws. While the king's actions "afford great joy to Catholics and seem to promise the marriage, they incense the people to a remarkable degree and may possibly sow the seeds of a civil war." No words spoken by the king could alleviate the distress of his Protestant subjects. They feared not so much Catholics as persons, for Protestants frequently protected and connived with their Catholic neighbors, but the Catholic connection with an international Church and Continental Catholic countries. Concessions to English Catholics were concessions to Spain and Rome. Spain was the principal prop of international Catholicism and would "plant the Pope's laws by arms, as the Ottomans do the law of Mahomet." But Spain could do the English no harm, "unless we have a Party here in England." English apprehension settled on what Protestants referred to as the "Spanish Party." To most English Protestants, those sympathetic to Catholics and the Spanish match had never seemed so strong.[32]

In response to rumors of an invasion, of bishops pushing for reconciliation with "the hope of a crosier staff or a cardinal's hat," of increasing numbers of Catholic sympathizers, of open conversions, and of the Prince of Wales's intended conversion to the Roman faith, Protestants reacted viscerally. Sir Edwin Sandys warned that the leniency shown Papists must be halted, for it not only struck at "Religion but at the State." His concern, which most members of the 1621 Parliament undoubtedly shared, was that if Catholics continued to increase and came to know their own strength, they would no doubt "attempt an alteration in church and state." In 1625, at the height of the plague, another member of Parliament expressed popular fears, saying there was "More Cause to fear the Plague of our Soules, than of our Bodies. The best Preservative, and Cure, is the Execution of the Laws against the Jesuits, &c."[33]

Such exaggerations captured the frenetic thinking of those who opposed the Stuarts' flirtations with Spain and Rome. The struggle with the papacy was no matter for compromise. It was a "struggle between light and darkness, between life and death. No innovation in faith or worship was of small account, if it tended in the direction of Rome." The peril in fact was too great to admit of tolerance or moderation.[34]

King James died unexpectedly in March 1625, having failed to define a legitimate role for Catholics in English society. Through his lax enforcement of the penal laws and his diplomatic initiatives toward Spain, James had stirred the hornet's nest, but it was his son Charles who was bitten. Charles I's policies and his inability to win the trust of his subjects brought the long-simmering crisis over religious and political unity to a head. The new monarch, like his predecessors, believed that it was his duty as king to protect the established faith: "There is nothing more dear [to me] than the preservation of true religion, as settled in this kingdom." As "defender of the faith" and "supreme governor of the church," he took seriously his charge to "conserve and maintain the church committed to our charge in unity of the true religion." The archbishop of Canterbury assured a colleague "that there is no man, nay, no Bishop in that Kingdom or this more truly, conscientiously, and constantly set both for the belief and maintenance of religion, as it is now established, than his Majesty (God be blessed for it) is."[35]

Church of England clerics readily reiterated their agreement with the accepted wisdom that the Christian magistrate had a sacred duty to protect the unity of the true faith. Indeed, church thinking had advanced little beyond its sixteenth-century formulations of church-state relations and seemed intellectually stagnant. One church thinker was William Laud, whom Charles elevated to the archbishopric of Canterbury because of his "worth and care, both for the good of God's church and the King's service." Unity in the Church was fundamental for Laud: "The ready way out of religion is to break the unity of it," which was best preserved by committing the Church to the protection of the magistrate. The care of God's Church, Laud contended, "is committed to kings in the scripture, that they are commended when the Church keeps the right way, and taxed when it runs amiss, and therefore her government belongs in chief unto kings."[36]

The archbishop also served as spokesman for the establishment's thinking on the relationship between church and state. Laud wrote in the king's name, "we have observed that the Church and State are so nearly united and knit together." Although they may seem two bodies, he continued, "yet indeed in some relation they may be accounted but as one, inasmuch as they both are made up of the same men," who differed "only in relation to Spiritual or Civil ends." In England the same subjects composed both church and state. For this reason, the Church could call on the state to succor and support her whenever "she is pressed beyond her strength." Likewise, the state relied on the service of the Church when needed. Laud reasoned that because God himself linked the two bodies, "the walls of the State cannot be broken but the Church suffer with it, nor the walls and fences of the Church trampled upon, but the State must be corrupted by it."[37]

Episcopal Protestants believed that without the dominion and protection of the civil government, the Church would not likely "enjoy all those rights that can any way belong to it." The concepts of unity and conformity in worship and the mutual dependence of the Church and the state for survival continued to dominate. As a result, it was difficult, if not impossible, to separate religious opposition from political.[38]

King James evidenced a willingness to tolerate Catholics under certain conditions. Popular fears, however, imposed severe restrictions on his behavior. At the end of his reign, life for English Catholics remained unsettled but manageable. Many loopholes existed for Catholics who had the status and the ingenuity to exploit them. A small but vibrant, widely scattered community continued to maintain their Catholic faith and their English loyalty.

CHAPTER TWO

"Conformitie to the form of service of God now established"

Building a Career at Court (1580–1620)

From his birth George Calvert had binding ties with the Catholic community. He was born into an environment that openly resisted the evolving state church. A decade earlier, Sir Thomas Gargrave had described Richmondshire in Yorkshire as an area where all the gentlemen were "evil in religion," that is, Roman Catholic.[1]

The records reveal remarkably little about George Calvert's family or his early life. He was born in late 1579 or early 1580, the son of Leonard and Alicia (aka Alice) Crosland Calvert of Yorkshire, where his family had resided for generations. His father, who achieved some prominence in the community, lived at Kiplin in the northern part of Yorkshire as a tenant of Philip Lord Wharton. George's mother died during his infancy; his father subsequently married Grace Crosland, a relative of Alicia.

Periodically between 1580 and 1592, Yorkshire authorities bedeviled the Calvert family for its Catholic leanings. In 1580 they bonded Leonard and Grace to assure their attendance at the state church. Although Leonard soon certified his conformity, local authorities continued to harass family members for nonattendance. In 1592 Yorkshire authorities discovered a school where the master taught from a "popish primer." Because two of the pupils were brothers George and Christopher Calvert, authorities again called the family to account for its illicit religious practices. Leonard gave bond that he, his wife, and his family would conform in matters of religion, and he quickly certified his conformity again. To guard against a relapse, the Yorkshire High Commission prohibited the family from engaging a Catholic schoolmaster or from having Catholic servants in the house. It ordered Calvert to keep "no popish books or other trumpery" and no relics of popery and required him to purchase, within the month, an English Bible, a Book of Common Prayer, and "Mr. Nowell's Catechism in English." The commissioners ordered Leonard to buy one other prominent Protestant book in addition, which was "to ly open in his house for every one to read." Finally, they instructed him to send his sons to a Protestant tutor in York and stipulated that, if required, he was to bring his children before the commission "once a quarter to see how they perfect in learning."

As ordered, Leonard sent young George and Christopher to study with a Protestant tutor, "Mr. Fowberry now schoolmaster at Bilton." George's stepmother refused to conform, and the authorities committed her in 1593 to the custody of the pursuivant Southwood. Pursuivants, whether in London or in the countryside, identified suspected Catholics and had them "apprehended, imprisoned, and prosecuted by the law." Some Catholics, to avoid the law, submitted to the blackmail and extortion tactics employed by some pursuivants. A notice eleven years later that referred to the "wife of Leonard Calvert of Kipling, non-communicant at Easter last" testified to her continued unwillingness to accept the Church of England.

The Calvert family fit a pattern that had emerged by this time in Yorkshire. The husband, for a variety of secular reasons, conformed but was unwilling or unable to bring his wife with him. Men frequently conformed in order to protect their status and property. Women who persisted in open allegiance to the ancient faith faced incarceration. The need for religious uniformity allowed the state to intervene in the most intimate aspects of family life. Within his own family, George Calvert witnessed the heavy-handed application of the law in matters of religion.[2]

When George Calvert was about twelve years old, secular authorities compelled him to conform to the established religion. Significantly, his state-induced conformity did not result from a religious experience or "spiritual awakening." How diligently had his Protestant tutor in York labored to win him over to the doctrines of the Church of England? Calvert left no written indication of what these two years meant or what he thought of his rather abrupt change of religion. Subsequent behavior showed that he accepted it. Conformity to the state church, however, could not erase the fact that he had been reared a Roman Catholic. Placing practical considerations at the forefront, George Calvert conformed externally to the practices of the established church. Although nothing in his subsequent life suggests that he was an avid Protestant, his correspondence revealed a committed Christian who frequently alluded to God.

Calvert conformed to the state religion from 1592 until well into 1624. After his two years of schooling with a Protestant tutor, George left home to attend Trinity College, Oxford, where he matriculated in the Lent Term, 1593–94. The statutes did not require students to take the oath to support the Thirty-Nine Articles and the Book of Common Prayer until their sixteenth birthday. No evidence exists, however, that he did not take the prescribed oath and thereby attest to his conformity. His Oxford experience "confirmed his acceptance of the doctrines of the Church of England."[3]

After he completed his studies in foreign languages, he probably returned home in February 1597. Young Calvert left his native Yorkshire in August 1598 to venture to London, where, at the urging of his father, he studied municipal law at Lincoln's Inn for the next three years. In 1601 he left on an extended trip to the Continent and did not return until April 1603, when he brought a packet from Paris for Sir Robert Cecil.[4]

Calvert's entrance into court politics was by no means a unique story: a talented and ambitious young man attaches himself to a powerful older politician and begins to make his mark. In Calvert's case the political mentor was Elizabeth's trusted adviser Sir Robert Cecil, "the principal manipulator of the dynastic change in 1603." James VI of Scotland owed Cecil for his ascension to the throne, and he generously bestowed titles on the man he called his "little beagle." On May 13, 1603, he made him Baron Cecil of Essendine, Rutland; on August 20, 1604, Viscount Cranborne; and on May 4, 1605, the earl of Salisbury. As secretary of state, privy councillor, and later lord treasurer, Cecil dwarfed all others who served at court during James's first nine years.[5]

With his extraordinary responsibilities, Cecil needed considerable secretarial assistance. He undoubtedly regarded Calvert's command of foreign languages, his intelligence, and the manner in which he carried himself as valuable attributes for a great man's secretary. Those talents, however, did not distinguish him from others who sought placement in Cecil's household. Patronage was critical in securing appointments, and Calvert apparently had someone willing to intervene. His appointment may have resulted from the sponsorship of his wealthy and influential cousin Ralph Ewens.[6]

By the spring of 1603, Calvert had taken the first step in building a career at court. Whatever the circumstances of his appointment, he recognized the advantages of serving the man who controlled court patronage. The appointment placed him at the center of court politics. As one of Cecil's secretaries, he crossed paths with English luminaries and foreign ambassadors who came to court to do business. Calvert, never a man of independent means, learned to use the system to his best advantage. For example, in October 1604 John More asked "Mr. Calvert to use his friendly offices" on another's behalf. Dudley Carleton sought to use Calvert's "nearness to my Lord" to deliver "an offer of service in general" to Cecil.[7]

The favors More, Carleton, and the many others sought from Calvert enabled him to build a circle of associates at court and in the diplomatic ranks. His influence with Cecil, a marketable commodity, helped to provide needed income. For example, Henry Serle, who sought Calvert's assistance for a refund for public business, promised to make Calvert a present out of the first allowance he received.[8]

Maintaining a position at court consumed his time, but not to the exclusion of courtship and marriage, beginning a family, and buying a house. On November 22, 1604, he married Anne Mynne, the daughter of George Mynne of Hertingfordbury in Hertfordshire, in London at the Church of St. Peter's Cornhill. The register listed Calvert as a gentleman and gave his residence as St. Martin's in the Field.[9]

Anne gave birth to a much desired male heir in the winter of 1605–6. In explaining to an associate that his cousin George would soon be writing, Samuel Calvert noted that "God hath lately sent him a son." George and Anne "named the child Cecill Calvert." He acknowledged his dependence on Cecil and on Henry Clifford, the earl of Cumberland, by naming them as godfathers. Cecil was probably born in Kent, and he was baptized in the Church of England on March 2, 1605/6. Two daughters, Ann (baptized April 1, 1607) and Dorothy (baptized August 18, 1608), soon joined his growing family. By midyear 1607 Calvert purchased a small house in Charing Cross. His financial situation was far from secure, however. Samuel Calvert, who took great interest in his cousin's advancement as well as his personal life, reported that he wanted to borrow four or five pounds from George but could not because of George's recent purchase of a house.[10]

George Calvert's personal behavior testified to his conformity. Calvert married Anne Mynne in a ceremony that accorded with the rites of the Church of England. They baptized their children, at least those for whom records are available, in the established church. They buried one child at St. Martin's in the Field, Calvert's parish church. When Anne died in August 1622, Calvert buried her in an elaborate sarcophagus in a Protestant church. A comparison with the behavior of Yorkshire gentry Catholics supports Calvert's conformity. They often buried their dead and not infrequently had their children baptized according to Protestant practices, but it was unusual for them to marry in the Protestant church. Calvert's unrecorded second marriage, which occurred after he was an avowed Catholic, strengthens the argument that he was a Protestant at the time of his first, recorded one. While suggestive, none of this can be taken as conclusive evidence that Calvert had renounced Catholicism in favor of Protestant doctrine.[11]

Calvert knew that advancement depended on maintaining the goodwill of his mentor, and he worked assiduously to gain Cecil's trust and respect. Did his continued service in Cecil's household reinforce his religious conformity? Given his position, Cecil had a variety of contacts with Catholics. In 1602 he recommended a Catholic for membership in the College of Physicians despite his "backwardness in religion." However, as any member of his household would have known, he hardly favored toleration for Catholicism, a religion he thought consumed by false doctrines and constituted a threat to the state. He especially resented priests, who he thought "were absolute seducers of the people from temporall obedience." He drafted a proclamation for the king that firmly enjoined "conformitie to the form of service of God as now established." He worried when James made overtures to Catholics. He urged the king to take a tougher line with Catholics, who recognized him as an enemy. Of all the powerful councillors between 1602 and 1605, Catholics considered Cecil among those least sympathetic with their aspirations. "The recusants say they have but 3 Enemies in England" whom they feared most: the lord chief justice, Cecil, and the lord high admiral. With regard to employing Catholics, Cecil declared that nothing "is more dangerous to the cause of God than when it appears to the vulgar that men of ability making open profession of popery are not only unpunished but graced and employed." Calvert realized that maintaining a secret connection to that church entailed too great a risk. He knew that Catholicism at court was a luxury afforded only those with wealth, status, and tradition on their side.[12]

Cousin Samuel reported that George "hath good favour with his Lord, and is diligent enough." Under the patronage of Cecil, now the earl of Salisbury, Calvert slowly but steadily grew in stature as he secured a number of lesser offices, honors, and sinecures that provided needed income for his growing family. In August 1605, Calvert was among many courtiers who attended the king at Oxford and received a master of arts degree. His first office came on July 10, 1606, when the king appointed him clerk of the Crown and assizes in the province of Connaught, County Clare, Ireland, upon the death of the incumbent. The growing rewards of office would in time make Calvert a rich man, but they never provided him the security of an independent financial basis.[13]

His work for Salisbury through 1608 went largely unnoticed by court gossips. But as a result of Salisbury's increased responsibilities—the king appointed him lord treasurer in 1608—Calvert began to attract attention. Court rumormongers soon made him an object of their speculations. In that year, one observer reported a rumor that Calvert was to be appointed clerk of the Privy Council. In 1609 Cousin Samuel wrote to William Trumbull, representative in Brussels, that through Salisbury's "private intention," the king appointed George as one of the clerks of the Signet office. He saw the appointment as significant and speculated that there "is a purpose to make him ere long an auricular minister in Court." Although that office carried no remuneration, it brought Calvert into close contact with the king. In his new capacity, Calvert drafted papers for the king's signature, a clear indication that both Cecil and the king trusted his discretion.[14]

A further indication of his improving status also resulted from Cecil's influence. Calvert had the opportunity to serve in James's first parliament, which sat intermittently between March 19, 1604, and February 9, 1611. In 1609 Cecil needed friends in the House of Commons. He secured a blank indenture for the seat in Bossiney in Cornwall and wrote in Calvert's name. Calvert, whose other duties restricted his attendance, left no mark on this parliament.[15]

In 1609 Calvert showed his first documented interest in colonial ventures. Swept up in the expansive enthusiasm for overseas enterprise displayed by the nobility and the gentry, he invested twenty-five pounds in the Virginia Company of London. The newly issued second charter expressly prohibited any "suspected to affect the superstitions of the Churche of Rome" from entering

Virginia "but as firste shall have taken the oath of supremacie." This wording apparently gave him no pause, because he did make the investment.[16]

A few months later, reflecting both his continuing interest and growing affluence, he ventured a more substantial sum in the East India Company. How much Calvert invested cannot be determined. It seems reasonable to conclude that his East India investments yielded substantial returns. Calvert "felt the pull of the great adventure of his day, the search for wealth in the expansion of English trade." His investments demonstrated that he now enjoyed ample financial benefits from his service as Cecil's secretary.[17]

That year brought mixed blessings for Calvert, however. In October his cousin recorded his concern for George's health and comfort if his wife should die in childbirth. He reported that she suffered from a lingering sickness. "I protest to you there are not many such friends living, nor many such women, such is the love she has gained (besides her own worth) amongst her husband's kindred, and for my particular, I shall but too soon miss her. Her life is in God's hands." Sam's pessimism, at least for the present, proved unfounded. A few weeks later he reported that Anne had "delivered a daughter on the day of the deliverance of the powder treason." His allusion makes it unlikely that he suspected that George and his family were crypto-Catholics.[18]

Calvert's diligence in his lord's service paid dividends in 1610. In March John Sanford reported, "others suspect Mr. George Calvert" would soon be named an ambassador. When his new appointment came, however, it was much closer to home. Salisbury recommended that the king appoint Calvert as one of the clerks of the Privy Council, and shortly thereafter he was sworn in as clerk and admitted into the council chamber ("with so much grace as never any better"). Calvert now had a position of considerable influence within court circles.[19]

His appointment as clerk of the Privy Council affirms his conformity. At about the same time, the king issued a proclamation against the Jesuits, and Parliament passed additional penal laws against Catholics. The appointment also meant that Calvert had to take the oath of allegiance. Oath-taking constituted a primary means of determining loyalty. During the summer the oath of allegiance was administered to both houses of Parliament and at the court, where it was first administered to the privy councillors. Because certain parts of the oath were contrary to Catholic doctrine, many Catholics refused to take it. Calvert appeared to have no scruples against taking it at this time, or at any time before 1625.[20]

In addition to his duties as clerk, he served as the king's agent on special diplomatic missions to the Continent. Soon after his appointment, Salisbury sent him on a mission that kept him on the Continent from August 1610 to March 1611. Not even the court gossips knew why Salisbury sent him on this lengthy mission. Cousin Sam stated what many wondered: "It will seem strange to you that Mr. Calvert should so soon upon his admission into the Council Chamber" go abroad. His reference to the trip as a vacation indicated that Sam did not know why "his little great lord" sent him on this mission. Salisbury set an extensive itinerary for him, provided him with letters to a number of ambassadors, and gave him one hundred pounds for his expenses. One of Trumbull's many correspondents wrote that George had been sent on a cursory employment through Holland, Cleves, and France and would return after he visited Sir Ralph Winwood. This gossip, too, could only speculate as to the purpose of the trip. He assumed that Salisbury sent Calvert to prepare for some future employment, perhaps as an ambassador. One correspondent reported from Paris shortly before Calvert's return that Calvert "gives everyone great contentment with his discreet conversation."[21]

Calvert returned to London in March 1611, "having been 2 days and one night at sea with foul weather." He went to court, where "I found my Lord in a disposition calm and sweet." Salisbury showed Calvert "that favorable respect wherewith he is pleased to grace those poor servants" he employs. But for all his graciousness, he gave Calvert no indication of what he intended for him. Indeed, Calvert confessed to one correspondent that he could provide no information on "the state of our Court here, our country, and our friends [because] I am yet but a stranger, and know little." Whether he knew it or not, speculation after his return from Paris focused on his appointment as Trumbull's successor. Thomas Edmondes, the English ambassador in Paris, wrote that he had heard from England that Calvert was to be named ambassador to Brussels. He speculated that if this was the case, "it is to qualify him for better employment later."[22]

His status remained a source of speculation. Not long after his return, More reported to Trumbull that Calvert's future employment remained in limbo. He noted that Calvert "is still spoken of" as Trumbull's successor but guessed that Salisbury wanted to keep him "near at hand." Rumors of a possible appointment persisted through 1611. The illness of John Corbit, the senior clerk, who "is very far fallen into a consumption, and comes not to Court," meant that his work fell to Calvert and his colleague Clement Edmondes. With Corbit's death in December, Calvert and his fellow clerk received the office of the commissary of Ireland, jointly, and each received half of the one-hundred-pound salary.[23]

Working for Salisbury brought Calvert into contact with the king, who observed him as he carried on his work. He impressed his monarch as a painstaking, cautious, and loyal servant who constituted no threat to his prerogatives. In 1611 the king employed him to research and transcribe his tract against the Dutch theologian Conrad Vorstius. Court gossip John Chamberlain reported that the king had been very busy in "writing somewhat in French against Vorstius." He reported that Calvert stayed close to the king and was totally "employed in reading and writing." Calvert confided to Cecil that he was busy in "writing out the discourse which the King began concerning Vorstius."[24]

By 1612 Calvert had established himself as a figure at court, and he appeared to be content to wait for whatever advancements Salisbury provided. The death of his mentor that year, however, disrupted his sense of security and threw the court into confusion. His cousin Sam summarized the feelings of many at court: "Our great, strange little lord is gone and as soon forgotten." But George had good reason to remember his late lord. Salisbury had named him as one of the four executors of his will, another indication that he trusted his former secretary. Serving as executor was no easy task, for Cecil died heavily mortgaged. His outstanding debts of more than thirty-eight thousand pounds complicated settlement of the will.[25]

The passing of a dominant figure like Salisbury left a void that James only haphazardly attempted to fill. He took two years to find a new secretary of state and lord treasurer, the offices so dominated by Salisbury. George Abbot, the archbishop of Canterbury, alluded to the unsettled conditions: A "great little man, who died a year or two past, left all out of order." The shifting political relationships that followed Salisbury's death challenged the now experienced Calvert to find his way through the maze of court politics. He had demonstrated few outward manifestations of ambition, but he showed no inclination now to drop out of the quest for status.[26]

In the decade or so after Salisbury's death, Calvert experienced his greatest advancement at court. His varied experiences before 1612 amply prepared him to become a courtier in the service of King James. Three salient factors emerge from an analysis of his maneuvers at court in the post-Salisbury period. First, he no longer enjoyed the favor of the king's primary adviser. For a man without an independent base, this was a potentially debilitating consideration. The second factor helped to offset the first: during his years in Salisbury's service, Calvert used his time and influence to build a network at court and in diplomatic circles. He referred to such individuals as "our friends" here at court. Third, Calvert's cautious, diligent, and loyal service marked him as a man well suited for James's style of leadership.

Even before Cecil's death, others challenged his dominant position. One of the new players was a Scotsman named Robert Carr. Samuel Calvert decried the state of affairs at court. He wrote to Trumbull, "[When you return,] you may find a change in Court, not from the houses or mansions, but the men and manners both growing from worse to stark nought," and he noted that "the King's minion Sir Robert Carr was made Viscount Rochester." The new favorite and his followers grasped for the power Cecil had exercised but showed a remarkable lack of responsibility in exercising it. Initially, the king seemed unwilling or incapable of remedying the situation. The Spanish ambassador sent the following unflattering commentary on the English court: "The Council is composed of men of little knowledge, some Catholics, but most schismatics or atheists, and … the King resolves on all business with Visct. Rochester alone, who is no persecutor of Catholics."[27]

Salisbury's death left Calvert without a patron. Try as he would over the next decade, Calvert never enjoyed the support of the king's new favorites, first Carr and then George Villiers. He harbored no illusions about his status. With a large family to support, he knew that he had to accommodate to the new favorite, whoever that might be, and his minions. He never was part of Rochester's circle, but he helped him manage the king's foreign policies. Rochester acted as secretary of state after Salisbury's death, but, significantly, the king never appointed him to the office. As a result, Calvert's work steadily increased. The king, without a secretary of state and reluctant to let anyone take complete control over foreign affairs, trusted Calvert to answer the Spanish and Latin correspondence and parceled out the remainder of the correspondence among the other clerks. Calvert's other duties entailed such things as executing warrants to search the lodgings or chambers of those whom the council suspected of harboring papers that "concern the state."[28]

His first significant new assignment came in 1613 when the king commissioned Calvert, Sir Humphrey Wynch, Sir Charles Cornwallis, and Sir Roger Wilbraham to go to Ireland to examine Catholic grievances and complaints made against the lord deputy. One observer thought the king sent the commissioners to "appease the Catholics." As was so often the case, however, the government's approach showed little empathy for the plight of Catholics. In an effort to chastise London supporters of the Irish Catholics, the government dispatched a lawyer named Talbot to the Tower for maintaining the pope's authority. The king would not reconvene an Irish Parliament until the Catholics "shall be better disciplined."[29]

The appointment afforded Calvert his first view of a land that would assume great import in his future. He and his colleagues spent almost four months in Ireland. Although he was the junior member of the delegation in both age and status, he actively participated in the investigation and helped to write the final report. Whatever his personal feelings may have been, the commissioners' recommendations evidenced little sympathy for Catholics. They decried the general neglect of "God's true religion" in Ireland and recommended strict enforcement of ecclesiastical conformity: All should be compelled to attend church or be punished. Popish schools must be suppressed. Priests must be found and punished. Able and religious schoolmasters should be recruited. Idle and scandalous ministers of the established church should be replaced with well-paid and conscientious successors.[30]

Calvert's signature on the report did nothing to hinder his advancement. The trip to Ireland was one of a number of activities during the next four years that foreshadowed his subsequent career both as a colonizer and as a proponent of religious pluralism. Calvert's quest of his principal objectives, wealth and land, eventually fused his interest in extending the empire and his views on religious diversity. The Irish sojourn provided an opportunity to witness the effects of religious oppression. His duties as clerk included a variety of experiences that gave him ample opportunity to observe the impact of enforced religious uniformity.[31]

His diligent work in handling foreign correspondence led to further speculation that he was in line for a diplomatic post. Gossipmongers at court dutifully noted his consideration for new assignments. Not one of them saw fit to question his religious loyalties as he advanced through the ranks. A rumor surfaced in December 1613 that the king would name Calvert as Sir Dudley Carleton's replacement as ambassador to The Hague. Cousin Sam, an incessant gossip, recognized what George undoubtedly knew, that "the track of the court is ever to name him first that last or never shall have the preferment." George showed little interest in possible overseas assignment. As Sam noted, his cousin "is talked on, but is not ambitious." Another gossip gave a better explanation. Chamberlain reported that Calvert was "reasonably well settled at home" with a wife and many children, who, he added, were no easy burden. More important, George directed his ambitions toward financial security, a goal best achieved in London. Here a succession of lesser offices and honors came his way. In 1616 the Privy Council appointed him one of the commissioners of musters for the county of Middlesex. James granted Calvert and another clerk one thousand pounds "out of the checks in Ireland" to reward them for their good service. Recognition of Calvert's increasing stature in James's government came in 1617, when, in honor of the marriage of the brother of the earl of Buckingham, the king conferred knighthood upon him.[32]

Beyond status, Calvert finally enjoyed considerable fiscal success. In January 1614 the East India Company allowed him, "in regard of his place," to add six hundred pounds to his adventure of one thousand pounds in joint stock. Calvert's success can also be measured in another way. In 1616 James granted Calvert the manor of Danby Wiske with all its appurtenances. This initiated his renewed interest in the land of his birth and brought him into contact with Sir Thomas Wentworth. Soon after his appointment as secretary in 1619, Calvert purchased lands in the parish where he was born. Here, between 1622 and 1625, he made his statement about wealth and status. If Kiplin Hall paled in comparison to Salisbury's Hatfield House, it still served notice to his fellow Yorkshiremen that George Calvert had arrived. These acquisitions put Calvert on the path that led first to Newfoundland and then to Maryland.[33]

Calvert did not avoid overseas assignments, but such errands were temporary and often involved delicate family matters that further evidenced the king's trust. In 1615 the king sent him to the Palatinate on a sensitive mission that was more a family concern than a matter of state. As part of a grand scheme to cement alliances with both Protestant and Catholic Continental forces, James married his daughter to Frederick V, the elector Palatine, in 1613. Elizabeth's marriage doomed her to an impoverished condition. When she discharged a gentlewoman who had served her faithfully for many years, she thought it dishonorable not to compensate her. Lacking money, she gave the woman jewels, a set of twenty-two ruby buttons. Calvert conveyed the king's displeasure at such an excessive gift while assuaging the anger and hurt felt by the young princess. Somewhat contrite, she explained to her father that she did not know her present was "worth so much." Calvert, having completed his mission, returned to England in the late spring, only to be sent on another personal mission to Heidelberg in July. These trips, although not of great diplomatic import, gave Calvert ample opportunity to observe an area that would provide his severest test in the king's service.[34]

Frederick's decision a few years later to accept the crown of Bohemia, in direct disregard of his father-in-law's advice, touched off a Catholic-Protestant firestorm that engulfed Europe for some thirty years. Whatever personal doubts Calvert may harbored about the increased tensions regarding religion, he continued to conform to the state Church. His political advancement came within a year after hostilities commenced between the impoverished Protestant forces of Frederick and the mighty Catholic Habsburgs. His appointment in 1619 as one of his majesty's principal secretaries of state took him by surprise. Court gossip centered on others; Calvert did not emerge as a candidate until the very end of the process. The appointment was unusual, for Calvert had no patron to advance his cause at court.[35]

At the time of his appointment, no one associated the new secretary with Catholicism. Four contemporaries later questioned his religious commitments during the years he served the king as secretary. Two of them, historian Arthur Wilson and former servant George Cottington, shed light on his religious commitments at the time of his appointment. The other two, Bishop Godfrey Goodman and Archbishop George Abbot, help to clarify when he ended his conformity. Although they referred to his possible Catholicism *before* February 1625, all wrote *after* that date, *when his Catholicism was public knowledge.*

Arthur Wilson (1595–1652), a contemporary historian, charged that "Papists and Pensioners of Spain, striving to promote the Catholic cause," infested the government of James I. Among those whom he named was the king's "Popish Secretary." According to Wilson, the king appointed Calvert secretary because he was Catholic. "Time and Age had also worn out Sir Ralph Winwood, the Kings able, faithful, and honest Servant, and Secretary." Wilson claimed that when he died, the king named Sir Robert Naunton and Sir George Calvert as secretaries. He characterized them as men of contrary religions and factions and said the king had matched the Protestant Naunton with Calvert, a "Hispaniolized Papist," to find a balance between their contrary views.[36]

Wilson's vitriolic account has generally served as the basis of the charge that Calvert was a Catholic when he was appointed secretary. However, Wilson's motives and his inconsistencies negate the charge. Wilson, a gentleman-in-waiting to the third earl of Essex, Robert Devereux, may not have been in the country at the time of Calvert's appointment. If he was not, he either relied on hearsay or juxtaposed Calvert's later avowed Catholicism with this earlier period. Wilson's account was highly partisan. In labeling Calvert as a "Hispaniolized Papist," he intended to slander the king rather than to render an accurate account. More important, his description is not of Calvert but of Sir Thomas Lake, a protégé of Charles Howard, lord of Effingham, and a Catholic. In 1614 Don Diego Sarmiento de Acuña, Conde de Gondomar, had noted that Lake was a Catholic, and in 1619, while Lake was on trial, Sir Thomas Wynne reported that "the papists are much dejected at it." Another person informed the king that Catholics at Louvain prayed for Lake's "good success."[37]

Lake's disgrace opened the door for Calvert. The king chose Calvert to replace Lake, a suspected Catholic who had been dismissed largely because of his wife's indiscretions with state secrets. Did the king appoint men of opposing religions to serve as his secretaries, as Wilson claimed? If so, all but Wilson missed it. In the considerable jockeying for position that took place whenever a secretariat came open, such a policy was not articulated. Of course, it would not have been publicized if it had existed. Moreover, Catholicism tainted very few applicants. Along with Calvert, gossips mentioned John Packer and Sir Dudley Carleton, two candidates not associated with Catholicism. Calvert's appointment also coincided with an anti-Catholic harangue by James. In this light Wilson's assertion seems even more doubtful.

Calvert's selection surprised many at court. Indeed, no one seemed more astonished than Calvert himself. When Buckingham told Calvert of the king's resolution to appoint him, he disqualified himself in diverse ways. He specifically stated that he thought himself unworthy "to sit in that place so lately possessed by his noble lord and master," Salisbury. Whether Calvert was genuinely concerned about his abilities or feigning humility, James was well pleased with his answer and his modesty.[38]

Why did the king choose him instead of candidates many court observers thought more deserving? Calvert mistakenly believed that he owed the appointment to Buckingham. His appointment came, however, in spite of the favorite's preference for someone—anyone—other than Calvert. That Calvert was the king's choice is indicated by an incident related some years later by Thomas Fuller. Believing that Buckingham had been instrumental in his elevation, Calvert followed court protocol. He presented a jewel of great value to the king's favorite. Buckingham returned it, stating that he had done nothing to advance him. Rather, he owed the appointment to the king, who, after reflecting on Calvert's abilities, designated him for the place. Buckingham's rejection of the gift further put the new secretary on notice.[39]

According to Buckingham, the king's motives did not flatter Calvert. The king did not want to appoint a more eminent man for fear of reflecting unfavorably on the other secretary, Naunton. Buckingham's caustic comments disregarded the most important factor. The king liked Calvert and trusted his work ethic. Moreover, Calvert's self-effacing and modest demeanor posed no threat to the king. Calvert had demonstrated his efficiency in handling routine and delicate matters of state on numerous occasions. Naunton, a literary buff, was not effective in dealing with the complexities of administration. The two were contrasting elements, but not for their religious commitments. The last thing the king wanted was a repeat of the nasty experience with Lake's wife. James blustered that the Catholic religion was composed of seven deadly sins and swore that Lady Lake was guilty of all of them. The king's sensitivity perhaps resulted from his inability to deal with his own wife's religious vacillation. He considered her commitment to Catholicism "as madness" but could only caution "her to be discreet in worship." Not surprisingly, he questioned Calvert more about his wife and her ability to be discreet in state matters than about Calvert himself. A week before the appointment, the king asserted that "women were the nourishers of Papistry in this Kingdom, and that a Papist woman and a whore were *voces convertibiles.*" Given James's strong prejudice against Catholic women, it seems unlikely that either Calvert or his wife was a practicing Catholic.[40]

James settled on Calvert in part because he was a known quantity. The Venetian ambassador noted that the king had chosen as Lake's successor "a young man of approved virtue." Calvert was an untiring worker, a loyal servant, and a discreet individual who could be depended on to carry out the king's wishes in foreign policy. Indeed, after observing him for a year, the ambassador characterized Calvert as "very cautious, prudent and restrained in his remarks." Beyond these qualities, James knew Calvert was thoroughly familiar with the European situation and the domestic scene. The king did not intend for Calvert to have any significant role in formulating those policies, and he sensed that Calvert would not try to rise above his station. Rather, as a proven administrator, Calvert's function was to execute policies conceived by others. The king recognized that Calvert, who was accustomed to following orders, would consult with his superiors before making crucial decisions and would not exercise independent judgment. In other words, Calvert was a safe appointment.[41]

Catholics apparently did not view Calvert's appointment as particularly useful. With the fall of Lake, they despaired regarding their loss of an active voice at court. Some Catholics lobbied to have Lake restored to favor or, failing that, to influence the king by some other means. Buckingham may have provided an opening when he mediated on behalf of a Mr. Lepton to gain access to the king.

Optimism prevailed among what Secretary Naunton styled the "practical Papists" that "a confident and active instrument" might overcome the loss of Lake at court. The efforts to have Lake at least restored as a councillor, some of which were attributed to the Spanish ambassador, continued into 1621.[42]

A letter from George Cottington, the second commentator on Calvert's religion during this period and a former member of Calvert's household, implies that Calvert was a Protestant at the time of his appointment. In 1628 he remembered that he had called on Calvert the day after he was sworn as secretary. He came to collect Calvert's letters to Spain and mentioned an ancient suit his relative Francis Cottington had before Calvert in his behalf. He asked the newly appointed secretary "whether he would accept of my service" and was admitted "into his family." Cottington departed a number of years later under less than friendly terms. He claimed that he never understood why his service ended, but money was certainly a factor. Cottington had invested in Calvert's Newfoundland enterprise and eventually sued him to recover some of his investment. Religion was another. His religion was incompatible with Calvert's now openly professed Catholicism. While he offered no firm date for Calvert's "new profession of Religion," his phrasing supports the argument that Calvert was Protestant at the time of his appointment in February 1619.[43]

As secretary of state, Calvert had the formidable responsibility of defending the king's leniency in matters of religion and his overtures toward Spain, policies that many Protestants found anathema. It was not necessary to be Catholic to support the Spanish alliance, but it was impossible to be a zealous Protestant and support it. His defense of the Spanish policy and its closely allied lax enforcement of the penal laws against Catholics marked Calvert in the eyes of some of his colleagues in Parliament. The Venetian ambassador noted the "various signs of contempt" shown by Commons against Calvert in 1621. Did Calvert's defense of the king's policies justify labeling Calvert a Catholic? Much depends on what is meant by *Catholic*. Under the conditions prevailing in 1621, one could be labeled, or libeled, a Papist for no more than supporting the king's policies. In Calvert's case the available evidence suggests that this is what happened. Calvert both defended and attacked the Spanish during the 1621 Parliament in accordance with what he considered to be the king's position. He was no more a "Hispaniolized Papist" than was the king.[44]

Calvert's hesitation to accept the secretary's appointment stemmed from his lack of wealth and an independent political base that left him dependent on his government offices for his livelihood. With some trepidation, he recognized that the king had chosen him over many other meritorious candidates. The king, he confessed, raised "me to that which I am." Unlike Salisbury, he functioned without the substance of power. He lacked independent wealth and status; he had only limited access to the king. Neither James nor Buckingham wanted strong-minded, independent councillors; men of lesser stature with a taste for administration fitted their needs. The new secretary would remain in London, where the king most needed his considerable administrative talents. There he would manage the intricate details of the king's foreign policy, direct the Privy Council, and see to the day-to-day operations of the government.[45]

These conditions left administrators like Calvert in an awkward position. The king's frequent absences from London complicated the process of transmitting information to his overseas representatives, and Calvert sometimes had to wait for his instructions before proceeding in matters of state. He lamented on one occasion that he could not send needed information until he heard from the king. In the absence of those instructions, he concluded that "we have the comfort of a good conscience to have discharged our duty and so leave it. I hope I shall heare from his Majesty shortly." Another time he confided to someone that he should not think it strange that Calvert's letters came slowly. The king was "in his progresses," far distant from London, and Calvert must "of necessity send by our slowe winged postes" to learn his majesty's pleasure before he could answer pressing questions. He accepted this as a condition of doing business and rarely vented his frustration. One observer reported, "For power he saith in plaine termes he hath none." Unwilling to risk rebuke from the king, Calvert rarely acted on his own and never overtly challenged the king's authority. He expressed his independence in subtle ways. For example, the manner in which he interpreted his instructions and communicated them to the ambassadors provided him with some control over the king's diplomacy.[46]

Calvert lived with the fact that he was not always made privy to the decision-making process and that others of lesser rank had more influence on policy or quicker access to information. John Packer, Buckingham's secretary who was rumored to be in line for appointment as one of the secretaries of state, had greater clout at court than Secretary Calvert. Indeed, Calvert's remoteness from the pulses of power scandalized the diplomatic corps in London. In September 1621 the Venetian ambassador reported that business was confined more than ever to the king, the prince, and Buckingham. The secretary of state "scarcely knows anything" about some important matters. A few months later the French ambassador provided a similar assessment. The control of public affairs rested with the king, the royal favorite, and the secretary of state. The king was apathetic toward public affairs, while Buckingham, although ignorant of domestic and foreign matters, interfered in both as his vanity dictated. As for Calvert, to whom most affairs of state were referred, the ambassador judged him "a very good man, of good sense and understanding, well-intentioned, courteous toward foreigners, full of respect toward ambassadors, zealously intent on the welfare of England; but because of all these good qualities, entirely without authority or influence." These limitations aside, Calvert met the king's expectations. He proved himself an assiduous and trusted servant, one on whom the king could rely upon for delicate matters of state.[47]

Given this tenuous situation, Calvert recognized the need to establish himself outside of London. His 1616 acquisition of Danby Wiske manor, which was located about five miles east of his birthplace, signified his intent to become an influence in Yorkshire. Beyond that, he needed strong allies, and he found one in Sir Thomas Wentworth. As Yorkshiremen, Calvert and Wentworth shared a common love for the northern reaches of England. Calvert confided to Wentworth in 1630, "I love Richmondshire with all my heart and it warms me when you talk of it, as cold a country as it is." But a shared love of the north and shared acquaintances did not alone form the basis of an alliance. Political designs did.[48]

Such ambitions clearly laid the foundation for the bond that shared friendship and common interests fostered. Calvert and Wentworth based their relationship on friendship and mutual advancement both locally and at court. They found a political home among the remnants of the Cecil faction. The Clifford family provided the link. The earl of Cumberland's son, Henry Clifford, married one of Salisbury's daughters. When Calvert was on a confidential mission for Salisbury in 1610, he spent much of his time with Clifford in Paris. Wentworth's connection with Clifford came through his marriage in 1611 to the eldest daughter of the earl of Cumberland (Henry Clifford's sister). After the marriage Wentworth traveled extensively on the Continent and spent much of his time in Paris with his brother-in-law. Upon his return in 1613, Wentworth assumed the role in local politics that his status accorded him. To strengthen his local base, he sought to advance his position at court through an alliance with the more experienced Calvert.[49]

Wentworth frequently journeyed to London on private matters between October 1617 and the summer of 1620. Given their mutual friends and Yorkshire backgrounds, Wentworth and Calvert undoubtedly met during these visits. Wentworth felt he knew Calvert well enough to call upon him for a number of favors. In late 1620 Wentworth reciprocated by managing Calvert's election to the House of Commons. That election was by no means a foregone conclusion, since the secretary eschewed a safe, government-controlled seat to seek election as a representative from Yorkshire. His long absence from the county of his birth, however, left him unknown to most of the electorate. He relied on Wentworth, who, as a prominent resident, had the requisite influence. The secretary met with Wentworth and Clifford in London. They agreed that Calvert's election could best be achieved if Wentworth ran with him. With all due humility, Wentworth reluctantly agreed to run, claiming that he did so not "out of any Ambition" but "to satisfy some of my best Friends, and such as have Power over me," that is, Clifford and Calvert, whom he described in another letter as his "nearest friends." This disclaimer aside, Wentworth saw an opportunity to advance his career at court and, with Calvert remaining in London, he returned to Yorkshire to secure their election.[50]

This episode left Calvert in Wentworth's debt. What had appeared in London to be a relatively simple task suddenly became a formidable operation when the election became enmeshed in local politics. Two complications emerged. Sir John Savile, who since 1615 had been challenging Wentworth for dominance in Yorkshire and who enjoyed Buckingham's favor, contested the election. Then a fall on the ice while on horseback incapacitated Wentworth for about ten critical days before the election. As an influential and lifelong resident, Wentworth believed his chances for success were excellent, but he despaired for the absent secretary's chances. To avoid any possible embarrassment, Wentworth brought considerable pressure to bear on the voters of Yorkshire.[51]

Savile had significant court connections based on his entente with Buckingham. Still, he made Calvert's court affiliation a bone of contention in the campaign. Wentworth reported to Calvert that Savile's "Instruments" were exceedingly busy in attempting to undermine the election, intimating to "the Common Sort underhand" that because Calvert was not a resident he could not by law be chosen to represent the county. Wentworth advised Calvert to consult the lord chancellor, Sir Francis Bacon, who "is very sensible of you in this Business," to obtain a letter clarifying the residency situation. Savile's people also charged that since Calvert was the king's secretary and a "Stranger," he was dangerous to the interests of the "Country." The youthful campaign manager assured Calvert that he would "omit nothing that my poor understanding tells me may do you service."[52]

When Savile attempted to turn Calvert's court connections against him, Wentworth extolled Calvert's influence at court, which he bartered as a marketable commodity. After soliciting the support of Sir Robert Askwith and asking that he in turn influence his friends and neighbors, Wentworth promised to introduce him to the secretary so Calvert could express his gratitude in person. He added, significantly, that Askwith would find the secretary more than ready to assist him in whatever ways he could. To another he promised to write to Calvert for a burgess ship at Richmond for him. Wentworth brought social pressure to bear where he could. To Henry Slingsby, he recommended a strategy that would result in an election challenge in Parliament. He asked him to have the high constables order the petty constables to list the names of the freeholders, designating those who had promised to be at York and to vote for the two of them. How much was done to make good on the promise is difficult to say. Calvert later sought favors from Carleton for Slingsby, whom he referred to as "a very worthy friend" whom he much esteemed.[53]

Wentworth had good cause to ponder "how the Country stands affected," for Savile was having telling effect. From Leeds a correspondent reported that Savile had received three hundred letters within a two-day span from "Gentlemen of Worth" urging him to stand for election. He reported that "the Country" was not that well disposed to Calvert because he was a "Stranger to the Country," because of his affiliation with the court, and for various other reasons that he did not relate. He did not attack him for his religious commitment. Savile appealed to the cloth-working interests, who may have been particularly turned against the government by the recent onset of a depression in the textile industry. His obvious success in exploiting his own influence at court aside, Savile decried Calvert's role as courtier, which he assumed would undermine support among Yorkshire voters. But Wentworth had carefully organized his support. When the election was held on Christmas day, Wentworth, standing first, carried the secretary to victory.[54]

Savile refused to accept defeat and challenged the validity of the election in Parliament. Much to Wentworth's chagrin, the leadership of the house submitted the disputed election to the committee on privileges. That committee, after hearing the testimony of three Yorkshire constables, cleared Wentworth and Calvert "of all Faults." Wentworth felt only partially vindicated by the decision. Addressing some of the Yorkshire freeholders a few months later, he justified his efforts in promoting Calvert's election. The secretary's faithful performance,

Wentworth told them, was more than any of your neighbors could have done for you. He asserted that Calvert provided better service than any representative elected in recent times. He hoped that the freeholders would see the perverse and depraved nature of those who labored to persuade them that Calvert's selection constituted a betrayal of the country.[55]

The knowledge that Buckingham was not well disposed toward either Calvert or Wentworth enhanced their relationship. Service in the House of Commons promoted the bond. While Parliament sat, Calvert, Wentworth, and other mutual friends, such as Clifford and Christopher Wandesford, had ample opportunity to meet and confer. Wentworth mentioned an example of Calvert's cooperation when he addressed the inhabitants of Rotherham about a bill in which they were keenly interested, an act that restricted those informing on violations of the penal laws (except those concerning popish recusants) to the county where the offense actually occurred. The bill originally prohibited the attorney general from informing, as he had formerly done, but when the bill was read, Calvert moved to strike the proviso limiting the attorney general, fearing it might unwittingly become a way to rob the people of a beneficial and needed law. Meeting privately with Calvert, Wentworth expressed considerable doubt that the king would assent to so general a law. The secretary assured his younger colleague that he need not worry, for Calvert knew well "his Majesties tender affection toward us" and that if rightly informed, he would not stop its passage. Calvert promised that he would not fail to apprise the king, out of his service both to him and to the commonwealth.[56]

The friendship, as it evolved, went beyond serving their mutual interests and became a relationship characterized by genuine respect and affection. Calvert later declared a commitment to Roman Catholicism. Wentworth, a staunch Protestant, eventually gained considerable notoriety for his anti-Catholic policies in Ireland. But religious differences mattered little to them. The friendship reflected, among other things, one of the key concepts that later came to fruition in colonial enterprises, namely, that people of differing faiths can work together to achieve common ends.

CHAPTER THREE

"But by God's help many have been lifted out of the mire of corruption"

George Calvert's Conversion and Resignation (1621–1625)

In the five years following his appointment as secretary, Calvert enjoyed his greatest successes and endured his foremost political—and religious—trials. His public experiences, along with profound changes in his personal circumstances, helped to forge the radical concepts he implemented later in his colonial enterprises. Two public activities were primarily responsible for entangling him in the web of church-state politics that resulted from the government's commitment to uniformity and its defense of the "true religion." His first challenge came in the Parliament of 1621, where he defended the king's resented religious and diplomatic policies. The second came after the dissolution of this parliament in February 1622 and arose from his supervision of the king's renewed effort to solve the Palatinate crisis through an alliance with Spain. Subsequently, two closely related issues, one personal (his conversion to Roman Catholicism) and the other public (his resignation as secretary of state), profoundly affected his life. The resolution of these matters in early 1625 permitted Calvert to focus attention on the overseas enterprises he had established while serving as secretary.

For Calvert, fidelity to the king and the king's policies remained paramount. Religion was one way he demonstrated that loyalty. As long as he served the king as secretary of state, Calvert conformed to the king's religion. He reaffirmed his loyalty on numerous occasions. Three public methods existed to confirm allegiance: taking the oaths of supremacy and allegiance, receiving Communion in the state church, and attending church. Service in the Parliament of 1621 afforded Calvert, and his colleagues, opportunities to affirm their loyalty. Members took the oaths together. Calvert also had a direct role in arranging the Communion service, "a means of Reconciliation" and the ultimate loyalty test.[1]

On its first working day, February 5, 1621, Commons ordered that "to prevent that noe person inflicted with poperye should sitt as a member," all members must take Communion at St. Margaret's in Westminster. The Communion service degenerated into a jurisdictional dispute between the clergy of St. Margaret's and the leaders of Commons and tested the secretary's ability to pacify the factions. The clergy objected to having the learned bishop-elect of Ireland, Dr. James Ussher, preach at the Communion service. Commons selected another church. The king, after complimenting the House on its pious and religious purposes, indicated that he wished to have the service at St. Margaret's. Commons sent word of its intention to use St. Margaret's, but the dean of St. Margaret's objected to Ussher's preaching without license. Commons sent Calvert to the king to mediate the matter. Calvert reported that the king graciously granted the requisite license for Ussher and that the dean had been duly informed. Secretary Calvert, who agreed with his friend Wentworth that no one is fit to serve without receiving Communion, joined his king and his colleagues.[2]

James opened the session by lecturing House members on their duties: enact laws he thought necessary; detail, without attempting to remedy, the grievances of the realm; and grant the much-needed financial assistance. His inability to live within his means forced him to convene this much dreaded parliament and to justify his policies for church and state. He explicated the origins of his Palatine policy and his attempts at mediation. He took pains to assuage doubt on the sensitive issue of religion. He had eased the enforcement of the penal laws on his Catholic subjects to facilitate the proposed marriage between Prince Charles and the Spanish infanta, the instrument by which he hoped to secure peace in the Palatinate. He reiterated that he would do nothing to sully the Protestant religion and cautioned members not to belabor grievances.[3]

The king left Calvert and the other counselors to assuage the considerable unrest his policies had aroused. But Calvert's reassurances fell on deaf ears, for members "began rightly with religion." They debated "promiscuously" four issues—defense and maintenance of the House's privilege under the rubric of liberty of speech, the best course "to abate the Insolence of the Papists," supply of the king's wants, and a redress of grievances accumulated since the last parliament—that would occupy their attention for the duration of the session.[4]

Even before this parliament convened, the king had stirred considerable resentment when he dismissed Calvert's staunchly Protestant fellow secretary, Sir Robert Naunton. The Spanish, who viewed Naunton as their greatest enemy, knew that the malcontents met at his house to discuss their opposition. Not surprisingly, many, including foreign ambassadors, attributed his disgrace to inappropriate influence of the Spanish ambassador, Diego Sarmiento de Acuña, Conde de Gondomar. Some members of Commons blamed Gondomar for the rapid increase in the number and influence of Catholics at home and the bumbling support for the Protestant cause abroad. Their discontent, which flowed from a deep-seated belief that English Catholics constituted a threat to the nation, energized them. As one member put it, "Religion and the Church [are] the Principal Matters of Parliament."[5]

Taking his cues from the king's opening speech, Calvert urged his colleagues not to let issues of religion and free speech divert Commons from the two main objectives laid out for them. He called on them to pass the "Good Laws" urged by the king and to vote the needed supplies. With a sense of urgency, Calvert addressed the deteriorating situation in the Palatinate and the king's needs to defend his errant son-in-law. This House was not called to examine why the situation existed or to evaluate past policies but to provide a remedy. He urged members to vote the supply, for "it is not honorable for the king to have his sword in his sheath" when so many are drawn. His plea, as well as those from other councillors, had little impact on the agitated members. Many thought Calvert's speech, which did not address grievances, "somewhat untimely." If they granted the king his money, members feared that "the parliament would be as good as done."[6]

Calvert quickly discerned the limitations that his role imposed. Mere words would not alleviate the anxiety, fear, and hostility aroused by the king's policies. Rather than uniting king and Commons, religious issues divided them. Both wanted their nation to restore James's son-in-law to his inheritance, but they disagreed on tactics. Zealous Protestants spurned a strategy that centered on an alliance with Spain. Spain was the enemy! Calvert's defense of strategies that members deemed pro-Spanish and pro-Catholic estranged him from them. They suspected him and his easy familiarity with the Spanish ambassador. His efforts to mediate between king and Commons all too often brought frustration.

The king expected Calvert to defend his policies, which he did to the chagrin of many members. Unable to attack the king directly, some members singled out Calvert as a target for maligning the king's domestic and foreign policies. Sometimes they ignored him; sometimes they treated him harshly; sometimes they humiliated him; and sometimes they sent Calvert to the king to mediate their differences.[7]

Religious issues, primarily the insolence of the Papists, prevailed. Calvert and others went to the House of Lords to request a conference regarding a petition to the king for the better execution of the laws against Catholics. Despite the intermittent sparring over matters of religion, which Calvert referred to as "rubs," a conciliatory mood existed between the king and Commons. Calvert reported that the parliament "(thanks be to god) proceeds happily." The lower house granted "two entire subsidies" to be paid within a year. The king, in turn, thanked them profusely and promised to spend all to benefit Elizabeth and Frederick. However, he gave no satisfaction regarding the laws against recusants.[8]

An incident that occurred early in the session illustrated the difficulty Calvert had defending the king's policies toward English Catholics and the Spanish. He and fellow councillor Sir Edward Coke clashed over the Spanish ambassador. Coke, who, according to the Venetian ambassador, "shows himself very opposite to his Majesty," delivered a scathing attack on the Spanish ambassador and the resort of English Catholics to his chapel. Coke took the popular position, "won a generall applause," and left Calvert to advocate for the government. The secretary defended the ambassador's house as a sanctuary under the laws of nations. His comment that visits to the ambassador's chapel by English Catholics were "by noe connivance of the State" touched off a firestorm. Calvert's statement enraged some members of the committee on recusants, who went so far as to call for the secretary's expulsion from the House. Cooler heads prevailed, however, and the committee resolved to ask the king how he proposed to conclude the Spanish marriage without prejudice to religion.[9]

After this parliament's first month, the usually modest secretary optimistically reported to Carleton, "I doubt not of good success for my part." He had been busy. The lower house had met on twenty-one days during February, and Calvert spoke once or more on at least seventeen days. In March he addressed Commons at least once on fourteen days. In addition, as one of the king's principal spokesmen, he spent considerable time conferring with the king and his other advisers. This left him little time to attend to his other duties. He complained near the end of March that he could not convene the Privy Council to conduct needed business because parliamentary affairs consumed so much time. Still, as the House adjourned for a three-week recess, the Venetian ambassador judged that it "is working harmoniously with the King." Each, he thought, aspired to see who could please the other most.[10]

Conciliatory gestures aside, the bitter hostility toward English Catholics and the Spanish continued and spilled over into the streets during the recess. A number of apprentices and "base people" insulted the Spanish ambassador while he traveled the streets of London, but the threatened violence did not materialize. Dissatisfied with the handling of the matter, James returned to rebuke the lord mayor and the alderman "for their slack and negligent government in not restraining the barbarous innocency of those people." He ordered the offenders to be publicly whipped throughout the streets of London. He issued a decree suppressing insolent abuses against persons of quality and charged the clergy to exhort the people to respect ambassadors. His efforts had no impact on the strong anti-Spanish, anti-Catholic feelings of most Londoners or of the returning members of Parliament.[11]

When members reconvened in mid-April, the king hinted that they would not be sitting much longer. He beseeched them to finish their work in a timely fashion. James wanted them to vote additional subsidies but without strings attached. Calvert continued to encourage members to implement the king's stated goals. He remained on the sidelines while the members debated issues on which the king permitted open discussion, relayed messages from the king, and when he thought the House challenged the king's prerogatives, he politely warned of the dangers of pursuing such a course. Wherever possible, he sought a middle ground that would satisfy contending loyalties between king and Commons.[12]

For the remainder of April and well into May, House members pressed for a resolution of their long list of grievances. Increasingly dissatisfied with members' willful behavior and unwilling to forsake his dream of a negotiated peace, James found Commons to be a source of embarrassment. In late May he resolved to recess Parliament until November. Faced with the prospect of returning home without any tangible gains, members pleaded for more time. The normally placid Calvert, exasperated with the House's dilatory tactics and its obsession with grievances, threw down a challenge. The king, he stated, would approve all bills that were good for the commonwealth and would hear and answer members' grievances. To this point, there had been a "uniting of the King's heart to his subjects, and the subjects to the King and woe be to him that would make a separation." Religion was certainly a contentious point, but the secretary ques-

tioned whether the strategy of Commons was the best way to help. Ever conciliatory, he implored members to "prepare as many bills as we may," realizing that
neither king nor Commons would get all desired results. Not all members
shared his willingness to compromise, and after a short, unproductive extension,
Parliament adjourned on June 4 without passing any bills or resolving any grievances.[13]

No longer consumed with parliamentary affairs, Calvert devoted his time to
council matters and foreign affairs. With the clamor for war with Spain abated
temporarily, James initiated another effort to secure peace by negotiation. Finally, after months of contemplation, he dispatched John Lord Digby to Vienna
to bargain for the restoration of the Lower Palatinate. Chamberlain captured
the despondent mood of the English when he lamented that "sure mens [i.e.,
staunch Protestants'] hearts begin to sinke, and fear that religion is hard in case
as well at home as abroad." From London, Calvert related the zealous manner
in which Gondomar solicited on behalf of the Catholics of England. The king
hoped that dealing frankly with Gondomar in London would facilitate Digby's
negotiations for a settlement. He ordered his judicial officers to proceed with
"all moderation and clemency towards that sort of his subjects." Relaxation of
the penal laws and closer ties with Spain ensured troubled relations between
king and Parliament. His diplomatic initiative, however, averted the necessity of
reconvening Parliament until February.[14]

By mid-October, Calvert reported an increase in the sharp differences between the king and his people. Until Digby returned, however, no one could
predict what would come of the Palatinate business. The king learned the full
extent of the failure only after the angry and humiliated Digby returned empty-
handed on October 31. James then altered his tactics and ordered members of
Parliament to reconvene on November 20. Calvert reported that the king now
wanted additional contributions from his people to support a war to restore his
son-in-law. The failure of diplomacy coupled with the lax enforcement of the
laws against Catholics intensified the distrust between the king and his parliament.[15]

This session, which lasted about a month, tried Calvert's patience in a num-
ber of ways. The dramatic shift to a war strategy left him in an awkward posi-
tion. The king dispatched others, Lord Keeper Williams, Lionel Cranfield, and
Lord Digby, to describe the "distressed state" of his children, Elizabeth and
Frederick, and to lay out a new course of action. Digby, who, according to
Calvert, made a plain and particular narrative of his whole mission, concluded

that all other means had failed and that war was the only recourse. The king had determined to recover the Palatinate by war but lacked the means to do anything about it without the assistance of his people. Cranfield, now lord treasurer, promised to ask for no money other than for that purpose and reminded Commons of its pledge to spend life and goods for this cause. Calvert was not part of the deliberations for war, and he assumed that these speeches established the general guidelines to be followed.[16]

He discovered, however, that Commons showed no disposition to supply the king's needs without resolution of the outstanding grievances. Lingering misgivings about free speech and misinforming the king took on new urgency. Williams, Cranfield, and Digby reiterated the king's command to discuss the business of the Palatinate. Calvert, ever the mediator, tried to appease anxieties regarding free speech. The king had issued a proclamation that forbade discussion of state matters in alehouses and taverns, but, Calvert said with a touch of sarcasm, "I hope this is neither alehouse nor tavern." The secretary's levity was lost on the sober House. Another member raised the issue of Sir Edwin Sandys's imprisonment. James had ordered his arrest soon after the June adjournment and, although long released from prison, his absence was conspicuous. Was Sandys arrested because of parliamentary business? Acting without any specific commission from the king, Calvert assured members that Sandys's incarceration was not for anything said or done in Parliament. One witness reported that "the House will scarce believe Mr. Secretary, but thinketh he equivocateth." Later a member expressed indignation with Calvert's explanation because he was a party to the arrest "and therefore no fit person in this case to give satisfaction."[17]

Members not only attacked the king's representatives; they also subjected the king's Palatinate policy to scathing criticism. Calvert tried to refute the false conclusion that this was not the time to vote a supply. In arguing for the supply, Calvert abandoned his usual discretion and strongly condemned both the Spanish and the English Catholics. He lectured that friendship among princes "is as their Strength and Interest is." The king of Spain can be trusted only so far. When James was ready, Calvert asserted, "he will be at defiance with the King of Spain; and for the false-hearted Christians, the papists, I would they were discovered and laid open." The king "hath been too long with his Sword in his sheath, but you would have it longer in." To fail to vote the supply was to make a farce of the House's previous commitment to the king's children. Inaction made a lie of earlier bellicose assertions. House leaders, who claimed not to know who "our true Enemie" was, endorsed the king's war in principle but disagreed with him on the tactics to be used. Limited warfare would accomplish little "against the Spaniard, unless we take from him his Purse, the West Indies." Calvert recognized the problem and informed his colleagues that the present supply was only sufficient to maintain the forces in the Palatinate; it would not sustain a long war. Finally after extensive debate, Commons appointed a committee to draw up a petition to the king on recusants, asked for a session before Christmas, and voted a subsidy for the "present Relief of the Palatinate," to be paid in February.[18]

At this critical juncture, with the Palatinate issue temporarily resolved, Buckingham's man, Sir George Goring, moved that Commons petition the king "to declare open War against the King of Spayne" if he refused to assist in restoring the Palatinate. Goring related to his patron that his suggestion took wonderfully well. The motion excited members but left them "much distracted" as they tried to sort out Goring's intentions. After considerable debate, Commons sent the king a petition that ranged over matters of religion and foreign policy at the close of business on December 3.[19]

Calvert, not knowing the origins of the motion and embarrassed by his ignorance, remained silent. He did not enter the fray until the next day. The secretary delivered what one member later described as a "soul-killing Letter from his Majesty." The king at last made his position clear in the form of a sharp rebuke. Confusion and anger reigned when members realized that the king had written his letter before receiving the controversial petition. The speaker of the House dutifully read the letter, which Calvert later characterized as "a brave one." The king had heard that his detention by ill health at some distance from Parliament had led some fiery spirits to meddle with matters far beyond their capacity and to encroach upon the prerogative. He excoriated members for interfering with state mysteries, namely, the prince's marriage, discussions about the king of Spain, and individual cases belonging to the courts of justice. He forbade any further debates on these matters. Concerning Sandys, the irritated king reiterated that he was not committed for misdemeanors in the House. Besides, he considered himself free to punish all insolence in Parliament. As for the petition, dated the same day as the king's letter, James asserted that he would neither listen to it nor answer it if it touched upon the forbidden points. Stunned, but enraged, House members realized that they had little recourse against the king's frontal attack. They sent messengers to recall the petition and resolved to discuss the matter further the next day. The letter seemed to rejuvenate Calvert. He told Buckingham that he did not know how others responded, but he applauded it. It was exceedingly comforting to "see his Majesty in such a princely manner" vindicate his honor "out of the hands of those who were so bold with it."[20]

The events of December 4 demonstrated the difficulties Calvert had as one of the king's men in the House of Commons. He, and the other councillors, received only general instructions concerning foreign policy matters. Digby's relation to the House seemed to indicate a shift in policy toward Spain. Acting on this assumption, and after the king departed for Newmarket, the councillors, left "to ourselves, wee neither spared the King of Spaine, nor the match, nor any thing that might concerne that Nation." For the next two weeks, they pursued such a course, and without any instructions to the contrary, "wee thought wee had done well." Calvert and the others now found themselves in the embarrassing position of having read the signs incorrectly and speaking in opposition to the king's position on Spain. Not surprisingly, suspicious House members vented their anger on the privy councillors. They concluded that Calvert's bold words were meant to trap them, and they singled him out for abuse. Only he knew that he had acted with sincerity. Only the king's strong assertion of his position ameliorated the stinging abuse.[21]

After virtually ignoring the House since he had recalled it, the lethargic monarch now attempted to reassert control. The king and Buckingham inundated Calvert with directions. The secretary was by this time damaged goods and had little credibility with his colleagues in the House. The Venetian ambassador wrote of the contempt expressed by some members toward Calvert when he spoke on many particulars in the king's name. One member openly ridiculed Calvert when he urged that the House not attempt to justify the petition by satisfying the piqued king "by Way of Excuse." Commons ignored his counsel that to offer the petition again would only "incense his Majesty the more." A few days later, Calvert brought a command from the king, but to his mortification, members ignored him and the order. He repeated it, only to be met with a frigid response that they needed more time to consider the matter. Calvert took these humiliations with as much dignity as he could muster but was unable to stem the tide. He could only quibble over the final phrasing of the petition, which was in its final stages. Calvert tried to return the House to the business of passing bills, but he faced a rebellion. The secretary informed Buckingham that many members desired to sit tight and conduct no business until they received the king's answer. He admonished members to abandon their course but to no avail. The now isolated secretary found few to help further "his Majesty's just and princely ends." He lamented to Buckingham that the king's supporters remained silent and did not speak on the king's behalf. Indeed, with such a charged atmosphere on the day the petition was sent, the secretary despaired of completing any business.[22]

Members continued to vent their anger at the king toward Calvert. On December 10, with the House sitting "long silent," he announced another message from the king, who expressly commanded Commons to pass the bills it had under consideration and "prepare to make an end of Session before Christmas." Members debated the matter. Calvert interjected a terse reminder that he had relayed not advice but a command from the king, adding that in his estimation the order did not prejudice the liberties of the House. More debate followed before members ordered the secretary to put the message in writing.[23]

A letter from the king on December 17 did little to assuage the doubts of members who adamantly believed that their liberties were under attack. The king decried the House's penchant for wasting time in "the curious wrangling of lawyers upon words and syllables." He informed House members that his earlier letter, which stated that their privileges were a toleration rather than an inheritance, was not meant to infringe on any privilege they enjoyed. The next day, with many members absent, Calvert moved that at "a certain Hour we shall proceed to Business," whether the House was full or not. Despite the fact that the king "was very desirous to make a session," no accord could be reached. On December 19, as Calvert put it, "Our ill handling of matters" led to the dissolution of the Parliament, which he thought was a "grave misfortune both to the king and people at this time."[24]

This acrimonious end disappointed Calvert. He suffered the double humiliation of serving as the king's spokesman in Commons without having access to the king or having the full confidence of his closest advisers, and of finding that his pleas for conciliation fell on deaf ears. Even if the king's men had spoken with one voice, even if the king had kept Calvert fully informed of his thinking, even if Buckingham had not interfered, Calvert could not have gained the king's objectives. The harassed secretary learned that he could not reconcile the interests of the king and members of the lower house on matters of religion and foreign policy. More important, he learned that religious uniformity confined the king and his subjects to perpetual conflict. Wentworth and Calvert could only lament that the dissolution was a "Disaster fallen upon this so hopeful a Parliament." There was blessing mixed with the disaster, however. The king, convinced that the Spanish match was the only way to peace on the Continent and the restoration of his son-in-law, dismissed the intense rancor evidenced in Parliament. In the absence of organized Commons-based opposition, the king and his only functioning secretary pursued the match without interference.[25]

To what extent did Calvert's continued involvement in these sensitive negotiations affect his subsequent decision to declare a commitment to Catholicism? His duties required closer involvement with Spanish representatives and greater contact with the English Catholic community. His pursuit of the king's objectives may have fostered a growing tension in his mind between his external conformity (Protestant) and his internal beliefs (Catholic) instilled during his childhood. If so, the tension placed him in a delicate position. In his actions, however, he never moved beyond the king's intended policy, a policy that favored leniency for English Catholics. William Aston wrote that Calvert held "his greatness soe with the Kinge as whatsoever the Kinge shall saye, he will doe."[26]

As circumstances dictated, he acted both for and against Catholics. In July 1621 he incurred the wrath of the newly appointed lord keeper, John Williams, for releasing "one Rockwood, a Papist," even though he undoubtedly did so on the king's instructions. After the Florentine ambassador solicited him on behalf of lay recusants imprisoned throughout England and Wales, he sought Buckingham's advice regarding the king's policy in the hope that he might be rid of further solicitations. In March 1622 he had the Privy Council issue a warrant banishing a seminary priest. His actions toward English Catholics stayed within the king's objectives, and never did he actively solicit on their behalf. Gondomar, who noted Naunton's dismissal in February 1622, described Calvert as friendly to Spain, but he did not identify him as a Catholic.[27]

The Protestant Calvert used his position to influence patronage decisions in the Church of England. In January 1622, after the death of the archbishop of York, he recommended a "Mr. Doctor Wright," for whom he had solicited appointments in the past. Buckingham chose another, but Calvert did not forget this man he styled as a friend and actively solicited on his behalf. About a year later he wrote to Conway asking that Wright be allowed to do homage to the king for the Bishopric of Bristol. The secretary also lobbied have a Church of England dean appointed for the Isle of Guernsey. The king rejected his suggestion because he did not want to alienate the French Huguenots ("those of the religion") on the island.[28]

His work as secretary defined his life, and at times it consumed him. He complained that, as the only secretary, he was stretched to the limit by a number of diplomatic crises. At the end of July 1622, he lamented to Carleton that his time was wholly taken up with what he called the miserable business of the Palatinate and the truce negotiated at Brussels. Reading and responding to the many dispatches from the king's ministers in those parts left "scarce a day free." The pace of negotiations frustrated Calvert, who vented his feelings to the earl of Bristol in a letter written near the end of October. He entreated Bristol to assure both king and prince that he would not lose an hour to bring the negotiations to a speedy end. Calvert did not, however, control the tempo. The cumbersome pace of the Spanish negotiators forced him either to accept their slow pace or ruin it with haste. He said he would "by God's assistance do that which to the best of my understanding" would advance his majesty's service. In December he apologized to Sir Thomas Roe for not punctually answering his letters. The burden of state business, which had multiplied "in this troublesome time," had left him not "without some excuse."[29]

In July the king appointed Buckingham's man, Sir Edward Conway, to the Privy Council. Rumors persisted throughout the fall that Buckingham wanted him named to replace Naunton as secretary, but the appointment did not happen until February 1623. The new secretary did little to lighten Calvert's load, but his coming did sow the seeds of Calvert's undoing. Buckingham did not choose Conway because he was a staunch Protestant. Rather, he elevated a man who was slavishly devoted to his service and who could be expected to do his bidding. As Sir John Hipsley told Buckingham in September, "Mr. Secretarie Conway is yours bodie and soul." Calvert had on number of occasions demonstrated that he did not fit such a description.[30]

Calvert continued at a feverish pace through the summer of 1623 as the government attempted to implement its Spanish policy. The king's frequent absences from London left Calvert responsible for the routine administration of foreign policy. He negotiated details of the treaty and its implementation with the Spanish ambassadors. He also managed the council. Although frequently bypassed by a system of personal government that avoided normal channels, the secretary seemed secure in his position in the government.[31]

His status at court still dictated caution when it came to his own religious sentiments. As well as anyone, Calvert knew the discrepancies between stated positions (filled with highly charged negative rhetoric) and government actions (usually moderate) toward English Catholics. As well as anyone, he sensed the tension between English and Catholic. As well as anyone, he knew that a significant minority of those at court either openly or quietly worshiped as Catholics. The discretion of James's wife, Anne of Denmark, notwithstanding, he surely knew that she attended Mass. As well as anyone, George Calvert understood the confused world of conflicting religious loyalties that pervaded the court of James I.

Equally so, his status dictated that he aggressively pursue his own interests. He used his influence to support his friends in the government and secure his interests outside of London. In a move that signified his persistent interest in overseas expansion, in July 1622 he obtained membership in the Council of New England. Left in London to administer the government, he still found time to pursue his interests in Yorkshire. He and Wentworth, who had returned to Yorkshire after Parliament ended, had two primary goals. Wentworth continued his efforts to increase their influence in the North in the face of Buckingham's continued support of Savile, while Calvert worked to advance Wentworth at court.[32]

Wentworth assisted with personal matters. He intervened when Calvert's father had difficulty in 1622 securing lumber for the construction of a new building on the secretary's estate at Kiplin. He urged his cousin Christopher Danby, who for some reason would not sell the trees to the elder Calvert, not only to sell them but to "freely bestow them upon him," since their value could not be great. In addition he reminded Danby that in the previous year the secretary had carefully, affectionately, and without any fanfare done him a kindness deserving a greater consideration than a few trees. Wentworth related to Calvert's father that he was grateful for an opportunity, however small, "to doe Mr. Secretary any Service" that conveyed his affection and zeal to him and his affairs.[33]

As Calvert soon discovered, it was easier to procure trees in the North than to secure appointments in the South. He had a few minor successes, such as the appointment of William Peasley, his own secretary and future son-in-law, as clerk of the Privy Council and an appointment for Christopher Wandesford, whom Wentworth styled as "my diligent and expedite Ambassador resident with his Majestie of Great Britaine." Wandesford soon after asked Wentworth and Calvert to be godfathers to his first child. Wentworth replied that he considered it an honor to be godfather to Wandesford's son and expressed his joy at Wandesford's linking him "with so noble a Friend as Mr. Secretary." During July and August 1623, Calvert repeatedly urged Wentworth's appointment as a deputy lieutenant for Yorkshire. Although King James spoke highly of him, the oppo-

sition was still too strong. Calvert did manage to secure his own appointment to
the Council of York in August, but this marked his last triumph in advancing his
and Wentworth's interests in the North.[34]

Wentworth's letters during the spring of 1623 and into 1624 reflected a
growing bitterness with his inability to secure a position at court, dissatisfaction
with his continued isolation in Yorkshire, and, paradoxically, his infatuation with
country life. He inveighed against what he termed Calvert's great goddess, political ambition, whose altars were so perfumed and smoking with the holocausts
of honor and greatness, "as meaner people may not presume to approach them
with their rurall and homely sacrifice." His comments revealed that Calvert had
shared his apprehension about his growing exclusion from the inner circle at
court.[35]

Political ambition finally ensnared Calvert. The critical event occurred in the
summer of 1623. The ailing king reluctantly agreed to allow his heir and Buckingham to journey to Spain to conduct the negotiations personally. The king
neglected to consult with the one person most knowledgeable about the negotiations, his secretary of state, who only learned of the plan after they departed
on their quixotic junket. Calvert's reaction to this rash initiative can only be surmised. As an experienced diplomatic who understood the ways of the Spanish,
he would have recognized the futility of this rash action. As an experienced
courtier, he would have grasped its implications for his own position.[36]

Calvert's standing continued to decline. While in Spain, the duke ignored
him and sent his correspondence directly to his "confidant" Conway, who then
informed the king. The tactic rankled the senior secretary, and news of his anger
reached Buckingham in Madrid. The duke dismissed Calvert's pique by writing
to Conway that "it is no matter." By September the situation was so obvious that
the Venetian ambassador reported that "this Conway constantly follows his
Majesty and grows in favour daily." The Spaniards "hate him extremely," refused to acknowledge him, and only negotiated with Calvert.[37]

Reports received from Madrid in mid-September that the prince might return without the infanta brought negotiations to a standstill. The Venetian ambassador remarked in a conversation with Calvert on September 26 that the
prince's return without the infanta clearly showed that the Spanish had ended
the matter. The secretary responded that two impediments stood in the way of
a favorable result, "the will of the favorite and the pope's blessing." He "could
not help agreeing" that if the prince could not arrange the marriage, the negotiations of other ministers offered little hope. The secretary could only add that

when the prince returned, the government would come to some decision. The ambassador appreciated that Calvert expressed himself freely. He knew that the secretary, who "makes a show of being a confidant of the Spaniards," was "a good Englishman" and the enemy of so many delays.[38]

Charles and Buckingham's return a few weeks later, empty-handed and much embittered, sealed Calvert's fate. Former secretary Naunton characterized the day of return as the happiest he had seen since James's "most joyful entrance" into the kingdom; he called it a "holy day." Conway gleefully reported that Charles and Buckingham spent three hours with the king, with as much freedom and love as ever. The prince's return altered the negotiations. Buckingham and Charles prepared to extricate themselves by destroying the Spanish treaties signed in Spain. Toward the end of October, those close to the prince began to speak against Spain, and the foundation was laid for scuttling the Spanish marriage.[39]

Calvert had little to do after October that did not relate in one way or another to Spanish affairs. As a member of a select group appointed to consider the treaty and English obligations under it, he sensed that James would consider it contrary to his will if the match did come to fruition. The aging monarch was no match for the two men closest to him. By the end of the year, the prince and the royal favorite spoke openly against the Spanish marriage and pressured James to call a parliament to consider their now repugnant treaties. In view of the new turn of events, many in the government scrambled to reassess their support for the treaties. Why did Calvert not shift his position once it became obvious that Buckingham opposed the treaties? First, the match and the concomitant Palatinate policy had served as a loyalty test. Calvert's support for the Spanish policy did not result from a desire to foster Catholic goals. It flowed from his loyalty to the king. Second, Buckingham spurned Calvert's weak gestures of conciliation. Third, Buckingham's alternative, a match with a French princess that offered equal dividends for Catholics, made little sense from the point of view of advancing English foreign policy objectives. The king's secretary continued to support a policy he thought was best for England. He remained loyal to a group of colleagues who had for years supported the Spanish match and to his king, who conceived of the policy in the first place. Without an army and lacking the money to pay for one, James, and his secretary, had no choice but to follow this strategy.[40]

Buckingham, whom Gondomar believed incapable of distinguishing between principled opposition and personal betrayal, effectively isolated supporters of the Spanish negotiations. The so-called Spanish party never favored that nation's interests over English interests. They supported the marriage and a lessening of the penal laws against Catholics and sought to bring peace to the Continent. In short, they supported the king. Now, with power shifting away from the king, his supporters found themselves in a intense fight to survive against a determined and reckless favorite. Calvert's votes in favor of the Spanish policy reveal that he was in a desperate fight for political survival. As long as those negotiations remained open, he served a useful purpose. He sensed that his position was tenuous and knew that his demise paled in comparison to the favorite's antipathy toward the earl of Middlesex and the earl of Bristol.[41]

By the end of the year, however, the situation looked bleak, and court observers referred to Calvert as damaged goods. One of Trumbull's correspondents warned him in mid-November not to rely on the secretary, who was now powerless. Chamberlain noted that talk of the match grew daily more cool, and Secretary Calvert felt the chill. The secretary had been around too long not to know that his career was in jeopardy. Despite the ominous signs, Calvert did not abandon the king and his Spanish policy. He could not have known that which became apparent with hindsight. The prince's return from Madrid marked the end of the king's reign. The prince and the favorite encouraged popular anti-Spanish sentiments to commandeer control of foreign and domestic policy. The shift to a French alliance left Calvert with little room to maneuver. His last vote in a majority supporting the Spanish match came late in January 1624. Those who remained loyal to the king's long-held policies, that is, supporters of the discredited Spanish alliance, found themselves a dwindling minority as Buckingham's strength grew.[42]

By the time a new parliament convened three weeks later, the royal pair controlled the government. Sensing victory, they pushed beyond the king's intentions and sought to use Parliament as the instrument to destroy the now despised treaties. Unable to secure a more prominent place in the House of Commons in 1624, the discredited secretary settled for the royally controlled seat at Oxford. His presence forced him to witness the destruction of the policy that he had labored so diligently to secure.[43]

Despite the reversals, Calvert maintained his conformity to the Church of England. As a member of the 1624 Parliament, Calvert, along with the other privy councillors, undoubtedly took the oaths of supremacy and allegiance, and surely he was in attendance when Communion was administered to the lower house. Because Calvert had long subordinated his religious feelings to his political career, it is understandable that the final resolution of them would not come until after his political career had been determined.[44]

James urged this parliament, which sat from February until the end of May, to pressure Spain in the futile hope of obtaining restitution of the Palatinate. Calvert heard the ambivalent king make "a very gracious and plausible speach confessing he had ben deluded in the treaty of the match." He promised that the prince, Buckingham, and the two secretaries of state would provide full particulars about the marriage treaty and granted Commons carte blanche on foreign policy matters. Buckingham took the lead and supplied the information about the Spanish negotiations that he wanted members to hear. In the vitriolic outpourings that followed the duke's revelations, Calvert, perhaps as confused as most members at the division between the king and the royal favorite, remained strangely silent, only occasionally interjecting messages from the king. Chamberlain caught the mood when he wrote that members on all sides were so wary and cautious that it seemed as if they were dealing with foreign enemies.[45]

Calvert knew, better than most of his contemporaries, how strongly the king had been committed to the match, but he was out of favor with Buckingham and out of touch with the king, who was insulated by a layer of men loyal to the duke. In stark contrast to his prominence in the 1621 Parliament, Calvert contributed little. He had little choice but to follow Buckingham's lead and bide his time. No longer did Calvert defend the royal prerogative and become the focal point of House members' hostility, as he had been before; now Calvert made no effort to defend the king's Palatinate and Spanish policies. The few messages he received from the king came through third parties, usually Conway, who enjoyed Buckingham's unqualified favor. Calvert found his assigned duties, usually pacifying the Spanish ambassadors, unpleasant and distasteful.[46]

The king's intention to use Parliament as a means of gaining concessions from the Spanish lost ground to the more popular notion of breaking the treaties and pursuing open warfare in order to restore James's son-in-law. In April the Spanish ambassadors attempted to turn the king's head by attacking Buckingham. Their failure increased hostility toward Spain. Calvert's isolation intensified, diminishing his chances of regaining his former stature. By the end of this critical month, gossips noted his declining status with the king and the prince.[47]

After considerable vacillation, the weary king agreed to break off the treaties. He named a council of war that *did not include* Calvert. Buckingham now moved toward a French alliance and prepared to send ambassadors to France to nego-

tiate a marriage with a French princess. He excluded Calvert from these negotiations for a Catholic consort and left him to placate the Spanish. Sensing his
delicate position, and completely out of favor with Buckingham, Calvert made
a bold move: he opened negotiations for the sale of his post as secretary.
Through his "chief instrument," William Peasley, he let it be known that the
daily decay in his health left him unhappy in so painful a place and that he was
content to resign the secretariat.[48]

The circumstances that led to Calvert's resignation and withdrawal from
public life attracted considerable interest in court circles. Dudley Carleton knew
that his uncle, Sir Dudley Carleton, ambassador at the Hague, coveted the position of secretary. During the first week of April 1624, he informed his uncle of
Calvert's reported poor health and his willingness to give up his place to the ambassador upon reasonable terms. Health may not have been Calvert's major consideration. Young Carleton wrote later that month that Secretary Calvert was
"on ill terms with the King and Prince" and was "called to account" for, of all
things, detaining diplomatic letters at the request of the French ambassador. As
the incident was over a year old when the king called Calvert on the carpet, it
can be viewed as pressure, instigated by Buckingham, to force the secretary's
resignation. The favorite let others know that he approved of the proposed retirement. The secretary indicated he would accept retirement if he could do so
without losing reputation and if there were some financial consideration for giving up an office said to be worth two thousand pounds per year. Some speculated that the secretariat would be a bargain at six thousand pounds. Speculation
regarding Calvert's possible resignation persisted, but once the crisis passed,
Buckingham, who wished to resolve other pressing issues first, appeared in no
great hurry to dispose of the discredited secretary.[49]

Although the situation appeared grim, Calvert had not abandoned hope. In
early May, he reiterated that he would part with the office "for the regard of his
health," which he must preserve for the good of his children. Young Dudley
Carleton remained skeptical about the health issue. He wondered if Calvert's
initial suggestion of resignation was not merely a ploy to gain a larger share of
state business. Secretary Conway, too, discounted the notion that reasons of
health led to Calvert's offer to resign. Rather, "distrust of standing" made "Mr.
Secretary Calvert utter this motion." Both young Carleton and Conway agreed
that Calvert's fate rested with Buckingham's success in toppling the earl of Bristol. As ambassador at the Court of Philip III, Bristol had labored diligently to
secure the Spanish match. However, he had quarreled with the duke in Spain,

and the king had summoned him home to defend his actions. If the king restored Bristol to good standing, Conway believed Calvert would not leave for any inducements. If Bristol failed, Conway judged that his colleague would "be easily persuaded" to surrender his post.[50]

The king commanded Calvert and Sir Richard Weston, who had recently made his peace with Buckingham, to draw up the "interrogatories" for Bristol's examination. A distressed Calvert faced a dilemma. Refusal would offend the king and make his position more untenable. Serving would offend his sense of justice. He could not deal leniently with his political ally Bristol and hope to avoid increased hostility from Buckingham, who was determined to humble the former ambassador to Spain. Cooperating with Buckingham meant Calvert would have to repudiate the position for which he had labored so strenuously. The commission report no longer exists, but it mattered little, for Bristol had been prejudged. Bristol's banishment from court made Calvert acutely aware of his precarious position.[51]

With the duke's power "wonderfull great" and with all business governed by the king, the prince, and the royal favorite "and none with them" but Conway, Calvert reluctantly concluded that he had no role in the preparations for the French marriage negotiations. Like his former colleague Naunton, he was secretary of state in name only. In August court observers noted his melancholy. Chamberlain heard a rumor that the seals had been taken from him the previous week, but he could not confirm it. Plagued by ill health and by his continued political humiliation, Calvert retreated from the heat of court politics. He retired for the remainder of the summer "unto the Country ... with my family at Thistleworth." He confided to Carleton that he was a "stranger both to busynesse and all men of busynesse." In his solitary confinement Calvert resolved the two issues—his political future and his religious allegiance—that had haunted him for some months.[52]

He was obviously unnerved, and his withdrawal marked an abrupt change in his established pattern of behavior. Not even during the period of anguish following his wife's death in August 1622 did Calvert excuse himself for such a long time from his duties. Now after years of service, mainly conducted from his residence on St. Martin's Lane, events at court isolated him and led to a self-imposed exile. The king broke Calvert's isolation when he recalled him to investigate a complaint brought by the Spanish ambassador regarding Thomas Middleton's play *A Game at Chess*. This diatribe against the Spanish and those English ("some councillors of state, some secretaries") who slavishly supported them offended the ambassador. He found no comedy in a play "so scandalous, impious, barbarous, and so offensive to my royal master." After an investigation, the council ordered a cessation of production until the king made his pleasure known. Except for this trip to London to conduct Privy Council business, Calvert remained secluded at Thistleworth. Soon afterward, as part of his effort to cut ties with the past, he leased his house on St. Martin's Lane.[53]

Calvert had to make his peace with Buckingham before he could sell his office. The needed reconciliation occurred sometime between September 20 and November 23. Conway informed Calvert that Buckingham wanted a copy of the king's letter to the pope and any other letters in his hands concerning the Spanish marriage. Refusal was probably the last thing anticipated, but Calvert did refuse. In leaving London, he had taken much of his correspondence as secretary with him. His trump card, which he played now, was his possession of these valuable state papers. Buckingham did not act magnanimously. He recognized that dislodging Calvert would be extremely difficult without the secretary's cooperation. Caught off guard by the bold move, he dissembled his anxiety to gain Calvert's trust. As soon as he retrieved the sensitive state papers, Buckingham took them to the king.[54]

If his ploy failed to win the king's trust (as Buckingham insinuated), it opened the door for reconciliation. Shortly thereafter, Calvert left Thistleworth to return to London. To atone for his political sins, he presented the duke with a painting by Rubens, hoping that Buckingham would find it worthy and accept it as a humble offering "from as thankfull and faithfull a servant as ever professed to serve you." By the end of November, they reached an agreement. Conway told young Carleton that Calvert had been reconciled "by putting his place" into the duke's hands. Buckingham, for his part, assured Calvert "that he should never have any offer made him for his place but that which should be in his power to take or refuse."[55]

On October 23, 1624, Chamberlain reported that Calvert "is still upon resigning." However, unwinding his "Courtly True-love-knot," as Wentworth poetically characterized it, was a prolonged process. His resignation hung in the balance until February 1625, when Sir Albert Morton, in consideration of three thousand pounds, had the seals delivered to him. Calvert seems to have made the bargain he wanted, financial remuneration and retirement with honor.[56]

As long as there existed some hope for the Spanish treaties, and for salvaging his languishing career, the religious question remained in limbo. Indeed, in all the speculation that preceded the secretary's reluctant resignation, no one in 1624 or even January 1625 suggested that Calvert was, or was about to become, a Catholic. Not even members of the Parliament of 1624, who listed all suspected Papists in offices of trust (and it did not take much to arouse their suspicion), seemed to have suspected the secretary.[57]

Calvert lost the secretary's office for political considerations, not because of his decision to convert to Roman Catholicism. His contemporaries attributed his resignation to Buckingham's hostility and to the general purge of all who favored the now discredited Spanish policy James had pursued. Zuane Pesaro, the Venetian ambassador, wrote that Calvert "to avoid a greater storm has saved himself by yielding up his post." And Pesaro's successor recalled in 1627 that Calvert, "being an acute man foresaw the duke's [Buckingham's] vexations on his return from Spain," resigned, and withdrew from court.[58]

George Abbot, archbishop of Canterbury, the third contemporary to comment on Calvert's religious life, attributed his change of religion to Buckingham's effort "to ridde him of all imployment and negotiations." Only then did Calvert turn Papist. However, Abbot provided no information as to when and under what circumstances Calvert had made the move. His March 1625 statement noted that Calvert had not looked happy since the prince returned from Spain. Since "it was thought" that he was very much interested in Spanish affairs, a course was taken to rid him of all employment and negotiations. "This made him discontented and, as the saying is, *Desparatio facit monachum*, so hee apparently did turne papist, which hee now professeth, this being the third time that he hath bene to blame that way."[59]

Did the archbishop report facts or repeat unsubstantiated rumors? Abbot strongly opposed the match and concessions to Catholics. His recollection even implied some contempt for his colleague's vacillation in matters of religion. Their differences aside, however, the knowledgeable archbishop seemed firm on the point of Calvert's wavering. If his childhood accounts for the first time, and his open avowal after 1625 is the third, what is the cryptic second time? No verifiable evidence of a deviation from conformity by Calvert exists. Only possibilities can be suggested. An aberration may have occurred in the summer of 1622 in the midst of personal tragedy: his wife died in childbirth, "leaving many litle ones behind." Anne Calvert had been sick only a few days. Unexpected, his wife's death was all the more difficult to bear. Two letters reveal the extent of his suffering. Shortly after his wife's death, he poured out his feelings to the earl of

Salisbury: "I am much bound to you for the sense you have of my sufferings." The "many images of sorrow" at the loss of his wife, "who was the dear companion and only comfort of my life," consumed him. He then related his conviction, which he shared a month later with Carleton, that God "laid this heavy cross upon me" for "my sins." As he told Carleton, his bereavement "is heavy indeed to me though my sins have deserved much more."[60]

Calvert deeply felt the loss of his wife, who "was the dear companion and only comfort of my life." Such comments and his introspective references to his sinful nature reflect a troubled man. Did the unexpected death of his wife cause Calvert to deviate from his practice of outward conformity? Did he seek comfort from a Catholic priest? Thomas Locke wrote that soon after her death Calvert removed himself to the home of the earl of Arundel (Thomas Howard, second earl) at Highgate. Arundel had been reared a Catholic but converted to the Church of England in December 1615. The king admitted him to the Privy Council seven months later and appointed him earl marshal in 1621. Arundel had been seriously injured in a carriage accident and was recuperating in 1622. Since he had a Catholic mother and a Catholic wife, his household undoubtedly maintained at least one priest. Did Locke mean *to infer* that Calvert sought the comfort of a priest? In itself, the evidence fails to validate the archbishop's charge or confirm a departure from Calvert's conformity.[61]

The bishop of Gloucester, Godfrey Goodman, the last contemporary to comment on Calvert's religious commitments, charged that the secretary converted to Catholicism early in the negotiations for the Spanish marriage treaty. Speaking of the period between 1619 and 1623, he recalled that Calvert, as the only secretary employed in the Spanish negotiations, "did what good offices he could therein for religion's sake." He asserted that Calvert was "*infinitely addicted to the Roman Catholic faith.*" Goodman, who died a Catholic, attributed Calvert's conversion to the Spanish ambassador, Gondomar, and to Count Arundell, "whose daughter Secretary Calvert's son had married." The bishop repeated the gossip that the secretary did usually "catechize his own children so as to ground them in his own religion, and in his best room having an altar set up, with chalice, candlesticks, and all other ornaments, he brought all strangers thither never concealing anything, as if his whole joy and comfort had been to make open profession of his religion."[62]

Goodman held two individuals responsible for Calvert's conversion. Thomas Arundell, the first Baron Arundell of Wardour, was a prominent court Catholic.

Calvert certainly knew him, and they had contacts before 1625. As early as November 1620, he served on a commission appointed by the king that included Arundell. When the Spanish ambassadors came to Calvert in 1623 because they could not find a lawyer to consult about pardons for recusants, the secretary sent for Arundell, who was in the country. Calvert dutifully reported this contact with such a prominent Catholic to his fellow secretary. Cecil Calvert did marry into the Arundell family, although not until 1627. The evidence, however, fails to support Goodman's assertion. The other person the bishop credited was the bête noire of English Protestants, the Spanish ambassador. During his long tenure as Spanish ambassador to England, from 1613 to 1622, with an extended absence from June 1618 to May 1620, Gondomar gained a reputation as a sinister force. Protestants believed that his specialties included bribing and converting Englishmen to Catholicism. If Goodman's assertion had been correct, Calvert's conversion would have to have taken place between May 1620 and May 1622, when Gondomar left England for the last time.[63]

Goodman's description of Calvert's infinite addiction to the Roman Catholic faith and lack of any fear of the consequences does not square with Calvert's reserved personality and his conduct while he was a member of the government. Neither does it accord with Calvert's generally cautious approach toward religion. In a government official, such an open devotion to the outlawed faith as Bishop Goodman described would have surely come to public attention, and there is no evidence that it did. Court gossips kept track of court conversions. Chamberlain reported on October 18, 1617, that he heard that Sir Herbert Croft had "turned Papist." Yonge noted in his diary on August 19, 1622, that the "Lord of Castlehaven is turned Papist Catholic." The royal favorite's status brought no immunity. Chamberlain reported in September that the "Countesse of Buckingham is relapsed into Poperie and makes open profession, whereupon she is sent from court." Calvert's absence from the accounts of court gossips neither proves nor disproves Goodman's contention, but it casts doubt on the charges. He did not live openly as a Catholic before late 1624 or early 1625; if he maintained a clandestine Catholicism, he hid it well. Despite the firmness of Bishop Goodman's charge, it was a recollection that remains unsubstantiated. As he remembered the past, he could have easily mistaken events following 1625 for those of an earlier time.[64]

Calvert apparently decided to make a clean break sometime between August 1624 and February 1625. No contemporary commentator firmly linked Calvert and Catholicism until February 1625. At that time, Chamberlain reported that "Sir George Calvert or Lord Baltimore which is now his title is gon into the North with Sir Tobie Mathew which confirmes the opinion that he is a bird of that feather." By this, Chamberlain meant that Calvert had recently acknowledged himself a Catholic. Mathew (1577–1655), the eldest son of the archbishop of York, was apparently ordained a Catholic priest after 1630 and had been knighted in 1623 ("for what service God knowes," as Chamberlain put it), no doubt for his ardent support of the Spanish marriage. Calvert had noted that the king, who "rests well assured" of his "loyalty and faithfulness," was sending Mathew to the Spanish court, "where he is no stranger." He suggested that Mathew's "profession in Religion" will permit him to seek to remove "all Rubbs arising that way, and to satisfy needless doubts and jealousies." The presence of Mathew, Calvert's proselytizing friend of school days, undoubtedly bolstered his decision and strengthened his determination to return to the Roman fold.[65]

His decision to return to his childhood religious faith was not sudden. George Cottington, who lived in Calvert's household, suggested that his conformity to the state religion was more than mechanical and that the decision to end it was not sudden. Indeed, given the magnitude of such a decision, and given Calvert's generally prudent nature, he certainly would have weighed the consequences of his actions. Cottington recalled that long before Calvert "declared him selfe Catholick, I felt was little or nothing for me, during which tyme I discerned and palpably sawe his preparation to a new profession of Religion, whereupon I came but seldome to doo my duty unto him." How many months or years Cottington meant by the word *long* is problematic, but his description likely applies to the half year or so preceding Calvert's open espousal of Catholicism.[66]

A letter written by a Carmelite priest and dated November 15 sheds light on his decision and answers the question about who converted him. Father Simon Stock wrote that "I have gained for Our Lord, by His Grace, two councillors of the King's Privy Council, the most intelligent and sufficient men that are of the Royal Council." He added that both were religious men who now live under "our government." The first may have been James, marquis of Hamilton, and the second "without the slightest doubt" was George Calvert. Stock's acquaintances in Spanish circles gave him access to the highest ranks of the Privy Council and the opportunity "to convert these two councillors." If Stock's claim is valid, then Calvert's conversion must have occurred between Stock's letters of late August and early November, with proximity to the latter date seeming most likely. The fact that Calvert did not return to London until early October further limits the timing to the five weeks between October 7 and November 14, 1624.[67]

Four points must be emphasized. First, Calvert had been faltering in his commitment to the state church for some time, and his decision to live openly as a Catholic was a long time coming. Second, Stock's description implied that Calvert's decision involved more than mere recidivism. Third, Calvert maintained his outward conformity until January 1625. Fourth, Calvert, like some of his contemporaries, willingly subordinated religious concerns to secular considerations. He suggested this when he tied Sir Kenelm Digby's conversion to the state church to future employability in the government. After January 1625, events allowed him to bring the secular and religious parts of his life together. By that time he had completed his journey back to the church in which he had been reared, an experience that contemporaries might have denigrated as a relapse.

Toward the end of December, for example, in his capacity as a privy councillor, he administered the oath of allegiance to a Cornelius O'Sullivan, a suspected Papist, who willingly took it. Less than four months later, as an acknowledged Catholic, Calvert eschewed taking the same oath. His move to change the wording of his patent for his Irish lands supports this interpretation. He surrendered that patent, which the king had bestowed on him in 1622, on February 12, 1624/25. The new patent, issued a month later, removed the religious prohibitions that would have precluded Calvert from holding the land. The new phrasing indicates that the language had not troubled him until he declared his open allegiance to Catholicism. More important, it discredits the notion that his decision to become a Catholic brought immediate disgrace and ostracism.[68]

Why did Calvert abandon his long-standing conformity? No one individual, not the Spanish ambassador, not Father Stock, not Lord Arundell of Wardour, not Sir Tobie Mathew, was responsible for his decision. Rather, it was the culmination of many influences. His increasing involvement in the Spanish negotiations and his constant contact with English Catholics played a role. The unexpected death of his wife in August 1622 influenced the decision. Contemporary descriptions indicate that the events that led to his resignation as secretary depressed him and led to a period of introspection and reassessment. He realized for the first time in more than two decades that he faced the prospect of exclusion from the nexus of power. He also came to see that the loss of office relieved him of a burden. It allowed him to resolve his conflicted religious loyalties.[69]

Amerigo Salvetti, the Tuscan representative in London, in his newsletter of January 28/February 6, 1625, took notice of Calvert's dismissal. Evidently quoting Calvert, the Tuscan resident wrote of Calvert's determination to withdraw from court and his willingness to place the office in Buckingham's hands for disposal. Then he noted that Calvert had added "that being resolved for the future to live and die as a Catholic, he knew that he could not serve him [the duke] where he was without the jealousy of the state and danger from Parliament."[70]

Salvetti's report left the impression that Calvert had resigned because he became a Catholic. But this statement, attributed to the fallen secretary, provided only a portion of the story. Calvert clearly anticipated that he could continue to serve as a privy councillor even after he announced his resolution "to live and die as a Catholic." During the protracted crisis that forced his resignation and led to his despair, he had resolved an inner conflict. He emerged from the ashes to turn the resignation to his best advantage. Chamberlain wrote in early January that "Secretary Calvert they say is upon his dismission (but not empty handed)." A month later, the Privy Council met to witness the swearing in of Sir Albert Morton as one of the king's principal secretaries of state. An extraordinary entry then followed. The lord president signified that his majesty graciously favored Calvert by allowing him to retain the dignity and place of a privy councillor.[71]

Calvert attached great importance to not leaving in disgrace, a disposition that was not lost on his contemporaries. In February a priest reported from London that the king had made Calvert "an Irish Baron," in order that the world should not conceive "he was put from his secretaryship in disgrace." Lord Carew echoed a similar sentiment a month later when he wrote that "Calvert is removed from his place of secretary, but *yet without disgrace*, for the king hath created him baron of Baltimore in Ireland, and remaynes a coucellor." Secretary Calvert engaged in some hard-nosed bargaining to gain his objectives. He left without disgrace, having secured an Irish title, receiving remuneration for his office, and maintaining his seat on the Privy Council. With the resolution of his secretariat and after a long internal debate, Calvert acknowledged his Catholicism.[72]

Word of his religious conversion spread. A priest reported in February 1625 that "Sir G Calvert, I am tolde, is *rectus* in C.R," that is, received into the Catholic religion. He also reported that Baltimore intended to voyage to Newfoundland, where he had a share in that plantation. Calvert, now in about his forty-fifth year, soon after left London to begin a new life as an English Catholic. The newly created Catholic Lord Baltimore emerged from the crisis precipitated by the prince's return in October 1623 not as a defeated man but as one who used his influence to gain an attractive settlement.[73]

The twists and turns of George Calvert's journey to Catholicism cannot be charted fully. Indeed, his religious life remains a picture of studied ambiguity. To argue that Calvert practiced his Catholicism openly before late 1624 defies the evidence. To believe that he was a secret, practicing Catholic distorts the case. To allow that he fully committed to the state church oversimplifies his very confused religious loyalties. The discrepancies in interpretation can be avoided by labeling Calvert as a schismatic. In common with so many Englishmen of his time, Calvert was torn between conflicting loyalties. As a loyal Englishman but unsettled in his religious life, Calvert better conforms to Arthur Wilson's description of one who had "the face of a Protestant, and the heart of a Papist." As long as he served the king, he subordinated religious considerations to political realities. His rude dismissal from political office, and the loss of the king's confidence, freed Calvert religiously and allowed him to declare his determination "to live and die as a Catholic." His forced conversion to the state religion in 1592 had been by no means a repudiation of the religion of his childhood, and his years as a conforming Episcopal Protestant had not resulted from deeply felt spiritual convictions.[74]

The connection between Calvert's resignation and his subsequent conversion establishes that his decision was not the desperate act of a defeated man who was harried from the government because he was a member of a hated and dreaded sect. He left the secretariat on very favorable terms. The usually cautious Calvert *chose* to identify with the outlawed religious community. In making the decision to embrace Catholicism, Calvert did not repudiate his Englishness. He did not seek martyrdom. He was not a victim of religious persecution. More important, he did not seek financial ruin or the destruction of his family. Better than anyone in 1625, he knew what it meant to be an English Catholic. He accepted this and, for the remainder of his life, labored to succeed in a world that was not favorably disposed to Catholics. But it was a world that he, as a former official, could and would manipulate for his advantage. He and his family did not dwell on the limitations they faced but rather thought in terms of possibilities.

Thus, the origins of Maryland can be traced to George Calvert's resignation as secretary of state only in the most circuitous manner. If Calvert had retained his offices through 1632 (and indeed he probably would have if Prince Charles had married the infanta), he would never have sought the Maryland charter. The evidence does not sustain the argument that Calvert founded Maryland because his conversion to Catholicism forced his resignation and led to his banishment. Calvert supported a losing cause, not a Catholic one as such but an English one, and lost. Whatever his motives were in seeking to found a colony in the New World, they were not the direct result of his resignation, a move forced for political considerations and not religious ones. His resignation, distasteful as it was, opened new doors for Calvert. As secretary of state, he acquired what was the first of his colonial properties, a grant of land in Newfoundland, and it was to Newfoundland he was bound. A new and different world awaited him as a loyal Englishman and a Catholic.

As a colonial Catholic entrepreneur, George Calvert acted on his conviction that the English penal legislation did not extend to the king's overseas dominions. He looked for a place to prosper, enjoy the fruits of his labor, and worship in accordance with the dictates of his own conscience. Within this context, the Catholic Lord Baltimore set out to found a new society in which those who joined him could prosper and live in relative peace. To advance his colony and ensure domestic tranquility, he adopted religious policies that ran contrary to the world in which he lived.

CHAPTER FOUR

"Upon this new shuffle of the packe"

The Catholic Lord Baltimore in Ireland and
Newfoundland (1625–1629)

From the wreck of his career as a prominent government official emerged a new, bolder George Calvert: the capitalist and Catholic colonizer. The cautious, conforming courtier gave way to a daring man who challenged some of his culture's most cherished political and religious concepts. In retiring from court and openly embracing Roman Catholicism, Baltimore significantly altered his lifestyle. He no longer enjoyed the profits of office, which, considering the sums he spent over the next seven years, must have been considerable. No longer would others come asking him to use his influence on their behalf. Instead, he had to approach the government as an outsider, which was made even more difficult by the fact that those who favored the Spanish match were out of favor. His profession of Roman Catholicism potentially exposed him and his family to an elaborate system of penal laws dating back to 1559.

As a Catholic and an Irish lord, Baltimore could have fallen into obscurity, but he did not. Despite the ups and downs of the next years, Baltimore does not seem to have succumbed to self-pity, despair, or bitterness. He was not a vanquished man who fled England to his overseas estates to avoid religious persecution. On the contrary, once he reconciled his religious commitments,

Baltimore enthusiastically entered into a new phase of his life that centered first on his Irish estates and then on his colonial enterprises. He took neither his rude departure from government service nor his open commitment to Catholicism as a defeat. With the 1624 crisis behind him, he had the time and energy to concentrate on his overseas investments.

Calvert's interest in overseas expansion predated his decision to live openly as a Catholic. If national goals inspired his first twenty-five-pound investment in the Virginia Company, the quest for profit motivated his substantial investment in the East India Company. An opportunity to link these two objectives on a grander scale came in 1620. Sir William Vaughan, a rabidly anti-Catholic colonizer, lost interest after failing to establish a colony in Newfoundland and assigned part of his grant to Calvert. In establishing an outpost in Newfoundland, the secretary hoped to expand the king's dominions and to exploit the valuable natural resources of the area. Administering the king's business at home and abroad between 1620 and mid-1623 left the harried secretary with little time to devote to his private enterprise, which at best was a diversion. Still, he was able to organize and dispatch a small expedition to his colony.[1]

An issue surfaced that directly affected the secretary's emerging colonial interests. In April 1621 Calvert risked the wrath of his colleagues in the House of Commons when he spoke forcibly against a bill for free fishing in America. The bill, which restricted the rights of the colonial proprietors by preventing them from taking prime locations for fishing and drying and allowed fishermen to cut wood, enjoyed considerable support with many members, who valued it "as a source of embarrassment to the government and as a means of extending Parliamentary control." Calvert vigorously defended the king's prerogative, to say nothing of his own interests, by arguing that plantations were not under the jurisdiction of Parliament. Plantations, he asserted, in an argument that presaged his family's view of colonial enterprises, "are not yet annexed to the Crown of England, but are the King's as gotten him by Conquest." He questioned whether Commons should move in the direction of making laws for the government of overseas plantations. As he understood the situation, the king governed new plantations by his prerogative and as he thought fit. He saw the value of keeping colonial enterprises under the direct authority of the monarch. Most of his colleagues thought differently and sent the bill to a committee for further discussion. Again in December he spoke against an act for freer liberty of fishing in Newfoundland and other parts of America. Calvert's influence "quite likely" ensured that the bill was "denied the royal assent after its second passage."[2]

Calvert's first venture as a colonial capitalist began with high hopes. He entrusted his objectives to Captain Edward Wynne and a number of Protestants. Wynne departed Plymouth in June 1621 and arrived at his destination in August. Within a fortnight, he reported favorably on the potential productivity of the soil and recited the many enticements that beckoned the investor. He enumerated salt-making, hemp and flax production, tar and iron supplies, timber for ships' masts and yards, the growing of hops, and the two fishing seasons that Newfoundland offered. He also extolled the climate, noting that the place he chose to plant and build was the "warmest, and most commodious of all about the Harbour." He predicted that after another year the colony would be self-sufficient. Wynne's comments, especially the latter one, must have encouraged Calvert to believe his investment a wise one.[3]

Calvert wrote Wynne at least four times between mid-February and mid-May 1622. Wynne, however, did not respond until July, some eleven months after his first letter. In a report that played to his employer's interests, Wynne rendered "a due account" of what had been accomplished through the group's diligent labor and extraordinary efforts. He reported that he and his company of twelve had dug a well, cut timber, dug the cellar of the main house, used the dirt to build an earthen embankment on the waterside, constructed a substantial house and other buildings, cleared land for a garden and crops, cut timber for boards, fenced the four-acre site, broken ground for a brew house room and other tenements, and begun construction of a wharf. He had great hopes, too. To create a pretty street, he intended to enlarge the small site by adding another row of buildings for the comfort of the neighborhood. Wynne concluded by saying the progress was beyond his expectations.[4]

Wynne sent another equally encouraging letter three weeks later. He touted the venturers' success with agricultural enterprises, and he extolled the masterful skill of "our Salt-maker." Indeed, he promised to send Calvert a barrel of the best salt that ever "my eyes beheld." Wynne gave a brief, cheerful assessment of the climate: "It is better, and not so cold as England." Another in the company echoed this view. "The Climate differs but little from *England*," he said, finding himself less cold that winter than "I did in *England* the Winter before, by much." Only when he wintered in his colony in 1628–29 did Calvert learn that he had been deceived by the "lying letters and reports of the Governors and such."[5]

His agent's letters left no doubt that Calvert's commercial venture had been established on a firm foundation. Descriptions of adequate housing, crop planting, defense measures, and potentially profitable activities dominated the correspondence between the Wynne and the secretary. Disingenuous? Perhaps, but others corroborated Wynne's glowing reports. Captain Daniel Powell, who took the new supply of men and women to the colony in late spring, recalled for Calvert the morning of May 27 when his ship entered the harbor at Ferryland. He found Wynne and his company in good health. The coast and harbors, which he described as bold and good, led him to conclude that "there can be no better in the world." The land on which "our Governor" planted "is so good and commodious, that for the quantity, I think there is no better in many parts of England." His house, which "is strong and well contrived, standeth very warme, at the foot of an easie ascending hill." More ominously, Powell added that Wynne had settled at the "coldest harbour of the land."[6]

On February 14, 1620, Richard Whitbourne, an experienced traveler who wrote of Newfoundland's many attractions, had presented his tract, *A Discourse and Discovery of New-Found-Land*, to Secretary Calvert and other members of the Privy Council for an endorsement. About six months later, the council recommended its publication to encourage those willing to assist that plantation either in person or otherwise. Calvert, who was in the forefront of those who rushed to exploit the many advantages Whitbourne so convincingly detailed, certainly found nothing to discourage the belief that Wynne had laid a firm foundation for a potentially prosperous colony. In the 1622 edition, Whitbourne wrote that the king's secretary had "most worthily" sent a great number of men and women to Newfoundland with the "necessaries" to sustain the enterprise. He, too, reported favorably on the colony's initial success. He noted the building of houses, the clearing of land, and the making of salt. Calvert's men had already sent home a good quantity of salt that had been approved as fit for preserving the "kind of fish as is taken on the coast."[7]

What did Calvert intend with his colony? Wynne closed his first letter by noting that Calvert had "greater hopes here" than he had previously discerned. To some extent, the secretary's hopes can be extrapolated from the second letter Wynne sent that summer. The captain's letter of August 17 spoke to Calvert's vision and the commitment he had made. The company, which numbered thirty-two, included a surgeon, a husbandman, two blacksmiths, a stone-layer, a quarryman, three carpenters, a tailor, three boat masters, a fisherman, a cooper, two married couples, three boys, and two girls. His request for personnel indicated an ambitious plan. He asked for six masons; four carpenters; two or three good quarrymen; a slater or two; a couple of strong maids who, besides other work, could both brew and bake; and a convenient number of west-country laborers, "to fit the ground for the Plough." He wanted a lime-burner, limestones, and a good quantity of hard lathes. He asked Calvert to furnish some guns and a gunner, another brewing cooper, some clapboards, and more iron, as well as steel, brick, lime, tiles, and a complete supply of all things, including victuals, linen, woolens for apparel and bedding, shoes of wet leather, Irish stockings, coarsely knit hose, coarse ticks, good flocks in a cask, and coarse mingled kerseys. He further requested another iron mill and two "Bridewell mills," along with a dozen leather buckets, a glazier, some glue, "rats-bane," and two fowling pieces.[8]

Although he provided for the physical well-being of his colonists, Calvert apparently made no provision for their religious needs. Only after Wynne's 1622 request for a "godly minister," did Calvert secure the services of a Mr. Richard James. His arrival in the colony provided for the spiritual needs of the colonists, who were most certainly Protestants, or "English heretics," as a Catholic priest later referred to them. James, who later became Sir Robert Cotton's library keeper, did not stay long and returned with a most unfavorable impression of the place.[9]

Calvert's commitment to creating a colony in Newfoundland reflected his growing confidence in his financial welfare. To what extent he tried to satisfy Wynne's expensive requests cannot be determined. While he shared the risks with other investors, Calvert invested a considerable amount of his own money to launch the Newfoundland enterprise. His actions to this point indicate that he clearly expected to gain a return on his investment by exploiting the natural resources of the island and that he had no particular religious mission in mind. The Newfoundland enterprise was an expensive investment, but only one of many he made. Accomplishing his major objectives of developing a profitable enterprise and expanding the empire proved more elusive than the secretary imagined.[10]

Buoyed by the favorable reports he received from his agent, Calvert made a fuller commitment late in 1622. Taking advantage of his position in government, he sought a grant of the whole country of Newfoundland. Although initially approved, the secretary's grant infringed upon so many extant claims that a new charter with defined geographical limits passed seals on April 7, 1623. Avalon, as he called his colony, was now his by royal charter.[11]

Calvert was at the height of his power. A week after the government granted the charter, he secured the appointment of his son-in-law William Peasley as clerk of the Privy Council. Early in the next month, a court gossip noted that "the King kept St. George's Feast at Windsor [and] Secretary Calvert was very gay and gallant there, all in white . . . , even to his white hat and white feather."[12]

An incident involving Captain John Nutt, described by some as a pirate, showed that Calvert vigorously wielded his power as secretary to defend his economic interests. In so doing, however, he inadvertently increased the tension between himself and his fellow secretary Conway. The English government did little to protect its nationals who risked their fortunes in an attempt to exploit the natural resources abroad and extend English dominance to America. The term *piracy* encompassed a host of naval adventures in the early seventeenth century, some legitimate and some less proper. Pirates infested the international waters off Newfoundland, and investors had to protect themselves from the marauders. Captain Nutt and some of his fellow sailors seized a French ship and began plundering other ships during the summer of 1621. That pirate offered protection from the French to English colonists, and in an effort to protect his enterprise in Newfoundland, Secretary Calvert established a connection with Nutt. In February Calvert issued a pardon for Nutt that could be extended for three months.

Before the pardon reached him, Nutt returned in the spring of 1623 to work the seas between England and Ireland. His activities came to the attention of Sir John Eliot, the vice admiral of Devon, who received orders to apprehend him. Short of ships, Eliot devised a subterfuge to lure the pirate to port. Although Nutt had "committed many wrongs," Eliot wrote to Conway to find out if he "is still worthy of pardon." Conway ordered him to ignore the pardon and send Nutt to the council, which he did. In an interesting turn, undoubtedly attributable to Calvert, the council summoned Eliot to explain himself and charged him with malfeasance in office. Eliot went to jail claiming his capture of Nutt had been misrepresented. Meanwhile, Nutt received his pardon. Calvert told Conway that he had "no other end but to be grateful to a poor man that hath been ready to do me & my associates courtesies in a plantation which we have begun in Newfoundland, by defending us from others which perhaps in the infancy of that work might have done us wrong." This incident demonstrated his ability to manipulate the council for his own interests (as well as those who sought to extend the king's dominions in North America). He had bested the duke's man, his fellow secretary Conway. His triumph, especially in view of Eliot's friendship with Buckingham, was a Pyrrhic victory.[13]

Following the return of the prince and the duke from Spain in October 1623, Calvert faced the political crisis that resulted from his unwelcome support of the

Spanish match. For well over a year, he paid no heed to colonial enterprise. Newfoundland awaited the disposition of his office and the resolution of his inner conflict concerning his religious commitments. In February 1625, now an Irish lord, a confirmed Catholic, and an investor, he again turned his attention to his colony.[14]

Did his decision to live as a Catholic alter his basic colonial objectives? No, he still sought to recoup the considerable investment already made and find a setting where he could enjoy the fruits of his labors. His decision did present some new problems, such as recruiting Catholics and priests who shared his vision. Whether he knew of earlier unsuccessful colonial attempts by prominent Catholics or the pessimistic attitude of Jesuit Robert Parsons cannot be known. He understood that most Catholics had little interest in fleeing their homeland for the wilderness. Beyond this, he never put Catholic goals ahead of his personal (recouping his investment) and nationalistic (increasing the king's dominions) objectives. Espousal of Catholicism did add a new dimension to the colonial enterprise, however: he and the Catholics who joined him needed to avoid the possible impact of the onerous penal laws. This, in turn, led to the most innovative departure: embracing freedom of conscience for a pluralistic society.[15]

In the first week of February 1625, Simon Stock, a Carmelite priest, noted Baltimore's intention to venture to Newfoundland. He claimed among his converts in England a gentleman who possessed "a land some three weeks distance by sea from Great Britain," a place "where our Holy Faith has never been preached." He added that "in spring this gentleman means to return [*sic*] to his land with his servants (some of whom I have converted)." Stock also laid some claim to naming the colony, which "we have called 'Avalon.'"[16]

Before making definite plans, Baltimore journeyed to Yorkshire to attend the February 25 wedding of Wentworth, his closest friend and political ally. His decision to embrace Catholicism had little or no effect on friends and political associates such as Wentworth. They even bantered about their religious differences. In informing Wentworth of the joyous manner in which the Spanish received the news of the birth of a son to King Charles, Calvert closed with "thus your Lordship sees that we Papists want not Charity towards you Protestants, whatsoever the less understanding Part of the World think of us."[17]

Baltimore returned from his visit to Yorkshire in early March. At this point, his expectations provide further evidence that his resignation as secretary resulted from political and not religious considerations. He expected neither social nor political ostracism as a result of his new religious commitment. He intended to remain on the Privy Council, albeit in a diminished capacity, in order to further his interests and to promote Wentworth's cause at court. He anticipated that with the support of his allies, the government would cooperate with and continue to support his renewed efforts to expand the English empire.[18]

To this end, Baltimore busily forged ahead with his plans. On March 11 he secured from the king a revision of his Irish grant that gave him better financial conditions and removed certain anti-Catholic provisions that were part of the original grant. Calvert held the original patent "by knights' service, in capite," which incurred a yearly financial obligation of about thirty pounds. James now granted Baltimore the patent in fee simple. Later that month Baltimore petitioned Secretary of State Sir John Coke to clear his two ships, the *Jonathan* and the *Peter Bonaventure*, stating merely, "I intend shortly, God willing, a journey for Newfoundland to visit a plantation which I began there some few years since." Everything was proceeding smoothly. Two days later Buckingham ordered Coke to release the ships, but with the clear stipulation that they return to England within ten days after arriving with a cargo of fish for use of the navy.[19]

Then the unexpected happened. After a severe illness, King James died on March 25, 1625. Baltimore's carefully laid plans began to unravel. As Wentworth put it, the death of the king meant an "intermission and pause for advisement on how to sett my cards upon this new shuffle of the packe." Baltimore, at the center of the game, had little time to ponder the implications of the death of the man he had so long served. Two days after James's death, as a member of the Privy Council, he signed the proclamation recognizing Charles as king. He assumed that he would continue functioning at court until he left for Newfoundland. The recently concluded marriage treaty with the French included generous guarantees for English Catholics. The imminent arrival of "the French Lady" made Calvert's assumption seem all the more reasonable. The assumption, however, proved unwarranted. Charles, in a maneuver designed to placate angry Protestants, adopted a harsh posture toward his Catholic subjects, a move that evidently took many by surprise. By public edict, the king commanded a stricter enforcement of the laws against Catholics than the statutes themselves commanded. Carmelite Simon Stock described the arrest and imprisonment of many of his fellow priests and declared it "a great persecution." The "worst omen" was the rumor of a new parliament, "for it is certain to be hostile to them and to their religion."[20]

The new king, who moved quickly to confirm his father's privy councillors, required them to take the oaths of supremacy and allegiance. The Tuscan resident in England reported that Baltimore refused the oath of supremacy. He told the king that since "everyone knew him to be a Catholic, he could not now serve him in the same high office without exciting jealousy in others, nor was he willing to take an oath so wounding his religious feelings." Salvetti quoted Charles as saying "that it was much better thus to state his opinions, rather than to retain his office by equivocation, as some did." Baltimore also balked at taking the oath of allegiance and asked for time to consider whether to take it. For the first time on record, he refused the requisite oaths of supremacy and allegiance, two oaths that he had frequently taken and tendered to others. He acted boldly by stepping down from an office he much cherished. More important, the king accepted his refusal to take the oaths and his withdrawal without rancor.[21]

Baltimore and other Catholics felt the sting of the king's hard-line policy. Charles barred Catholics from participating in James's funeral by ordering that "no Recusant Papist shall have any mourning of what rank soever he be." This denial epitomized Baltimore's new status: with the old king's death, his former life was a thing of the past. His departure from the Privy Council marked the end of the road he had followed since 1603. For over twenty years, he had identified with the government and especially the late king. Even after the humiliating negotiations that led to his resignation as secretary, and even after the resolution of his religious commitments, he fully expected to retain some foothold at court. Undaunted, he turned from the pomp and circumstance of court to plan for a visit to his languishing colony.[22]

Archbishop Abbot simply noted that Baltimore "is withdrawn from us [i.e., the Privy Council], and having bought a ship of 400 tuns, hee is going to New England, or Newfoundlande, where he hath a colony." Here, too, Baltimore experienced disappointment as outside circumstances stymied his projected voyage to Avalon. A court gossip reported on April 13 that Baltimore, "now a profest Papist," was going to Newfoundland, but the government prevented him from doing so. He chose instead to sail to Ireland.[23]

Did the decision to stay his journey to Avalon and his determination to move to Ireland result from his profession of Catholicism? No evidence exists to suggest that he felt threatened by the penal laws at any time between 1625 and 1632 or that the government intended to charge him under the penal statutes. Other factors beyond the renewed persecution of Catholics account for his move to Ireland. For one thing, he underestimated the magnitude of the preparations necessary to provide for his family on a lengthy voyage to a land about which he really knew very little. Having received no recent reports on the condition of the colony, he postponed that more arduous journey until the next spring. Stock reported that the "Avalon gentleman, of whom I have already written, is to remain in Ireland until the coming Spring."[24]

Newfoundland was his first priority, but it was not his only one. The condition of his Irish estates in the county of Longford concerned him as well. He needed to assess his holdings, which consisted of "many castles, villages, and lands." He possessed an estimated 2,304 acres of arable and pasture land and 1,605 acres of wood and bog. The move not only allowed him to focus on his neglected Irish estates; it also gave him time to reassess his position in light of the death of King James.[25]

Beyond these considerations, there may have been a more pressing concern: another eruption of the dreaded plague. Like his contemporaries, Baltimore did not know what caused the periodic outbreaks, but he understood that abandoning population centers was the safest course. Faced with the threat that surfaced in the spring of 1625 and became epidemic from July through September, Baltimore may have been prudent to get away from London. Finally, his ability to manipulate the government for his own purposes over the next few years belies any suggestion that the government hounded him out of England. On April 26, a few weeks after this delay, the Privy Council granted permission for Baltimore, "his family and whole retinue, bag and baggage, to pass into Ireland without search." In spite of the anti-Catholicism prevailing at court, Baltimore secured in early May a letter signed by the king. The king instructed his deputy and chancellor in Ireland to see that Baltimore was discharged from any financial obligations due under the 1622 grant and ordered him to draw up a new recognizance based on the 1625 revision. More important, Sir Arthur Aston, the man who led the Newfoundland expedition in Baltimore's place, was also a known Catholic.[26]

Baltimore may have changed his plans even before the court gossip's letter noted his stay. As early as April 5, he secured a pass from the Privy Council for Aston to travel to Newfoundland with the proviso that he procure some hawks and elks for the king. Stock described Aston as "a Catholic Knight and dear friend, who for many years fought in the wars against Turks and infidels, [and who] is resolved to go thither in May, with two faithful servants." Entrusting leadership to a Catholic soldier of fortune, an appointment for which Stock claimed credit, was a natural consequence of Baltimore's conversion and marked a significant development in the colony's history. Until Aston sailed in late May, accompanied by at least two other Catholics, Protestants had managed the colony. But Baltimore did not choose a Catholic to take charge of the colony solely for religious considerations. Wynne's dismissal followed years of dismal results: he had failed to establish a profitable enterprise and had to be replaced.[27]

Baltimore delayed leaving London until after Aston sailed in late May. From this time until David Rothe, the bishop of Ossary, noted his presence in Ireland in September 1625, Baltimore remained out of sight. The bishop offered the best intelligence on Baltimore in Ireland. After repeating the report of "a gentleman of the Lord of Baltimore's retinue lately comme from England," he explained that Baltimore was a known and professed Catholic, who, with his wife and children, had come to dwell in the country. Ossary reported that Baltimore had taken up residence in Ferns in County Wexford, where he purchased lands valued at sixteen hundred pounds from Sir Richard Maisterson. Baltimore planned to build at a place called Cloghammon, but in the interim he lived in the manor house at Feames. He left two of his young children at Waterford, where they were to be educated at a private school of the humanities.[28]

Ossary mentioned "dame Joane Baltimore now wife" of Calvert. The absence of any record of the marriage in Church of England documents suggests that the marriage was Catholic. The wedding undoubtedly took place earlier in 1625. This event, especially if it occurred in Ireland, may have been another reason for postponing the Newfoundland trip.[29]

The bishop also sermonized about an "infection," which he attributed to a gentleman in Baltimore's retinue. Although circumstantial, the commentary reinforces that interpretation that the plague was another reason for departing London with a sense of urgency. Ossary related that we "live here in continuall feare of the infection," which in England, but especially in London and the surrounding areas, had killed many thousands. After noting the excessively high death rate in London, the bishop reported that he had heard that "few or no Catholics died although many on every side of them were carried to their graves." The bishop thought it ironic that "the Protestants, but especially the Puritans, spare not to say that this plague is comme from God to punishe the nation for their remisses and toleration with Catholicks."[30]

The Catholic colonizer faced an unexpected problem as he prepared for his overseas adventure. As a recent convert, Baltimore had no intention of sailing without a spiritual presence, but he found no priests willing and able to join him and his company. Recruiting priests proved a vexing problem, and a number of years passed before he found a solution. Initially, he left the matter in the hands of Father Stock. While Baltimore and his family established themselves in Ireland, the Carmelite remained in England, where he continued to press Rome for support for the Avalon colony. Stock reported to the Sacred Congregation "de Propaganda Fide," which had been created in 1622 to spread Catholicism among the heathens and protect the faith in countries where Catholics were in direct contact with heretics and infidels. His letters provide a glimpse of what one priest thought Avalon might become, given proper encouragement from Rome. More important, Stock's commentaries offer insights on the problems a Catholic colonizer had in recruiting priests.[31]

The priest and the colonizer based their affiliation on mutual advantage. The only specific thing Baltimore sought from Stock was his assistance in recruiting priests for Avalon. By his own testimony, the Carmelite also attempted to recruit prospective Catholic colonists. He had a number of other goals, too, not the least of which was the founding of a Carmelite novitiate in England. He found Baltimore's Avalon colony advantageous for meeting that end. Beyond this, he seems to have envisioned an important role for the fledgling colony in furthering Propaganda's task of spreading Catholicism throughout the world. His urgency in seeking priests for Avalon was closely bound up in both of these purposes.[32]

Stock broached the subject of priests for Avalon in his first letter. Baltimore (identified as "the gentleman"), he wrote, "desires to take with him two or three brethren to sow the Sacred Faith in that land." Because two of the three Carmelites in England were sick and unable to provide spiritual assistance, he implored Rome's "help in the sacred undertaking." In early March, before Propaganda could have possibly responded to his earlier letter, Stock sent another missive, updating the progress of the Avalon matter. Writing from London, he claimed that fifteen or twenty more Catholics "are to accompany the first that I converted." With greater urgency, he renewed his pleas for two priests "with authority sufficient to found and continue in this Avalon mission." Although he received assurances of assistance from Rome, by May Stock lamented that the promised priests could not arrive in time because no ships would depart for those parts after May. He lamented that he could only "teach them acts of contrition, and pray that our Lord may assist them." Stock also noted Baltimore's intention to sail for Avalon in spring 1626, and he declared his hope that by then Propaganda would be able to "provide him with two or three priests to accompany him and his men in that zeal which he so eminently possesses, to the admiration of all here" in England.[33]

The Carmelite perceived the advantages of the Church's involvement in this colonial project. He augmented his plea for priests by broadening the mission of Baltimore's colony. From his initial contact with Calvert, he imagined Avalon as a staging area "to sow the Sacred Faith." Stock's "grand missionary design" envisioned the colony "as a bridge-head for the spiritual conquest of America," a base from which missionary priests would travel to other English colonies converting the natives, checking the growing Protestant influence in the New World, and winning to the Catholic faith not only America "but Japan, China, the Philippines and the East Indies" as well. Stock emphasized two closely related points. First, the Church now had the opportunity to plant the faith in a land where the leaders were Catholic. Second, English heretics were busy in the New World. With a mix of fact and fiction, he chronicled their activities, predicting boldly that without the needed missionary priests in Avalon, the Indians "will become pernicious heretics." His letters touched a sensitive area. At Propaganda his news of how the English heretics were perverting the Indians of North America "was heard with great disgust."[34]

Despite a sympathetic ear, Rome was not of much help. Promised laborers were long delayed. Stock reported in September that the two recently arrived Carmelites from Flanders lacked both the faculties and the abilities for such a mission. Besides, Aston's ship had sailed long before they arrived. Five weeks later, Stock confronted a deteriorating situation. Father Bede, recently sent to England and given authority over Stock, rejected Stock's proposal for Avalon. Stock wrote his superiors that he had laid the whole project before "my companions," Fathers Elisers and Elias, and urged them to go on the mission. Neither showed any inclination to depart. After citing the reasons for their reluctance, they judged that the project was "a matter of much greater difficulty than mister Simon believes." Bede concurred in their recommendation that this "is a matter for mister Simon," since he initiated it.[35]

By March 1626 the inactivity regarding Avalon deeply frustrated Stock. Another chance to send missionaries was fading: "But since Your Most Illustrious Worships have failed to send missionaries as promised, and now as come another Spring with nothing done, I have lost hope, and we shall lose both the occasion, and the souls there." In the meantime, Propaganda ordered Stock to go to Avalon. By gaining firsthand knowledge, he would facilitate the recruitment of additional priests. His continued reports concerning the harsh treatment accorded Catholics notwithstanding, Stock could not bring himself to venture to Avalon. Pleading a host of reasons, he demurred. He made his acceptance conditional on gaining his primary goal, license to establish a mission in England to assist him in supplying the Avalon mission. After a year's activities on Baltimore's behalf, even with an apparent surplus of priests in relation to the number of Catholics in England, Stock still had no priests to accompany the expedition to Avalon.[36]

Other pressing problems besides acquiring the service of priests demanded attention. As long as the war against Spain continued, Baltimore was in no position to utilize their services in his colony. He remained in Ireland, forgoing any plans he might have had to sail in the spring of 1626. That fall, Baltimore observed a meeting in Dublin to discuss what he called the "new military scheme," a proposal to maintain an army in Ireland. Those present decided to postpone any action until they gathered additional intelligence from the counties. That Baltimore reported his observations directly to Buckingham indicated that he remained on reasonably good terms with the government in England. Furthermore, the report of the meeting by the earl of Westmeath and others contained this significant remark: "Lord Baltimore was present and will testify as above." By February 1627, the situation had changed dramatically. Buckingham, having dabbled disastrously in wars against both Spain and France since 1625, desperately sought to extricate himself (and England) from the Spanish conflict. To handle the intended delicate peace negotiations, he turned to the remnants of the discredited faction that had supported the Spanish match. The anti-Spanish tide had turned.[37]

Buckingham summoned Baltimore back to court. Supposedly, he was to be entrusted with the delicate negotiations with Spain in Brussels, along with the second earl of Salisbury, Sir Richard Weston, and Sir Humphrey May. Baltimore returned to England in March and for a brief moment was back at the political center. Buckingham took him to Newcastle to discuss the Spanish situation with the king and the Privy Council. According to the Venetian ambassador, "should this new scheme obtain the king's assent, he [Baltimore] will be employed in it, because they consider him to be a staunch Spaniard." Two weeks later, however, the ambassador reported that although Baltimore met frequently with the duke, some "assure me that because he is so notoriously a Spaniard the king cannot employ him from lack of confidence."[38]

Although keenly interested in playing a role at court, Baltimore took advantage of his recall to pursue other interests. Without office, he had to be sensitive to his financial needs. In April he sought to renew his 1621 grant of the duties on silk imports. It had expired on the death of James I, and his departure to Ireland intervened. Charles granted Baltimore the silk customs for a fifteen-year period. As a further courtesy, the king also exempted him from repaying any duties collected since the death of James. The grant included a stipulation that if the subsidy was stopped, Baltimore was to receive full value from other customs.[39]

His recall, and his efforts to pursue more aggressively his colonial interests, demonstrate that his religion did not particularly restrict his activities. He requested a warrant exempting the *Ark of Avalon* and the *George of Plymouth* from the stay imposed because of the war with Spain. In his letter to Buckingham's secretary, he stated that Sir Arthur Aston was waiting to sail to the "young plantation." His hope that he might have an important role in the negotiations led him to postpone his own journey to Newfoundland. However, by May it was obvious to him, having been "here now some two or three months a spectator upon this grand scene of state," that "I have no part to play."[40]

Attention now shifted to the long-anticipated voyage to his colony. To his friend Wentworth, he wrote in haste that he was bound for a long journey to a place that he had long desired to visit "and have now the opportunity and leave to do it: it is *Newfoundland* I mean, which it imparts me more than in curiosity only to see." He confided, "I must either go and settle it in a better order than it is" or else give up the grant. Unwilling to lose all that he had invested, Baltimore told his friend, "I had rather be esteemed a fool by some for the hazard of one month's journey, than to prove myself one certainly for six years by past, if the business be now lost for want of a little pains and care." He added that he was going to sail in a three-hundred-ton ship with twenty-four pieces of ordnance. With two or three good ships to accompany him, he assured Wentworth, the expedition had no need to fear either the French or the Dunkirkers.[41]

Wentworth remained out of favor and did not secure his long-desired place at court until Buckingham passed from the scene. Sir Arthur Ingram had informed him in November 1625 that the "Duke's power with the King for certain is exceedingly great." Those he favored, he advanced, but those he frowned upon "must go down." Ingram advised Wentworth that the lord marshal, a close associate of both Wentworth and Calvert, lost favor with the "Great Duke" and, as a consequence, the king "will hardly speak to him."[42]

Wentworth's steadfast opposition to the forced loan of 1627, the king's effort to exact money from his subjects without the consent of Parliament, made him especially odious at court. Baltimore, busy with preparations for his departure to Newfoundland, took time to offer his friend some sage advice drawn from his experience at court. His letters, while revealing his deep concern for his friend's well-being, also evidenced Baltimore's pragmatic approach to politics. After warning him that his refusal to pay played into the hands of his enemies (in this instance, Buckingham and Sir John Savile) who hoped "to see you act your own notable harm," he urged Wentworth to redeem himself at the lowest price he could. He pleaded that Wentworth not be blind to the advice of those who "have no Interest in the Counsel they give you but your own Safety and Preservation" and advised him not give the commissioners an absolute refusal; rather, he should either pay the money in the country, which would disarm his adversaries, or reserve his right to answer until he went to London. Three weeks later Baltimore wrote in haste that he was sorry he would not be able to see Wentworth; he was departing within three or four days for his colony in Newfoundland and did not intend to return until fall. Having conferred with mutual friends, he reiterated his worry that Wentworth's "too much Fortitude" would lead to a misfortune that his heart might endure but from which his body would suffer grievously. Calling on his long experience in these matters, Baltimore philosophized that "the conquering Way sometimes is yielding" and implored Wentworth to send the money to the collectors without further ado. When Baltimore returned from Newfoundland in late November or early December, he learned that his advice had been ignored and that his friend had been incarcerated for a time.[43]

In addition to outfitting ships for the voyage, Baltimore at last secured the services of two secular priests, Anthony Pole (alias Smith) and Thomas Longeville. Again, Stock claimed credit. Having abandoned his hope that Rome would supply Carmelite missionaries, he reported to Propaganda, "I have procured two secular priests to go thither, one to remain with the Catholics there, who are approximately twenty, the other to return here in hope of further help in the spring." Smith and Longeville provided a new spiritual presence in a land previously served only by Protestant clergy, and their joining the expedition marked another obvious and dramatic change in Baltimore's colonial activities.[44]

Lord Baltimore, the two priests, and a contingent of colonists sailed for Avalon on the first of June 1627 "to lay the ground of his plantation." A later report written by the Belgian nuncio indicated Baltimore's willingness to colonize with a religiously mixed population. He "took with him besides Protestants also *some* Catholics who gladly went along to avoid the persecution which was just commencing." They arrived on July 23 only to find an uninhabited site. According to the nuncio, they did not see anybody else for some months.[45]

The scene must have been disappointing for one who had already expended so much money on the project. Another Newfoundland entrepreneur, Robert Hayman, a participant in plantation building, indirectly spoke to Calvert's situation. Hayman gave serious thought to how the imperfect business might be improved to the best advantage of the king and his subjects. He emphasized the importance of resident proprietors and noted that all the planters had been wronged by the dishonest, idle, unfit men they had employed. He singled out Baltimore, who had much injury done to him, for wisely taking charge of his business.[46]

Baltimore did not allow the disintegrating state of his colony to trouble him long. He found one hopeful sign of permanence in his deserted colony. As the proprietor, he took up residence in the manor house built by Captain Wynne in 1622. From there he supervised the establishment of a firmer foundation for his colony. In an effort to secure the desired religious harmony within his religiously diverse population, he permitted the priests to celebrate Mass "in one part of the house, while the heretics held their services in another part."[47]

The summer sojourn whetted his appetite to do the job properly. Baltimore, his family, Father Longeville, and a number of other Catholic colonists returned to England in late November or early December. According to the nuncio, they "praised the Newly Found Land very much, thereby raising a desire in others to see that country." The proprietor of Avalon returned to England determined to establish residency in the next spring. He expected to turn the enterprise into a profitable one. After a short stay in England, he went to Ireland to plan the next adventure.[48]

Before departing for Ireland, Baltimore gained the king's support. He informed Charles that he could no longer commit the managing of his colony in Newfoundland to the trust of others, "by whose negligence and otherwise" his estate had been "already much wasted," to his great prejudice. To succeed, he had to take up residency for a number of years, and he told the king he was prepared to make that commitment. Calling it a good and laudable work, the king strongly endorsed Baltimore's enterprise. He was no less inclined to favor and protect the plantations of "our good and faithful subjects" in those remote parts of the world than was his father. He, too, knew they tended much to the honor

of "our Crowne the enlargement of our dominion and to the good of our people." Charles, "well assured by long experience" of Baltimore's "loyal fidelity"
and of his zeal to serve and honor him, licensed him to return to his colony. By
the king's command, his lord deputy, Henry Cary, Viscount Falkland, was to
allow Baltimore to travel from any port in Ireland and to assist him in all lawful
ways in matters that concerned him or the furtherance of his Newfoundland
voyage. Thus, this avowed Catholic's fortune had come full circle. Despite his
religion, once again he enjoyed the confidence of his king, who knew him to be
a loyal Englishman committed to an enterprise that served the interests of the
empire.[49]

From his second departure for Newfoundland until his death in 1632, Baltimore depended primarily on two men, Wentworth and Sir Francis Cottington,
to protect and further his interests in England. Beyond using their good offices
at court, Baltimore also entrusted to them substantial personal responsibilities.
These arrangements indicated the strong bond of trust that existed between
Baltimore and his friends.

Cottington had served many years at court and had ample opportunity to
come to know his cousin Calvert. Between 1611 and 1616 their careers as clerks
of the Privy Council had coincided. This service had brought status and wealth
to both and served as stepping-stones for future advancement. More important,
their responsibilities for handling the Spanish correspondence had provided
background for their subsequent negotiations for the Spanish match. When
possible, Calvert had used his influence to further Cottington at court.

Of greater importance, both men had become deeply involved in the Spanish marriage negotiations. Cottington, despite triggering Buckingham's temper
when he warned against the trip to Spain, accompanied the duke and the prince
in February 1623. The failure of those negotiations in 1623 and 1624 had
proved disastrous for both Cottington and Calvert. Out of favor with the ever
powerful Buckingham, they were forced to corroborate his fanciful tales of the
role he played in the negotiations of the Spanish treaties. In addition to wit-
nessing the destruction of the treaties, neither had been able to aid their friend
Bristol, the former ambassador to Spain, whom Buckingham had blamed for his
own ineptitude. Like Calvert, Cottington had suffered from the duke's wrath.
He had been virtually banished from court but later had ingratiated himself with
the duke. He did not, however, reestablish himself fully until the government
reversed its anti-Spanish policy. Largely through the intercession of Sir Richard

Weston, Cottington reached a pinnacle of success when he was sworn in as a privy councillor in November 1628.[50]

In addition to their shared beliefs in matters of foreign policy and their uneasy relationship with Buckingham, Baltimore and Cottington had in common an unsettled spiritual life that culminated with a commitment to Roman Catholicism. At various times, indecision and doubt related to the established church bedeviled both men. Cottington had shuttled back and forth between England and Spain during the summer of 1623. He became ill that August and nearly died. Apparently, he summoned a priest and made a (temporary) profession of faith in the Catholic church. Cottington never acknowledged that episode. That he continued in outward conformity to the state church until he began to live openly as a Catholic in 1652 suggests a parallel to Calvert's life. To what extent, if any, they discussed religious issues cannot be determined.[51]

Assured of the king's support, and assisted by his two friends whose fortunes were on the rise, Baltimore forged ahead with preparation for a lengthy stay in Newfoundland. He entrusted a substantial sum of money to Cottington and Sir William Ashton to be used for his children. In an August letter to Cottington, he wrote, "I hope the trust of those moneyes assigned for my children is now clear out of that Jewes hands of Lincolns Inne, and setled upon you and Sr. W. Ashton."[52]

Before taking most of his family to Newfoundland, Baltimore settled two related matters: his need for new funds and a suitable marriage for Cecil. In "a will that I hope shall be performed in my life time," he made a contract with his son Cecil, who was not going to Newfoundland. Baltimore bartered his main assets, his land in England and Ireland, for the much-needed cash to undertake his imperial adventure. Cecil received all his father's English lands, two-thirds of his silk farm, and his Irish lands, the latter to be held by his father during his lifetime. In return, Cecil consented to marry within a year, accepted that Wentworth and Cottington must approve his choice in marriage, and agreed to pay his father, or his father's attorneys, the sum of three thousand pounds in two installments.[53]

With his eldest son's future secured, Baltimore got ready to depart for his colony. Amid the busy preparations to sail, he took time to write Wentworth, even though he was "loathe to part in a letter." His letter seemed filled with apprehension. He pondered whether he would ever see England again and reminded Wentworth of "the promises yow made to visit me in Newfoundland," although he knew full well that his friend would never fulfill it. He closed this letter to his Protestant friend with "God send us a happy meeting in heaven and in earth if it please him."[54]

Accompanied by his wife, many of his children, two sons-in-law, a secular priest named Hackett, and at least thirty other Catholics, Baltimore landed safely in Newfoundland in June. The Catholic colonizers, some of whom Stock claimed were "among my spiritual children," remain anonymous. Whatever their background, they and the Calverts faced the overwhelming task of carving out a new life in a howling wilderness. In return for their commitment, they expected a chance to prosper and to be able to practice their religion in a freer environment.[55]

How any of the planters reacted, especially those seeing the country for the first time, can only be imagined. Certainly awe-inspiring, the land must have been equally daunting. Unfortunately, few besides Baltimore left any record of "this remote wilde part of the worlde where I have planted my selfe." He wrote two letters, one to the king and one to Buckingham, that provided a glimpse into the colony during the summer of 1628.[56]

In his planning for his colony, Baltimore never envisioned that a running naval battle with the French would occupy so much of his time and energy. When he sailed, he knew that preparations were under way to send a fleet to relieve the Huguenots at La Rochelle. To his dismay, he found that the war between England and France had spread to Newfoundland and that the responsibility for defending English interests fell to him. As he lamented to Buckingham, "I came to builde, and sett, and sowe, but I am falne to fighting with Frenchmen," seamen who were troubling the king's loyal subjects, who had come only to fish. He described the confrontation to his king. The French came with three good ships and four hundred men and quickly seized two English ships with all their fish and provisions. Had he not sent his own ships to intervene, the French would have continued to plunder English mariners and fishermen. Baltimore's ships came upon six French ships that "had Almost made theire Voyage" and were nearly ready to start home. His men seized them and sent them to England. Cecil Calvert later stressed that his father had engaged the French with his own ships, manned by his own planters, and that his defense of English interests had been at "his great charge and losse."[57]

Baltimore understood that this success was but the opening round in a conflict that would carry over to the spring. He worried that the return of his ships and the French prizes to England would leave the English in Newfoundland defenseless in the face of a renewed French assault. Thus Baltimore petitioned the king for the loan of one of the prizes. His letter to Charles emphasized his loyal service to his sovereign and detailed the difficulties that he had encountered in his struggle to enlarge the king's dominions. While acknowledging that colonial enterprises commonly have troubled beginnings, he noted that they "cannot be easilie overcome by such weake hands as myne" without the king's special protection. Baltimore entrusted his letter to his son-in-law William Peasley and charged him to secure the loan of one of the prizes taken that summer. Given the sad state of the navy, acquiring the loan of a valuable ship would be no easy task; this again tested Baltimore's influence at court.[58]

The French were not Baltimore's only problem. To his consternation, internal disputes over religion also breached the peace of the infant colony. In bringing thirty to forty Catholics into a colony where the dominant element had been Protestant, Baltimore acted upon the assumption that he could colonize successfully with a religiously mixed population. He saw religion as a private matter and expected that his colonists would share that view. However, his novel approach scandalized both Protestants and Catholics.

Erasmus Stourton, "Preacher of the Word of God, and Parson at Ferry-Land," returned on the same ship that brought Baltimore's letters to the king and Buckingham. Upon landing in England, Stourton brought the religious practices in the colony to the attention of authorities. The two priests in the colony, Hackett and Smith, he exclaimed, say Mass every Sunday "and doe use all other the ceremonies of the church of Rome in as ample manner as tis used in Spayne." He even witnessed the priests, Baltimore, and the Catholics at Mass. Stourton also charged that against the will of Protestant William Poole, Baltimore had his child "baptized according to the orders and customs of the church of Rome." Stourton said nothing about his own behavior in the colony during the examination, but he must have been disruptive, for Baltimore, who considered him audacious, had banished him on account of his misdeeds. Immediately after giving his testimony, the irascible knight errant of Protestantism in Newfoundland set off to entertain the Privy Council with his scandalous charges. With his petition for the loan of a fighting ship also on its way to the council, the last thing Baltimore needed was a hue and cry about priests and religious practices in the colony.[59]

Ironically, Baltimore's religious practices fared no better with some of his fellow Catholics. According to the report that made its way to Rome two years later, he scandalized at least some members of the hierarchy with his effort to be fair to his Protestant colonists. "As to the religious usage, under one and the same roof of Calvert, in one area Mass was said according to the Catholic rite, while in another part of the house the heretics carried out their own." In 1627 Propaganda had prohibited missionaries from using churches in which heretics held divine services. If the pragmatic proprietor knew about the decree, he chose to ignore it. His house was the only practical place to hold services.[60]

The events unfolding in London in the fall of 1628 provided a significant test for Baltimore. The Catholic colonizer, stranded far from his power base, needed his friends to protect his interests. His survival seemingly rested on whether Stourton or Peasley would carry the day. Both, in their own ways, had good cases. That "knave" Stourton, representing militant intolerant Protestantism, had the weight of history and the club of the penal laws on his side. Baltimore had the king's approval and friends at court. More important, though, he was fighting the national, *Catholic*, enemy France, defending English interests, and extending the king's dominions.[61]

Buckingham's death at the hands of an assassin on August 23, 1628, strengthened Baltimore's influence at court. His two patrons, Wentworth and Cottington, began to enhance their positions at court in the new scramble to gain influence. One commentator reported that some thought Sir Richard Weston, the lord treasurer, would "have the greatest power with the King." This, he thought, would exalt "the Popish faction," for "he will bring in Arundel, Bristol, and Sir Francis Cottington his great friend." Within months of Buckingham's death, and through the lord treasurer's influence, the king elevated Cottington to the Privy Council and soon after appointed him chancellor of the exchequer.[62]

Wentworth was not outside the lord treasurer's circle of influence. He shared with him first a desire for peace with Spain and then closer relations between the two powers. Weston supported his appointment to the Privy Council, where he joined Cottington and the other new members. The government further rewarded Wentworth in November and December 1628. Advancement to the Privy Council, elevation to viscount, and appointment as president of the Council of the North consummated his ambitions as a courtier. In the aftermath of the Spanish war and Buckingham's death, Calvert's two closest friends and associates had made their way to the seat of power.[63]

Wentworth's service as president of the Council of the North produced contrasting reactions from the Calverts, who were favorable, and some Yorkshire Catholics, who were fearful. Christopher Wandesford wrote to Wentworth that "the Papists already hang down their heads like Bulrushes" at the rumor of his appointment. They "think themselves like water spilt upon the ground which cannot be gathered up again," saying openly that "the days of Security and Quietness, in which they were lulled asleep by the Indulgence of the last" president were gone. Cecil Calvert's reaction to Wentworth's appointment differed remarkably from that of these Catholics. He quickly congratulated Wentworth and wanted him to know that no one was more joyful than he at the news. Eventually the news reached his father. He wrote to Wentworth in 1629 that he was infinitely glad for the honor the king accorded to him and grateful to see that "there is no change of fortune" that would make him forget your "old servants and friends." While such remarks were at once perfunctory and self-serving, there is no reason to believe them insincere. English Catholics, as much as other Englishmen, acted in ways that best served both their temporal and spiritual interests. Yorkshire Catholics long had supported Sir John Savile, Wentworth's chief rival for control in Yorkshire. The reckoning they feared stemmed from political realities, not religious factors. For the Calverts, succeeding as Englishmen and Catholics meant maintaining influence at court, and Wentworth was their friend and ally.[64]

Baltimore's friends at court held firm in their support of his endeavors. Stourton, perhaps despairing of his chances of success, never presented his case to the Privy Council. Cottington took Baltimore's petition for the loan of a ship to the king. When informed that Baltimore feared that the French, whom he had defeated the previous year in defense of his and the king's interests in Newfoundland, would seek revenge, Charles granted the "sayd humble request." Cottington instructed the lord treasurer to loan Baltimore one of the six prize ships, in this case the *St. Claude,* for a twelve-month period. Baltimore further tested his influence in the government when he sought a letter of marque, predated to before his seizure of the French ships, in order to receive his share of the prize money. The behavior of this Catholic Irish baron belies the notion that his religion impaired his ability to manipulate the government for his advantage. The government showed remarkable concern for Baltimore's interests. The Privy Council worried that a commission sought for New England might encroach on Baltimore's plantation and consulted with him. The proprietor of Avalon assured the council that the commission did not "concern him at all," for "it is far removed from Newfoundland." Charles and his government extended royal protection to a loyal English Catholic.[65]

The Stourton incident highlighted two critical elements for Baltimore. First and foremost, his former political status afforded sufficient protection to counter the attacks. Whatever the validity of Stourton's charges, they paled in light of Baltimore's influence at court. His religion notwithstanding, his loyalty and devotion to the government were not in question. Quite correctly, he thanked Charles for "protecting me also against calumny and malice" of those who sought "to make me seeme foule" in your eyes. The king's government showed that it had no interest in allowing internal religious disputes to overshadow the more important matter of the day, the war with France. For the moment, Baltimore's influence held.[66]

Second, the Stourton episode illuminated the most significant consequence of Calvert's decision to live as a Catholic. His new religious commitment opened him to attack by those willing to resort to anti-Catholicism. His religion placed him and his heirs in harm's way. Their enemies could, and would, play the religious card at the most inconvenient times. This left the Catholic Lords Baltimore vulnerable. The incident certainly foreshadowed the problems that lay ahead and helps to explain why the second Lord Baltimore spent his time in England defending his charter instead of colonizing personally in America.

Neither the banishment of Stourton nor the loan of the *St. Claude* ended Baltimore's difficulties, for he had yet to feel the lash of his most formidable opponent, the Newfoundland winter. Unfortunately, he did not have access to French explorer Samuel de Champlain's wisdom: It "is impossible to know this country without having wintered there, for on arriving in summer everything is very pleasant owing to the woods, the fair landscape, and the good fishing for cod and other species which we found. But winter in this country lasts six months."[67]

Robert Hayman, no stranger to Newfoundland, euphorically extolled in a series of verses the land that Baltimore visited in 1628:

> The Aire in *Newfound-land* is wholesome, good;
> The Fire, as set as any made of wood;
> The Waters, very rich, both salt and fresh;
> The Earth more rich, you know it is no lesse.
> Where all are good, *Fire, Water, Earth, and Aire.*
> What man made of the foure would not live there?

By August 1629 Baltimore was prepared to answer with a resounding "Not I!"[68]

Shortly before leaving, he wrote three letters, one to Cottington, one to the king, and one to Wentworth, that summarized events in Ferryland between August 1628 and August 1629 and provided a rationale for his departure. These letters indicated that Baltimore, although discouraged that his enterprise showed so little promise, remained committed to succeeding in his colonial ambitions. They also make clear that Baltimore's decision to abandon the Newfoundland enterprise had nothing to do with religion. The letters to his closest friends, Wentworth and Cottington, solicited their support for a new charter that would allow him to colonize in a more suitable climate. His letter to King Charles recounted his difficulties and declared his ambition to shift his colony to a warmer climate. He admitted to the king, "I have had strong temptations to leave all proceedings in plantations, and being much decayed in my strength to retire myself to my former quiett." However, he was not ready to quit at this low point. His "inclination carrying me naturally to these kynd of workes, and not knowing how to better employ the poore remaynder of my dayes," Baltimore assured his monarch that he was prepared to continue his work "to further, the best I may," enlarging your empire in this part of the world. This English Catholic colonizer confidently laid before his Protestant king a request for a grant of a precinct in Virginia with all the privileges he had enjoyed in his Newfoundland patent. With incredible audacity, Baltimore announced his continuing intention to serve his king and country by "planting of tobacco" in Virginia.[69]

Problems with religion did not affect his request for a new colony. As a matter of fact, religion was the one area in which Baltimore achieved some success. Simon Stock, who continued to monitor developments from England, informed Propaganda that two Fathers of the Society of Jesus had gone to Newfoundland to serve as missionaries. Precisely how in 1629 Baltimore came to acquire the services of Fathers Alexander Baker and Lawrence Rigby remains unclear. Also unexplained is why Baltimore took so long to secure an entente cordiale with the Jesuits. Relying on Stock had been convenient and encouraging, given Stock's promises. After a number of years, however, he had tired of Stock's grandiose posturing. Once the Carmelites and the seculars had been eliminated, the Jesuits became the obvious choice. For their part, the Jesuits were interested in a base for a missionary effort, and this may explain their willingness to venture with Baltimore when other priests rejected his overtures. Beyond this, the Society's ability to act decisively now seemed attractive and served to overcome any doubt that Baltimore may have had regarding its reputation within the Catholic community. Stock later reported that the "fathers of the Society have a mission or a special commission for those places in America." The coming of the Jesuits may have resulted from a letter Baltimore wrote to Father Andrew White some-time during the fall of 1628. The letter, no longer extant, perhaps sought to as-certain the priest's interest in colonization. In any case, as a result of this contact, the Calverts secured an important partner in White, who would serve as their major publicist in their "Maryland designe." But this was in the future, and the arrival of the two Jesuits did nothing to bolster the troubled psyche of Lord Bal-timore, who by now contemplated shifting his base of operation to the Chesa-peake.[70]

His letter to Cottington, which focused on the money he and Ashton held in trust for his children, implored his friend to use his influence to secure a similar grant in a more favorable climate. He reiterated this theme in his letter to the king. Thanking the king for his continued confidence, Baltimore detailed the difficulties and encumbrances that made it desirable for him to leave his colony. "I have found," he lamented, "by too deare bought experience," that which other men "always concealed from me" for their private interests, that from mid-October to mid-May "there is a sad face of wynter upon all this land." He found that with land and sea frozen solid, no life sprang forth until the begin-ning of May. The air was "so intolerable cold, as it is hardly to be endured." His house was no longer a home, but a hospital, with half of the hundred or so in-habitants sick at any given time. Nine or ten of his company had died. The harsh winter had taken its toll on his own health as well.[71]

Before boarding his ship, Baltimore wrote in haste to Wentworth. With the prospect of another long winter facing him, he confided to his friend that he had "suddenly resolved" to leave the barren waste of Newfoundland for a warmer climate. He feared that "I shall rayse a great dust of talke and discourse and be censured by most men of giddiness and levity" for leaving. He realized that the foundation there was ill laid in a miserably cold country located "in the coldest corner of all the country: tis not terra Christianorum." Baltimore made no spe-cific reference to his destination; nor did he ask for Wentworth's support for a new charter. He asked Wentworth to protect him if "my name came in question upon any grubbing complaint of those fishermen with whom I have had con-tynuall quarrels," and whom he considered "the most barbarous people that ever man had to do withall."[72]

This letter closed an important chapter in his life. Newfoundland, which had occupied so much of his time for the previous four years, taught him some valu-able lessons. Begun on such a hopeful note, the experience was still another stinging defeat for George Calvert. Religious considerations, especially his open espousal of Catholicism, played but a small part. His difficulty in attracting priests exasperated him, but the 1629 arrival of the two Jesuits laid that matter to rest. The braying of the intolerant Stourton frustrated him, but the matter had been resolved in a favorable manner. He never mentioned religion as a factor in his decision to leave.[73]

Sir David Kirke, who seized the mansion house from the agent of the second Lord Baltimore in 1638, offered a less charitable scenario ten years after Baltimore's departure. He told Archbishop Laud that the air of Newfoundland agreed perfectly well with all God's creatures except Jesuits and schismatics, adding, "A great mortality among the former tribe so affrighted my Lord of Baltimore that he utterly deserted the country." Kirke opined that the best security was a strict observance of the rites and service of the Church of England. Religion served as a convenient cover for the Kirkes' effort to displace the Calverts.[74]

Baltimore invested in the land, and he expected to profit from the natural resources in Newfoundland and the fishing industry. Three factors, the harsh and unforgiving Newfoundland winter, the savage fishermen with whom he had to interact, and the French whom he had to fight, conspired against him. They seemed too formidable to overcome in view of his declining health. As he confided to Wentworth, he had engaged in the enterprise at great expense. A later appraisal claimed that he had risked between twenty thousand and twenty-five thousand pounds. Baltimore's assessment was simple and direct: "I have lost."[75]

The decision to leave in 1629 must have been difficult, but he saw his departure as only a temporary setback. His mind raced ahead, forming new possibilities, this time in Virginia. He expressed cautious optimism to Wentworth. Having ventured this far, and with "grave probability" that he could overcome the difficulties in the end, he told Wentworth that "by the grace of God" he would persist. He believed he was better equipped to offer a new colonization plan than someone starting anew in England. That said, under Peasley's care he sent to England his children and his letters signaling his interest in a new patent. Leaving a remnant of "some 30 heretics and two or three Catholic women, with no priest or minister," Baltimore, his wife, and the rest of the colonists, along with whatever personal belongings he salvaged, set sail for the Chesapeake, where new challenges and new obstacles lay in wait.[76]

CHAPTER FIVE

"If your Majesty will please to grant me a precinct of land with such priviledges as the king your father my gracious Master was pleased to graunt me"

Securing the Charter (1629–1632)

Avalon's disintegration was Maryland's genesis. By "deare bought experience," the first Lord Baltimore learned some of the hard lessons of his predecessors, who also found the winter "in this woefull land" beyond endurance. Starting over would not be easy for a man whose futile enterprise had sapped his energy and his fortune. To begin anew, Baltimore had to find a better location, secure authority from the government to colonize in a new land, rewrite the New-foundland charter, seek funds to supplement his depleted reserves, and attract individuals willing to venture forth under his leadership.

It was an ironic turn of events that the frigid Newfoundland winter drove Baltimore to the sultry Chesapeake. He arrived in late September after the op-pressive heat of summer had dissipated and spent only a few weeks in the area, which from a climatic perspective must have seemed like the promised land. Had he arrived during the steamy Chesapeake summer, he might well have con-cluded that in its own way that climate was just as oppressive as a Newfoundland winter. For now, he remained optimistic that the Chesapeake offered a respite from the excessive weather, foreign wars, disease, and religious squabbling that had been his fate in Avalon.[1]

Baltimore did not anticipate a welcome as cold as the Newfoundland winter. Nor did he anticipate that his intention to create a new colony within the former boundaries of Virginia would provoke intense and prolonged resentment among the Virginians. He knew that the defunct Virginia Company charters had not encouraged Catholics to reside in the colony. While the 1609 charter did not exclude people "suspected to affect the superstitions of the Churche of Rome," it did require those who wanted to reside in Virginia to take the oath of supremacy. The 1612 charter authorized Virginia authorities to tender the oaths of supremacy and allegiance to anyone venturing to Virginia.[2]

His unexpected arrival troubled the governor and the council of Virginia. They summoned Baltimore for an interview. In recounting the meeting, they informed the Privy Council of their ready inclination to give Baltimore the respect due to a person of his status. When they learned that Baltimore intended to "plant and inhabit among them," the Virginians followed their instructions from the Privy Council and tendered the oaths of supremacy and allegiance to him. Having refused the king, Baltimore could hardly comply with the demands of these churlish frontiersmen. "Making profession of the romishe Religion," he utterly refused to take the oaths. The councillors, not inclined to exercise any independence where it did not suit their interests, refused to accept an alternative oath offered by Baltimore. They told the hapless interloper that "they would not admit any man into their society which would not acknowledge all preeminence belonging to his majesty, and so prayed him to provide himself for the next ship, wherein they have shipped him home." The government sentenced one zealous Virginian to two hours in the pillory for "giving My Lord Baltimore the lie and threatening to knock him down."[3]

Why did the Virginians react so viscerally? One explanation leaps forward: as loyal churchmen, they responded negatively to Baltimore because of his religion. Governor John Pott and the council members wrote that they were happy in the free exercise of their religion and implored the king's privy councillors not to allow any Papists to settle among them. But their reaction entailed more than religious hostility. Some of them knew that the king had appointed Calvert, among others, to manage the business of the Virginia colony in 1624. At that time, company leaders accused the king's commissioners "of extreme partiality" and attributed the king's actions to Gondomar and his successors. The Virginians saw Calvert as the enemy whose involvement in the nullification of the company's charter had nearly destroyed them economically.[4]

The Virginians left no doubt of their opposition. Leaving his wife, servants, and most of his possessions behind, Baltimore took the first available ship to London. He returned hopeful that his influence and previous faithful service would secure the coveted "precinct of land in Virginia." He intended to outmaneuver the Virginians by working through the more friendly government in London. While he sought a grant of "unplanted" land within the former bounds of the old company, the Virginians, led by William Claiborne, initiated actions to thwart his plans.[5]

In spite of the developing opposition, Baltimore had good reason to be confident. By the time Charles replied to his August petition, the peripatetic Baltimore had sailed from Virginia and may have already reached England. He undoubtedly saw a copy of the king's November 22 letter soon after he arrived in England. The letter was indeed a princely one and must have blunted some of his distress. It was hardly a persecuting letter. Men of "your condition and breeding," the king told him, are more fit for other employments than the framing of new plantations, which commonly have rugged and laborious beginnings. He urged his loyal, *now Catholic*, subject to return to enjoy all the respect his former services and late endeavors justly deserved. Given his situation, the king's generous offer must have tempted the fallen courtier, who never fully abandoned his interest in statecraft. Baltimore undoubtedly understood that Wentworth or one of his other friends had influenced the king's invitation. He accepted that the king and his friends acted in what they thought were his best interests, but he also realized that he could never return to his former status. Neither the king's advice nor the counsel of his friends dissuaded Baltimore from pursuing his goal of acquiring land along the Chesapeake, a country he extolled "to the skies."[6]

Stock reported that Baltimore regretted his return to England and wanted to resume his colonial enterprise. The king, who thought otherwise, expressed concern about Baltimore's declining health and ordered him to desist from further personal involvement in his imperial designs. Baltimore petitioned his former colleague, Sir Dudley Carleton, now viscount Dorchester and a secretary of state, for three favors. First, he asked him to "procure a privy seale" for the use of the *St. Claude* as the king promised. Second, he solicited a letter from the Privy Council to the governor of Virginia "in favor of my wife now there," directing him to assist her return to England. Finally, he requested that Dorchester lay before the king his suit made from Newfoundland for "a portion to be granted unto me in Virginia." He informed the secretary that Sir Francis Cottington had already informed him of the king's intention that "I should have any part not already granted." He confidently asked that the grant contain powers and privileges similar to those granted to him by the king's father for Newfoundland. For his part, Baltimore promised that "I shall contribute my best endeavors" to enlarge the king's empire in America. Because he could not go in person, he intended to accomplish his goal through such gentlemen and others who would willingly adventure with him. In February a court observer reported that he had secured a vessel "to fetch forth his lady and servants" from Virginia.[7]

Baltimore pursued his charter despite the many calamities that befell him within a relatively short time. Personal tragedy struck in the spring. The ship carrying his wife and servants foundered on the rocks off the Irish coast in early 1630, leaving Baltimore a widower for the second time. He also lost whatever of his worldly possessions he had left behind when he departed hastily from Virginia. Upon receiving the news, Baltimore may have gone into seclusion at Kiplin Hall, for he literally disappears from the record until the summer.[8]

In addition, the man who was to become the Calverts' bête noire, William Claiborne, launched a systematic campaign against any outside incursions into the Chesapeake. In March 1629, months before Baltimore left Avalon, the governor of Virginia, noting that diverse places in the colony had yet to be discovered, authorized Claiborne to explore areas to the south of Jamestown as well as "some particular places" to the north and in Chesapeake Bay. Since Baltimore sought a patent for unclaimed lands, the move gave proponents of the old Virginia Company an advantage in the struggle over a charter. The next year Claiborne returned to England to oppose any grant that might infringe on the claims of the former Virginia Company.[9]

On top of these afflictions, Baltimore's Newfoundland enterprise had exhausted his financial resources. While he was still in the colony, his brother-in-law George Mynne transferred four thousand pounds of his stock and two thousand pounds that represented Calvert's share of the second joint stock venture to Philip Burlamachi, a merchant-financier, to cover a portion of the money borrowed to finance the colony. In August 1630 one of Wentworth's correspondents painted a bleak picture of Baltimore's condition. Although Baltimore would never admit it, he did not have the means to support himself in England without assistance. William Robinson opined that Baltimore could not in good conscience borrow more money without "knowing some probability to pay again." As Wentworth's informant heard it, Baltimore had resolved to return to Ireland, where "melancholy and the barbarous carriage of the Irish (little differing in that part from savages) together with the sad thoughts of his past, and present fortunes, will quickly devour him." Robinson implored Wentworth to intercede on his friend's behalf. Wentworth dutifully wrote to reassure Baltimore and to inquire of his plans. But Baltimore, unwilling to commit his plans to paper and perhaps not having anything firm to disclose, preferred to wait until they met. Although he did not admit it, he had, much to his chagrin, made little progress on the charter.[10]

At some point during the summer, Baltimore returned to London to resume his quest for the new charter. His ability to exploit his connections for concessions testifies again that his choice of religion did not inhibit his quest for government favor. For example, in July he received an endorsement from the Privy Council in a letter ordering the lords justice of Ireland to assist him against a possible fraudulent land transaction. The council reminded the lords of Baltimore's former status as a privy councillor and his present status as a peer of that kingdom. Although he had no formal role at court, Baltimore tracked foreign affairs and provided Wentworth with court intelligence. In August 1630 Baltimore received a packet from Lady Cottington that he sent to Wentworth. The king had sent Cottington, who, like Calvert, supported repairing the fractured relationship, to Spain in the previous October to serve as ambassador extraordinary. The packet contained the news that Cottington's negotiations with the Spanish were close to completion, news that Baltimore knew Wentworth longed to hear. Soon after he wrote, Cottington dispatched a copy of the treaty to London.[11]

In the same letter, Baltimore reported that he and his family were "yet in Health" but noted that the dreaded plague had returned and that some fifty-six died. A month later, his news was more ominous. An outbreak of plague in his household, he confided to Wentworth, meant that "no man hath come to me nor I to them." He had become something of a recluse and confessed that he could not provide news either from court or from abroad.[12]

Outbreaks of plague played a significant role in his life. Fear of England's greatest scourge, rather than the threat of religious persecution, had led to his decision to transport his family to Ireland in 1625. Now again in 1630, plague returned to taunt him. His bout with plague offers a rare personal glimpse of Baltimore during the last twenty months of his life. His narrow escape also provides an opportunity to highlight how important he was for securing the charter.

Baltimore wrote the letter dated September 12 in two sittings. The first part described his encounter with plague, while the second responded to a letter from Wentworth, now missing, that arrived after Baltimore had penned his initial words. Baltimore told his friend that he was in "a retirement here at Greenwich," where he had fled with his children and a servant or two "from the infection of the plague." The outbreak had occurred about three weeks before in his lodgings at Castle Yard. He thought he knew the source of the infection and could barely contain his anger. The carrier, he thought, was "a boy," the son of Lord Arundel's housekeeper. Arundel, the lord marshal, was one of Baltimore's closest friends, so traffic between their household servants was not unusual. The boy had returned from an infected house and stayed with Baltimore's servants "some 2 or 3 days, till he fell down right sick and was removed out of the house." The information had been "very dishonestly concealed" from him by the boy's father. Despite Baltimore's fears, bubonic plague rarely spread from human contact.[13]

For seventeenth-century Londoners, plague remained a deep mystery, and many saw its outbreak as an act of God. In 1630 they had no idea of how plague spread; they only knew it came regularly to their neighborhoods. Scarcely a year passed without a visitation by the feared disease. Five major outbreaks occurred between 1563 and 1665. After 1609, only the 1625 outbreak took a greater toll in human life than the one in 1630. The more than thirteen hundred deaths associated with plague in 1630 brought terror to all. Those most at risk were London's poor, who lived in overcrowded houses, had few changes of clothing, and had little appreciation of hygiene. In such conditions fleas easily moved from rats to humans. Not surprisingly, plague took its greatest toll among servants. The elite fled the crowded cities for the country, as Baltimore did in 1625.[14]

For rich and poor alike, each outbreak reawakened dread. Baltimore confessed that the arrival of the deadly disease caused much alarm within his household. Because no one knew what caused plague, no one could predict who would be the next victim. Baltimore was not terribly clear on the "preparations" taken or how he applied them. He merely stated that he used sweats, electuaries, and other remedies generally used against plague. Further, he wrote Wentworth, "There was no going out of the town then, nor safety in it, unless we had known which of us were sound and which tainted."

Baltimore also hesitated to flee to a safer environment because he feared that he would not be able to secure medical treatment for anyone who became ill. Soon the feared disease struck again. A servant woman named Bridget Draycot (or Draycoate) appeared infected and "fell deadly sick." Baltimore elaborated on her symptoms, which corresponded to bubonic plague. He did not think his servant would live after two sores appeared and she went into a frenzy. If her symptoms followed the usual pattern, her temperature rose dramatically and she suffered headaches, vomiting, and pain. Draycot was in the fortunate minority, for Baltimore noted, "God be thanked," that she since had recovered. In an effort to prevent the disease from spreading, he isolated her and brought in someone from out of town to attend her. Baltimore stayed in the household a week longer, "until she was past danger," and then removed his family to Greenwich. From there he reported to Wentworth that those who had fled remained in good health, as did those servants left behind at his lodging in Castle Yard.[15]

Draycot was not just one of the servants. She was "a woman of my wife's" (referring to his late wife Joan), who "had the charge of my little boy," his son Philip, who was about three years old. The bills of mortality indicated that plague affected children more severely than adults. Small wonder that Baltimore concluded this section of his letter on a humble note: "Blessed be God for it who hath preserved me now from shipwreck, hunger, scurvy and pestilence and from many other dangers," which, he felt, more honest "men have not escaped."[16]

Despite the impediments—the loss of his wife, his worsening financial situation, and plague—Baltimore never wavered in his determination to follow through on the quest for the new grant. He persisted despite another flurry of activity by the government against recusants in the early 1630s. The Venetian ambassador reported that the Privy Council had ordered "the renewal of the edicts against Catholics" and stated its resolution "that for the future they shall be rigorously observed." He noted that the king recognized "that the liberty with which the Catholics for some time have performed their exercises in the houses of ambassadors creates a great scandal among the generality of the people here and causes a notable prejudice to the state." These and other anti-Catholic actions against recusants, however, never directly threatened Baltimore or his family. Having witnessed periodic anti-Catholic posturing, he accepted it as a necessary pandering to popular fears. With the exception of an aside to Christopher Wandesford, he left no indication of his reaction. After telling his Protestant friend of the queen's pregnancy, he said he wrote only to urge him to "spare us poor Catholiques and try God Almighty" to bless the rest of Wandesford's labors and endeavors beyond his approbation. In keeping with his tolerant demeanor, Baltimore told his friend, "I will pray for you." The government's delay in responding to Baltimore's petition must be attributed to other factors than the government's stricter enforcement of the penal laws.[17]

The financial condition of the government of Charles I prolonged Baltimore's pursuit of the Chesapeake grant. In general, and in common with his father, Charles faced expenses that exceeded his revenues. Baltimore's petition coincided with a push by the king's bureaucrats to cut expenses. The king's curt dismissal of the 1629 Parliament with his botched attempt to arrest its leaders exacerbated the troubles of a government already hard pressed to make ends meet. Charles needed Parliament and its ability to draw upon the wealth of the country. His decision not to meet it forced him to live on his own limited revenues. Baltimore, like the king, desperately needed money to fund his objectives. In the face of this austerity, additional government grants to provide much-needed revenue seemed unlikely, and without them a charter would do him little good. That he gained both objectives was no mean feat.

Baltimore secured the requisite support by patiently exploiting his court connections. The reemergence of the Spanish faction favored Baltimore. The war with Spain had not secured any English advantage, and Charles was anxious to extricate the country from an expensive and counterproductive war. In some ways it was like old times, for the advocates of friendly relations with Spain had finally gained ascendancy in Charles's government. Although no longer an insider, Baltimore followed the treaty negotiations with the Spanish closely and served as an unofficial consultant for those involved in the effort. His correspondence indicated a keen interest in the outcome. With renewed vigor, he carefully cultivated his relations with those men with whom he had labored to conclude the Spanish match who now had influence in the government. Suspicious Protestants, who saw them swarming like locusts at court, greatly exaggerated the number (but not the influence) of those who supported closer ties with Spain. The confidential letters of Juan de Necolade, Philip's agent in London, revealed that only a relatively small number of courtiers favored friendship with Spain. Among the most prominent were Sir Richard Weston, the earl of Portland and now the powerful lord treasurer; Sir Francis Cottington, who negotiated the Spanish treaty; and Sir Thomas Wentworth, who would soon be named lord deputy of Ireland. Others included Sir Francis Windebank, one of the secretaries of state, and the earl of Arundel. At no time did these men indicate any scruples over Baltimore's religious affiliation. Only in part can this be explained by the Catholic leanings of Cottington, Arundel, and even Sir

Richard Weston. Granting the charter did not depend on Baltimore's religion, one way or the other. Wentworth, Cottington, and Arundel, among others, aided and abetted Baltimore's quest for his charter without any concern about his religious commitments.[18]

As a result of information supplied by Sir Tobie Mathew, Baltimore informed both Wentworth and his associate Christopher Wandesford of the state of the Spanish deliberations as of September 26, 1630. He wrote of Sir Kenelm Digby, another Roman Catholic and participant in the Spanish match negotiations, who recently had "his eyes opened" and converted to the Church of England. Baltimore harbored no recriminations about Digby's politic switch to the Church of England. He merely observed that the move made him eligible for whatever employment for which the government might think him fit. Indeed, he recognized the utility of supporting his former associate, regardless of his religion. Still dabbling in matters of state, he urged both Wentworth and Wandesford to write to the lord treasurer to support Digby's appointment as the ambassador to Spain.[19]

Meanwhile, in a move that had monumental consequences for his colonial enterprise, Baltimore solidified his ties with members of the Society of Jesus. Why he had not moved sooner to an association with the Jesuits is a puzzle. He undoubtedly had had contact with them before 1628. No layman knew more about the controversies that surrounded members of the Society of Jesus and split the Catholic community than the former secretary. Perhaps this knowledge had made him wary. He realized that the king saw the Jesuits as the greatest threat to civil harmony. More important, many Catholics still regarded the Society, which was established in England in 1623 as a separate province under Father Richard Blount, with suspicion and fear. The English recognized the Jesuits as very aggressive proselytizers. The best organized, most numerous, and most militant of England's priests, Jesuits alienated some Catholics, who resented their forcefulness. Calvert's cautious side may have made him reluctant at first to associate with an order identified by many as extremist and unfavorably characterized by King James as the Puritans of Rome. In any case, few decisions were of greater magnitude for Calvert's son and for Maryland than the one that led to an association with the Jesuits in the late 1620s.[20]

After he returned from Virginia, Baltimore replaced the ineffective Carmelite Stock with an English Jesuit named Andrew White. Baltimore had now found a priest willing and able to assist the enterprise as a recruiter and adventurer. As long as they shared common goals, such as attracting Catholics into the enterprise, the entente served both parties well. White and Calvert were born to Catholic parents within a year of each other, but unlike Calvert, White remained a Catholic throughout his life. Born in London and educated in both in France and Spain, he returned in 1605 to his native land only after ordination as a priest. By this time, the *now Protestant* Calvert had launched his career in Cecil's service. After a brief stay in England, White journeyed to Louvain, Belgium, where he joined the Society of Jesus at the age of twenty-eight. He returned to England as a Jesuit missionary in 1612. Between 1615 and 1619, he taught in Louvain and gained a reputation as a prickly scholar. In 1619 he came back to England again and served the English mission until 1622. White may have been known to Calvert, who, as the secretary of state, tracked the activities of priests in England. White's return to teaching at Jesuit colleges after 1622 precluded any personal participation in the budding Avalon project. That the *now Catholic* Calvert wrote in the fall of 1628 to White at Liège, Belgium, indicates that he knew the Jesuit might be interested in joining forces. White returned to England before June 1629 and spent some of his time at the mission of St. Thomas in Hampshire County. The priest and the colonizer finally joined forces in the spring or summer of 1630.[21]

Baltimore knew that the Society of Jesus had assumed an increasingly major role in Catholic survival. More than any other clerical group, the Jesuits recognized the relationship between the gentry and maintaining the faith. They flourished because they understood the limitations imposed by the penal laws. Functioning like itinerant preachers, the Jesuits enjoyed the greatest success in bringing the sacraments to scattered families where Catholicism tenaciously hung on, notably among the gentry and the nobility. These ubiquitous missionary priests encouraged greater gentry and nobility control over their own religious affairs as part of their survival/mission strategies. For example, they accommodated the laity by providing individual priests for gentry households. In return, Catholic nobles and members of the gentry sheltered the priests and provided requisite sustenance to carry out their clandestine mission. As a further quid pro quo, some of their sons, educated overseas, returned as priests to nurture the religion among the gentry, who employed them in their households. In the absence of the Church hierarchy, the English Catholic nobility and gentry had grown accustomed by the 1620s to asserting their authority over the clergy.[22]

Baltimore's association with the Jesuits had an immediate impact: it transformed his views on the jurisdictional dispute between regular clergy (priests under the control of religious orders) and secular clergy (priests under the control of the Church hierarchy). As Calvert had struggled with his own religious commitment during the fall of 1624, Rome had sought to bring some order to the chaotic conditions that confronted Catholics. The destruction of the Catholic hierarchy during Elizabeth's reign had left the clergy and the laity on their own. Efforts to bring some organizational order had proved inept. In January 1625, the pope appointed Dr. Richard Smith, a convert who had received a Jesuit education, as bishop of Chalcedon in an effort to unify the clergy and the laity in their struggle to survive. The archpriest, as Smith was known, arrived in England in April and spent most of the next eighteen months acclimating himself to the English mission. He enjoyed a modicum of peace as he visited Catholics in various parts of the realm. The question of jurisdiction then erupted into a nasty, protracted struggle between the regular clergy, who opposed his authority over them, and the secular clergy, who supported the bishop. The Carmelite Stock reflected the turmoil within the Catholic community. He told Propaganda that the discord resulted from ambition (who will be the greatest) and liberty (the avoidance of punishment for disorder and scandal). He professed "indifference whether I live in obedience to bishops or generals" as long as he could discharge his duties. The only solution he saw, given Smith's inability to fulfill the "duty of office or to govern the secular clergy," was papal intervention. The controversy embroiled lay Catholics, who tended to support the position of their confessors. Supporters of the bishop sought to restore traditional church order in England; his opponents saw the need to accommodate Catholicism to new realities imposed by the penal laws.[23]

The Jesuits took the lead in opposing the bishop, who seemed to enjoy the support of the majority of the laity, including Lord Arundell of Wardour, Cecil's future father-in-law. Baltimore joined the minority of Catholics who supported the Jesuits. He offered his support in spite of Smith's goal to demonstrate the loyalty of the English clergy. What resonated with Baltimore was the Jesuits' opposition to the appointment of a bishop with far-reaching authority over both clergy and laity. The Jesuits took the position that the laity should be free to admit into their homes priests of their own choosing, a position that undoubtedly enhanced their appeal among the gentry. They recognized that having a bishop in England was not in step with the realities faced by the laity and supported the "Lay Catholics of England," who protested the authority that Smith tried to exercise. These Catholics saw that the penal laws, which forced them to harbor priests, rendered the clergy dependent and permitted greater lay control.

They viewed Smith's assertion of authority as a threat not only to their property but also to their safety. In 1631, after years of generating considerable heat within the Catholic community and attracting the attention of the government, Smith withdrew to France, a defeated cleric.[24]

His involvement in the archpriest controversy did not prevent Baltimore from lobbying the Protestant government for additional monetary grants and a new charter. Nor did he abandon his interest in statecraft. Calvert wrote *The Answer to Tom-Tell-Truth, The Practice of Princes and the Lamentations of the Kirke*, a vigorous defense of King James and the policies he had pursued to regain the Palatinate. He alerted King Charles to the firebrands who aimed to set the "whole State on fire," embroil the realm, and alienate "the hearts of the people from their Prince." The usually moderate Baltimore used strong language to characterize the radical Protestants who demanded revenge for Frederick, the king's brother-in-law. These men who "take Gods word for their guide" were saying things "that can never go well with the Religion and State of *England*." Under the guise of religion, these "Maskers," that is, the authors of the three pamphlets Baltimore named in the title of his tract, sought to undermine loyalty to the king. With ponderous detail, he argued that Frederick had unlawfully usurped the crown of Bohemia and cautioned Charles not to intervene on behalf of his brother-in-law in a desperate cause that was unjust and dishonorable. He hoped that the king would pursue and ponder "these few lines" in order to quench the fire "when it shall flame."[25]

Baltimore denied any particular interest in "this scribbling presumption, but my owne fidelity, and the love of some of your servants here that pray for your happiness." Calling on God as his witness, he protested "that I write by no instructions of Forreigners, nor for no pension, nor obligation to any forreigne Prince whatsoever." He told Charles that he had written the tract solely for the king's edification and had not shared the analysis with others. His disclaimer aside, Baltimore was not an impartial observer. As secretary he had labored diligently to implement the policies that James had devised for dealing with Frederick. More important, he had a real interest in neutralizing the pressure from those who wanted the hostile relations with Spain to continue. In taking up his pen, Baltimore bolstered his friends in the government who also sought peace with Spain. His staunch defense of English foreign policy, his enduring commitment to monarchism, and his ample protestations of his loyalty as an English subject could not be lost on those who had to decide the fate of his much-desired grant.[26]

The former secretary understood, perhaps better than others, that the government moved slowly. Except for his impecunious situation, he remained in good spirits as he waited for his petitions to run their course. He joked to Wentworth about meeting with others on numerous occasions at Arundel House to win the lord marshal's "money at tables." Finally in March 1630 he won a small victory. He procured a warrant for two thousand pounds to be paid out of the increase of the subsidy on the raw silk imports; these funds bolstered his sagging fortunes.[27]

The pace of the negotiations, however, wearied even the veteran bureaucrat. Baltimore's high hopes drooped as negotiations with the government stalled. After a "solitary vacation" during the summer of 1631, he confessed to Wentworth that he had made little progress in gaining access to their former colleague, Lord Treasurer Portland, "that great man" who had the responsibility for cutting drastically the king's expenses. He watched the sluggish pace of his silk patent, but he knew he would not "receive one penny by it" for another year at the earliest. He noted that passage would be costly and lamented that he had to begin "the world a new in buying household stuffs, (all that I had being lost), and in removing my self and my children into Ireland" at great cost. He told Cottington he could see his way clear if his friend either secured a grant of some duty or custom that might produce quicker revenues or persuade the king to give him a gift of one thousand pounds. But his words were of no avail, for he knew that Cottington's duty to the king transcended their friendship. Baltimore feared he would have to sell his patent for the revenue on the increase from the silk imports at an extreme loss, since few were willing to bid on patents and grants of customs and risk the wrath of the lord treasurer. He wanted Wentworth to know that he had not written for the purpose of gaining his further intercession and that he was grateful for all he had done on his behalf. The two years of anticipation had deeply frustrated and discouraged Baltimore, who, faced with ever dwindling economic prospects and no certain guarantee that he would secure his charter, momentarily succumbed to self-pity. "I shall make as good shift as I can, and be as little troublesome to them [his friends] hereafter as I may."[28]

Upon learning in October of the death of Wentworth's second wife, Baltimore responded with a most elegant letter. If his own "Occasions" did not force him to stay, he told his friend, he would not convey his sentiments through a letter but would come with all speed in person "to express my own Grief, and to take Part of yours, which I know is exceeding great, for the loss of so noble a

Lady, so virtuous and so loving a Wife." Recalling his own losses, he added that there were few who "can Judge of it better than I, who have been a long time myself a Man of Sorrows."[29]

The "Occasions" to which Baltimore referred were his efforts to sell his silk patent and to secure his charter. Toward the end of the month, he obtained one of his goals. In consideration of the surrender of his former letters patent on the increase of the subsidy from every pound of raw long silk and raw Morea silk, and for his good service to the Crown, he was granted a pension of one thousand pounds per year, which was to be paid out of the duties of all sorts of wine imported into England. After paying the arrears in the rent, Charles granted Baltimore the pension, which was to run for twenty-one years beginning March 25, 1632.[30]

Baltimore's good fortune continued. In February 1632, through the influence of his friends at court, he secured a warrant directing the attorney general to prepare a grant in Virginia. Councillors Wentworth, Cottington, and the earl of Dorset ordered the attorney general to prepare a grant for Lord Baltimore that included a precinct of land extending from the Chesapeake and the James River on the north to "the River of Passamogmus on the South." The new patent carried the same conditions of honor and advantage as his previous Newfoundland grant. The bill authorizing the grant reached the privy seal on March 17.[31]

News of the impending grant aroused adherents of the old Virginia Company, who initiated a campaign to defeat the Calverts. They carried their virulent campaign to the Privy Council, where they succeeded in having a special committee appointed to investigate the matter. The committee, composed of some of George Calvert's closest associates in the government, ruled against the Virginia Company supporters and ordered the Maryland grant to be drawn. Baltimore's enemies persisted, now claiming that the Maryland grant encroached on plans to settle the south side of the James River, and again challenged the grant.[32]

Unwilling to risk what he had accomplished, and having no inclination to "disgust" his opponents, Baltimore offered a compromise. He proposed to change the boundaries of his grant to a location he considered less desirable. The Privy Council ordered that the attorney general draft a revised grant for land to the north. To bolster his case, Calvert wrote to the earl of Middlesex asking for his recollection of the actions taken "with the old Virginia Company." He told his former colleague that some former stockholders "pretend" the charter was "still to be in force" and that he sought a new patent for "some part of that large Territory" once part of the "old Patent," but unplanted. Baltimore's supporters on the Privy Council acted as if the company had been "damned for ever" and pushed through the second warrant. That one, signed in March 1632 by Arundel, the earl of Carlisle, Cottington, and Wentworth, authorized the attorney general to prepare a new and amended grant of land in Virginia. At long last and against all odds, Baltimore was well on his way to gaining his charter.[33]

With victory at hand, however, fifty-two-year-old George Calvert succumbed to illness and died at his lodgings at Lincoln's Inn Fields in London. In his will, signed the day before his death, Baltimore described himself as sick of body but sound of mind. The precise nature of his illness is not known—fevers and agues were generic terms. He had suffered periodic bouts with illness since at least April 1623 and had been weakened by his winter in Newfoundland. His son buried him in the churchyard at St. Dunstan, Fleet Street, London.[34]

George's death left his son and heir more dependent than ever on his court connections. In his will, the first Lord Baltimore implored his friends Wentworth and Cottington to be Cecil's guardians and supervisors. He asked them to take care of his poor family "and to Patronize, and love it as they have been pleased to doe unto mee since our first" acquaintance at court and elsewhere. George Calvert's friends rendered the assistance the young lord needed. After describing how the Virginians had harassed him in 1632 and 1633, Cecil wrote Wentworth that "by the Help of some of your Lordship's good Friends and mine," they "overcame these Difficulties." Wentworth, for his part, told the young Lord Baltimore that he supported his enterprise in memory of his "Noble and Excellent father," whom he characterized as "soe worthy a Person, and my Dere friende." If Wentworth, who left in July to assume his new post as lord deputy of Ireland, had an ulterior motive, it was no more than to secure the favor of Cecil, now a young Irish baron, as a potential ally in that troubled land. The support of Wentworth, Cottington, and other friends of his father, prevailed and allowed Cecil to move forward with his plans to launch the colony that the June charter authorized.[35]

Five weeks after the death of his father, on June 20, 1632, the charter for Maryland passed the seals. The second Lord Baltimore inherited the depleted family fortune and the colonial enterprise now in gestation. His father had pinned on the new colony his hopes for recouping the considerable investment already made in his Avalon adventure and for creating a place where he and those who followed him could live in material and spiritual comfort. Indeed, the problems that Cecil inherited with the Maryland enterprise would have severely tested the most skillful and hardened manager. Success or failure depended not only on his managerial skills, but also on the influence of those at court who supported the enterprise.

The charter did not end the second Lord Baltimore's troubles. His father's willingness to redefine its location did nothing to assuage Maryland's adversaries. They dogged the youthful Baltimore and his enterprise and did everything in their power to prevent the founding of the colony. "Some of the dissolved Company of Adventurers to Virginia" proved far more tenacious than he expected. Perhaps believing that the elder Calvert's death strengthened their position at court, they again endeavored "to overthrow my Business at the Council-Board." In May the Virginians presented the government still another petition. The council assigned it to the lords commissioners for foreign plantations, where Baltimore was on fairly secure ground. Many of the lords were numbered among his father's closest associates and were both sympathetic toward and supportive of the Maryland colony. Still, the proceedings were troublesome and fraught with danger. The council ordered both Baltimore and his adversaries, "the Adventurers and Planters of Virginia," to present their written propositions and justifications of their positions on June 28, 1632.[36]

The attacks, couched in language that appealed to the prevailing anti-Catholic sentiments of the English people, put Baltimore on the defensive. His paper, *Objections Answered Touching Maryland*, summarized the religious, economic, and imperial charges against his colony and offered his rebuttals. The first two objections questioned the colony's effect on English Catholics. Objection one charged that the government would lose any hope of inducing conformity if it allowed Catholics to migrate to a place "where they may have free liberty of their religion." Objection two charged that the government would appear to countenance a kind of toleration of (or at least a connivance with) popery if it granted the charter. The next two objections related to the financial implications of a Catholic withdrawal. Objection three worried about the negative impact of allowing recusants to leave England and escape the penal laws. Furthermore, if the government permitted Catholics who left to take their wealth with them, it would damage the kingdom. Objection four centered on "the Catholic as subversive" theme that formed the basis of Protestant fears and fueled their anti-Catholic prejudices. Roman Catholics could not be trusted to serve English interests. Permitting the Catholics to leave, the argument ran, could prove dangerous to Virginia and New England. Maryland Catholics "may be suspected" to bring in the Spaniards to suppress the Protestants in those parts. Worse still, the Catholics (having control of the government) could and would shake off any dependence on the English Crown.[37]

The answer to objection two noted that the preamble of Baltimore's patent "recited" the "enlargement of the Kings Dominions" as a motive for the grant, and the response to objection five, which enumerated some of the reasons why Maryland did not threaten Virginia or New England, elaborated on Baltimore's English goals. The distances between Maryland and the other colonies and the fact that Protestants in those areas outnumbered "Roman Catholiques in all of England" by three to one precluded a Catholic conquest. The "poverty of those parts" made it improbable that a foreign prince would undertake "the hazard and charge of such a remote designe." Finally, if Marylanders suffered no oppression in their spiritual or temporal concerns, they would have no reason to turn to foreign princes. With regard to the likelihood that Maryland would cast off dependence on the English Crown, the author made a number of points. Interestingly, he did not deny the possibility. But even if that happened, he argued, it was better for "English men, although Roman Cathollique," and not dependent on the Crown, to possess that country than for foreigners like the Dutch and the Swedes, who daily encroached in North America, to have it. More important, Baltimore spoke of the ties that would bind Maryland to the Crown and the state of England. These included protection from foreign enemies and from "wrongs which may be done unto them by his Majesties Protestant subjects in those parts" and the benefits of trade with England. Baltimore intended to serve English interests, but as this tract made clear, such service had to be mutually beneficial.[38]

Baltimore's answers persuaded members of the council to reaffirm their support for his patent. The lords directed the Virginians to seek their redress in the courts if they desired to pursue the matter further. Building on his success, Baltimore used his influence to secure a letter from the king ordering the governor and the council of Virginia to accord him the respect due to a person of his rank. At the end of July, the Privy Council granted a pass for the *Ark* to proceed unmolested.[39]

His antagonists refused to concede defeat. Baltimore postponed the mid-September sailing until October as his adversaries made their final efforts. Having exhausted their political influence, they now resorted to false rumors to prevent the expedition from sailing. Writing to Wentworth, Baltimore confided that his adversaries troubled him in many ways. He lamented how they delayed the expedition by carrying vicious tales to the Privy Council. The council, he wrote, had been informed "that I intend to carry over Nuns into Spain and Soldiers to the King" of Spain. Not only were no formal charges made, but Baltimore reported that the lords had laughed at the patently absurd rumors. However, they treated seriously the charges "that my Ships were departed from Gravesend without any Cockets from the Custom-House, and in Contempt of all Authority, my People abusing the King's Officers, and refusing to take the Oath of Allegiance." As a result, the council issued orders to recall the *Ark* and the *Dove* before they could reach open seas so they could be searched. All of this was done in great haste and without so much as consulting Baltimore, who mistakenly thought that his ships were now well advanced on their voyage. He went before the lords and convinced them that the attorney general "was abused and misinformed" and that there was no basis for "any of the former Accusations," which he considered "most notoriously and maliciously false." The council, having received word that the 128 colonists on board the *Ark* and the *Dove* had taken the required oath of allegiance, restored Baltimore's ships to their former liberty. The accusations, which forced Baltimore to appear before the council, meant another expensive delay before his ships could be on their way.[40]

The council's edict failed to resolve the matter. Baltimore believed that his adversaries had corrupted "and seduced my Mariners." Right down to their departure from Cowes on November 22, nagging fears continued to plague him. He implored the leaders of the expedition to discover what they could from both the sailors and the passengers about the private plots by his adversaries in England, "who endeavored to overthrow his voyage." They were to send the report to him as soon as possible. Giving credence to Baltimore's anxieties, Father White, who was on board the *Ark* anchored at Yarmouth, advised that "the seamen secretly reported that they expected the post with letters from the Counsell at London" that would prevent the ships from sailing. However, a sudden strong wind forced the *Ark* and the *Dove* to put to sea. As Father White interpreted the event, "thus God frustrated the plot of our seamen." A few months later, Baltimore reported that, having overcome tremendous difficulties, he had sent "a hopeful Colony into Maryland, with a fair and probable Expectation of good Success."[41]

Baltimore's adversaries failed to achieve their primary objectives, the restoration of the Virginia charter and the prevention of the dreaded Maryland patent. They succeeded, however, in irrevocably altering the course of the colony's development. Baltimore believed the Virginians attacked solely "to molest him in his proceedings, well knowing how prejudicial" they would be to him financially.

In this sense, the Virginians bear some responsibility for the many legal actions taken against Baltimore by his creditors when he failed to pay his debts in a timely fashion. More important, his debilitated financial condition, along with the unrelenting threat to his charter and the nascent colony, forced the proprietor to reassess his decision to sail with the first expedition. By not sailing, he removed, at least temporarily, the singular element of his charter, a resident lord proprietor to overcome the obstacles that accompanied new societies. He had to control events remotely through surrogates, who, no matter how devoted, never quite met his expectations.[42]

He appointed his brother Leonard to go in his place and penned a set of instructions to guide him and the others who ventured with him. His carefully crafted 1633 instructions embodied the hopes and fears that resulted from reliance on a religiously diverse population. His admonitions regarding Catholic behavior and the treatment of Protestants reflected the influence of his recent struggles with the Virginians' appeal to anti-Catholic prejudices. As Roman Catholics in a nation that legally proscribed their religion, they were vulnerable. Baltimore anticipated the strategy and did what he could to parry its thrust. In the end, the proprietor's influence held: the Virginians lacked the influence to prevent the Calverts from implementing their new charter.[43]

The two colonial charters that George Calvert wrote reflected his thinking on a number of issues important to him. His circumstances changed dramatically between the writing of the two. In April 1623 he was on the inside, had ample funds to support a variety of activities, and conformed to the state church. In April 1632 he approached the government as an outsider, a Catholic who lacked the financial ability to finance a colony. More important, the first Lord Baltimore negotiated for the new charter as a seasoned colonizer who had experienced the rigors of colonization. Did his new religious commitment after 1625 exert a major influence on the provisions of the second charter? An analysis of the differences between the Newfoundland and the Maryland charters regarding religion, government, and landholding indicates that Calvert made only a few significant revisions. These adjustments reflected his experiences in Avalon and his new status as a Catholic in England.[44]

Changed circumstances aside, the charters showed remarkable similarities. The 1632 charter scrupulously followed the structure of its predecessor, adding or deleting in only a few instances. In both charters the proprietors received extensive grants of power, subject to a few specified limitations. The second charter, for example, repeated the bishop of Durham clause. Durham, established as a county palatine by William the Conqueror, remained as the last example of this extensive grant of royal power at the time Calvert wrote the charters. He included this clause, which conferred powers on the proprietor that rivaled those of a king, to gain as much independence within the king's dominions as was possible. Other minor alterations addressed the new leadership (the second Lord Baltimore), the location (the Chesapeake), and morphology (i.e., changes in spelling, capitalization, etc.). King Charles granted the Maryland charter to George Calvert's son and heir, who he knew was pursuing his father's intentions. Similar to its predecessor and consistent with the elder Calvert's exchange of letters with the king, this charter emphasized the Calverts' commitment to enlarge the king's empire and dominions.[45]

Both charters acknowledged the existence of "certain Barbarous people" who lived without the "knowledge of Almighty God," but the Maryland charter added the Calverts' intentions "to trade with the Natives" and to foster "the propagation of the Christian faith." These two additions recognized that the Chesapeake region had a more substantial native population. The latter addition reflected the Calverts' new association with the Jesuits and provided an umbrella under which priests of the Society of Jesus could achieve their objective of proselytizing among the natives. English charters perfunctorily included statements about converting the native population. English Catholics, of course, shared a zeal for "propagation of the Christian faith" with English Protestants and were no more cynical nor sincere than their "heretical" counterparts. In this instance, conversion of "barbarous peoples" had a specifically Catholic context, and the clause was included because of Calvert's conversion. An overseas missionary effort to the Indians was a great attraction for some English Catholic priests and a motivation for them to participate in the dangerous and arduous task of colonization.[46]

George Calvert's association with the Jesuits proved beneficial for his son. To the impecunious Calverts, the zeal of Father Andrew White was a godsend. The willingness of English Jesuits to serve led to the inclusion of the missionary clause in the Maryland charter and signified a definite Catholic goal. The intention "to trade with the Natives," added another incentive. Pacified and converted Indians made for better trading partners. If neither the first nor the second Lord Baltimore made the conversion of Indians their highest priority, their spiritual partners did. Once again, the Calverts artfully fused their material interests with their spiritual concerns.[47]

The new language regarding the natives may have indicated a lack of concern on the part of the English government about an openly Catholic colonizer who was now closely associated with the Jesuits, but another clause shows that the government did not entirely turn a blind eye to the situation. Consistent with the Avalon charter, the Maryland charter granted the proprietors the privileges of patronage and advowson for all churches erected "(as Christian Religion shall increase)." The new charter, however, contained a significant restriction, which took into consideration Baltimore's recent conversion. It empowered the Calverts to build and found churches, chapels, and oratories "in convenient and fit places" in the colony but required them to be dedicated and consecrated according to the ecclesiastical laws of England. It seems likely that someone in the government rather than the Calverts added this clause. If the purpose of the provision was to prevent the building of Catholic churches, it failed. In the eyes of the Calverts, the clause only restricted the government. They did not see the prohibition as extending to private chapels, and they had no intention of building public churches. This clause reinforced the Calverts' evolving strategy of keeping religion out of the public arena. As father and son envisioned their enterprise, the proprietary government would assume no role in developing or sustaining religious institutions.[48]

Another significant change had to do with how the proprietor received his land from the king. He held the land forever, but the conditions were altered dramatically. The second Lord Baltimore held his land in free and common socage, by fealty only. The change eliminated the uncertain military service required by the *in capite* obligation of the Avalon charter and fixed an annual fee. In this case, the king required only "two Indian Arrowes of those parts, to be delivered at Our said Castle of Windsor, every yeere on the Tuesday of Easter weeke." By removing the military obligation that their tenants incurred under the Avalon charter, the Calverts hoped to make their new enterprise more attractive to prospective planters. With free and common socage, the proprietor's tenants paid a quitrent but otherwise owned the land.[49]

The Calverts made only minor changes in the civil and legal provisions of the Maryland charter. The charter left the role of the freemen the same and expressed their role in the political process in equally ambiguous terms. As his father had done for the first Lord Baltimore, King Charles acknowledged his special trust and confidence in the fidelity, wisdom, and justice, and "Provident circumspection" of the second Lord Baltimore. He too granted the proprietor full and absolute power "for the good and happy government" of the province. This included enacting and publishing laws pertaining to the public state of the province and the private utility of particular individuals under the king's seals as well as Baltimore's own. Each charter enjoined the proprietor to seek the assent of the freemen, or the greater part of them or their deputies, to the laws that affected them, and as often as needed. Both documents authorized the proprietors to take member or life if an offense so required. The language authorizing the appointment of judges and justices and the pardon of crimes remained essentially the same, but the Maryland charter expanded the jurisdiction of the judges. Both charters required that the laws, which were to be reasonable, be published and enjoined the king's subjects to observe and keep the laws absolutely. These laws, as well as laws the proprietors made on an emergency basis, were not to be repugnant or contrary to the laws of England. This provision created a delicate situation for the Catholic Lords Baltimore when it came to religious legislation. How could they extend freedom of conscience to all colonists, Catholics included, when such a concept ran contrary to English law? Would not laws negating the penal legislation repudiate English law?[50]

Religious liberty raised the touchy question of allegiance. The king usually employed the oaths of supremacy and allegiance to gain assurances of loyalty from his subjects. By the late 1620s, Charles never doubted the loyalty or fealty of the Catholic Lord Baltimore. But what of the planters? The Maryland charter, like its predecessor, did not require the planters to take the oaths of supremacy or allegiance. However, they were tendered the oaths before they left their native land. A provision in the Maryland charter subsumed the issue of allegiance. The king commanded "that the said Province shall be of our Allegiance" and that all people and their descendants "shall be Denizens, and Lieges of Us" and be protected in their property rights. Further, another phrase, "and Soveraigne dominion due unto Us, Our Heirs and Succesors," implied recognition of the king's supremacy. The king assumed the allegiance of the proprietors and those who ventured forth to the colonies.[51]

The second Lord Baltimore received the same grant of power as his father had to confer favors, rewards, and honors on deserving inhabitants "with what titles and dignities" he thought fit. This clause took on greater relevance for the Maryland enterprise. The Calverts added a most significant change, conspicuously absent from the Avalon charter, that reflected their status as Catholics. Charles granted Cecil "full and absolute licence, power and authoritie" to create a manorial system. The charter authorized the proprietor to assign parcels to those willing to purchase them in fee simple, fee tail, or for term of life or years by such services, customs, or rents as seemed fitting to him. The king exempted "the said now Baltimore" from the statute passed in the Parliament of Edward I, "commonly called the Statute *Quia emptores terrarum*" and any other relevant statutes. Circumventing this statute meant that the Marylanders held their land from the proprietor and not from the king. The proprietor, as the king's tenant, owed fealty to the king, but his tenants owed their fealty to the proprietor. This assumption informed the clause that authorized Baltimore to create manors. Each manor was "to have, and to hold a Court Baron, with all things whatsoever, which to a Court Baron doe belong, and to have and hold viewe of Franck-pledge; (for the conservation of the peace, and the better government of those parts)." The manorial system was central to the Calvert vision for Maryland. This innovation became the basis for building a new society in Maryland. The first Lord Baltimore was not a backward-looking Catholic who wished to return to an idealized form of the past. Neither he nor his son looked to institute a feudal system as an end in itself. Rather, the manorial system was part of an evolving plan designed to attract wealthier planters, to assure the allegiance of the planters, and to ensure that religion would remain a private matter.[52]

The Maryland charter introduced a clause that spoke to the first Lord Baltimore's unhappy experiences with the Virginians. It exempted "the Inhabitants of the said Province of Mary-land" from being held as a member of Virginia or any other colony. By granting Lord Baltimore the patent, the king separated Virginia and Maryland and made both subject to the Crown. The charter concluded with a statement from the first charter. By the king's expressed wish, any questions about the sense or understanding of the wording of the charter were to be interpreted in the proprietor's favor. The king entered one caveat: "Provided alwayes, that no Interpretation bee admitted thereof, by which Gods Holy and Truely Christian Religion, or the allegiance due unto Us ... may in any thing suffer any prejudice, or diminution."[53]

With the possible exception of the missionary objective, the second charter, written after the first Lord Baltimore's open espousal of Catholicism, betrayed no obvious Catholic goals. Still, Charles's advisers knew the grantee was Catholic. Why did the government grant a Catholic lord proprietor the right to exercise such extensive political and religious powers? Did members of the Privy Council not realize that those who brought Christianity to the natives would be Catholic priests? The only explanation that makes sense in the context of the turbulent 1630s is that those in positions of authority trusted the man to whom they were willing to grant the charter. They never doubted his loyalty as an Englishman. The government supported another effort to expand the king's dominions by a trusted and valued servant.

The charter of Maryland was a remarkable document. On the surface, it appears to be a contradiction in terms. Most English subjects viewed their Catholic counterparts as potentially subversive to the English nation. In 1632 no one—not the king, not the privy councillors, not George Calvert's friends—doubted that the Calvert family had embraced Catholicism. Yet, amazingly, the government gave these Catholics the right to thousands of acres of land and asked for little in return beyond Baltimore's loyalty as an Englishman and a willingness to extend the empire. Even more amazing, the king and his councillors entrusted to a Catholic family allied with the Jesuits the propagation of the faith to the barbarous people who lived within the charter's boundaries. No one held a gun to the king's head. Why did he follow the recommendations of his advisers? The charter clearly expressed the government's confidence in Baltimore's loyalty and his desire to further the interests of the king's growing empire.

Although George Calvert died before the king granted the charter, it was his legacy. His vision would significantly influence the colony founded by his son. In some ways the charter epitomizes his efforts to reconcile what for most men were divergent interests. With only limited success, he sought harmony in the confusing and tumultuous world in which he lived. In the House of Commons, he tried to harmonize relations between king and Commons. No one individual could have accomplished this, but he tried. In the delicate negotiations between the English and the Spanish for a royal marriage, he attempted to bring increasingly divergent goals together. The match was too unpopular in both countries to have succeeded, but he tried. When the adherents of the old Virginia Company attacked his proposed charter, he tried to reconcile the differences but to no avail. On a personal level, he tried to reconcile his conflicting loyalties to Church and state. His commitment to Catholicism never negated his loyalty to king and state. As a Protestant and as a Catholic, he sought to advance his financial interests and expand the king's dominion by establishing new colonial enterprises.

The full story of Catholic survival in early-seventeenth-century England remains to be told. Nevertheless it can be asserted that families like the Calverts, who were willing to risk practicing their faith openly and pursue public goals, helped to keep the Catholic religion alive. But without seasoned friendships of influential Protestants like Wentworth and Cottington, for whom religious differences were of no consequence, it is doubtful that the Calverts, even with all their courage, wit, and cunning, could have succeeded in securing their generous charter to Maryland, which enabled them to carry on their grand designs in America. By their cooperation, the king and Calverts' friends demonstrated that in the early seventeenth century personal loyalty could indeed transcend religious differences. They knew that Maryland served England's best interests. The Calverts carried that same spirit over into their Maryland colony.

CHAPTER SIX

"Such a designe when rightly understood will not want undertakers"

Selling Lord Baltimore's Vision (1632–1638)

The historical shadow cast by his father obscures the critical role played by Cecil Calvert. The elder Calvert rose to prominence in the government of James I and established the family fortune. He made the initial overseas investments. He secured a favorable charter for the Avalon colony. He financed the Newfoundland enterprise, largely from the profits of his office. He took charge of the faltering enterprise after 1624 in an effort to salvage his investments. He experienced the rigors of colonization. He moved his family to Avalon on a permanent basis in an effort to build the community on a firm foundation. He decided to shift the operation to the Chesapeake, and he petitioned the government for a new grant. Maryland was his dream. But he died. The vision, the "Maryland designe," now belonged to the second Lord Baltimore.

When his father's death thrust the family enterprise into his inexperienced hands, Cecil was not unprepared to step into the breach and put his stamp on the project. He had remained in England to marry and to manage the family's estates while his father journeyed to America. His active involvement commenced after his father returned from Virginia in 1629. By that time, George's health made the king's prohibition against further direct participation in colony founding more palatable. In the two years before the government granted the charter, Cecil served as his father's partner and secretary. He knew of the family's precarious financial situation and shared the determination to create a successful enterprise in the Chesapeake region. Although he had not participated initially in the family colonial enterprise, he knew the troubles his father had experienced in Avalon. Likewise, he had a good sense of what his father wanted from the new effort and knew that his desire to colonize had not been dampened by his experiences in Avalon. He assisted in rewriting the Avalon charter in anticipation of the new grant.

The zeal with which the young Irish lord approached his "Maryland designe" belies the notion that he acted merely to fulfill an obligation inherited from his father. He devoted his life purposely to building a successful colony. The responsibility for formulating and articulating the vision, for organizing the first expedition, and for attracting the requisite investors and willing emigrants fell to him. His situation was far from enviable. Indeed, no other English colonizer launched an enterprise in the face of such pronounced opposition as he did.

The historical record yields little of his early life. The date of his baptism, March 2, 1606, suggests that his birth took place within the previous two months. He was named for Sir Robert Cecil, his father's patron, and the baptism took place at his grandmother's home in Bexley in Kent in the Archdiocese of Canterbury. He spent most of his youth in London, primarily at the house on St. Martin's Lane, where he and his siblings lived. Cecil attended Trinity College, Oxford, but did not graduate.[1]

The absence of hard information on Cecil's spiritual life confounds any definitive resolution about his religious commitments. His father, a nominal Protestant, had his children baptized in the state church. In his formative years, Cecil had at least a perfunctory introduction to the doctrines and practices of the Church of England. To what extent, if any, he embraced its doctrine cannot be known. More than likely, Calvert resisted instructing his children in Catholic doctrine until after he resolved his own religious commitment in late 1624. In 1629, after George made public his commitment to Catholicism and after he associated his enterprises with the Jesuits, he sent three sons to study at the College at St. Omer. No evidence exists to suggest that Calvert sent his eldest son to an overseas Catholic school or that he employed a Catholic tutor before 1624.[2]

In 1624 the government issued Cecil a pass, which contained the usual prohibition against visiting Rome, to travel to the Continent. Whether he embraced Catholicism while overseas or waited until he returned in 1625 or 1626 to England, he lived openly as a Catholic after that. He took the name Cecilius when he was confirmed in the Catholic faith. Whatever the vicissitudes of his early spiritual life, after he converted to Catholicism, he never wavered in that commitment. His subsequent behavior conformed to the accepted practices of seventeenth-century English Catholics.[3]

Like his father, he did not believe his profession of faith kept him from aggressively pursuing his economic interests. After recounting the many problems he had in sending his ships to Maryland, he confided to Wentworth "the great Desire I have to wait upon your Lordship" in Ireland. Baltimore indicated his readiness to journey there for the opening of the 1634 Irish Parliament, where he was entitled to a seat in the House of Lords. Wentworth's strategy, however, did not include Baltimore or any of the absentee English landlords. He wanted to control as many votes as he could in his own hands. He confided to secretary John Coke that he would rather "have their Proxies than their Company." As a result, the Irish lords in England received word from Charles that they should absent themselves from Parliament and send their proxies to the lord deputy. Denied opportunity to serve in the Irish Parliament, the disappointed Baltimore complied, and he wrote Wentworth that he had confidence "that you will not putt it into such handes as shall make use of it such things wherein it may be infallibly conceaved, I would not have given my voice, if I had beene present."[4]

His disappointment did not dampen his Irish ambitions. Before Wentworth left England, he promised the second Lord Baltimore that he would fulfill the ancient promise to his father "for a Horse Troop in this Army." During the early 1630s, Baltimore continued to press the lord deputy for the first troop in Ireland that came under his patronage. Unable to satisfy Cecil, Wentworth assured him that the promise made to his father had not been forgotten, as can nothing else that "I owe to the memory of soe worthy a Person, and my Dear freinde." He offered Baltimore a five-hundred-pound payment as a token until he could clear the obligation in some other way. If Wentworth bought out of his obligation cheaply, he at least offered Cecil something in return. The lord deputy saw no place for Baltimore in the patronage system he intended to build. For his own part, the cash settlement probably satisfied the cash-strapped Baltimore, who had committed all his resources to Maryland. His Irish aspirations revealed an ambitious Catholic who sought to manipulate the system for his own benefit, whether in England, Ireland, or America.[5]

In seeking his fortune in these places, Baltimore studiously shunned the limelight. Few contemporary accounts of him exist. One associate, Robert Wintour, provided a rare and valuable glimpse of the man he deemed critical to Maryland's success or failure. He considered Baltimore to be a man of excellent parts who, though young, had given the world ample testimony of a ripe judgment, approved worth, and solid virtue. He used adjectives such as *noble, real, courteous,* and *affable* to describe Baltimore and judged him to be sharp and quick-witted, but not willful, of singular piety and filled with zeal for the conversion of the Indians. His judgment that the young lord was disinterested in his own profit but most solicitous of the common good was half right. Baltimore's personal behavior was beyond reproach. He was an excellent master of his passions and lived an "innocent life" free from all vices.[6]

Baltimore's careful formulation of his objectives led Wintour to conclude that he did not make idle promises. For example, he compensated for his lack of experience by reading and consultation. Wintour stressed that the proprietor talked to others in London who had been to the Chesapeake in an effort to avoid those "inconveniences" that hindered other plantations. Wintour remained confident that the "Maryland designe," when rightly understood, would not lack for interested parties. He commended the proprietor's caution and wariness in admitting adventurers into so noble a society as Maryland. Wintour thought Baltimore was such an excellent person that all colonists "may promise themselves with assured confidence all content and happines" under his government. He completed his sketch by noting Baltimore's intention to emigrate with his family and a number of noble and able gentlemen.[7]

No matter how valid Wintour's assurances were, the young manager faced a wide array of challenges in implementing the family plan for an overseas empire. Some of the difficulties he confronted were endemic to the colonization process, but others resulted from his peculiar circumstances. Comparing his circumstances on the eve of launching Maryland with those of his father before he sailed to Avalon demonstrates how poorly positioned he was for the undertaking. The elder Calvert had the requisite resources (or so he thought) to sustain the colony during the expensive initial building phase. More important, no concerted opposition challenged his claim or resisted his effort to colonize in Avalon. His resignations notwithstanding, the former secretary and privy councillor still had the status and influence to protect his interests. The second Lord Baltimore had no lucrative government offices and lacked the prestige, power, and money that came with those offices. He faced formidable foes with a depleted financial base.

Organizing and then launching a major colonial enterprise under these conditions tested his leadership at every turn. Baltimore had to surmount five major obstacles: First, he had to neutralize the continuous threats emanating from the adherents of the old Virginia Company. Second, he had to recruit enough planters willing to take the risks inherent in founding a new plantation. Third, he had to find investors willing to share the financial risks. Fourth, he had to identify capable leaders to assist him in governing. Fifth, he had to keep his Catholicism in the background, because it separated him from the English mainstream and exposed the enterprise to attacks crassly based on anti-Catholicism. Five factors worked in his favor: First and foremost, he continued to enjoy the support of influential members of Charles's government. Second, and closely related to the first factor, Parliament, a focal point of anti-Catholic sentiments, had not met since 1629. Third, the proprietor had an abundance of land to distribute and trade rights to barter in his quest for supporters. Fourth, he enjoyed the support of members of the Society of Jesus. Fifth, he had a deep reservoir of tenacity to complement his enthusiasm for the enterprise.

Baltimore's plan could succeed only if he attracted other English men or women who would willingly forsake their native land to cast their lot with him in a risky venture. He had to articulate his vision of the colony's potential, and that image had to offer something of value to those whom he courted. He relied on two primary methods of communication: word of mouth and a limited campaign using printed material and public statements. This meant that the message came across in a piecemeal fashion.

Baltimore never articulated in any single document a comprehensive objective from which all other statements of purpose flowed. His responses to the crisis during the turbulent times between 1649 and 1651 provide some insight to his thinking. In 1649 he affirmed this maxim as certain and true: "By Concord and Union a small Collony may growe into a great and renouned Nation, whereas by Experience it is found, that by discord and Dissention Great and glorious kingdomes and Common Wealthes decline and come to nothing." Two years later, he wrote that "a Government divided in it self must needs bring Confusion and Consequently much misery upon the People under it." These two statements constituted the core of his vision, the creation of a society where English men and women could live together in peace and prosper. He wanted to eliminate those elements, such as religious wrangling, that divided societies. He needed a unified society that was loyal to him as the lord proprietor. His religion precluded using religious tests, such as Communion in a specific church or church attendance, as the means of unifying society. He desired to unite Marylanders "in their affection and fidellity to us" by providing for their "temporal felicity in this World." This, he projected, would bring "complyance with us in all reasonable things." His success hinged on the creation of a *peaceful* society in which he and his people, regardless of their religious predilections, could *prosper* and *worship* without any interference from the government.[8]

A number of documents, which he wrote, edited, or approved for publication, explicated his vision of what the colony *might* become. Four of them appeared before the *Ark* and the *Dove* sailed. These included the Maryland charter, the revised Avalon charter modified by his father with his assistance, and a pamphlet entitled *Objections Answered Touching Maryland*, which had a very limited circulation. Published anonymously in 1632 or 1633, the *Objections Answered* attempted to alleviate the fears of those troubled by the colony's association with Catholicism. Baltimore's direct confrontation of the issue demonstrated his uneasiness over the potential impact of anti-Catholicism on his vision for Maryland. Another short pamphlet, *A Declaration of The Lord Baltemore's Plantation in Maryland*, written in late 1632 or early 1633 by Father Andrew White, S.J., accentuated the positive and appealed to literate Englishmen who had sufficient resources to invest in the undertaking or who had reasons to venture in person. In it Father White deftly spun the spiritual and secular threads together in an effort to attract as many clients as possible. This pamphlet, which Baltimore revised before its publication early in 1633, demonstrated his willingness to risk public attention. It was his only printed source intended for prospective planters and adventurers. Finally, immediately before his ships sailed for America, he wrote instructions for his brother Leonard, the designated lieutenant governor, and the two councillors, articulating his policies for the founding years.[9]

The remaining documents added to the vision by offering data from the recently established colony. The prolific White chronicled the journey to Maryland, his first impressions, and the activities of the first weeks. He sent the Latin version of his manuscript, entitled "Relatio Itineris in Marylandiam," to the provincial of the Society in England, who, in turn, sent it as a report to his superiors in Rome. Governor Leonard Calvert relayed the English version, "A Briefe Relation of the Voyage into Maryland," to his business partner in London. The Latin and English manuscripts differed only in that the Latin one was more pious and contained frequent references to divine favor, while the English version placed greater emphasis on the nature of the climate, the soil, and the products of the earth. Baltimore, or someone working under his direction, used the 1634 manuscripts to publish the 1634 *A Relation of the Successful beginnings of the Lord Baltimore's Plantation*. Designed primarily to attract planters to the colony, it conveniently deleted the harrowing details of the long and perilous voyage of the *Ark* and the *Dove* as graphically narrated in White's manuscripts. Still another *A Relation*, this one published in 1635, described the actual settlement more fully than the previous manuscripts and publications. It contained another, more detailed version of "The Conditions of the plantation," which delineated the proprietor's revised land-distribution policy.[10]

But Father White did not write *A Relation of Maryland; together with a Map of the Countrey, the Conditions of Plantation, with his Majesties Charter to the Lord Baltemore, translated into English*. According to Peasley, Jerome Hawley, one of the two commissioners who sailed with the first expedition, and John Lewger, soon to be appointed the first secretary of the colony, composed this 1635 *Relation*. Also designed to lure prospective emigrants to Maryland, it focused on the attractions of the colony, the equipment they needed to exploit these resources, and the generous conditions under which they could acquire land in Maryland. It also provided many new details of the colony's first year, beyond those found in White's narratives. Like most promotional literature, the *Relation* painted a rosy picture of the condition of the colony as of early 1635, stating that in only six months, the colonists had established the colony of Maryland on a firm foundation. The authors proclaimed that the way had been prepared. Compared to the first adventurers, who were "ignorant both of Place, People, and all things else, and could expect to find nothing but what nature produced," the newcomers could proceed with more ease and confidence.[11]

White's post-sailing narratives and the Hawley-Lewger *Relation* presented favorable views of the colony's first year or so. They emphasized the key point of Baltimore's vision: come to Maryland and prosper; but they added little else to the vision. That task fell to Robert Wintour, whose unpublished "Short Treatise" exemplified a form of colonial promotional literature, the personal report written by an interested observer. Wintour responded to a series of questions from a Captain John Reade, who presumably contemplated emigrating to Maryland. The answers he gave, often light-hearted in nature, provided a knowledgeable account by someone intimately involved in the "Maryland designe."[12]

More than the other literature, the "Short Treatise" clarified Baltimore's vision for his colony. At the same time, it exposed the motives behind Wintour's decision to forsake his native England in search of a new life, elaborating one Englishman's image of what Maryland could be. Thus it helps to explain why a select group of Englishmen, of whom Wintour is a classic example, came to venture their lives and fortunes in Baltimore's "Maryland designe."

As a Catholic, Wintour avoided the attention of authorities. Most likely, he was a younger brother of Sir John Winter (1600[?]–1673[?]), a Roman Catholic and secretary to Queen Henrietta Maria, Maryland's namesake. Wintour possessed impeccable credentials in the small English Catholic community active in court circles. His parents were wealthy, ambitious at court, and Catholics. Wintour's Catholic grandfather, the earl of Worcester, achieved prominence in the courts of Elizabeth I, James I, and Charles I before his death in 1628. His father commanded a ship with Sir Francis Drake in 1585 and 1586, fought against the Armada in 1588, and served as a member of Parliament in 1589 and 1601. His mother, Lady Anne, the daughter of Edward Somerset, the fourth earl of Worcester, sent two sons to Maryland on the *Ark* in 1633. Her sister Blanche married Thomas Arundell, the brother of Anne Arundell, Cecil Calvert's wife. These familial and religious connections linked Wintour to the Calverts and their Maryland enterprise.[13]

Wintour's easy familiarity with Horace marked him as a man who gained his knowledge not only through extensive travel but through books as well. Initially he followed his grandfather and his father by pursuing a career at sea. He attracted the attention of English authorities after he began helping English Catholics get to the Continent without the necessary legal formalities. According to the deposition of Elizabeth Hafteville given on February 14, 1633, Wintour had established twenty-eight Benedictine nuns at Brussels and made two trips to Rome on their behalf. A few weeks later an informant reported to Secretary of State Sir Francis Windebank that Wintour had recently trimmed the *Black Lion*, a ship of 240 tons that he had purchased at Dunkirk. The informant claimed that Wintour was the captain but confessed his inability to ascertain either the intended destination of the vessel or its purpose. Aiding and abetting people in Catholic religious orders was a hazardous occupation subject to severe penalties if one was caught.[14]

By October 1633 Wintour was employed by, or associated with, Lord Baltimore and the "Maryland designe." He first became acquainted, "sometimes familiarly," with Calvert "for divers yeares both in his father's lifetime and since." Sir John Coke's urgent letter to Admiral John Pennington dated October 19, 1633, referred to complaints made before the Privy Council that Baltimore's ships had "gone for Gravesend" contrary to orders and that the company (that is, the people leaving for the plantation) had not "taken the oath of allegiance." The ship, incorrectly identified the day before as the *Charles of London*, was the *Ark of London*. The record stated that "Richard Low is Master and Captain Winter hath charge of the companie." Baltimore, too absorbed other matters, needed someone he trusted who did not intend to emigrate to take charge of the colonists. When it became obvious that the challenges against his charter and intended colony were serious enough to prevent him from accompanying the expedition, Baltimore drew up his "Instructions" on November 13, 1633, and delegated the authority he had intended to exercise to his brother. At this point, Wintour's responsibility for the planters on board the ships ended.[15]

Wintour's relationship with the proprietor after the *Ark* and the *Dove* sailed cannot be ascertained. Although wealthy, he did not participate in any commercial activity with the adventurers. He postponed his departure until 1637, most likely for reasons of health, but remained keenly absorbed by the unfolding Maryland drama. He monitored events by gathering information from impartial and experienced men who had returned from the colony and from others who had participated in similar enterprises. This data, along with his many conversations with the proprietor, formed the basis of his insightful letter, the "Short Treatise."[16]

The published statements and the manuscript accounts made by Baltimore and his associates provide the fullest elaboration of his vision and reveal his attempts to negotiate the treacherous terrain of conflicting religious loyalties. In founding his colony, this ambitious Catholic colonial entrepreneur acted neither exclusively from religious considerations nor for the sole purpose of furthering a specifically Catholic goal. This did not mean, however, that he lacked concern for his coreligionists. Quite the contrary. He made a special effort to recruit Catholics, but under the same conditions he offered to others. He offered them an *opportunity* to prosper under his benevolent leadership. Baltimore, as an English Catholic, embraced a multiplicity of motives, all of which were to enhance his well-being and that of those who committed to his enterprise. His colony was English and England was Protestant. Until circumstances changed in England, Maryland Catholics had to tread softly as they sought greater freedom of worship and economic prosperity.

Baltimore knew better than anyone else that an exclusively Catholic colony was not possible. Therefore, he actively recruited Protestants as well as Catholics. Because of the religious diversity of the company and the omnipresent fear and suspicion against the Catholic Church, religious considerations always had to be factored into the decision-making process. Even if religion did not motivate the Virginians' challenge to Baltimore's charter, the intensity of the confrontation meant that Baltimore had to be ever vigilant for the next anti-Catholic assault. Further, as a Catholic, Baltimore and those with whom he closely associated could ill afford to be too open in attempting to attract Catholics. In marked contrast to Massachusetts Bay Colony, where the Puritan leadership desired to be "a Citty upon a Hill," with the eyes of all people on them, Baltimore eschewed attention. He sought to plant his little colony as unobtrusively as possible.[17]

Baltimore delivered a succinct summary of his intentions on the eve of his ships' departure for his colony. He instructed his brother to make, upon arrival, a short declaration to the people regarding his (Baltimore's) intentions. The proprietor listed as his first motive "the honor of god by endeavoring the conversion of the savages to Christianity." Wintour's conversations with the proprietor furnished additional information regarding his desire for a peaceful and prospering society, which included harmonious relations with the Indians. Baltimore believed that the leaders of the Virginia colony had mismanaged their relations with the Indians, and he wanted to avoid a repetition of their mistakes. The charter, which named conversion of the natives as one of his goals, fit his vision in two ways: bringing Christianity to the Indians, "who are undoubted idolators," and cultivating them as trading partners.[18]

In his conversations with the Jesuits, Baltimore held out the possibility of converting the natives in return for the order's support for his enterprise. Father White overstated the case when he wrote that Baltimore's expressed and chief objective was to "bring to Christ that land" and the adjacent area, "which from the beginning of the World to this day never knew God." The animated priest boldly stated that Baltimore's intention to plant Christianity there ought to be shared by those who ventured their fortunes with him. He could hardly contain his excitement at the prospect that "many thousands of Soules may be brought to Christ by this most glorious Enterprise." His sources led him to believe that the Indians eagerly desired teachers to instruct them and baptize them. Beyond this, he knew that Baltimore offered the only prospect for an English Jesuit mission. Establishing a mission to the natives was the Jesuit raison d'être.[19]

Like White, Wintour emphasized the higher inducement of converting the

Indians to Christianity. He argued that Baltimore's vision was of a far different and nobler nature than that of the other plantations, and he gave many reasons to support this contention. He argued that Maryland originated from a concern for "the conversion and civilizing those barbarous heathens that live like beasts without the light of faith." This gave Maryland its nobility, and he asked what higher goal there could be than the "winning of soules from our common and greatest enemy," the Devil, to our "eternall Soveraigne."[20]

The missionary objective complemented the Calvert vision in another way. The Indians interested the proprietor as partners in the desperately needed fur trade. Converting the natives was a necessary first step in pacifying them and ensuring stability for the colony, goals that were uppermost for the proprietor. He may have been skeptical of the authenticity of the conversions, but the missionary effort, however poorly implemented, should not be dismissed as merely a means of serving the proprietor's material interests. The missionary effort reflected Baltimore's inclination to bind spiritual and material interests.[21]

Baltimore, more than his Protestant counterparts, felt the need to proclaim national goals. He told his brother to make certain the colonists understood this point: by their actions, they augmented the king's dominions in those parts of the world. The very concept of an *English* colony established by Catholics that would, as the charter stated, enlarge the king's empire and dominion reflected the tension that existed between English and Catholic. This idea alone justified the support of the Protestant government for a Catholic undertaking. Protestant fears centered on foreign elements that they saw dividing the loyalties of English Catholics. Spain and Rome remained the enemies of England. In the Protestant mind, and indeed in the view of some Catholics, Englishmen who favored Rome favored Spain. Even the Venetian ambassador believed that the "Catholics of this country are for the most part Hispanophiles." The phobia journeyed to the Chesapeake. Father White reported that in anticipation of the arrival of the Maryland expedition, Claiborne had spread a rumor that six Spanish ships were coming to destroy the Indians, who "were all in armes to resist us." Baltimore could not prove his "Englishness" any more than he could alleviate the fears most Protestants had about the Spanish and Catholics. These perceptions aside, Baltimore always acted as an Englishman.[22]

The proprietor's instructions addressed the sensitive issue of allegiance. He sought to alleviate Protestant fears that English Catholics were more Catholic than English and that their loyalty to their Church overwhelmed their loyalty to their country. He also appealed to the national instincts of English Catholics. A year or so later, Wintour amplified the latter theme in his letter to his friend. He specifically confronted the plight of Catholics who were not destined to inherit large estates or enjoy independent wealth. As an English Catholic, he wrote that it grieved his "very soule" to hear his country, its worth, and its government "so much wronged and blasphemed" by young Catholics. Their complaint that "their country affords them no employment" served as an excuse for idle loitering at home or rushing to enlist in a foreign army. He expressed contempt for those who served foreign princes to the detriment of his England, which he described in hyperbolic terms. Wintour considered the peopling of English colonies far more laudable and useful for the country and in "every way more worthy and becoming a true English heart" than any foreign service. Englishmen, he preached, should spend their time and endeavors "in the service of our owne King and State," enlarging "our Soveraignes dominions" by the addition of new provinces. For English Catholics, Maryland offered the possibility of serving their country and its monarch while resolving the tensions between religious and secular loyalties. They should employ their time and talent by expanding the king's dominions on the Chesapeake frontier, which offered prosperity and religious liberty.[23]

Finally, Baltimore's instructions assured the Protestants and Catholics who ventured their lives and fortunes of his own commitment. He stood ready to assist them so that they could enjoy the benefits of their costs and labors with as much freedom as they could desire. The promotional literature clearly emphasized the natural resources of the colony and detailed the conditions under which prospective planters could acquire their land, the foundation for prospering.[24]

Baltimore, White, and Wintour all recognized that lofty ideals such as God, country, and conversion did not motivate all individuals. The missionary priest knew that converting Indians excited few potential planters. He acknowledged that most men "are not so noble-minded, as to hold their levell purely at this end, so great and glorious, but commonly Pleasure, wealth and honour, are the great Adamants that draw them." Fortunately, "Gods deerly-good Providence hath wrapped also all of these together in this one Action, that neither higher nor lower inducements might be wanting." White reflected Baltimore's thinking when he commingled the spiritual and the temporal. Venturing to a strange new land required material rewards as well as spiritual. The proprietor envisioned a stable society based on a hierarchy created through the distribution of his major asset, the land. This part of the vision aimed to attract relatively well educated and affluent individuals. Wintour described how they might take advantage of the material attractions Maryland offered for achieving a quiet life sweetened with ease and plenty.[25]

Under Wintour's deft pen, Maryland became the land of milk and honey, the haven that men throughout the ages had sought. It offered "the true happy country life so much extolled by ancient and moderne writers." He painted a vivid picture of an idyllic life, a princely condition, and then set about to demonstrate how that life was to be accomplished. He used Baltimore's land policy to create the image. Land was at the heart of his enterprise, and the proprietor offered it as the primary inducement for prospective immigrants. To develop his holdings, the proprietor traded land on generous terms in return for a modest quitrent and loyalty. Wintour, flushed with excitement, filled in the details. An investor needed only to invest £500 to live after the first two years "in far greater plenty" than if he had £500 per year in England. Wintour calculated how to use the investment for the greatest advantage. Wealth in the Chesapeake to a considerable extent resulted from accumulating servants. The greater the number, the greater the gain. In the scenario he created, the greater portion of the investment, £300, would be applied to securing fifteen able laboring men, to purchasing a year's supply of the commodities necessary to feed and clothe them, and to obtaining the materials required for working and fighting. Another £100 would be used to purchase merchandise appropriate for trading with the Virginians for a herd of twenty cows. Another £30 would secure an equal number of breeding sows. He allotted £20 more for merchandise to trade with natives, which would bring the adventurer more corn and venison than he or his men could eat. Another £20 would be spent on wines, spices, and other such conveniences for his own house, which Wintour predicted would quickly be erected by the labor of his fifteen men from the superabundance of materials easily at hand. With the remaining £30, the colonist would purchase a shallop for trading, voyages of discovery, and fishing.[26]

In England people were plentiful ("throngs of loyterers and wasters") and land was scarce (a "bald schorne earth"). Maryland, in contrast, was a spacious country of untouched soil, with an infinite treasure of wood only awaiting the opportunity to be collected. Under Baltimore's generous conditions of plantation, the adventurer who transported fifteen servants would receive 3,000 acres of good and fertile land, "richly laden with fruit, firr, and timber trees." The conditions for acquiring land listed in the 1633 *Declaration* were the most generous. For every five men between sixteen and fifty transported to the colony, the adventurer received 2,000 acres of land at the annual rate of four hundred pounds of wheat. By 1635 Baltimore reduced the amount of land he would award to those transporting servants. The manorial grant entailed "all such royalties and privileges, as are usually belonging to Mannors in England." The conditions required that the adventurer pay an annual quitrent of twenty shillings "in the Commodities of the Country." Wintour used the new conditions, which had been published four days before he wrote. He did not deem it necessary to call attention to the promise of the special political privileges inherent in the manorial system.[27]

Wintour described, quite unrealistically, how the 3,000 acres could be utilized to bring about the idyllic life he thought so commendable. An enclosed deer park, the mark of economic and social distinction in England, merely entailed setting aside the first 1,000 acres as "a park for deere." Of the next 1,000 acres, half would be enclosed for the swine and cattle, and half would be cleared as quickly as possible for planting. In common with the authors of the 1635 *Relation*, Wintour emphasized the great variety of crops that could profitably be grown and the necessity of diversification. He recited without "rhetoricall exaggerations" the several ways by which the profit from the land was to be found. By employing only his servants upon this land, the planter would have after but two years an ample surplus of tobacco, wood, rapeseed, hemp, flax, wheat, and hops. So great would the profit be that he predicted in the third year the adventurer would be able to bring an additional ten servants, thereby proportionately increasing his profit. Careful breeding of the cattle and swine would yield an equally large profit. Other profitable employments included the manufacture of pipe staves, the planting of tobacco ("the profitt to be made of it is a thing so knowen I need not speake of it"), fishing, and the manufacture of silk and potash. Sassafras, copperas, clapboard, and "a world of commodities for medicine, druggists and dyers" were there for the understanding adventurer to enrich himself with and, when combined with the produce of the earth, made for a very profitable trade with the ships that eagerly plied the Chesapeake. He projected that the remaining 1,000 acres should be set aside for distribution to his servants when their five-year contracts expired.[28]

After five years, the planter would be well established. Wintour envisioned him with a solid house (or houses), a fine deer park close to his door, cattle and swine grazing and growing fat on his land, ponds and rivers teeming with fish, and fowl in abundance right at hand. All of nature's bounty was to be complemented by the company of "goodfellowes and cheerfull free holders," the "loving and friendly neighbourhood of halfe a dozen or half a score [of] gentlemen," his friends and partners who in a similar condition "accompany him in his sports and consummate his felicity by sharing gladly in it." In Maryland, he pontificated, there is "nothing to doe but to be merry and grow fatt, eate, drinke & recreate, and give God thanks."[29]

Baltimore's vision encompassed how Marylanders might "give God thanks." Worship, however, exposed the English-Catholic tension, which lay at the very foundation of his enterprise. He publicly stated his Englishness in various venues. How could he express his Catholicity? He now faced his religious liability: attracting Catholic colonists on the one hand, and protecting them from molestation on the other. The penal legislation coupled with rampant anti-Catholicism dogged him at every turn.

Paradoxically, the Catholic proprietor's vision of establishing a viable English colony in America necessitated muting the public appeal he made to his coreligionists and his intentions to subvert the penal legislation and the established church. His first publicist, Father White, included little in the text that could be readily identified as Catholic. An early reference in *A Declaration* noting that the colony's name honored "our most gracious Queene" may have served that purpose. Few would have missed mention of Charles's controversial Catholic consort. White concluded his pamphlet by urging those desiring more specific information to contact Lord Baltimore at his house in the Bloomsbury district of London. A critical reader might have identified Bloomsbury as an area with a significant Catholic population. White avoided any other references to the Catholic connection and couched his arguments for venturing to Maryland in general terms that would appeal to the widest audience.[30]

Wintour, too, highlighted the colony's namesake, but he deftly tied the association to the national connection. His Majesty, as an indication of "his Princely affection" toward the undertaking, bestowed upon it the name of his royal bedfellow, "our most gracious Queene Mary, commanding it to be called Maryland." Wintour signaled that by this act Charles placed his royal stamp of approval on the colony, a meaningful action for an enterprise under the leadership of a Catholic and absolute lord proprietor.[31]

More complex and left unsaid publicly was Baltimore's vision of the role religious institutions would play in his effort to achieve his primary objective: a society consisting of men and women of differing religious persuasions living together in relative peace. Like his father, Baltimore recognized that some men could divorce their religious sentiments from their loyalty to the state. His father's willingness to subordinate religious commitments to political realities had not been lost on Cecil. This established the context within which Baltimore sought to build a society that encouraged a diversity of religious opinions. He acted upon the assumption that religion was essentially a private matter and that the colonists would be able to overcome their religious differences for the greater good of the colony and the lord proprietor. Unlike the leaders of Massachusetts Bay, a community built on the necessity of religious unity, he rejected religious uniformity and appealed to secular loyalties. He was not so naive as to believe that religious differences could merely be swept aside, but he acted on the assumption that they could be blunted.

For obvious reasons, the proprietor accentuated these altruistic goals, while downplaying the materialistic personal and familial objectives that drove the project. When Baltimore looked toward America, he envisioned a small kingdom with himself firmly situated at the top as the head and heart of the new community. He saw himself as the linchpin of the enterprise. It was not flattery, but a fair assessment, that led an associate to call him "the prynce" of Maryland. In Baltimore's mind, he was lord of the Maryland manor, supported by his liege people, each of whom was lord of his own manor.[32]

Baltimore had well-laid plans for using his power for the advancement of his plantation. He knew that to achieve his princely vision, he needed to develop quickly a relatively stable society incorporating people of varying social status and religious commitments. Stability would result from the distribution of land to a few individuals, who would ensure social peace and tranquility among the rest of the community. To realize his grand vision of a stable society, he had to convince others to join his ranks by risking life and fortune. A means to this end was his willingness to share political power with the freemen who ventured with him. As resident proprietor, he calculated that he would be able to exercise the control necessary to restrain legislative excesses.

Wintour, for one, had no quarrel with the extensive powers granted to Baltimore in the charter. In Wintour's understanding, as in Baltimore's, the proprietor received from the king the requisite favors, privileges, and prerogatives to encourage and sustain the effort. Wintour described the colonial government as monarchical in form, with the lord proprietor, whose good character he had already enumerated, occupying a position similar to a kingship. He endorsed Baltimore's vision of government because it reproduced forms familiar to the English. A council of select men would assist the proprietor, and a parliament, where each freeholder had a voice, would be convened when needed. As

Wintour interpreted the charter, the king's subjects in Maryland would be governed only by the laws they made in their assembly. He, and presumably Baltimore, believed that the Maryland charter devised a form of government that avoided the inconveniences that occurred in other colonies. Through his judicious leadership, the proprietor intended to avoid the chaotic beginning that had so marred the development of the other endeavors.[33]

Baltimore and his colleagues identified potential planters and adventurers and tried to sell the "Maryland designe" to those Catholics and Protestants who might be interested. The campaign fell far short of their hopes. Months after the departure of his ships, Baltimore informed Wentworth that 325 colonists had sailed. Why did the proprietor report a figure more than doubled the number who had ventured with his brother? Either he did not know, or he lied. Others, such as the Venetian ambassador (who said there were 800) and an English Jesuit ("a considerable colony of Englishmen, largely Catholics") misjudged the numbers. The expedition numbered closer to 140, with the majority of the immigrants Protestants of some sort. The minority Catholic element dominated leadership of the colony. More than likely, Baltimore's contemporary reckoning represented the number he thought necessary to build the enterprise on a solid foundation.[34]

Why did Baltimore, and those who assisted him, fail to satisfy their recruitment goal? It was not from want of effort. Simply put, the risks and disadvantages outweighed the inducements. Baltimore's religion hindered the effort and placed him in a delicate situation. It left him open to attacks from the Virginians while denying him access to the English pulpit, the most effective means of disseminating information to Protestants in Caroline England. More important, his identification with Catholicism limited the colony's attractiveness to planters (those willing to move to Maryland) and adventurers (those willing to invest in the enterprise and perhaps move there as well). It hampered his appeal to Protestants, the vast majority of whom uncritically imbibed their culture's negative feelings toward Catholics. A handful of daring or desperate Protestants embraced the "Maryland designe," nonetheless, based on the promises of prosperity and liberty of conscience. Although they were few in number, they constituted a majority in the expedition. And English Catholics showed little inclination to join their coreligionist. Although the government never troubled the Calvert family on account of religion before 1633, the penal laws had taken their toll on the Catholic community. Of all prospective migrants, Catholics were the least likely to risk further exposure to the dreaded penal laws.

The nature of Catholic survival dramatically affected the young Irish lord's ability to attract English Catholics. As well as any Catholic, he understood the nature of the community in the late 1620s and early 1630s. His residences in London and in the countryside and his marriage into a prominent Catholic family enhanced his awareness of the strengths and weaknesses of the community. He knew that most Catholics had abandoned their faith as a result of the government's efforts to enforce uniformity. The way Catholicism persisted among the aristocracy and gentry and the dependence of poorer Catholics on their protection meant that he had little opportunity to attract them.[35]

The periodic efforts to force Catholic conformity continued, but they no longer resulted in many conversions. Despite a creeping numerical increase, the English Catholic community in the 1630s remained isolated and splintered, badly disorganized, and divided over a number of long unresolved problems. On the eve of colonization, those who had not surrendered to the penal laws had made the necessary adjustments to persist as Catholics. This relative security, which encouraged most Catholics to remain within their protected surroundings, presented the young proprietor with one of his greatest challenges: luring Catholics to his colonial enterprise. Moreover, these characteristics limited the methods of recruiting that Baltimore could use.[36]

Better and richer Catholics, many of whom were active at court, benefited from the apparent leniency of Charles I. They believed they had some cause to be optimistic for the future of the community. If they worked for any goal other than the enhancement of their own wealth and status, it was to bring religious change from the top down through significant court conversions, by facilitating negotiations between the papacy and representatives of the English government, and perhaps from a gradual elimination of the penal laws. The openness of court life, in concert with the company of numerous fellow-travelers who conformed religiously only to exercise political power, and the presence of a Catholic Queen, made it possible for them not only to survive but also to enjoy life and practice their religion in private. Some even entertained the vain hope, however fanciful, that Charles might convert and restore Catholicism in England. Court Catholics—conspicuous beneficiaries of the king's moderate policies—remained a small, and in many ways self-centered, minority. Even if he reached these Catholics, Baltimore had nothing to offer them.[37]

Catholics living outside court circles, who could ill afford such openness, offered a more fertile recruiting area. A papal agent in England in the 1630s accurately noted that these Catholics tried "exteriorly to live in such a way that it may not be known that they were Catholics, from which it follows that other Catholics derive little or no use from them." By choice and by force of law, many Catholics remained isolated, attempting to live as unobtrusively as possible. The problem for Baltimore was to find these Catholics. Many Catholic members of the nobility and gentry also lived outside of the court circle. The same emissary noted that their social status allowed them to make "almost open profession" of their religion, facilitated by uneven enforcement of the penal laws and a long tradition of civility that existed between Protestants and Catholics in local areas. Friendship and social standing prevented the penal laws from having full effect. Outside of London on scattered manors, family members, servants, and tenants sustained their commitment to Catholicism. These largely self-sufficient and relatively self-contained enclaves maintained their own priests, tutors, and other professionals. By providing access to the Mass and the sacraments, they also allowed other less influential Catholics in their vicinity, who might otherwise have been forced to conform, to persist in their religion. Unless the entire manor was willing to emigrate, the "Maryland designe," no matter how attractively presented, had little appeal.[38]

Only London offered easy access to a concentrated Catholic population. Bloomsbury, where Baltimore resided, was one such area. In a petition to the Privy Council imploring assistance against Catholics, William Haywood, the rector of St. Giles in the Fields, and three of his church wardens described the parish as a hotbed of Catholicism. They deplored "the miserable estate" they were in because of the "great increase of those of the Romish church." They suggested that in Bloomsbury the number of Catholics might even exceed the number of Protestants. For Catholics, London offered many advantages and conveniences that Maryland could not. These included ready access to foreign chapels and their priests, so necessary for their spiritual well-being, and to the professional classes necessary for their material well-being.[39]

For his vision to succeed, Baltimore knew he must attract a suitable number of artisans, laborers, and servants. Given their dependence on the Catholic nobility and gentry, he realized there were few unattached Catholic servants. They had either succumbed to governmental pressures and "converted" to the state religion, or they had secured employment with a Catholic whose social standing afforded protection against the penal legislation. The poorer Catholics, thus dependent on their betters for protection, were not about to risk what little security they had by emigrating. By the time Baltimore initiated his search for emigrants and investors, these Catholics were not looking for an escape route.

They submitted to the penal laws when they had to and quietly avoided them the rest of the time, but they were not disposed to leap foolishly into colonization. Baltimore therefore concentrated on recruiting members of his own class, who could bring the needed servants with them.

Baltimore inherited his colonial enterprise at a propitious time in the history of the expanding Jesuit community. The support and protection offered by the expanding Catholic social elite facilitated a significant increase in the number of priests, who conducted their illicit missions in the face of the penal laws. The number of Jesuit priests steadily grew during the reigns of James I and Charles I. The English Province, including those in overseas houses, totaled 218 in 1623. By 1636 that number rose to 374, with 183 priests working in England and Wales. This growth as well as the need for closer supervision of priests, led the Society of Jesus to form a separate Province in 1623 under the jurisdiction of its own provincial. The Jesuits and Baltimore accepted the need for greater lay control over priests.[40]

But Baltimore had a harder task than merely locating Catholics: he had to strike a responsive chord in them. He and the missionary priests promoted the enterprise in the context of his vision. The later testimony of Catholic commissioner Thomas Cornwallis indicated that freedom of conscience ranked high among the inducements offered. But like nationalism and the opportunity to prosper under Baltimore's benevolent leadership, religious liberty failed to excite many Catholics. Ultimately, their reluctance, and for that matter Protestant reluctance, to emigrate to Baltimore's colony dampened his high hopes for an auspicious beginning. Even the Jesuits failed to recruit a significant number of Catholics willing to go to Maryland as their servants and had to rely on Protestants to fill their quota.[41]

English Catholics, however, did not entirely turn a deaf ear to the recruiters for the "Maryland designe." A few, who saw enticing possibilities in Baltimore's vision, found their interest piqued. His greatest success came in enlisting those with whom he intended to share political power and social status. He envisioned these men, on whom he would bestow generous grants of land, as lords of the manors. Working with him in their common cause, they would share responsibility for maintaining social stability. He admitted no one without good recommendations and a knowledge that he was free from any taints in life and manners. With those he deemed worthy, he freely shared himself and his fortune, making them as much as possible "his companions and free sharers in all his hopes." The master adventurers, whom Wintour described as gentlemen, wellborn, of noble education, and good friends, formed the backbone of the settlement. They were men of means, experienced in employments both at home and abroad, who were not fleeing their country. Wintour believed that they could, if they chose, live in England with repute and esteem.[42]

It was left unsaid that these gentlemen were for the most part Roman Catholics. The majority came from gentry families who had long been interested in colonization or had connections with the Calvert family. Maryland resonated with the younger sons, who had little chance of inheriting the family estate. Their religion generally precluded careers in the professions or in politics, but in Baltimore's enterprise they could better themselves without having to compromise their religion. It offered to young Catholic gentry an alternative to dissipating themselves in the service of foreign princes.[43]

Not only did the proprietor scrutinize potential leaders, but according to Wintour, he screened, or tried to screen, the emigrants who went as servants. The servants, Wintour emphasized, were not like those who went to other colonies, idle vagabonds promiscuously gathered from the jails, outlaws forced to flee their country, or servants enticed away from masters or children from their parents. Rather, they were fellow countrymen, neighbors—the tenants of Catholic gentry families—who went to Maryland under no false pretenses and secure in the contractual obligations of their service. Wintour contended that Maryland servants accompanied their masters out of love, confident and resolved to live and die with them, ready to share their prosperity or suffer in adversity. As it turned out, few servants fell into this idyllic category.[44]

In the end, however, the minimal response, especially among Catholics, profoundly influenced the Calverts' management of their "Maryland designe." It forced them to rely upon unknown quantities who had neither religious nor familial ties. The result was, in the words of Charles Calvert, that his father had to depend upon such as for "some Reason or other could not live with ease in other places. And of these a greate parte were such as could not conforme in all particulars to the severall lawes of England relating to religion." The necessity to depend on individuals representing a variety of religious persuasions—from Roman Catholics, members of the Church of England, and Englishmen with Puritan leanings, to a number who were indifferent toward religion—placed a premium on keeping religious strife from destroying the enterprise.[45]

Robert Wintour convinced himself, if no one else. He embodied the "pushes" and "pulls" that led many to forsake their native land for a new life in a new England along the shores of the Chesapeake Bay. Two salient and closely related factors influenced his own decision. One was his economic and social status in England and the prospect for their improvement, and the other was the extent to which that position could be enhanced by casting his fortune with Lord Baltimore. The most important economic consideration was the amount of money he could invest. The most important social-status consideration was his religion. In the face of overwhelming odds, Wintour remained a Roman Catholic, and his Catholicism linked him to the Calverts and to Maryland. Nevertheless, Wintour hardly fits the image of a religious pilgrim, devout as he may have been; his choice therefore must be viewed against the appeal that Maryland had for English Catholics.

Wintour epitomized the upper stratum of the immigrant society. He was persistently Roman Catholic. He was a younger son of a Catholic gentry family that had a history of interest in the New World. He was related by marriage to the Calverts. Above all, he was adventurous, single, ambitious, and affluent.[46]

He based his decision to emigrate on the attractions he had enumerated for Captain Reade. Two statements in particular shed light on his decision to emigrate. Adventuring to Maryland, he thought, should not be done for the wrong reasons: it should not be undertaken for company or fun or because of dissatisfaction with life in England. Rather, colonists should have as their main motives the honor of God, a thorough understanding of the nature of the "Maryland designe," and a confidence of success. Maryland was "a highe vocation rather then a temptation." In addition, he saw the necessity of making the commitment as quickly as possible. The best of the business, he told his friend, "is now at the first." Consistent with his recommendations to Captain Reade, he transported six adult male servants and a fifteen-year-old male servant. Judging by the inventory of his estate, he also brought a considerable amount of personal property, by which he intended to create the gracious style envisioned in his letter.[47]

Wintour projected a bright future in Maryland. Even accounting for his optimism, he miscalculated on a number of matters. The "Maryland designe" suffered from a want of adventurers. Either he and his colleagues did not reach enough people, or the vision they saw failed to excite a significant number of people. He got it wrong in another way as well. His dream of a well-settled plantation within five years failed to materialize. While the record reveals nothing about the condition of his house and the possible existence of a deer park, Wintour seems to have made progress toward capturing the dream he put forth. But, as it happened with so many emigrants to the Chesapeake region, his death brought it to an end. He left no heirs when he died in 1638, but he did leave for posterity a statement describing a vision of a land where English Catholics could put their time and energies to good use by casting their fate with Lord Baltimore. His legacy was his optimistic portrait of the "Maryland designe." These worthy goals, to serve God and monarch, to have the honor of participating in the founding of a new society, to satisfy intellectual curiosity, drew Wintour to the Chesapeake.

Wintour seemed ideally suited to serve the proprietor's interests and his own. However, his brief tenure in Maryland reflected a hard reality for Baltimore, who found that even those with whom he most closely associated himself could not be relied upon to carry out his will in *his* colony. They either resisted or modified proprietary goals or, worse still, died prematurely. The sparring over a code of laws for Maryland was to reflect the inherent problem for an absentee proprietor. Those Catholic and Protestant landowners, servants, and clergy clearly had wills of their own and their own interests to pursue.

CHAPTER SEVEN

"With free liberty of religion"

The Calvert Model for Church-State Relations (1633–1655)

Careful planning expedited establishment of a colony on a firm foundation, and early reports gave Baltimore cause for hope. Under his subordinates, mainly relatives or family associates, the immigrants established an outpost along St. George's River. As the proprietor instructed, the leaders sought and achieved amiable relations with the local Indians. On March 27, 1633, they agreed to "live friendly and peaceably together" by giving mutual satisfaction for any injury done. To avoid any misunderstanding with the Yoacomaco Indians and to build a relationship on an equitable foundation, the government bought thirty miles of land from them for payment consisting of axes, hoes, cloth, and hatches. The Indians happily sold land that they intended to abandon.[1]

The early optimism gave way to discontent; by 1637 the "Maryland designe" was floundering on the shoals of dissent and discord. Acquisition of Indian lands unmasked the divergent interests of the proprietor and the Jesuits, leading to a confrontation that divided the loyalties of Maryland's Catholic inhabitants. The fur trade, on which so much of Baltimore's financial hopes depended, proved disappointing and exacerbated tensions within the nascent community. By the late 1630s, the proprietor, mired in legal disputes and troubled by a deteriorating financial condition, lived on his father-in-law's charity. The irascible Virginians, perhaps only Governor John Harvey excepted, continued their hostile posturing and diverted attention from building the requisite infrastructure. More significant, Baltimore's own colonists seemed unreceptive to his distant leadership and contested his princely prerogatives on matters such as the initiation of legislation. And, of course, the religiously diverse nature of the population presented the greatest challenge to creating a peaceful and prospering enterprise.[2]

Conditioned both by his father's experience and by practical necessities, Cecil Calvert rejected the beliefs that his colonists had to profess his religious faith and that he had to control their religious practices. In effect, he sought to transform the structure of his society within a conservative (sometimes described as feudal) framework. His novel concept that religion was a private matter, free from government assistance or restraint, marked a significant break with the dogmas of the age. When he removed the prop of religious uniformity, which contemporary rulers considered essential for political stability, he was calling on the immigrants to behave in radically different ways. Their culture distrusted religious differences, but he urged them to put their differences aside, to act with Christian charity toward one another, and to prosper. Baltimore understood the importance of religion and knew that differences could not be easily swept aside by proprietorial edict. He believed, though, that under his enlightened leadership, religious contentiousness could be minimized.[3]

The proprietor's policy reflected a philosophical commitment to religious liberty as well as a pragmatic one. The penal legislation, designed to enforce uniformity, forced English Catholics to reexamine their perspective on the relationship between religious allegiance and political loyalty. Baltimore's minority status denied him the privilege of an established church, which eliminated two major tenets of English thinking about the state's role in religious matters, the magistrate's obligation to protect the "true religion" and religious uniformity. Cecil, here reflecting his father's demeanor, was far more accepting of religious differences than his contemporaries were. As he saw it, civil harmony did not depend upon enforcing religious conformity. He accepted his condition for what it was and worked to prosper within the world that existed in the 1630s, 1640s, and 1650s. The potentially explosive nature of religious questions within a pluralistic community meant that he had to step carefully and devise a religious settlement that at the least would not further exacerbate those tensions.

In moving toward a more secular society, the proprietor did not envision one that would be devoid of religious commitments or institutions. Rather, they would be voluntary. The state, his government, would *privilege* no particular religious group. To ensure civil peace, Baltimore sought to avoid the appearance that any particular religious group received special treatment. Individuals and not the state had to take responsibility for fostering their own religious institutions—unlike the practice in other English colonies. That meant no established church or publicly supported educational institutions. Religious freedom was the modus operandi of the "Maryland designe," but not the purpose of the founding of Maryland. It was a means to an end, which was the creation of a prosperous society.

Even under the best of circumstances—and Baltimore's were not—the successful execution of a vision requires luck and good timing. Quickly changing circumstances in the colony and in England forced him to scramble to stay ahead of events. The outbreak of hostilities between king and Parliament in 1642 threatened the king's protection and brought Baltimore face to face with new penal legislation implemented by Parliament. He found himself living under increasingly chaotic conditions. Questions of allegiance, not English or Catholic, but to king or Parliament, made life precarious in both England and the colonies. Past loyalties served only as a partial guide for the present confused and tense conditions. To his credit, Baltimore showed an uncanny ability to adjust to unforeseen situations. Among these unanticipated factors, his inability to recruit more Catholics and his decision not to sail with those who had committed dominated his thinking about religious practices in the colony.

Initially, his religious policies reflected three considerations. First, the men he chose as leaders, mostly his fellow Catholics, constituted a minority of the general population, just as Catholics did in England. The difference was that in Maryland, Catholics (mostly gentry) dominated the political scene. This boded well for Baltimore's desire to establish a stable society. Less encouraging, the majority of the population shared to some extent the anti-Catholic thinking that prevailed in England. Baltimore knew full well that these tensions lurked beneath the surface, and he took precautions to prevent an eruption of religious dissension, whether between Catholic and Protestant or between Catholic and Catholic. A third component, and perhaps the most important, was his relative weakness as the "absolute" proprietor. Circumstances prevented him from achieving the power envisioned by the language of the charter. As his ships prepared to depart in November 1633, the disappointed Baltimore realized that unexpected "accidents" necessitated his remaining behind. More than the personal satisfaction that would derive from assuming his place as the head of his community, he wanted to exercise close control over the implementation of his vision. The success or failure of his policies depended on two groups of people: those he chose to implement his will and those colonists who opted to seek their fortune with him. Could they fulfill his vision?[4]

Of the immediate family, only Baltimore's son, Charles Calvert, the third Lord Baltimore (1637–1715), explicated the origins of the Calverts' religious policies. In his reply in 1678 to queries from the English government, he described the situation as he understood it some forty-five years later. Charles noted that his father had an "absolute Liberty given to him" to transport to Maryland "any Persons out of any of the Dominions that belonged to the Crowne of England who should be found Wylling to go." The recruitment campaign attracted those who "for some Reason or other" could not live with ease in other places because they could not conform in all particulars to the "severall Lawes of England relating to Religion." Many who declared their willingness to venture with his father did so in order to enjoy a general toleration. He added that unless his father had met certain conditions concerning toleration, in all probability Maryland *might* never have come into being.[5]

Charles implied that the impetus for toleration originated with the people who did not conform to all particulars of the Church of England and that they made toleration a precondition for emigration. As he understood it, his father's policies resulted more from some kind of negotiation than from a vision. But the son overstated the situation when he attributed religious policy to the adventurers and planters recruited by his father. Catholics, and perhaps some of the Protestants, who contemplated emigrating did want assurances with regard to religion. Thomas Cornwallis later recalled a conversation he had had with the second Lord Baltimore before departing for Maryland. He informed the proprietor that his security of conscience was the first condition he expected from Baltimore's government. However, the proprietor, who saw religious liberty as a given, found his commissioner's request for a written guarantee impertinent. Because of the uncertainties of his world, he offered little more than general assurances of security of conscience to those who sailed to the colony.[6]

The third Lord Baltimore failed to realize that his father's basic vision was nonnegotiable. The colonists did not force Cecil to take a position with which he felt uncomfortable. Like his father before him, he initiated religious policies designed to foster his vision of a peaceful and prospering society. These concepts fitted their liberal personalities, but beyond that, what choice did they have? The status of the Calverts notwithstanding, the penal laws could not be ignored. Supporters of the defunct Virginia Company made that point. A willingness to risk colonization with people of differing religious views remained fundamental to the Calvert strategy. Cecil succeeded because he recognized that if he was to recoup the family fortunes in Maryland, provide an opportunity for Catholics to worship without fear or burdensome laws, and still attract a sufficient number of colonists, he had to keep religion out of politics. The process by which he attempted to achieve this goal, however, must be viewed as having an evolutionary character.[7]

Another statement further indicated that the third Lord Baltimore had a faulty understanding of the origins of his grandfather's and his father's religious policies. He thought that "soone after the first planting" his father had had a law enacted that guaranteed Christians "Liberty to Worshipp." Instead, his father rejected legislation and relied on executive fiat. The less committed to paper, the better the chance to avoid scrutiny of a practice potentially contrary to the laws of England. Cecil sought a legislative solution only after rapidly changing circumstances in England and in the Chesapeake region in the late 1640s forced his hand.[8]

The third Lord Baltimore undervalued the "Maryland designe." His grandfather and his father had created an integrated and sophisticated plan. They yoked religious policies to another important component of the vision, the manor. The inclusion of the manorial system in the Maryland charter indicates their commitment to finding innovative ways to keep religious conflict from engulfing the entire community. They wanted to recreate to the extent possible the system that had ensured Catholic survival in England. If successfully transplanted, these enclaves would provide the necessary privacy and safety for religious practices while at the same time offering a way to keep religious squabbles from becoming notorious. Maryland was to be the manor writ large. The gentlemen, tied to Baltimore in a variety of ways, imported the requisite servants, gained the land needed to prosper, and had the authority to deal with secondary concerns in their manorial courts. Allowing the Jesuits to establish manors on the same terms as the other gentlemen made it possible for them to provide for the spiritual needs of the Catholics. Cecil did not, however, limit land distribution to manor lords; his need for colonists demanded flexibility. He offered lesser amounts of land (fifty to one hundred acres) to men and women who transported fewer people to Maryland. Ironically, this initiative helped to undermine Baltimore's vision of himself as lord of the Maryland manor. Smaller independent landowners eventually triumphed over the lords of the manors. Nevertheless, the manorial system served him well when he had to dodge tricky questions of allegiance in the 1650s.[9]

The proprietor committed his thoughts to paper only after he abandoned any hope of sailing with the expedition. His instructions, issued on November 13, 1633, placed the responsibility for civil peace squarely on the shoulders of his Catholic relatives and friends. By executive fiat, he required them to be very careful "to preserve unity & peace amongst all the passengers on Shipp-board, and that they suffer no scandall nor offence to be given to any of the Protestants, whereby any just complaint may hereafter be made, by them, in Virginia or in England." To prevent discord, he ordered his officers to "cause all Acts of Romane Catholique Religion to be done as privately as may be" and to "instruct all Roman Catholiques to be silent upon all Occasions of discourse concerning matters of Religion." Finally, Baltimore ordered that government officials treat the Protestants with as much mildness and favor as justice would permit. He expected his injunctions to be observed "at Land as well as at Sea." This strategy aimed to curb disputations and prevent potentially contentious religious issues from destroying the project before it had a chance to succeed.[10]

The "Instructions" admonished Catholics to keep their religious practices as private as possible. But on March 25, 1634, Father White celebrated a Mass, the Catholics erected a cross, and the leaders "with devotion took solemne possession of the Country." Was it an act of celebration or act of defiance, or both? By their exuberant actions, Catholics proclaimed that private no longer meant secret. How private the colonists kept their thoughts was another consideration. Would William Smith, who later stated in his will that he died a member of the Roman Catholic Church, "out of which there is no salvation," keep his thoughts private, or would he challenge Protestants on this point? Would David Wickliff, a former pursuivant and "now a chiefe protestante," keep his thoughts private, or would he flaunt his past to the Catholics? Would the Jesuits create tensions by their very presence? Would they refrain from proselytizing among the unchurched Protestants? To survive in this small world, Catholics and Protestants had to acknowledge their differences and accept the visible presence of each group's religious practices.[11]

Baltimore's Maryland was unique in another respect. In the three colonies founded before Maryland, the civil government actively promoted religious activities; this was especially true in Plymouth and Massachusetts Bay, where religion had been the principal reason for the colonies' founding. Baltimore's strategies differed from those employed by the leaders of the Massachusetts Bay Colony. There the General Court passed a law that made political freedom an attribute of membership in one of the churches, and the magistrates took seriously their role as "nursing fathers," that is, their special role to foster and protect the religious institutions. Although viewed as a paternalistic feudal lord who concerned himself with all aspects of his settlers' lives, Baltimore certainly does not fit the image of a "nursing father" in matters of religion. Under his leadership Maryland assiduously avoided any taint of a religious test for voting or holding office. All male residents, excluding servants and Jesuits, were eligible. Nor did the Maryland proprietor not establish a church and require all inhabitants to support it through taxation, as was done in Virginia. His government founded no churches. The Jesuits, who lived in Maryland at their own expense, seized the initiative and took over an Indian longhouse, where they conducted worship services for the Catholics. Baltimore's policies left the Protestants, who brought no ministers, unchurched.[12]

Not sailing with the first expedition genuinely disappointed Baltimore, who chafed at his status as an absentee landlord. He very much wanted to assume his role as head of state on site. Circumstances there, such as Claiborne's encroachments on Kent Island, forced him to relinquish more authority to those in the colony. But worse, his representatives failed to resolve the tensions with the Virginians and to produce the profits needed to sustain the proprietor and his family. Not willing to rely only on his brother to resolve the Kent Island dispute on favorable terms, Baltimore pursued solutions outside of the Chesapeake region. By acting on his conviction that a solution could be found along the banks of the Thames, Baltimore again demonstrated his confidence that Charles's government would continue to support his effort to expand the English nation, in spite of his religious commitments.[13]

Baltimore's status as an absentee landlord and as an English Catholic sensitized him to questions of loyalty. He ordered his brother and his Catholic commissioners to assemble as soon as possible after landing "all the people together in a fit and decent manner." He wanted his officers to read the patent to them, make a short declaration of his intentions, and then, after publicly taking the oath of allegiance to King Charles, administer it to the colonists. He needed them to "testify to the world that none should enjoy the benefits of the grant without public assurance of their" fidelity to the king. Less than two years later, he created a new oath as a substitute for the controversial 1606 oath. Whether the proprietor acted in fear that he might be stripped of his colony, from a desire "to win over" the king, or because he needed to provide a method by which his people could express their allegiance without damaging their religious scruples, he devoted considerable time to writing it. He incorporated the substance of this work into a bill, "An Act for Swearing Allegiance," that he sent to Maryland for approval in 1639. The act called upon all Marylanders of age eighteen and older to swear their allegiance to the king within a month of the assembly's adjournment and for newcomers to take the oath within a month of their arrival. Oath-takers acknowledged in their conscience and before God that Charles was the lawful and rightful king of England. They swore to bear true faith and allegiance to the king and to defend the Crown to the uttermost of their power against all conspiracies or other actions made against the king. They also attested to their willingness to disclose all treasons and traitorous conspiracies that they knew or heard of against the king. They took the oath on their faith as Christians. This oath, by not setting loyalty to the king in the context of denying papal power, reflected Baltimore's desire to find a middle ground. Safety for Baltimore, for his colony, and for Maryland Catholics meant avoiding the choice between secular and religious loyalties. He expected his Catholic colonists, lay or clerical, to recognize the wisdom of this policy.[14]

Baltimore's loyalty to the Crown was not altruistic. He expected a return on that commitment and used his court connections to further his interests and the well-being of his colony. Resolving tensions with the Virginians remained a high priority during the first years of his proprietorship. He attempted to force better relations with the older colony along the Chesapeake Bay by initiating changes at the highest level. He acted on the increasingly doubtful proposition that he could somehow control events from England. John Harvey, appointed to govern the unruly Virginians in 1629, found himself at odds with those in his colony who opposed Baltimore's claims. The Virginia oligarchs, who perceived their royally appointed governor as a threat to their land and trade interests, treated him with disdain and eventually expelled him. The governor admitted in 1634 that his power in Virginia was not great. His commission forced him to abide by the will of the majority of those present at the council table. When it concerned Maryland, he lamented, "I have almost all against me in whatever I propose." The Maryland charter and the arrival of Baltimore's colonists were the most serious threat to the future of Virginia since the 1622 Indian attack. Harvey was the closest thing Baltimore had to an ally. Before the *Ark* and the *Dove* sailed, the Privy Council, at Baltimore's behest, instructed Harvey to assist "them at their first beginning." Harvey complied but gained no friends thereby among those he governed. Virginians were so adverse to trading with the newly arriving Marylanders "that they would rather knock their cattell on the heads then sell them to Maryland." The governor's willing assistance contributed to his expulsion in the spring of 1635. Baltimore unsuccessfully tried to use his influence to have Harvey's detractors recalled to England to answer for their actions.[15]

Harvey's favorable treatment of the Marylanders raised the specter of Catholicism along the Chesapeake. He denied before the king's Privy Council on December 11, 1635, that he had failed to administer the oath of allegiance and that he was "a favourer of the Popish Religion." Virginia planter Samuel Mathews sent a long letter rationalizing the tactics used against Harvey. He concluded by beseeching God to direct the king to appoint "some worthy, religious Gentleman" to govern his colony. The Virginians took a risk in throwing out the royal governor, but they never imagined that their actions might provide an opportunity for the last man they wanted, the Catholic proprietor of Maryland.[16]

With matters on the Chesapeake at an impasse, Baltimore once again demonstrated his audacity by seeking appointment as governor of Virginia. Sometime before February 1637, Baltimore broached the subject with one of his supporters on the Privy Council, Secretary of State Windebank. He wrote on February 25, "since I waited on you, I have (heere in the Country) further considered of the proposition" concerning the governorship. Baltimore confidently predicted that he had the ability to do what the appointment demanded and asserted that the king would benefit greatly by naming him governor. He conceded that the appointment would be "of good consequence to him" as well. Finally, he thanked Windebank for his "present care of my Newfoundland business that concerns me very much." Baltimore followed this letter with a memorial to Windebank that, if used, would have provided the king with ample justification for the appointment. The proprietor first urged the secretary to extol his virtues to the king. Windebank should let Charles know how much Baltimore appreciated the great favors he had received from him. Further, he should inform the king that Baltimore desired to do some acceptable service, "wherein hee may express his duty and gratitude to his Majesty." But Baltimore understood that gratitude only went so far. He knew the appointment had to be in the best interests of the king. Thus, he coached Windebank to examine the present state of Virginia so that he would understand well "the great prejudice the King suffers there, by not receiving so much profitt from thence, as he ought to have, and is due." Baltimore promised to increase significantly the king's revenues "without laying any new, or other taxe or imposition on the Planters." The catch was that the advancement of the king's revenues "cannot be effected, unless the Lord Baltimore do repaire and reside some time there," and he could not do this safely unless the king gave him authority as his royal governor. Then, regaining his humility, he told the secretary that he had no ambition or affection but for the advancement of the king's service, and he authorized him to tell the king that he thought Baltimore "would accept the government, and two thousand pounds yearely for the support thereof, payable out of that improvement of Rent." Baltimore promised that if he received the appointment, he would resolve his personal affairs in England and be ready to sail as soon as the king ordered.[17]

From Baltimore's top-down perspective, the appointment made sense. In one bold stroke, he could remove the greatest threat to his colony and at the same time guarantee a substantial income for himself. He and his family could embark for America knowing that the charter was secure and that he had effectively neutralized the Virginians. It made sense, but had the financially strapped proprietor taken leave of his senses? Was it feasible for a Catholic to be governor of the royal colony?

Baltimore still had "great friends" in the government. Sir Edmund Plowden recognized his fellow Catholic's influence when he sought Baltimore's support on behalf of his New Albion charter in 1639. Equally important, precedent existed for Catholic colonial governors. The brother of Maryland councillor Jerome Hawley was governor of Barbados, and he was Catholic. Beyond precedence, the timing seemed right. In the period preceding the Bishops' War in 1638, court Catholics had cause to be optimistic. Without Parliament, which had not been in session since 1629, anti-Catholic forces lost much of their impact. Charles's chronic revenue shortfalls encouraged voices, whether Protestant or Catholic, that promised to enhance his financial well-being. Still, Charles did not appoint Calvert to the post. Baltimore's scheme failed, but not because he was a Catholic. Rather, his fellow Catholic and his commissioner, Jerome Hawley, effectively undercut Baltimore's initiative. Hawley, also arguing that he could significantly improve the king's revenues, sought and secured appointment as Virginia's treasurer.[18]

The proprietor's desperate financial situation made the Virginia governorship very attractive. From the mid-1630s Baltimore lived at Wardour Castle or its environs and served as his father-in-law's aide. Lord Arundell, in a letter depicting his own problems, revealed Baltimore's woeful condition. After writing of his declining health and increasing indebtedness, he described how demands by one son-in-law, Lord Eure, exacerbated his situation. He then noted, "My son Baltimore is brought so low with his setting forward the plantation of Maryland, and with the clamourours suits and opposition which he has met with in that business, as that I do not see how he could subsist if I did not give him diet for himself, wife, children and servants." This from an eighty-year-old man who admitted having a debt of twenty-three thousand pounds![19]

Unable to establish himself as a manorial lord in Maryland, Baltimore did what he could to improve his fortunes at home. This included taking advantage of the limited opportunities offered by his father-in-law. With Baltimore's encouragement, in October 1638 the aging Arundell directed the trustees of his estate not to sell Hooke Farm, the principal messuage in Semley Manor, but to convey it at his death to Baltimore and his heirs for the remainder of the ninety-nine-year lease. Arundell also ordered that his daughter Anne receive two thousand pounds, the amount paid to his other married daughters as part of their settlements. Before he died on November 7, he made it known that Baltimore had "never importuned me in anything" and stated his wish that Baltimore "might be able to live like himself," seeing that much of his "weak fortune" had been sunk into his plantation.[20]

Believing that he had his father-in-law's blessing, Baltimore and his family took possession of Semley Manor, its stone manor house, and Hooke Farm in August 1639. Baltimore paid his rent and received a letter from Arundell's second son, William, congratulating him on his acquisition. Mr. Lewin, the steward, held court on August 19 at Hooke Farm house, where the tenants accepted the authority of their new landlord, Lord Baltimore. The value of the produce from the manor, estimated at between £240 and £280, seemed like a godsend to the impecunious proprietor. However, the trustees, who believed that Arundell did not have the power to limit the land to Baltimore, dampened his sense of relief when they refused to transfer the manor to him or pay him the £5,000 that Arundell had earmarked for him. Then, acting on advice from the trustees, the tenants let it be known that they would not pay rents to Baltimore. The actions of the trustees led to a series of court proceedings that put additional strains on Baltimore's resources. The other heirs claimed that Baltimore took advantage of Arundell in his final sickness, a time when his memory had failed him, to secure in a clandestine manner the deed to Semley. They charged that Baltimore illegally cut down woods, levied fines, and collected rents for his own profit. If their accusations were true, his ruthless exploitation of the Wiltshire lands testified to his desperate financial condition.[21]

Baltimore's failure to generate revenues in his colony contrasted with the success he had in implementing his religious policy. Considering the potential for animosity among the religiously diverse population, the relatives and friends to whom Baltimore had entrusted the implementation of his policies did a remarkable job of preventing religious disruptions during the first years. His surrogates ably defused two incidents in which Protestants tested his policy by complaining against Catholics. Baltimore's policy offered the colonists religious freedom but no assistance for developing religious institutions. Church of England communicants did not respond well to their new circumstances. For the most part, they remained without the services of their priests until about 1650. Without ministers and without government support, the unchurched Protestant majority relied on lay readers or a visiting clergyman from Virginia.

Protestant immigrants sensed the government's delicate situation. One dispute involved William Lewis, overseer of the Jesuit plantation of St. Inigoes. In their Annual Letter of 1638, the Jesuits recited their success in proselytizing among the lowly Protestant servants. Not only was the attendance on the sacraments large, but "the most ignorant have been catechized" and the sick and dying "have been assisted in every way, so that not a single person has died without sacraments." Nor were the Protestants forgotten. Unable to secure a "station among the barbarians," that is, among the Indians, the Jesuits were able to devote themselves "more zealously to the English" and boasted of their accomplishments in bringing numerous Protestants to the Catholic faith.[22]

Against this background the Lewis case emerged. Lewis, on the first Sunday in July 1638, reported that some of his servants intended to circulate a petition to the governor of Virginia in chapel that morning that delineated "the abuses and scandalous reproaches which God and his ministers doe daily suffer" from the Catholic overseer. The servants claimed that Lewis said "our Ministers are the Ministers of the divell" and that "our books are made by the instruments of the divel" and that he had ordered them not to keep or read any books pertaining to the Protestant religion. The "poore bondmen" under his subjection claimed this a "great discomfort," especially for those in a "heathen country where no godly minister is to teach and instruct ignorant people in the grounds of religion." They alleged that when anyone came to Lewis, he "taketh occasion to call them into his chamber," where he labored "with all vehemency craft and subtlety to delude ignorant persons." The Protestants concluded their petition with a plea that the Virginia governor ("you who have power") do what he could to relieve them of "these absurd abuses and herediculous crimes." This petition threatened the very foundations of Maryland's existence, for the last thing the proprietor and his officials in Maryland wanted was outside interference from Protestant Virginia.[23]

Once the dispute became public, the government treated it seriously. Maryland authorities moved quickly to prevent the social fabric from being torn apart by religious dissension, much as Massachusetts officials had done in the cases of Roger Williams and Anne Hutchinson. But leaders of the Maryland colony added a curious twist. In this instance the dominant element took action against one of its own who had violated the principles enunciated by Baltimore in his instructions. A warrant directed the sheriff to bring Lewis and the Protestant servants into court, where three Catholics (Governor Leonard Calvert, Commissioner Thomas Cornwallis, and the newly appointed secretary to the colony and recent convert John Lewger) heard the particulars.[24]

Lewis testified that the servants had been reading from a book of sermons by an Elizabethan Puritan minister, "Silver Tongued" Henry Smith. When he entered the room, "they read it aloud to the end he shoulde heare it, and that the matter being much reproachfull to his religion," Lewis responded by branding the book a "falsehood," charging it "came from the Divell, as all lies did, & that he that writt it was an instrument of the divell." Two witnesses affirmed that Lewis had also charged that Protestant ministers "were the ministers of the divell," and another claimed that Lewis had forbidden Francis Gray, a freeman who evidently conducted lay services, to read Smith's book of sermons in the house nor any other "such base fellowes as he [Smith] was." Gray's testimony about a conversation on the matter with Father Thomas Copley that went unchallenged in court frustrated Lewis's chances for acquittal. He reported that Copley, who had arrived in Maryland in August 1637 to manage the secular affairs of the Jesuit mission, "had given him good satisfaction" and "blamed much William Lewis for his contumelious speeches and ill-governed zeale and it was fitt that he [Lewis] should be punished."[25]

The court found Lewis guilty of disturbing the peace. Lewger found him guilty of "offensive & indiscrete speech" and said that he had exceeded his authority in forbidding the Protestant servants "to read a booke otherwise allowed & lawfull to be read in the state of England." He stated that Lewis's "unseasonable disputations" on religion tended "to the disturbance of the publique peace & quiett of the colony," in direct disregard of a "publique proclamation sett forth to prohibit all such disputes." Lewger fined him five hundred pounds of tobacco, as did Cornwallis, who found him guilty of acting against the proclamation "made for the suppressing of all such disputes tending to the cherishing of a faction in religion." The court then put Lewis on bond of three thousand pounds of tobacco until "tenth of November next" and ordered him not to "offend the peace of this colony or the inhabitants thereof by injurious & unnecessary arguments or disputations in matters of religion" or use "any ignominious words or speeches touching the books or ministers authorized by the State of England."[26]

For Maryland the threat from hostile authorities in Virginia and enemies in England loomed very large. With Baltimore's adversaries eagerly awaiting an opportunity to undermine the charter, every effort had to be made to deprive them of ammunition. The burden of this policy fell most heavily on his coreligionists, in this case the overseer of St. Inigoes, William Lewis, a man of "ill-governed zeale." His servants could sneer that "the Pope was Anti-christ" and that the Jesuits were anti-Christian, but he could not answer. To do so promoted "faction in religion." The Lewis case clearly indicates the Catholic leadership's recognition of the precarious nature of their foothold. Determined to avoid any charges that they had come to plant "the Romish religion," Lord Baltimore's agents tolerated no breach of the peace over religion (regardless of a case's merits). The leadership would not even countenance suppressing a book that spoke in unflattering terms about Catholic beliefs and practices.[27]

The second incident further confirmed that the Catholic government adhered to Baltimore's policy. In this instance some Protestants turned to the government in an effort to redress a grievance against a socially prominent Catholic. For reasons unknown, Thomas Gerard, a wealthy Catholic physician who was married to a Protestant woman, took away the key to the chapel, a small house or room on his manor that Catholics shared with the Protestants, and removed the Protestants' books. David Wickliff, a Protestant from St. George's Hundred, petitioned "in the name of Protestant Catholicks" for a redress of the grievances. The assembly found Gerard "Guilty of a misdemeanor." It ordered him to return the key and the books and fined him five hundred pounds of tobacco, to be used "toward the maintenance of the first minister as should arrive." The Catholic leadership in the legislature punished a fellow Catholic who violated the proprietor's policy of religious diversity. To ensure their own freedom, Maryland's Catholic leaders accepted Baltimore's progressive views.[28]

The Lewis and Gerard cases displayed the fragility of a policy designed to keep religious questions out of the public arena. On one level, the resolution of the cases without any further intervention from the proprietor worked toward the creation of the harmonious society that Baltimore sought. On another level, these two cases revealed the limitations of his policy. An executive fiat could not eliminate religious tensions in a society in which people identified themselves by religious labels. When the cases became egregious, civil authorities acted to keep peace within the community and to avoid possible intervention by outside authorities. They acted neither to support a particular religious doctrine nor to provide for the spiritual needs of the inhabitants. In marked contrast to the other English colonies, religion remained a private endeavor that concerned the government only when it became disruptive. With Catholic civil authorities punishing Catholics for their behavior, non-Catholic members of this fledgling society saw that the proprietor and his representatives had indeed made good on their promise of liberty of conscience. It is significant, however, that during this same period the records reveal no Protestant charged with breach of the peace in matters of religion. It remained to be seen whether Baltimore's government would be able to punish Protestants who disrupted the community by publicly expressing anti-Catholic sentiments.[29]

A more destructive confrontation within the Catholic community occurred in the early 1640s. The Jesuits wanted the government, which they considered Catholic, to grant them greater freedom to carry out their missionary efforts to the Indians. They also wanted special tax privileges, exemptions because of their priestly office, and the right to acquire land on their own. Unlike the Lewis and Gerard cases, these disputes left Baltimore's surrogates confused and demoralized. The challenges necessitated the proprietor's intervention because they risked alienating many of his supporters. The confrontation, which threatened his vision for the colony, forced Baltimore to consider whether his colony was indeed a Catholic province.

Up to this point, the proprietor and the Jesuits had benefited from their entente. Each side brought into the relationship liabilities directly related to their English and Catholic commitments. Father White had reflected the dual loyalty the first colonists faced when he ceremoniously took possession of "this Country for our Saviour, and for our Soveraigne Lord the King of England" on March 25, 1634. The Jesuits, however, embodied the international character of Catholicism. Their "prince" was in Rome. They viewed events from a global perspective and thought in terms of church government (canon law). For Baltimore, whose "prince" was in England, the Jesuits highlighted the potential conflict between English and Catholic that he wished left unexplored. From his perspective, Jesuit demands threatened the delicate balance that he sought between English and Catholic loyalties. Moreover, the priests threatened the claims of loyalty he placed on the colonists. Their insistence on a privileged position in his community coincided with increasing tensions over religious matters between king and Parliament. Their acquisition of Indian lands threatened him financially and politically. Still impoverished, and with the world he knew breaking apart, Baltimore reacted viscerally to Jesuit activities.[30]

With hindsight, the association with the Jesuits seems unavoidable. The only statements regarding the origins of the partnership came from the Society. Father Edward Knott, the English provincial, recalled in the early 1640s how the relationship had developed. When Baltimore received in propriety a province "on the sea coast of North America, inhabited by infidels," he immediately contacted Father Richard Blount, the provincial in England at that time, to seek Society involvement. He also wrote to the "Father General, earnestly begging" him to give "certain Fathers" permission to participate in the mission. According to Knott, Baltimore laid before the general three roles for the priests: strengthening Catholics in their faith, "converting heretics" who would assist in colonizing that country, and propagating "the faith amongst the infidels and savages."[31]

Knott's statement needs explication. Baltimore did seek the requisite permission, perhaps at the urging of some Jesuits who fancied the opportunity to carry on an overseas mission under the auspices of a Catholic lord. He viewed the acquisition of the services of the Jesuits in much the same manner as if he were securing a priest for his own household. He accorded the holy fathers no privileges beyond those available to other planters. To satisfy English laws, the Jesuits were not priests but gentlemen adventurers. His willingness to allow members of the Society to emigrate on the same terms as the other gentlemen was as far as Baltimore would or could go in providing for the spiritual needs of his Catholic settlers. He benefited from the willingness of Jesuits priests to migrate. They fulfilled his objectives in a number of ways. He gained a spiritual presence dedicated to carrying out one of the expressed goals of his colony, bringing Christianity to the natives, which in turn would aid in reaching an unexpressed goal, a lucrative trade with the Indians. More important, the priests came at no direct cost to him. He further anticipated that they would tend to the spiritual needs of the Catholics. In addition, they actively recruited needed colonists to sustain their mission and served as agents for pacifying the native population of Maryland. Despite their initial eagerness, in Maryland the Jesuits chafed under the bargain, in part because the government restricted their movements among the natives.

The matter of converting heretics troubled the proprietor. The commitment to religious freedom surely permitted the Jesuits to proselytize among the colonists. A 1641 account claimed that about 10 percent of the less than four hundred colonists had been converted to Catholicism. Yet, conversions in a small evolving community could only exacerbate religious tensions brought from England. However attractive the conversion of heretics may have been to the clerical hierarchy, the proprietor had to approach this issue with great caution. He undoubtedly had discussed conversions among the English with Father White. That priest surely understood the limitations under which the Catholic proprietor functioned.[32]

Unable to persuade the proprietor to provide any contribution to support their work, either from his own funds or from any common source, the Society had agreed to accept "the same conditions, agreements and contracts as the rest of the colonists, and act accordingly." In the allotment of lands, the Society agreed that it "should accept a portion tallying with the conditions and agreements." The clause in the charter that exempted Maryland from the statutes of mortmain may have been added to allow the priests to hold land without royal license. This concession aside, the Jesuits thought the proprietor offered too little and failed to recognize sufficiently their role as priests. Baltimore, however, could not have approached the priests at a better time with such a parsimonious proposition. The English Province of the Society of Jesus never possessed greater wealth during the seventeenth century than during the few years surrounding the founding of Maryland. At that point it had more income than it needed to support its missions and could afford to take a risk on the Maryland venture. Only a few years later, that changed, and the father general of the Society urged the English Province to implement more frugal practices.[33]

Both the Jesuits and Baltimore understood that in Maryland the priests would have to fend for themselves with little or no assistance from the proprietor. They accepted these terms and sought private solicitations to finance the "pious undertaking." Many Catholics "showed great liberality," contributing both money and servants to secure a Jesuit presence in English America. Once in Maryland, the priests quickly learned that they could not expect "sustenance from heretics hostile to the faith," nor from Catholics, most of whom were poor. The status of the priests was similar to what it was in England. The notable exception, or so it seemed, was the freedom they had to conduct their missionary efforts.[34]

Contemporaries such as papal envoy Gregorio Panzani thought the Jesuits had greatly influenced Baltimore. In 1635 he reported the view that Baltimore was "wholly devoted" to the Jesuits whom he sent to his colony to convert the natives. With the exception of Father White, however, Baltimore did not seem close to any of the Jesuits. His reasons may have been as much strategic as spiritual. Allowing the Jesuits to go to Maryland entailed considerable risk. Panzani reported rumors that the archbishop of Canterbury contemplated asking the Privy Council to strip the proprietor of his colony, "since there is much fear that the Jesuits will make such a nest there for themselves as to be able to do harm to the State." Panzani predicted that Baltimore's influence with Cottington would be sufficient to thwart such an effort if the archbishop did undertake it.[35]

Panzani's observations about the Jesuit influence contained more than a kernel of truth. Baltimore, with the tacit approval of the English government, sent the best disciplined and most controversial English Catholic priests to assist in expanding the English empire. He wanted priests in the colony; however, he had to be careful not alienate the king, who had grown increasingly dissatisfied with the Jesuit presence in England. Charles, through his Catholic queen, gave secret instructions to Arthur Brett to carry to Rome. The queen instructed Brett to get the Jesuits, who are "overbusy in matters of state," recalled from England before her husband used "remedies which our laws do provide against them."[36]

Baltimore put some distance between himself and the Jesuits in Maryland by relying on secular priests in England. It may have been because his negotiations regarding the governorship of Virginia were at a delicate stage that he delayed the departure of Father Thomas Copley, alias Philip Fisher, the newly appointed superior for the Maryland mission. More likely, Copley did not receive Baltimore's permission because of "certain difficulties" between the proprietor and the Jesuit provincial. The problem may have stemmed from the provincial's expressed concern that Baltimore's oath "would not be acceptable at Rome." The papal envoy received his information from a secular priest whom he described as Baltimore's confidant, which suggests that Baltimore was not depending on the Jesuits for his spiritual sustenance. By 1636 the entente between the proprietor and the priests had begun to unravel.[37]

The Jesuits in Maryland soon proved to be a greater problem than Baltimore had anticipated. Copley's arrival in August 1637 aggravated tensions between the proprietor and the priests. The new superior descended from a distinguished English Catholic family. He entered the Society of Jesus at Louvain between 1611 and 1615 and after ordination returned to London. He was in residence at Clerkenwell when the government raided that Jesuit residence in 1628. A few years later the English provincial Father Henry More judged Copley to be of good talents but "deficient in judgment and prudence." Copley, who served as minister and procurator of the Jesuit residence in London, had worked closely with White to further the Maryland colony and its missionary work.[38]

John Lewger, a second immigrant destined to play a major role in the controversy, arrived later, in November 1637. The proprietor, having disallowed the laws passed in 1635 by an assembly he did not authorize, decided he would provide statute law for the nascent colony. He entrusted Lewger with a draft of laws for which he wanted assembly approval. The newly appointed provincial secretary seemed to fit Baltimore's model for surrogates. They met at Trinity College, Oxford. Lewger, then a member of the Church of England, eventually received ordination as a priest in 1632 and became the rector of Laverton, Somerset. Doubt led him to abandon his clerical career, and he converted to Catholicism in 1635. In London, the impecunious Lewger renewed his friendship with Baltimore. The proprietor recognized Lewger's potential as a loyal supporter and offered him a fresh start in Maryland. Unable to finance his family's move to the colony, to say nothing of the requisite number of servants, Lewger turned to the Catholic clergy for financial assistance. His status as a manorial lord and provincial secretary placed him among the elite in the small community and put him squarely in the middle of the developing controversy between the priests and the proprietor. Father Knott described Lewger as "formerly a minister and preacher" who, despite his conversion, "retained much of the leaven of Protestantism." Lewger, bedeviled by his own religious loyalties and deeply obligated to both the proprietor and the clergy, embodied the contradictory issues of a controversy that initially focused on Baltimore's draft of the laws.[39]

Copley did not read the draft before the assembly convened in January 1638. He assumed that temporal matters belonged to the proprietor and that on matters of conscience the proprietor had followed good advice. He asked rhetorically, "what occasion could I have to intermeddle" in those affairs? If Copley knew of the initial agreement between Baltimore and the Society, he chose to ignore it. The entente could only work if both parties accepted the fiction on which it rested. Baltimore, to circumvent the penal laws, permitted Jesuit involvement on the understanding that the priests would be treated as gentleman adventurers and fend for themselves. Copley, who assumed that Maryland was a Catholic country and not an English colony, wanted full recognition of the authority of the Jesuits as priests.[40]

Copley's dissatisfaction precipitated a crisis that, in the proprietor's estimation, threatened the colony's existence. The Jesuits refused to attend the assembly but "excused their absence by reason of sickness." When summoned, they made it known that "they desired to be excused from giving voices," a move to which the legislators agreed. This recognition of their priestly office proved to be the opening salvo in a campaign intended to gain a privileged position within the evolving community.[41]

Refusal to participate in legislative deliberations did not result from disinterest. Their overseer and other Catholics kept them informed, a fact not lost on the small St. Mary's community. Still, Father Copley could maintain that he did not see the laws passed by the legislature until the governor was about to send them to his brother. Despite only a "hasty reading" of the laws, he quickly enumerated a list of grievances for the proprietor.[42]

The Jesuit lamented that the laws made no provision to promote the conversion of the Indians. He also objected that no effort had been made "to provide or to shew any favor to Ecciesiasticall persons, or to preserve for the church the Immunitye and priveledges which she enjoyeth every where else." Lewger's assertion that the church had no privileges until the commonwealth granted them particularly offended the priest. Copley feared that Lewger wanted to bind the clerics to the laws and tax them as laity. In anticipation of the proprietor's approval, Lewger demanded fifteen hundredweight of tobacco from the Jesuits to help pay for the erection of a fort. Copley objected to paying "such kind of taxation" but offered to assist gratis if Baltimore freed them from having to pay it.[43]

The priest objected to the law pertaining to manors, the law requiring the planting of two acres of corn, the law governing the beaver trade, and the land tenure laws. He assured the proprietor of his resolution "*to take no land but under your lordships title*" but warned that he would take as "much land as might suffice to build a church or a house"—land given by a converted Indian king. He advised Baltimore to find out whether anyone who attempted to restrain ecclesiastical liberties in this way did not incur the "excommunications of Bulla Coenae." This 1627 papal decree covered a multitude of sins. Copley evidently referred to the prohibition against the citing of ecclesiastical persons before a lay tribunal, the condemnation of those who pass statutes destroying or impairing ecclesiastical liberties, and the prohibition against imposing taxes or other burdens on ecclesiastical property without papal permission. Finally, he protested section 34 of the act for the arbitrary punishment of some enormous offenses. That law, which prohibited exercising jurisdiction and authority without the proprietor's approbation, authorized hanging any Catholic bishop who should come to the colony and also any priest, if the exercise of his functions were interpreted as the exercise of ecclesiastical jurisdiction or authority.[44]

After urging the proprietor to take the good advice of the Church in all things concerning the Church and "not to trench upon the church," Copley entreated Baltimore to privately authorize the Society to enjoy certain privileges while the government was Catholic. First, he wanted the Church and the Jesuit houses to be sanctuaries, that is, safe from the invasion of secular officials. Next, he wanted the Jesuits and their domestic servants and at least one-half of their planting servants to "*be free from publique taxes and services.*" As for the rest of the servants, "though exteriorly they doe as others in the Colony, yet that in the manner of exacting or doing it," Copley wanted a private agreement that the customs of other Catholic countries observed. Without this arrangement, the priest worried that Catholics "out of bad practice" will forget "those due respects which they owe to god and his church." Baltimore's terse marginal notes conveyed his reaction: "All their tennants as well as servants he [Copley] intimates heere ought to be exempted from the temporall government."[45]

Beyond the financial issue, Copley forced Baltimore to confront his paradox: how to be Catholic without being too Catholic. What obligation did he have to the Church? Could civil authorities deny the Catholic Church in Maryland the rights and privileges it enjoyed in other Catholic countries? The letter posed a delicate, almost embarrassing problem. An aroused Lewger prepared a set of twenty questions that he called "The Cases" to assist the proprietor in addressing the paradox. His composition signified that defining the role of the clergy and the nature of the colony engrossed the Catholics in the small community.

Before asking his questions, Lewger established the factors that informed his cases. First, as a colony, Maryland depended entirely on England for its subsistence. Second, Catholics constituted less than 25 percent of the population. He concluded that neither the assembly nor the proprietor could acknowledge the Church in any public way until England was reconciled with the Catholic Church. This meant they could not establish any ecclesiastic discipline, allow provincial synods, erect spiritual courts, accept canon law, or admit priests or bishops "(as such)." The secretary believed he was on solid ground in arguing that the Catholic Church, as represented by the Society, must subordinate its interests to those of the colony. He had recently spent time with Baltimore and felt confident that he was expressing the proprietor's thinking. The priests had become too public, and Lewger saw the need for restraint. Father Knott in England, however, thought that the recently converted secretary maintained dogmas "offensive to Catholic ears."[46]

Baltimore, for a variety of compelling reasons, wanted to avoid a direct confrontation with the priests. First, he did not want this disagreement to become public. Such notoriety might further damage his efforts to attract colonists. Having invested his depleted fortune in the enterprise, getting people to the colony remained his highest priority. Second, he needed the priests in order to satisfy the spiritual needs of the Catholics already there, to attract new Catholic colonists, and to pacify the natives. Third, he did not have replacements readily available. Fourth, he was in many ways beholden to the Society. Father Copley tersely, but correctly, reminded him that in the peopling and planting of Maryland, no one had contributed more than the Jesuits, and he thought it unlikely that anyone would do as much in the future. Finally, the priests enjoyed the support of influential members of the fledgling community, and Baltimore could not forfeit their support. Thomas Cornwallis, one of the original councillors and now one of the colony's most prominent inhabitants, beseeched Baltimore to acknowledge the privileges of the Catholic Church, "which is the only true Guide toe all Eternal Happiness." He urged that he reconcile the differences between Church and government as quickly as possible. Baltimore negotiated with the Society in England, but the matter dragged on for years before he achieved final resolution.[47]

During the summer of 1638, he opened negotiations with the English provincial Father Henry More, who favored reaching an understanding. The proprietor also ordered his brother not to patent any land for the priests until he achieved a settlement with the Society. After reaching the accord, Baltimore sent a sharp rebuke to Maryland, censuring both the governor and the secretary for the errors committed against the Jesuits. Since Baltimore's letters of July 30 and August 2 no longer exist, the exact nature of the settlement he thought he had worked out with Father More and the nature of the rebuke to his officers in Maryland remain unknown. Lewger, writing to the proprietor on behalf of the governor and himself, protested that they knew not what errors they had committed against the priests. The repudiation stung more since both thought they had implemented the proprietor's will. Lewger denied any evil intentions against the Jesuits. In this same letter, Lewger informed Baltimore that he had spoken with Father Poulton, Copley's successor. To Lewger's amazement, Poulton disclaimed any knowledge of the instructions and directions from the provincial for future behavior by priests in Maryland. He desired "a note of what was written concerning them that they might conforme themselves to it in all points so far as in conscience they might." Poulton, however, refused to believe that the provincial would concede that a Catholic "magistrate may in discretion proceed here, as well affected magistrates in like cases doe in England." Whatever the understanding was between the leader of the colony and the leader of the Society, it did not find a friendly reception in Maryland.[48]

A further blow to any agreement came from the assembly that convened shortly after Lewger wrote his letter. The assembly passed as part of the Ordinance of 1639 an "Act for Church liberties." It seems unlikely that the proprietor included this act in the package of laws sent for approval and which the 1638 assembly rejected. This meant the act originated with the freemen in Maryland. Why did they choose this particular time to champion the liberties of the Church? No direct evidence links Jesuits to the act, but they may have swayed legislators to pass a general statement of protection. The reports the proprietor received convinced him that the Jesuits had actively lobbied lay Marylanders to gain a concession that he would not have granted.[49]

Did the assembly pass a vague and ambiguous act in an attempt to mediate the burgeoning differences between the priests and the government? As adopted, it read, "Holy Churches within this province shall have all her [*sic*] rights liberties and immunities safe whole and inviolable." A similar bill, which stated that the "Holy Church within this Province shall have and enjoy all her Rights liberties and Franchises wholy and without Blemish," passed the next assembly. The cryptic phrasing of the law, allowing variant interpretations, seemed to satisfy all parties but settled nothing.[50]

In practice, and in keeping with Baltimore's intent, the colonial government circumscribed "rights and liberties" to the point where the blanket guarantee meant little. The 1639 assembly enacted at least one piece of legislation directly infringing upon the rights that the Church "hath in other Catholick counryes" when it placed the proving of wills and granting of administrations in the hands of the secretary of the colony. Since Maryland had no ecclesiastical court system to fulfill this function, the action was more pragmatic than philosophical. The 1640 assembly passed "An Act touching Marriages," which closely paralleled Lewger's thinking as expressed in Article II of his "Cases" and restricted the clergy's traditional role. The Jesuits may have gained a few concessions, but they failed to secure the blanket endorsement of their rights that they wanted. Their challenge not only threatened Baltimore's prerogatives and financial well-being; it endangered the very existence of the colony. After 1640 he moved away from reconciliation.[51]

In so doing he clarified his thinking on his and the colony's relationship to the Society. On the issue of acquiring land in Maryland, he remained adamant and recognized no superior, the Catholic Church notwithstanding. When he failed to win support for this position in the assembly, he issued new "Conditions of Plantation" in November 1641. The new conditions consisted of six articles. He ordered the first four, which were similar to the previous conditions but less generous, published in the colony. The remaining articles, directed at the Society, introduced significant changes. The fifth stipulated that no ecclesiastical or temporal body would have the benefit by the preceding conditions "of possessing or enjoying any lands" without "special license first had and obtained for this end under the hand and seal of his Lordship." With the sixth article, the proprietor attempted to introduce the English statute of mortmain to prevent the Church from holding lands in perpetuity.[52]

Seeking recognition of his position, Baltimore prepared a statement consisting of four points that he wanted the English provincial to issue in the Society's name. Had this document been accepted, the Society would have forthrightly recognized Baltimore's authority. The statement stipulated first that the Society would relinquish all claims, direct or indirect, to trade or traffic with the Indians without a special license from Baltimore or his governor. Second, the Society would relinquish any legal right to land in Maryland unless Baltimore granted it. The provincial was to "disavow" all purchases of Indian land not acquired by the Society in a lawful manner. Baltimore's extraordinary third point indicated how far he was willing to go with the clergy. He asserted that the laws of Maryland "doe binde all persons whatsoever as well spiritual as lay." His colony's dependence on the state of England required that it "must be (as neere as may bee)" in conformity with English law. This meant that "in conscience" neither he nor any of his officers (even if they were Roman Catholics) were obliged to allow Maryland priests any greater privileges than the king or his magistrates offered to like persons in England. Furthermore, no ecclesiastical person whatsoever in the province should expect such concessions. He concluded by asserting that he and his officers could proceed against ecclesiastical persons, lands, and goods "for the doeing of right and justice to any other person" or for maintaining and preserving all the rights, prerogatives, and jurisdictions granted to him, just as they could do against the laity, without committing any sin or incurring the censure of Bulla Coenae. The final point concerned "causes testamentarie, probate of wills, granting of letters of administration, &c., and the granting of licenses for marriages," which ecclesiastical courts handled in Catholic countries. Until he established these courts, such cases were to be heard, determined, and punished only by the officers authorized by Baltimore.[53]

Not surprisingly, the Society resisted this bold attempt to define its role in Maryland. "The Fathers of the society," the English provincial wrote, "do purposely withhold from subscribing to what the baron exacts of them, because they consider some of the points quite adverse to ecclesiastical immunity." With negotiations stalled, Baltimore moved unilaterally. He imposed an embargo on Jesuits intending to go to Maryland and took steps to replace the remaining Jesuits in Maryland with secular clergy. One Jesuit sought an intervention to get the embargo lifted. This led to a "bitter falling out" between family members. William Peasley's earnest entreaties failed to move his brother-in-law. Likewise, Ann Peasley found her brother unwilling to relent until the priests agreed to all his conditions. Only Baltimore seemed to have recognized the threat posed by an uncontrolled Catholic clergy to Maryland's survival.[54]

The surreptitious sailing of an English Jesuit in contempt of his prohibition irritated the proprietor. Exasperated by what he considered the Society's devious tactics, by its refusal to acknowledge his authority, and provoked by family pressures for concessions, he vented his anger in a letter to the governor in November 1642. He believed, "upon very good reason," that the priests aimed to destroy him. Then in a statement that Protestants would later employ, he aroused fears about a Jesuit-Indian alliance: if the Jesuits could not maintain a party among the English colonists "to bring their ends about," they would endeavor to do it with the Indians, arming them to go against all who opposed the Society's ends. Circumstances convinced him that the priests had masked their seditious activities under the pretense of "God's honor" and the propagation of "the Christian faith."[55]

The proprietor acted on his understanding of the individual's relationship to the clergy. "If all things that Clergie men should doe upon these pretenses should bee accounted just and to proceed from God," he professed, "Laymen were the basest slaves and the most wretched creatures upon the earth." Should "the greatest saint upon the earth" invade his household against his will with intention of saving the souls of all his family but worked toward his "temporall destruction," he concluded that survival dictated that he must expel "such an enemy." To fill the spiritual void, Baltimore sought other priests who had no intention to do "mischiefe towards mee." The Society, confirming the proprietor's suspicions, used its influence to block his request for permission to send secular priests to the colony.[56]

In founding an English colony in America, the Catholic proprietor did not intend it to be a Catholic refuge that publicly flaunted English laws or that allowed the Jesuits all the privileges and immunities they enjoyed in Catholic countries. When the Jesuits threatened the proprietor's temporal destruction, no matter how much spiritual good they may have done, they had to go. He would tolerate no more from "those of the Hill," as he contemptuously referred to the Jesuits, whose actions were of "dangerous consequences" to him and to his colony. Baltimore chided his brother for his misguided loyalty to the Jesuits. You would, he wrote, have no reason to love them very much "if you knew as much as I doe concerning their speeches and actions here [in England] towards you." By the time he wrote his brother, Baltimore had resolved in his own mind the efficacy of Copley's 1638 threat of excommunication. Baltimore demanded that his brother remain strong. Excommunication would be no more than an inconvenience. The proprietor stated his position without ambiguity: if Leonard did not act accordingly, he betrayed his brother.[57]

Acting as Baltimore's agent, George Gage sought permission for secular priests to travel to Maryland. The opposition that he encountered he attributed to the unethical and unfair tactics employed by the Jesuits. The Society opposed both the secular clergy and the temporal lord in order to maintain their absolute rule and power in the colony. In attempting to supplant the Jesuits, the proprietor followed an accepted practice of English gentry Catholics, to pick and choose their own priests, a policy the Jesuits in England championed. Ironically, Cecil found himself in the same position his father had been in in 1627: he needed priests willing and able to venture to America under the conditions he established. As he too discovered, finding priests who would accept his position on the role of priests and pay their own expenses proved vexing.

Baltimore reached agreement with two or three priests who were "prepared for the journey." One of them, Mr. Gilmett, not only filled the spiritual need but offered a major temporal inducement as well. The priest had connections with six or seven families who would emigrate if he did. Jesuit behavior had so agitated Baltimore that he seemed willing, if necessary, to support these secular priests out of his own limited resources. He told his brother to find accommodations for the two priests and the "Boy" who attended Gilmett. He agreed to pay the necessary costs of the priests' stay, but only if their expenses could not be covered in some other manner. However the governor managed the situation, the proprietor hoped that his brother would "husband my expence herein the best you can." Baltimore instructed Father Territt, the other secular priest sent to Maryland, to acquaint the governor with "my mind" and the thinking of diverse pious and learned men whom the proprietor had consulted about the controversy. He expected, based on a number of consultations, that Father Gilmett would reinforce Territt's message to the governor. He did not, however, and Baltimore's gambit to replace the Jesuits with more pliant priests fizzled. The Jesuits in their Annual Letter of 1642 from Maryland reported that the secular priests had failed to support Baltimore's exalted claims.[58]

The confrontation with the Jesuits revealed the tensions that existed for English Catholics. The events of 1632–33, a time of relative tranquility, made Baltimore painfully aware of his handicap as an English Catholic. He knew that the triumph of those who used anti-Catholicism as a pretext placed all Catholic interests in jeopardy. A decade later his religion made him more vulnerable. The proprietor's harsh language and actions reflected his severely limited options. If he overreacted in his feelings toward the Jesuits, it was because he acutely perceived the threat. Whatever his personal feelings, he could not put the interests of the Catholic Church (as defined by the Jesuits) above the interests of his colony. To acquiesce to the Society entailed too great a risk. As an English Catholic heavily invested in founding a successful enterprise, he demonstrated his willingness to do whatever it took, short of abandoning his religion, to protect his colony and see it prosper. He derived small satisfaction when the general of the Society in 1643 ordered the priests not to accept any land offered them, "whether by the faithful or by infidels," without Baltimore's consent. Other crises soon engulfed the colony and pushed the land dispute with the Jesuits to the background.[59]

Baltimore envisioned that his religious policies would ensure for his coreligionists as much security as they had had in England—perhaps, in time, more. His confrontation with the Jesuits deepened his conviction that he had to keep religious forces in check. By the mid-1640s, however, two factors forced him to rethink his position. One was the rapidly changing scene in England. After August 1642, conditions in England worsened as king and Parliament went to war over highly politicized religious issues. The other was the increasing independence of the freemen in Maryland, who used the assembly as their main vehicle of expression. The new circumstance made it imperative that he keep religious tensions in his colony from undermining an already attenuated position at home. How could he protect his coreligionists while at the same time not alienating the radical Protestants who were turning the world upside down?

The outbreak of hostilities between king and Parliament created special problems. Court Catholics especially supported the royal prerogative. A few years before, in 1639, Arundell had petitioned for the continuance of the king's favorable treatment of "the nobility of the Roman Catholic religion." Baltimore, like his father-in-law, depended on the king's beneficence to survive. However, only in those areas where the king's men dominated, and only when Catholics lent their weight to the king's cause, could they expect favorable treatment. The proprietor, an adroit politician bent on saving his province from external and internal threats, faced the Rubicon: should he cling to his traditional base of support, the monarchy, or should he sound out the opposition? To survive, he had to have the support of whichever side grasped political power in England.[60]

As the crisis mounted, Baltimore again explored the possibility of emigrating. Relocating would allow him to assume control of his colony at a critical juncture. This time his in-laws intervened. His brother-in-law, William, sought from the House of Lords a writ *ne exeat regia* to prevent Baltimore's departure. He wanted his brother-in-law to satisfy the family in court as to the manner in which he took possession of Semley Manor and other property. Two days later, Baltimore petitioned to have the writ stayed until he presented his case to the House of Lords. He also attached an affidavit that he had no intention of *suddenly* leaving the kingdom.[61]

Civil war in England accentuated the unsettled conditions along the Chesapeake and quickly sucked Maryland into the vortex of civil confusion. In April 1643, Governor Calvert left for England, where he learned that his brother remained committed to the royalist cause. After an extended stay, he returned to Maryland in September 1644, bearing a commission from the king, who directed him to go to Virginia and, with the aid of Governor William Berkeley, seize all ships and property of all who were in "actual rebellion." Baltimore expected to profit from his loyalty to the king. The commission stipulated that half of the revenues from such seizures should go to the proprietor. The Calverts never profited from the commission, but it did provide ammunition to their enemies.[62]

About the time Governor Calvert received his commission, a confrontation directly related to events in England began to unfold in the colony. On January 18, 1643/44, the provincial court issued a warrant for the arrest of Richard Ingle "upon high treason." Captain Ingle, a tobacco trader who had conducted business in the Chesapeake region since about 1632, made the mistake of speaking against the king when he visited Maryland in 1642. The acting governor ordered Ingle arrested for saying that Charles I was no king. The decision to try him for high treason came to naught when Ingle escaped and returned to England. Events in England and America clearly identified the Calverts as royalists.[63]

In supporting the king, the Marylanders gained an implacable enemy who wanted revenge. On August 26, 1644, Commons authorized eight vessels trading with Virginia "liberty to transport ammunition, cloaths, and victual, custom free." One of the vessels was Ingle's ship, the *Reformation*. Having taken the covenant to support those opposed to the king, Ingle sailed under letters of marque from Parliament to Maryland. His invasion again demonstrated the colony's vulnerability on matters of religious and political loyalty. In the words of Jesuit Henry More, the English provincial, some "enterprising heretics, thinking to gratify the Parliament, invaded the colony of the Catholics." The attack by "that ungrateful Villaine Richard Ingle" in 1644 came very close to destroying Baltimore's little colony.[64]

The knowledge that Governor Calvert had a commission from the king "to execute a Tyrannical power against the Protestants" or any one else who adhered to Parliament spurred Ingle to action. He ventured his life and fortune by landing his men in an effort to assist "the said well affected Protestants" against those he called the tyrannical governor, the Papists, and their malignant adherents. Ingle recounted several encounters he had had with them and concluded that "it pleased God" to enable him to seize a number of locations in the colony. Indeed, he routed the governor, who fled to Virginia, leaving Ingle in control of the province.[65]

This period, later known as "the plundering time," inflicted pain and loss on the Catholics. Some "Credible persons" later informed Baltimore that only one Roman Catholic took the rebel's oath against him. Ingle's men pillaged, burned houses, killed cattle, and destroyed or stole the personal property of prominent Catholics, including Thomas Gerard, the Brents, Cornwallis, and Lewger. They struck especially hard at the Jesuits, who collectively owned the most substantial estate in Maryland. Copley claimed that Ingle destroyed or stole property valued at eighteen hundred pounds. That priest, who described himself as "a sober honest and peaceable man not given to contention or sedition nor any way opposing or in hostility to the King and Parliament," fell victim, as did his colleague, the ancient priest Andrew White. Ingle took a number of Catholic prisoners and transported them to England, where he justified his behavior by claiming that the people of Maryland were "Papists and of the Popish and Romish Religion" and that most of them had assisted the governor in putting his commission from the king in force. He claimed that only Papists held office and that it was generally held in Maryland that if he had not come, the Papists would have disarmed the Protestants. Finally, he rationalized his seizure of property by stating that all that he took or destroyed had belonged to Catholics.[66]

Ingle, who carried his malevolence to London, spearheaded an assault on Baltimore's charter. Ingle probably brought a petition from "diverse Inhabitants" of Maryland. It listed the grievances against the "Tyranicall Government of that Province ever since its first setling, by Recusants; whoe have seduced, & forced many of his Majesty subjects, from their Religion." Among other things, the petitioners objected to the governor's commission from the king and the tendering of an oath by Maryland officials against Parliament. They further recommended that both houses do "a very good service" and settle the plantation and government in Protestant hands. The Committee of Lords and Commons for Foreign Plantations, the recipient of the petition, judged the governor and the deputy governor unfit "to be longer continued in the said charge." It also determined that the proprietor had broken the trust reposed in him by the charter. A month later, the committee received orders to write an ordinance to settle "the Plantation of Maryland under the Command of Protestants."[67]

A number of other hostile petitions to the House of Lords further undermined Baltimore's credibility. A petition read on April 25, 1646, referred to Baltimore's poisoned purposes and the designs of his papist inhabitants to plant their superstition between New England and Virginia and to rob, murder, and destroy whoever opposed them. Seven months later, a member of the Committee of Lords and Commons for Foreign Plantations presented an ordinance that closely followed the wording of the petition from "diverse Inhabitants" of Maryland to the Lords. It charged that Baltimore "hath wickedly" broken the trust of the English government and instructed the committee to appoint an able governor and other Protestant officers who were "well affected" to Commons.[68]

These actions put the Maryland charter in jeopardy. On February 26,

1646/47, the Lords ordered Baltimore's case to be heard a fortnight later and assigned two members "to be counsel with the state and the merchants, against the Lord Baltimore." On March 4 the proprietor responded to the ordinance for repealing his patent with his own petition. He tried to buy time by noting that he knew neither the particulars of the charges leveled against him nor the names of those who accused him. He stated that he expected some ships to arrive from his province between March and June with "some persons" whose testimony he needed for his defense. He asked the Lords to present him with written charges so that he could prepare his defense in a transaction that so "dearly concernes his inheritance." That same day eighteen merchants from London who traded in Virginia and other English Plantations petitioned to have the ordinance passed. Their attack centered on the proprietor's religion and his royalist leanings. They asserted that not only did Baltimore and his agents commit horrible acts in the colony but they also operated "as papists and enemies" under the king's commission to seize the estates of those loyal to Parliament. The Lords, perhaps in response to the vague nature of the petition, ordered the merchants to bring in their charge against Baltimore in writing.[69]

Baltimore's delaying tactics worked. The threatening ordinance dropped from view. The news he received from his colony also boded well for the future. Near the end of 1646 his brother returned to the province with a force of Maryland refugees and Virginia volunteers. He reestablished proprietary authority and instituted policies to bring reconciliation to the fragile society that Ingle's attack had nearly destroyed. Within a remarkably short time after he reasserted proprietary authority, dispersed inhabitants returned and new immigrants began to arrive. The proprietor had weathered another storm, but the near loss of the charter unnerved him. He initiated new policies designed to keep his bold experiment from destruction.

Faced with increasingly chaotic conditions at home and in his colony, Baltimore sought to counter Ingle's influence with Parliament and to restore some stability to his decimated colony. Moving boldly in 1648, he initiated a coup d'état that cast out all but the head of state. One effect of the confrontation with the Jesuits was a loss of confidence in his brother's ability to follow his commands. Another was the recognition that he could not necessarily rely on the Catholic gentlemen, his liege lords. Even his friend Lewger seemed to fall short of the mark the proprietor set for leadership in the colony. Two events presented Baltimore with the opportunity for bold change: the premature death of his brother in June 1647 and Lewger's return to England. Acting in concert with the proprietor's instructions, Leonard, before his death, named Catholic councillor Thomas Greene as governor until his brother acted. Baltimore, in an effort to outmaneuver his adversaries in Parliament, fostered a revolution in his own government. On August 17, 1648, he named William Stone, a Protestant with close ties to Parliament, as Greene's successor. He followed this appointment with others that put Protestants in most of the important colonial offices. These appointments dramatically altered the nature of the proprietary government. As one of his critics later put it, "His Country, till he employed Captain Stone, never had but Papist Governours and Counsellors." Now Protestants dominated his government. Baltimore gambled his success and the colony's future on these Protestants' loyalty to him as the Catholic proprietor.[70]

Baltimore acted for two primary reasons. With charges before the Committee of the Admiralty, he undermined Ingle's contention that only Catholics held important offices in Maryland. Stone strengthened his hand in any subsequent negotiations concerning the repeal of his charter. Equally important, Stone, as his commission noted, undertook "in some short time" to recruit five hundred people who were willing to reside in the province. Unable to attract Catholic landowners in any significant numbers, and faced with a dwindling but still religiously pluralistic population, Baltimore sought to stabilize the colony with new leadership and an infusion of new immigrants. He also made a final effort to get the Society of Jesus to recognize his charter rights and to acknowledge the restrictions English law imposed on the priests.[71]

These newcomers would help the proprietor solve his persistent challenge: to put rent-paying farmers on his land. When efforts to attract inhabitants from England and Ireland collapsed, he turned his attention to other English colonies. In 1643 he recruited in New England, a place described by the Jesuits a year earlier as "full of Puritan Calvinists, the most bigoted of the sect." Undaunted by such prejudices, he commissioned Cuthbert Fenwick to journey to New England in search of prospective tobacco farmers. Fenwick carried a letter and a commission to Captain Edward Gibbons of Boston. Massachusetts governor John Winthrop recorded that Baltimore offered land in Maryland "to any of ours that would transport themselves thither, with free liberty of religion, and all other privileges which the place afforded, paying such annual rent as should be agreed upon." To Winthrop's obvious relief, "our captain had no mind to further desire herein, nor had any of our people temptation that way." This initiative demonstrated Baltimore's confidence in his vision and his desperate need for planters. He even recruited among those most likely to possess strong anti-Catholic sentiments.[72]

Undaunted, the proprietor again looked to Virginia as a possible solution for his problems. Unlike Maryland, which welcomed all potential rent-paying comers of whatever persuasion, Virginia did not. The Virginia assembly passed a law against dissenters in 1639, "though as yet none" lived there. Within three years, however, the nonconformists created a congregation and appealed to New England for clergymen. In 1642 the new governor, Sir William Berkeley, executed his instructions "to be careful that Almighty God is served according to the form established in the Church of England." Under his leadership the assembly required the conformity of all ministers to the "orders and constitutions" of the Church of England. In the next year, the assembly ordered nonconformists "to depart the Colony." In 1648 Berkeley again raised a "persecution against them" and dispersed the congregation at Nansemond. Virginia's intolerance made Maryland's invitation welcome. With the potential to prosper with no impositions on their practice of religion, many of Virginia's nonconformists sought refuge in Maryland. As one of the emigrants put it, "In the year 1649, many, both of the congregated Church, and other well affected people [i.e., supporters of Parliament] in Virginia, being debarred from the free exercise of Religion under the Government of Sir William Berkeley removed themselves, Families and Estates into the Province of Maryland." They accepted Stone's invitation, which promised them freedom to worship and the privileges of English subjects.[73]

Why did Baltimore entrust his government to Protestants and seek recruits among iconoclastic Virginia Independents who were hostile to his religion? He took the risk because he had no other alternative. Beyond the obvious, two other factors must be emphasized. First, these apparently radical departures were consistent with his original vision. He imagined that his policy of religious freedom and the lure of rich lands would overcome traditional religious antagonisms. He would work with whatever group best served his interests. Despite setback after setback, he remained confident that he could devise policies to maximize his chances of success.

Second, his maneuvers coincided with developments in England. Contrary to what might have been anticipated, given the anti-Catholic rhetoric that united them, the ascension of radical Protestants to power in the mid-1640s did not prove detrimental to Catholics. English Catholics succeeded in maintaining, even apparently increasing, their Church alongside the national one. More important, as the proprietor struggled to formulate and implement his radical changes, English Catholics sought permission from Rome to negotiate with the Parliamentary Army for toleration. Baltimore did not participate in these discussions, but he must have been aware of them. The 1647 negotiations between English Jesuits and the army came down to an argument over an oath of allegiance, something in which the proprietor had a keen interest. These talks eventually collapsed, largely because of divisions between Catholics, and showed once again "how difficult it was to unite the Catholic minority on any point." From Baltimore's perspective, these exchanges showed that toleration had gained a new respectability. In his mind, they must have validated his long and laborious struggle to establish a pluralistic society based on religious liberty.[74]

The changes implemented by the proprietor created new problems. How was he to protect his coreligionists in the exercise of their religion without jeopardizing his relationship with Parliament or antagonizing his new recruits from Virginia? With political leadership in the hands of Catholics and family members, Catholics had been relatively free to practice their religion. No urgent need for formal legislation existed. Now, in response to the new circumstances that emerged after 1645, Baltimore jettisoned his previous policy of trying to remove religion from the public arena through informal means. He now adopted a public policy that entailed oaths for his officers and legislation. He launched a two-pronged strategy designed to formalize the guarantees of religious freedom that he had sought from the beginning.

Baltimore first moved to secure safeguards for Maryland Catholics through a series of oaths to be administered to all of his principal officeholders, most of whom were now Protestant. The proprietor placed considerable confidence in the utility of oaths. In 1635 and 1636 he drew up and revised an oath of allegiance that allowed Catholics to attest their loyalty to the king. His oath, taken "upon the faith of a Christian," undoubtedly served as the basis of "An Act for swearing allegiance to our Soveraingn Lord King Charles," which the 1639 assembly passed.[75] Before that date, he required oaths from his councillors, sheriffs, and judges, as well as an oath of fealty to him as proprietor. He compelled his brother to take an oath "for the Equal Administration of Justice." The new oaths prescribed in 1648 demonstrated his intent to protect religious freedom in Maryland. The governor, for example, had to swear not to trouble, molest, or discountenance any person professing to believe in Jesus Christ and in particular no Roman Catholic for or in respect of his or her religion nor in his or her free exercise thereof, as long as the person remained faithful to the proprietor and did not disturb or conspire against his government.[76] Equally important, the governor attested that he would not discriminate in conferring offices, rewards, or favors on the basis of religion, but would confer them on inhabitants found "faithful and well deserving of his said Lordship." The governor pledged to use his "Power and Authority" to protect Christians in the free exercise of their religion from molestation (without Baltimore's "consent or Privity") by any other officer or person in the province. The proprietor required a similar oath from members of the new council and the proprietary secretary. These oaths, by which he hoped to control his major appointive official, followed the basic policy that he had articulated in his 1633 "Instructions." His government would neither interfere with the free exercise of religion on the part of Christian Marylanders, nor would it discriminate on account of religious affiliation in appointing persons to positions of authority. As long as (Christian) Marylanders demonstrated their fidelity, his government would protect their right to worship as they chose.[77]

With his major appointive officers under control, and in advance of the Virginia migration, the proprietor turned his attention to the remainder of the inhabitants. His solution to the potential for calamitous religious wrangling in his increasingly pluralistic society was a law. "An Act Concerning Religion" recognized that the proprietor could no longer rely on the efficacy of his original informal instructions. The assembly, which was to convene on April 2, 1649, only needed to accept his wisdom.[78]

More than ever, the proprietor wanted to unite the now increasingly diverse people of Maryland in their affection and fidelity to him while avoiding anything that tended toward factionalism. He strove for unanimous and cheerful obedience to the civil government. "As wee are all members of one Body Politique of that Province," he advocated, "wee may have also one minde in all Civill and temporall matters." Herein lies the novelty of the "Maryland designe." Nothing was said about uniting all Marylanders in religion. What was important was loyalty to the head of the civil government, not to a religious doctrine. Baltimore had designed the Act concerning Religion to avoid discord and harmony, to achieve concord and union. To the extent that it was humanly possible, he intended to remove religious concerns from politics.[79]

Religious issues did not stand separate from other issues that Marylanders deemed important. One issue that concerned the freemen of the colony was their right to initiate legislation. The 1638 assembly had forced Baltimore to concede that right. Now buoyed with the colony's prospects, the proprietor complicated matters by returning to a practice he had abandoned in 1638. He submitted a body of sixteen laws "written in three Sheets of Parchment" to the 1649 assembly, the first under a Protestant governor. He wanted the whole body to be passed without alteration and raised again the issue of the assembly's right to initiate legislation. The freemen balked at the proprietor's code, which would have replaced all existing laws for the colony. They argued and debated and finally wrote their own version of the bill. Then, having made their point, they juxtaposed their bill and some of the proprietor's as part of the code of twelve laws that they passed.[80]

Although modified by the assembly, this Act concerning Religion formed the foundation of Baltimore's modified "Maryland designe." It assumed that place, however, only by default. For one thing, the act tacitly conceded that the attempt to implement the manorial system as a means of keeping religion private was not working. For another, the act responded to heightened religious tensions in both England and America. Baltimore not only wished to neutralize Parliament; he wanted also to assure the well-being of the Catholics who ventured to his colony. The proprietor reacted to the growing anti-Catholic sentiments openly expressed before and after Ingle's intervention. One Marylander complained in 1644 that another had slandered him by quoting him "that he hoped there would be nere a Papist left in maryland by may day." An ardent supporter of Parliament reportedly told another supporter that "concerning the government now established that hee hoped within a while to see a confusion of all Papistry here." One resident testified to seeing another go into Giles Brent's loft and throw down his books, saying "Burne them Papists Devills, or words to that effect." The will of Thomas Allen, a poor Protestant, exemplified the fear and distrust evident in the society. Although he left his children with little in the way of estate, he stated that he did not want his children to live with any Papist. Whether based on fear or cupidity, the rising anti-Catholic sentiment could not be ignored. The anticipated arrival of Virginia Protestants needed to be considered as well. Baltimore intended to cushion their arrival with a law controlling public discourse on religion.[81]

A dearth of legislative records for 1649 makes it impossible to determine precisely who added what to the mix. The hybrid legislative Act concerning Religion reflected the concerns of the freemen, who also saw the need to deal more formally with religious differences. In an effort to secure peace within the religiously polarized community, the legislation imposed severe penalties for fomenting religious disputes. Any person under the authority of the "absolute Lord and Proprietary of this Province" who would "blaspheme God," or deny Jesus Christ to be the Son of God, or deny the Holy Trinity, or utter reproachful speeches against the Holy Trinity" risked death and forfeiture of all lands and goods to Lord Baltimore.[82]

In a similar vein, the law subjected any person who used or uttered any reproachful "words or Speeches concerning the blessed Virgin Mary the Mother of our Saviour or the holy apostles or Evangelists" to fines and whippings and, for a third offense, banishment. The act provided similar penalties for reproachfully calling any person a "heretic, schismatic, idolater, Puritan, Independent, Presbyterian, Popish Priest, Jesuit, Jesuited Papist, Lutheran, Calvinist, Anabapist, Brownist, Antinomian, Barrowist, Roundhead, Separatist," or any other disparaging epithet relating to religion.[83]

In addition, the act punished those who profaned "the Sabbath or Lords day called Sunday by frequent swearing, drunkennes or by any uncivill or disorderly recreation, or by working . . . when absolute necessity doth not require it." Baltimore, who may have already been negotiating with Robert Brooke, "a well-to-do English Puritan" who intended "to transport himself his wife eight sons and family and a Great Number of other Persons" to Maryland, might have seen such a provision as a way to induce further migration of radical Protestants from England. More likely, assembly members saw it a means to encourage the anticipated immigrants from Virginia.[84]

The act concluded on a more generous note. Because forcing the conscience in matters of religion frequently led to dangerous consequences, and in order to procure a more quiet and peaceable government in Maryland, and to preserve mutual love and amity among the inhabitants, the act proclaimed that no one "professing to believe in Jesus Christ, shall from henceforth bee any waies troubled, Molested or discountenanced for or in respect of his or her religion nor in the free exercise thereof." In Maryland, in contrast with other English colonies, no person was in any way to be compelled to believe in or exercise any "Religion against his or her consent." The only condition imposed on this freedom was that the residents remain faithful to the proprietor and not engage in hostile actions against the government.[85]

This part of the act represented a major breakthrough in contemporary thinking about the relationship between religious and political institutions. For the first time in the English world, a legislative enactment guaranteed to all Christians the right to worship without molestation from secular authorities.

Events before 1648 had demonstrated that not even in the free air of the New World could Englishmen put aside their religious differences. Maintaining religious freedom became yet more problematic in the turbulent English world of the 1650s.[86]

The miscreants who rejected Baltimore's generous offer of religious liberty were the nonconforming Virginians. Baltimore's officers quickly moved to apply the new policy to them. That policy entailed mutual obligations that fostered the interests of both parties. The Virginians received liberty of religion and conscience in return for political obedience to the proprietary government. They received land on the same terms given others in return for a yearly rent and subscription to an oath of fidelity to the proprietor. Finally, Baltimore's officials erected a new county (Anne Arundel) to encompass the Virginia Independents and allowed them to choose their own officers and to hold their own courts. If a 1650 document signed by the leading Protestants, including elder William Durand, meant anything, the proprietary government fulfilled the bargain. An incident involving Walter Pakes, who accused the Protestant secretary Hatton of speaking evil about "Roman Catholickes," indicated that the proprietor avoided trouble at all cost. He absolved his secretary of any wrongdoing, once again supporting a Protestant against a Catholic. Another case involving Hatton further demonstrated that Protestants could use the courts to protect their own. Hatton's niece, Elinor Hatton, served in the household of Luke Gardiner, a Catholic. Concerned with Gardiner's attempts to convert her to Catholicism, her mother and her uncle had demanded Elinor's return, but Gardiner had refused. The court issued warrants for the arrest of both Elinor and Gardiner on the basis that "insufferable" acts impugned the government, injured the girl's mother and uncle, and had dangerous and destructive consequences for the peace and welfare of the province. From Baltimore's perspective, he had taken the necessary steps to balance contentious religious commitments at this tense time.[87]

These extraordinary measures, however, proved insufficient to ensure the civil peace Baltimore so much needed for his colony to prosper. Once more outside forces intervened to disrupt the colony. In 1651 Parliament, which had defeated and executed Charles I in the Civil War, dispatched a commission to reduce Virginia to obedience to the Puritan commonwealth. After accomplishing their mission in Virginia, the commissioners, interpreting their instructions broadly, decided to force obedience in Maryland also. Between 1652 and 1655, intermittent war raged between the commissioners and their supporters, mainly the recently arrived Independents from Virginia, on one hand and Governor Stone and Calvert loyalists, on the other. When Governor Stone capitulated in 1655 and submitted to the presumed authority of the commissioners, the proprietor again lost his province without benefit of legal proceedings.[88]

Having gained control of Baltimore's province, the Independents set about to undo his innovative and radical religious policy. The "Act concerning Religion" of 1654, passed in an assembly that excluded all inhabitants who had supported the proprietor or who were Roman Catholic, stands in marked contrast to Baltimore's 1649 act. Considerably shorter than its predecessor, the 1654 act differed in two significant ways. It dropped the extreme provisions against blasphemy and name-calling, and it excluded Roman Catholics, Episcopal Protestants, and those who "practice licentiousness" from the protections assured to others. For the first time, Maryland authorities denied some Christians equal opportunity to pursue their economic, political, and religious rights on account of religion. Lord Baltimore had not used religion as a basis for excluding persons of a particular faith from the full enjoyment of those privileges.[89]

Acting within the context of the anti-Catholicism of their times and sensing that Lord Baltimore's defense of religious freedom reflected his weakness within the English Protestant world, the Independents disregarded their promises of fidelity and unseated the proprietor. At this point, the Virginia nonconformists, supported by the commissioners and religiously in accord with the dominant elements in Parliament, acted from what they thought was a position of strength. They instigated a rebellion that temporarily brought an end to Baltimore's liberal proprietary rule. Their Act concerning Religion marked a significant step backward in the quest for religious liberty.

The events of the first two decades of Baltimore's proprietorship might have driven a lesser man to despair. He had expended his meager inheritance launching a risky enterprise, only to be greeted by various challenges to his authority. Some flowed from an innate desire of the English to protect their property and interests through a legislative body that acted independently of the executive. It is likely, though, that these challenges had religious overtones, which, in one way or another, jeopardized proprietary economic interests. Each challenger failed to recognize Baltimore's lofty goals and sought to secure its interest at the expense of the proprietor's vision of a prospering pluralistic society. He met the Jesuit challenge, but not without damaging relations with family in England and his coreligionists in Maryland. Under the guise of religion but for economic gain, Ingle came close to destroying the colony. The Virginia Independents, who had accepted Baltimore's invitation only to find that they could not accept his authority and his demands for allegiance, proved to be the most serious threat. In response to multiple attacks against his charter and his economic and political rights, the proprietor tried to take the requisite steps to offset danger. The triumph of radical Protestants in England made his situation ever more precarious. The Virginia Independents, allied with the parliamentary commissioners, deposed him by force of arms. Governor Stone's inability to secure a military victory led these unappreciative Protestants to believe they had defeated the papist proprietor. The fate of the "Maryland designe" came down to a contest between a radical Catholic proprietor and the radical Protestants in his colony, aided by those who had defeated, tried, and executed his benefactor, Charles I. In the face of the transatlantic alliance between zealous Protestants, Baltimore's chances to recover his colony seemed remote.

CHAPTER EIGHT

"The People there cannot subsist & continue in peace and safety without som good Government"

A Second Testing of Religious Freedom (1653–1676)

The 1649 Act concerning Religion failed to achieve the stable body politic that Lord Baltimore desperately desired. His troubles accelerated rapidly at home and in America after its passage. In England, as an open Catholic, he now incurred the financial penalties imposed on Catholics by the new radical Protestant authorities. The government forced him to compound, that is, to pay hefty fines, to keep his estates. Lawsuits from family members that challenged his use of lands he had acquired from his father-in-law lingered into the 1650s. Having recently become a widower, he had sole responsibility for his young son Charles. In the early 1650s, Baltimore engaged in a protracted legal struggle with Sir David Kirke and his family, who, he charged, had illegally acquired his interests in Avalon. In Maryland, his opponents seemed poised to strip him of his rights and his lands. Virginians Richard Bennett and William Claiborne, the parliamentary commissioners who had long harbored grievances against him, justified seizing control of his colony under a spurious reading of their instructions from the English government. Radical Protestants—Independents or congregationalists—from Virginia accepted the proprietor's generous terms to relocate in Maryland but failed to patent their land, to honor their financial obligations to him, and to swear fealty to him. His officials proved incapable of sustaining his authority as the Virginia émigrés, who now constituted about half of the colony's population, seized power and ruled in the name of Parliament or the lord protector of England.[1]

His responses to the many crises of the 1650s indicated that Baltimore had no intention of quitting. Too much time, money, and even blood had been expended. He persisted in his Catholicism and in his belief that he could succeed and prosper as an English Catholic colonizer. The deposed proprietor spent little time pondering whether his noble experiment had come to a troublesome end. Rather, he fought for the restoration of his charter rights.

His decision to remain in England forced Baltimore to fight on two fronts. He developed a two-pronged strategy, conducting both parts simultaneously, to regain control of Maryland. In the colony, he pursued an aggressive policy. He displayed considerable impatience in dealing with Bennett and Claiborne and urged his officials to do their duty and reestablish his authority by whatever means were available. A negotiated settlement with the men who had "reduced" the colony amounted to an abnegation of his charter rights. In England, he lobbied the new government(s) to regain control. Here, he more than met the challenges his opponents posed. In his colony, however, he encountered disaster after disaster in his attempts to establish his authority. His impatience, a lack of timely news from the colony, and his inability to find the right men to implement his orders offset his skills at orchestrating a solution in the English political arena.

Restoration of the Calverts' charter rights in Maryland certainly was not a foregone conclusion. Cecil had no trusted friends on the Council of State, and ultimately he had to deal with Oliver Cromwell, a man whose reputation for anti-Catholicism was hardly comforting. Still, while the personalities had changed, the basic structures of English politics remained in place. He had to make a compelling case and find influential individuals to argue it for him. A number of factors strengthened his ability to negotiate with the English government. The occupation of his colony by the parliamentary commissioners remained controversial. The absence of legal proceedings against his charter bolstered his claim. In addition, he seemed better equipped than the commissioners to bring some degree of stability to the North Atlantic empire, a major objective of Cromwell's government. He had support from prominent Protestants who had influence with Cromwell. Finally, Cromwell's conflicted but pragmatic approach to dealing with individual English Catholics aided Baltimore's chances.[2]

The Catholic proprietor advanced his cause cautiously. As an Irish land-owner, Baltimore knew that Cromwell had exhibited virulent anti-Catholicism during the conquest of that land in 1649–50. As an English Catholic, he knew the Instrument of Government, the legal basis for Cromwell's assumption of power in 1653, excluded Catholics from political or religious freedom. The Instrument banned all Roman Catholics from voting in parliamentary elections, excluded them from service in that body, and denied them (and prelates) the freedom to worship that it extended to other Christians. Cromwell had expressed his hostility toward Catholicism on numerous occasions. He found the Roman Catholic religion repugnant and distrusted anything in the Protestant Church that resembled the customs or beliefs of the Catholic Church. Some four years before assuming all power, Cromwell expressed his view: "For that which you mention concerning liberty of conscience, I meddle not with any man's conscience. But if by liberty of conscience you mean the liberty to exercise the Mass, I judge it best to use plain dealing, and to let you know where the Parliament of England have power, that you will not be allowed of it." The lord protector also pursued a stridently anti-Catholic foreign policy.[3]

Baltimore's Catholicism identified him with a religion that English Protestants still found inimical to their national image. The commissioners assumed that the liberating elements of the English Civil Wars and the interregnum had done little to change attitudes regarding English Catholics; and for the most part, they were not wrong. Legal and psychological impositions remained in place, and occasional calls to tighten the restrictions on Catholics surfaced.

Anti-Catholic posturing did not close every door for a skillful politician, however. Baltimore sensed that he might find that Cromwell, like his Stuart predecessors, needed to appease Catholics who did not threaten his rule. Like Baltimore, Cromwell had to accommodate subjects of diverse religious commitments in an age of shattered uniformity. His actions toward his Catholic subjects stemmed less from anti-Catholicism than from political prudence and a commitment to liberty of conscience. Liberty in terms of religious thought was fundamental to Cromwell. A fellow radical quoted Cromwell's theoretical position: "he had rather that Mahumetanism [Mohammedanism] were permitted amongst us, than one of Gods Children should be persecuted." Cromwell believed that he imposed on men's consciences far less than Parliament did and that he had plucked many from "the raging fire of persecution." At one point he even stated optimistically that he intended to remove the impediments for Catholics "as soon as I can." Parliament's repeal of the Act of Uniformity in

1650 marked a significant break with the past and brought the English closer to Baltimore's position.[4]

But in the final analysis, Baltimore's feelings about the lord protector mattered little. The displaced proprietor had no option but to negotiate with Cromwell's government. To secure restoration, Baltimore had to assume that there would be some continuity. He accepted the onerous penal laws, whether under the Stuarts, Parliament, or the lord protector, as a given. His challenge was the same in each case: find ways to circumvent them.

Cromwell's pragmatic attitude frustrated the commonwealth commissioners and their supporters, who focused on the proprietor's religion and employed vicious anti-Catholic sentiments to attack him. The antiproprietary pamphleteers and petitioners mixed truth with distortions and falsehoods in their effort to justify their actions and to rid the Chesapeake region of an undesirable Catholic element. They sought to rile long-standing fears of political absolutism and religious intolerance usually identified with international Catholicism. The author of *Virginia and Maryland, or the Lord Baltimore's Printed Case Uncased and Answered*, in reviewing the history of the colony, made a number of false statements about it: The English colonists at their first arrival professed "an establishment of the Romish Religion onely" and suppressed "the poor Protestants among them." Other charges twisted the truth: Baltimore, a professed recusant, imposed oaths "to protect chiefly the Roman Catholick Religion," made his colony a "receptacle for Papists, and Priests, and Jesuites," and until he employed Governor Stone, appointed only papist governors and counselors, who were committed "to St. Ignatius, as they call him." The Protestants were "for the most time miserably disturbed in the exercise of their Religion." From subtle practices or hope of preferment, many converted. The author reprinted the oath for councillors and then selectively and incorrectly noted two parts of the 1649 act that bolstered his case against the proprietor. Anyone who called another person an "Idolater, Papish Priest, Jesuite, Jesuited Priest" incurred financial penalties. However, no "Papist shall be troubled for the exercise of his Religion, so as they be faithful to his Lordship." Leonard Strong argued that those of the "congregated church and other well-affected people in Virginia" could not forfeit "the present liberty which God had given to the English Subjects" by submitting to Baltimore's "Arbitrary and Popish Government." Nor could they swear to uphold a government and officers "who are sworn to countenance and uphold Antichrist," that is, the Roman Catholic religion. Captain Roger Heamans, the captain of the *Golden Lion*, whose support made Captain

William Fuller's victory at the battle of the Severn possible, referred to Stone's supporters as a "party of Roman Catholics, malignant and disaffected persons." Bennett and Mathews filled their petitions to English authorities with anti-Catholic invectives or innuendos.[5]

This strategy should have worked, but it did not. Mathews and Bennett vented their annoyance in 1656: "The covenant, laws, and platform [instrument] of government established in England, declare the suppression and extirpation of popery." His highness's oath supported this, but, they added, "the lord Baltimore's government declares and swears the upholding and countenancing" of that religion. They failed to grasp that Cromwell preferred a liberal proprietor of royalist background to the orthodox Puritan commissioners of republican background. At opposite ends of the religious spectrum, and for very different reasons, the Catholic lord proprietor of Maryland and the Puritan lord protector of England shared a commitment to liberty of conscience.[6]

Baltimore defended his actions in his 1653 pamphlet *The Lord Baltemore's Case*. He shrewdly molded his argument around two motives, nationalism and capitalism, with which the English could resonate. First he stressed the imperial importance of his colony. The English government had granted his charter to "prevent the Dutch and Swedes from incroaching any nearer to Virginia." Baltimore then called attention to the costs involved in accomplishing that goal. He asserted that he and his friends had disbursed more than forty thousand pounds, of which at least half was "out of his own purse." He further noted that two of his brothers had died founding the colony. Simply put, he had every right to recoup his expenses and to profit from the enterprise.[7]

The proprietor recapitulated the state of affairs beginning in 1651. He highlighted two plaited points, the illegitimacy of "the Pretended Commission" and the loyalty of his officers. After the commissioners reduced Virginia, they invaded Maryland to reduce it to parliamentary authority. Baltimore emphasized that his government was not in opposition to Parliament. The Council of State in England had recognized his loyalty and ordered Maryland's name struck from the commissioners' instructions. His officers subscribed to the engagement and declared their allegiance to "the Government of the Commonwealth of England in chief under God." Not good enough! The commissioners demanded that all writs and proceedings emanating from his courts be done in the name of the Keepers of the Liberty of England and not in the proprietor's name. When Baltimore's governor and other officers objected to the order, the commissioners removed them from office, seized all government records, and appointed others to manage the government independent of the proprietor until the Council of State acted. This extreme action troubled Baltimore, who saw it as a direct assault on his rights and prerogatives. He argued against the innovation, noting that the act of Parliament changing the form for writs applied only to writs that employed the king's name. He issued writs in his own name, not the king's.[8]

At first glance, then, the Virginia-Maryland controversy seems to be another manifestation of a continuing boundary dispute. It was that—but it was much more. The Maryland charter lay at the heart of the controversy. The Virginians, represented in England by Colonel Samuel Mathews, on August 31, 1652, sought affirmation of their claim to Maryland in the House of Commons. The Virginians wanted a restoration of their ancient boundaries. Sanctioning such a move would obliterate Maryland. Legal arguments aside, Maryland's opponents, led by Bennett and Claiborne, wanted nothing less than the rescindment of the Calvert charter and the end of a Catholic presence along the Chesapeake.[9]

Baltimore countered Mathews with his own petition, cosigned by about twenty prominent "Protestant Adventurers and Planters to and in Maryland" who were well known to many members of Commons. He petitioned for a hearing before the Council of State and the restoration of his officers until the council adjudicated the boundary question. The House referred the matter concerning "the old limits of Virginia" to the Committee of the Navy and instructed it to hear all parties, consider the merits of their claims, and report its findings to the House.[10]

The proprietor delivered a copy of the Maryland patent to the committee and requested that any new charter granted to the Virginians not encompass Maryland. He argued that for the previous twenty years his province had not been part of Virginia. The committee received in writing certain "Exceptions against the Lord Baltimores Patent, and his Proceedings" in Maryland. Baltimore submitted his own written responses, which summarized the complaints made against him and provided the council with his analysis of the controversy. First he refuted the charge that Maryland had illegally infringed on the Virginia patent of 1609. Next he countered his opponents' claims that his people had wronged Claiborne by stripping him of Kent Island. The third objection seemed timely, namely, that Maryland constituted a "hereditary

Monarchy," which was inconsistent with the Commonwealth of England. Finally, he had to confront having given his consent to a 1650 law that referred to the late Charles Stuart as king.[11]

In responding to the third objection, that his patent created a hereditary monarchy, Baltimore revealed some of the thinking that had informed his effort since the inception of his proprietorship. The charter, he argued, created not a monarchy but a county palatine that was subordinate to "the Surpreame Authority of England." He, as the proprietor, owed allegiance and a fifth part of any gold or silver found to the heirs and successors of the late king—in this case Parliament. He drew a parallel between his position and the lords of manors in England, who, he conceded, may well be considered monarchs *within their domain*. Writs for their manor courts did not emanate in the name of the Keepers of the Liberty of England. Tenants took oaths of fealty to the manor lords. Manor lords in England had in varying degrees great royalty and jurisdiction within their manors. Despite the problems that he had encountered with implementation of the manorial system, Baltimore was not willing to abandon the concept. But he willingly altered his approach. For example, after the mid-1650s he increasingly granted patents for manors to Protestants.[12]

In defending the manorial nature of his province, Baltimore noted one significant difference from his English counterparts. He had the power to make laws involving life and estate, grant pardons, and the like, a necessity for any man undertaking a plantation in "so remote and wild a place." The charter, however, commanded that these laws be made with the consent of the freemen in the colony, be reasonable, and not be contrary to the laws of England. He defended his "negative Voyce," his power to veto legislation, as a reasonable method to protect his investment. Without it, "factious people as usually new Plantations consist of" could make laws to strip him of his authority and property.[13]

With regard to his charter, Baltimore deftly brought together nationalism, enterprise, and religion. He reiterated the importance of Maryland for the English nation. It was, he argued, advantageous "to the interest of this Commonwealth" to have an Englishman in possession of this part of that great continent of America rather than Indian kings or foreigners such as the Dutch or Swedes. The patent allowed him and his friends to invest the "greatest part of their fortunes for the honour of this Nation, as well as their own particular advantage."[14]

Baltimore then alluded to a fundamental issue raised by his opponents. He acknowledged that he was a recusant but indicated that he did not see this as a problem. He added, parenthetically, "Lord Baltemore knows of no Lawes here against Recusants which reach to America." Bennett repeatedly emphasized the commissioners' desire "to put the laws of England to execution" in Maryland. He wanted the penal laws passed by the various parliaments to extend to the colonies. Colonial enterprises made sense for English Catholics only if that legislation did not apply to overseas holdings. Here the second Lord Baltimore followed the thinking of his father, who argued that Parliament should not make laws for the colonies. The elder Calvert reasoned that since the king acquired plantations by conquest, they were his to govern. The execution of the king and the subsequent rule, first by Parliament and then by Cromwell, complicated thinking on this issue. In the absence of any resolution of it by various English governments, Cecil continued to act on the assumption that English law did not directly extend to his colony. As long as his laws were not contrary to English laws, he felt he was on safe ground.[15]

Baltimore made the 1649 Act concerning Religion, passed by his religiously diverse assembly, the focal point of his defense. He presented its contested passage in the best light. By the general consent of Maryland Protestants and Catholics, the assembly promised all inhabitants who "profess to believe in Jesus Christ" freedom of conscience and freedom to practice religion as they saw fit. Here he had to tread carefully. Did this act abrogate the penal laws? Bennett and Mathews certainly thought so. In their summary statement submitted three years later, they inveighed against an oath "to defend and maintain the Roman Catholic religion, in the free exercise thereof." No one seemed willing to explore the implications of this charge. In any case, Baltimore argued that this act reflected that the English inhabitants "are so well pleased with the Government constituted there by the said Patent."[16]

The precarious political situation within the English government diminished opportunities for a quick resolution and complicated Baltimore's efforts at rational long-term planning. About all he knew for certain was that the Virginians would not quit the field until every possible means to unseat him had been exhausted. He could only conclude by expressing his hope that Parliament would see the wisdom of his brief and not deprive him and the inhabitants of the colony of "so an important a privilege (which is their inheritance and dearly purchased by them)" by placing them under the jurisdiction of the Virginia government.[17]

Unstable political conditions in England and Maryland continued unabated. In late 1653 and into 1654, power shifted from Parliament to Oliver Cromwell, who assumed control as lord protector of England. The Instrument of Govern-

ment bestowed supreme authority on him and gave him the title of "Lord Protector of the Commonwealth of England, Scotland, Ireland, and the dominions
thereto belonging, for life." As this transition took place, the Council of State
responded to a petition from Mathews. It ordered on December 29, 1653, that
a letter be prepared for the governor and council of the colony to encourage
them and to "establish the present Governor till further order." The council also
created another committee to investigate the conflicting land claims put forth
by the adversaries and report its findings to the protector.[18]

Baltimore did not wait patiently for the English imperial bureaucracy to render a judgment. Instead, he moved to reassert his authority in his colony.
Cromwell's ascension called into question the original parliamentary commission issued to Bennett and others. John Langford argued that Cromwell's dissolution of the Long Parliament in April 1653 terminated the commission. The
absence of any confirming act by the succeeding supreme authority in effect restored Baltimore to his proprietorship. Luke Barber, a recent immigrant to
Maryland who had served in both Cromwell's army and his household, made the
same point later in a letter to the lord protector. He referred to a "partie of men
at a place called Anne-Arundell" who, "pretending a power from your Highness," had taken "the Lord Baltemore's Country from him" in 1654. Meanwhile,
Baltimore's interpretation of these events had encouraged him to act. In late
1653 he took the risk and instructed his governor to resume his authority.[19]

The proprietor dealt first with land and loyalty, two of the three pillars of his
enterprise. The recent émigrés from Virginia had neither taken out patents for
the lands they claimed nor taken the oath of fidelity as his "Conditions of Plantation" required. The first step in his plan was to bring "those of Patuxent and
Severn" under his administration. On February 7, 1654, Stone announced that
the proprietor, "out of his Good affection to them," was giving inhabitants three
months to remedy the situation. They had to appear before his secretary to
patent their land, pay his receiver-general all arrears of rent, pay his lordship's
officers the fees that rightly belonged to them, and take the oath of fidelity. By
not complying, inhabitants forfeited their claims to the lands and gave the governor the right to seize the land for Baltimore's use.[20]

Less than a month later, Stone dealt with another matter of utmost importance to the proprietor. The governor announced that he would issue all writs
in Baltimore's name. Acting on the principles he had set forth in *Baltemore's Case*,
the proprietor was claiming this "privilege" under his patent, which reserved
"sovereign dominion, faith and allegiance" to the commonwealth. In his view,

resuming this practice in no way abridged the obedience he and his officers owed to the commonwealth in chief under God.[21]

Stone directly addressed the issue of allegiance on May 6, 1654. Cromwell, as commander of all commonwealth forces, had been named lord protector. The charter subordinated the proprietary government to that government. Publicly, and "in a solemne manner," Stone called on all inhabitants to submit themselves to Cromwell's government and recognize him as "Soveraign Lord." Baltimore's characterization of Maryland as a manor and the degrees of allegiance that were implied seemed to resolve the problem of serving two absolute superiors. Marylanders owed allegiance to Baltimore as lord of the manor. He owed allegiance to Cromwell as the head of state. From the proprietor's perspective, shifting from Charles I to Oliver Cromwell did not affect how he conducted business in his province. Stone, on Baltimore's orders, made changes on the council to lessen the influence of the Independents.[22]

The Virginians did not publish a response until 1655. *Virginia and Maryland* revealed their frame of mind and the events of the previous year. The author offered a point-by-point refutation of the proprietor's view on allegiance. He asserted that the people of Patuxent and Severn declined to take an oath of fidelity to the proprietor because it was incompatible with their subjection to the Commonwealth of England. Taking the oath placed them in the incongruous position of having to "serve two absolute Superiours." John Hammond shed light on proprietary thinking. He believed that the former Virginians conspired to get Bennett and Claiborne to intervene to ease their pretended sufferings. They picked quarrels with "the Papists" and questioned the oath before "declaring their aversness to all conformity." It was not religion, but "that sweete, that rich, that large Country they aimed at." Whether they acted to deprive Baltimore of "all his interest in that country" or out of genuine religious scruples, the Independents saw no reason to capitulate to Stone's demands.[23]

Bennett and Claiborne, unsure of their own status as parliamentary commissioners, hesitated to intervene further into Maryland's affairs. Nevertheless, Stone charged them with leading some Marylanders "into sedition, and rebellion" against the proprietary government. Acting in compliance with Baltimore's directions, Stone repudiated his previous settlement with the commissioners. When the commissioners did venture to St. Mary's City, they found a tense situation. A heated exchange failed to resolve any issues. The commissioners, with some people from Patuxent and Severn, crossed the Patuxent River and prepared to do battle with Stone. The governor, expecting the imminent arrival of an armed band of Virginians, and at the urging of "those few Papists that were in Maryland," who feared they would be held accountable for the bloodshed, decided that discretion might be the better part of valor. On July 20, 1654, he "condescended to lay down his power lately assumed from Lord Baltemore" and submit ("as he had done once before") to a government appointed by the commissioners.[24]

The parliamentary commissioners named Captain William Fuller, a radical Protestant who may have left Virginia in 1651 because of religious persecution; Richard Preston; William Durand; and seven others as commissioners "for the well Ordering, directing and Governing the affaires of Maryland." They empowered this new council to rule in the name of his highness, the lord protector, and no other. Further, the parliamentary commissioners ordered the council to summon an assembly for October 20, 1654, and expressly prohibited those who bore arms against Parliament or professed the Roman Catholic religion from voting or serving in the assembly. By restricting the political rights of Catholics and adherents of the Church of England, these radical Protestants acted in conformity with the Instrument of Government. The commissioners concluded by ordering Baltimore's secretary to deliver the provincial records to their secretary.[25]

The proprietor's initiative to reassert his authority unilaterally proved premature and costly. He misjudged Stone's ability to seize the moment, and he miscalculated the strength of his supporters and their competence. Most important, he misread the strength of his opponents, who decisively thwarted his plans. They added insult to injury when the October assembly passed the repressive "An Act Concerning Religion" that repudiated the third pillar of his enterprise, freedom of conscience.[26]

Baltimore reacted viscerally to the news of this latest defeat. In January 1655, Governor Stone received fresh news and instructions from England. The author of *Virginia and Maryland* reported that Baltimore rebuked his governor for cowardice and threatened him with removal if he failed to reestablish proprietary authority. Stone gathered his courage, rallied the old council, and mustered the militia. Emotions ran high. According to the hardly impartial Leonard Strong, Stone threatened to hang those to whom the commissioners had entrusted the government of Maryland. The governor first sent Josias Fendall and William Eltonhead, with about twenty militiamen, to capture one of the opposition leaders at Patuxent and to secure the return of the official papers. Soon after, Stone and a force variously estimated to be between two hundred and three hundred marched north to Providence. The Virginia émigrés refused an offer from an advance party to surrender and prepared to defend their holdings.

Stone arrived at the mouth of the Severn River on March 24, only to be soundly defeated the next day in fierce fighting. After suffering heavy casualties, Stone asked for terms. Two days after the battle of the Severn, the victors tried ten proprietary supporters for their opposition to Fuller's regime and executed four of them. The victors also imposed an oath of silence on proprietary supporters to prevent them from writing to the proprietor. Hammond echoed the proprietor's thoughts when he wrote that the Independents had "brought to desolation, one of the happiest Plantations that ever Englishmen set foot in." Bennett and Mathews chided Baltimore for choosing "to adventure his title" this way rather than waiting for the determination of the supreme authority in England.[27]

The Virginia émigrés and their supporters now controlled Maryland. Stone's defeat, and the subsequent execution of some of the proprietary leaders, effectively ended Baltimore's rule. The defeat left him with one alternative. To overcome his opponents, to resume his legitimate charter rights, and to bring relief to the inhabitants of Maryland, who were "in a very sad, distracted, & unsettled condition," he had to resolve the conflict in London. The battle for Maryland now had to be won or lost in England.[28]

Even before he knew the outcome of his actions in Maryland, Baltimore pursued his cause on this second front. To make his case to Cromwell, he emphasized that the Virginians' occupation of his land was de facto, not de jure. The proprietor, and diverse persons of quality, informed the lord protector that Bennett and a force of Virginians had entered his plantation, where they encouraged people to oppose his officers. This gained Cromwell's attention. In January 1655 the lord protector reproached Bennett and his associates. He may have been more aggravated by Bennett's precipitous and unauthorized acts than by the justice of Baltimore's case. The differences between Baltimore and the inhabitants of Virginia regarding their respective boundary claims were "pending before us and our Council, and yet undetermined." Cromwell ordered Bennett and those under his authority to forbear disturbing Baltimore, his officers, or his people in Maryland and to put matters as they were "before any disturbance or alteration made by you" until he adjudicated "the said differences above mentioned" and issued further orders. Cromwell signaled his impatience, his desire to make the final resolution in the dispute, and his intention not to be pressured into an ill-advised decision.[29]

This quarrel never commanded Cromwell's full attention. He had his hands full trying to consolidate his power, stabilize a badly fractured society, fend off plots to restore the monarchy, and parry a variety of threats from foreign countries. In addition, the nature of the dispute did not encourage an easy resolution. Beyond the legal issues, the Virginians constantly and consistently attacked Baltimore's religion. The dispute languished before the Council of State for more than two years with only intermittent steps taken to prevent additional violence.

Baltimore's situation showed some small signs of improvement by the end of June 1655. To be sure, the occupation of Maryland continued as the Independents solidified their control of the government. In April the Provincial Court commissioned military commanders for both sides of the Patuxent River and ordered them to prepare to repel "enemies of the Lord Protector." The council ordered all the officers "to take the Solemn Engagement of faithfulness" to Cromwell. Some changes also took place in Virginia, the source of most of the proprietor's troubles. Colonel Edward Digges, the new governor, proved more conciliatory than Bennett. In June he issued a proclamation that enjoined Virginians not to meddle in the "troubles in Maryland." That same month, he let Cromwell know that Virginia had no role in "the business which hath lately happened between the men of Severn and the Lord Baltimore his officers in Maryland." That was the work of commissioners Bennett and Claiborne. Recognizing that countenancing either side might lead to more bloodshed, Digges pledged not "to interest ourselves in that business" until Cromwell made his pleasure known. With Fuller firmly in control in Maryland, he could afford to take the high ground and dissociate his colony from the violent proceedings in Maryland.[30]

Bennett responded by sailing for England to defend the commissioners and move the case more speedily through the bureaucracy. Cromwell's sporadic interventions in this dispute lacked consistency. Bennett did have some small successes, which, if nothing else, prolonged the proceedings and kept Baltimore from enjoying the benefits of his colony. As a result of the Virginian's entreaties, Cromwell sought in September to clarify what he had stated in his letter of January 12. He declared that he did not intend to stop "the proceedings of those commissioners who were authorized to settle the civil government in

Maryland." He intended only to prevent and forbid any violence over the boundary dispute between the two colonies, an objective clearly not achieved. Cromwell, not well versed in the specifics of the protracted dispute, failed to grasp the intimate connection between the commissioners' actions since 1650 and their attempt to overthrow Baltimore's charter, which he always referred to as the boundary dispute between Maryland and Virginia. When he wrote to Digges two weeks later, the lord protector again distinguished between the work of the commissioners and the boundary dispute. He reiterated that the latter issue remained under consideration by him and his Council of State. For now, the lord protector seemed willing to live with "what hath been done by the Commissioners for settling the civil government" in Maryland in "pursuance of the late Council of State their instructions." Whatever the vagaries of his messages, he consistently made this point: he expected all parties to await his decision.[31]

Over the course of the next year, the controversy lingered before the Council of State or one of the many other committees that examined colonial affairs. In November, after a long silence, Baltimore again put his case before the lord protector. He complained that Bennett and others had interrupted his rights and jurisdictions in Maryland. Cromwell assigned two advisers, the lord commissioners Bulstrode Whitelocke and Sir Thomas Widdrington, to examine the charges and to recommend remedies.[32]

For the first time in many years, Baltimore could anticipate recognition of his proprietary rights. In 1656 the Virginia House of Burgesses, which wanted to dissociate itself from the parliamentary commissioners, sent Governor Digges to England to placate Cromwell and to seek an agreement between the warring parties. Whitelocke and Widdrington, who had the unenviable task of making sense of the conflicting claims, reported to Cromwell in May 1656. The report no longer exists, but the reactions of the concerned parties indicated that it favored Baltimore over Bennett. The Virginians appealed the decision and petitioned to have the Committee of Trade reconsider the entire case.[33]

The recommendations of Whitelocke and Widdrington gave Baltimore the advantage but not the final resolution he wanted. The many-sided negotiations with Cromwell's government dragged on endlessly through late fall and into the spring of 1657. If Bennett and Mathews recognized that their enemy now had the upper hand, they refused to acknowledge defeat. In July the Council of State referred the Bennett-Mathews petition; the representations from the Virginia governor, council, and burgesses; the Whitelocke-Widdrington report; and several other papers to the Committee for Trade. That committee read the material and heard from both parties. It required Bennett and Mathews "to make some Proposals for the Settlement and Peace of the Said Province." When they did, the committee gave Baltimore the opportunity to respond to them. On September 16, 1656, the committee reported its recommendations to the council. Baltimore stated that Cromwell was sufficiently satisfied to promise him a final decision "with all convenient Expedition."[34]

Three weeks after the council received the Committee for Trade's report, Bennett and Mathews sent a protest to Secretary of State John Thurloe that rehashed their quarrel with Baltimore. Their petition, "Objections against the Lord Baltimore's patent, and reasons why the government should not be put into his hands," ostensibly pleaded on behalf of the people of Maryland. They implored that the lives and estates of his highness's good subjects not be abandoned to the mercy of Lord Baltimore "merely for their submission and engagement to the Parliament and to his highness." The two Virginians made the proprietor's religion a focal point in their effort to persuade Cromwell not to reestablish Baltimore's popish rule. Once more, they attempted to marshal the forces of anti-Catholicism in an effort to make a weak case stronger. Once more, Bennett underestimated Baltimore's adroitness and the efficacy of the 1649 Act concerning Religion as a means of neutralizing that stale charge. If Baltimore knew of Bennett and Mathews's last desperate effort to circumvent the process, he chose to ignore it. Confident that he would eventually prevail, he sent instructions to his new governor.[35]

In December the Council of State referred the Baltimore-Bennett conflict to the Committee of the Council for Foreign Plantations with instructions to speak to the parties and to recommend actions to be taken. In the meantime, the battle of the petitioners continued into January 1657. Baltimore and the adventurers of Maryland referred specifically to the violent acts committed by Fuller and others in Maryland. They held Bennett and Claiborne responsible for shooting four of their men in cold blood, for the imprisonment of others, and for the plundering of the planters loyal to the proprietor. Bennett and Mathews also submitted another petition, which was referred to the Committee for Plantations.[36]

Baltimore's emerging success in England gave him another opportunity to establish his proprietary authority and his plan in Maryland. In view of the disastrous results of his previous attempt to reassert his authority, he moved cautiously. He had taken a tentative first step on July 10, 1656, acting because "the

People there cannot subsist & continue in peace and safety without som good Government be settled & established as well for the cherishing & supporting of the good People & well affected for us." Ignoring for the moment that Fuller still retained control of the government, he revoked his commissions to Stone and other officers, appointed Josias Fendall as the new governor, and named a new council consisting of Stone, Thomas Gerard, John Price, Job Chandler, and Luke Barber. Gerard, the only Catholic appointed to the council, turned out to be the most troublesome.[37]

The dilatory tactics of Cromwell's administration, which seemed incapable of resolving matters, spurred the warring parties to negotiate their own settlement. Governor Digges, who used his influence with both sides to bring them to the bargaining table, was the needed catalyst. Resolution finally came on November 30, 1657, when both sides signed "The Agreement between the Proprietary and the Commissioners." The document reviewed the many controversies that had produced "much bloodshed & great distempers" and threatened "the utter ruin" of Maryland. It further rehearsed the negotiations in London that had failed to determine an outcome. The report previously made by the Committee for Trade on September 16, 1656, established a basis for the agreement. Perhaps luck, certainly weariness, but mostly Baltimore's extraordinary political savvy and patience provided the much-needed victory.

The proprietor shaped events in his chaotic colony, or at least tried to shape them, primarily through the instructions he wrote and the men whom he trusted to carry out those instructions. The various directives that he penned over the next few years defined his approach for restoring tranquility in the battered colony. They indicated that he had not abandoned his original "Maryland designe" and that he wanted to test anew the religious policies he had implemented before 1650. Enforcement of the Act concerning Religion became part of his strategy to gain the loyalty of his colonists, to foster stability, and to neutralize his critics in England. His instructions to Fendall and the council, dated October 23, 1656, closely paralleled the report from the Committee for Trade submitted six weeks earlier. First, he desired that the people at Ann Arundell and other places who had opposed his government return to the status quo antebellum. He wanted them to submit quietly and peacefully to living under his patent as was the case "before the troubles began, vizt. in the year 1650." Next, he required Fendall and the council to duly observe the law entitled the Act concerning Religion, "*whereby all Persons who profess to believe in Jesus Christ* have Liberty of Conscience and free Exercise of theyr religion."[38]

Emphasizing this act made good sense. It embodied, albeit in an altered form, his policy since the beginning. It put him in good standing with some English radicals. The 1649 act resonated much better with the lord protector than did the commission-inspired repressive 1654 act. Finally, it served to dampen the religious rhetoric of the previous few years and demonstrate that the claims made by his enemies lacked substance. Assurances that Christians would not be troubled because of their religious beliefs and that they had the freedom to worship as they pleased countered charges of a Catholic establishment in Maryland.

His instructions further demonstrated his dependence on those to whom he entrusted the execution of his goals. As an absentee landlord, he had preferred to empower members of his family, such as his brother Leonard, and people with whom he had a personal relationship, such as John Lewger. Beginning in 1648, recruiting loyal and able subordinates had become more difficult. Fendall's appointment as his lieutenant governor in 1656 exemplified the obstacles Baltimore encountered in finding trustworthy men who not only understood his objectives but had the skills to accomplish them. A number of circumstances had prevented him from fulfilling his long-term goal to reestablish a leadership coalition based on family and, by implication, religion. Conditions in both the colony and England were too unsettled. With his case still not finally resolved, and with the Virginians continuing to nip at his Catholic heels, Baltimore could ill afford to appoint a coreligionist at this critical juncture. Augustine Herrman in the New Netherlands reported hearing of the "violent animosity against the Papists" and that the inhabitants "will not bear a Papist governor."[39]

Without question, Baltimore would have designated his Catholic brother Philip as his representative at this critical moment. Philip was the only child from his father's marriage to his second wife, Joan. As an infant, he must have stayed with Cecil when his father and the rest of the family went to Newfoundland. In 1630, after his mother's death, he lived in London with his father. Before George died in 1632, he entrusted the care and education of young Philip, who was about six years old, to Cecil. Philip, as a member of his brother's impoverished household at Hooke Farm in Wiltshire, came of age during Maryland's first decade. Baltimore's dispute with the Jesuits impacted on Philip in one significant way. Rather than providing a Jesuit education for his brother, Baltimore sent him to the recently founded English College at Lisbon. Secular clergy had established this college in 1626 with a donation from a wealthy Portuguese nobleman who had stipulated that the Jesuits were to have nothing to do with the college. The English College at Lisbon was the only institution of higher learning open to English Catholics that was free of Jesuit influence. Father Gilmett (Henry Shirley), one of the secular priests dispatched by Baltimore to replace the Jesuits in Maryland, had been procurator at Lisbon between 1634 and 1636.[40]

Philip's time in Lisbon and his education at the English College prepared him for his later service in Maryland. Portugal openly proclaimed religious toleration, an anomaly for Catholic countries. Philip's education also reinforced the Calvert thinking on religious freedom. The second president of the college, Father Thomas White (also known as Blackloe) and his followers supported Catholic accommodation with the English government and rejected excessive papal claims to temporal power. Philip had ample opportunity to absorb the baroque architecture and city planning of his host country. Before he could apply any of his learning, however, he had to bide his time in England, where he returned in 1647 at the age of twenty-one. Philip most likely spent a significant portion of the next ten years in his brother's household assisting him with his effort to reestablish his proprietorship.[41]

For now, Baltimore took his chances with radical Protestants whose loyalty he thought he could secure through office and land. Several factors recommended Fendall's appointment. He had demonstrated his loyalty in the battle of the Severn, and he had been imprisoned by the parliamentary commissioners' government for disturbing the peace. Fendall, who had lived in the colony long enough to know its problems, embodied the colony's unsettled condition. Fuller's regime had remanded him to prison in 1655 for disturbing the peace by pretending power from Captain Stone. In the next year, Fendall took an "oath in the presence of God and before the face of the whole Court" that he would not directly or indirectly disturb the present government "till there be a full determination from England of all matters relating to the government."[42]

The Protestant Fendall, however, must have realized that his appointment was a stop-gap measure and that the proprietor would eventually turn to members of his family. His reaction to the arrival of Philip Calvert sometime between January and April of 1657 cannot be known. He would have welcomed the additional instructions from the proprietor that Calvert carried. In anticipation of a definitive statement from London, Fendall and Calvert began to assert control over the southern part of the colony in April and May of 1657. The entrenched government led by Fuller at Patuxent, however, refused to go out of business.

The stalemate continued into the summer. In June, in preparation for a meeting in England with Baltimore, Fendall named a Protestant loyalist, Luke Barber, to serve in his absence.[43]

When news of the settlement finally arrived, Philip Calvert had every reason to celebrate. After more than seven years of turmoil, the agreement restored Baltimore on very advantageous terms. It required those in opposition to Baltimore's government to relinquish any government powers, to deliver all government records and the proprietor's former Great Seal, if it should be found, to his officers, and to give all due obedience and submission to Baltimore's government. Further, the agreement left resolution of all offenses or differences that had arisen in the colony to Cromwell and his council. A concession to the people in opposition concerned their land rights. Baltimore agreed that they could patent their lands under his "Conditions of Plantation" as if none of the controversies and differences had happened. He stipulated that they had to patent the land within nine months of notice, take an oath of fidelity to the proprietor, pay all arrears of rent due to him, and remit the required fees to the proprietor's officers. He agreed that the people in opposition had up to a year to leave the province if they desired.[44]

Finally, Baltimore promised that he would never give his assent to the repeal of the 1649 law that assured freedom of conscience to all persons in the province who professed to believe in Jesus Christ. He faithfully promised upon his honor to observe and execute that law to the best of his ability and stipulated that his officers in Maryland would give assurances to the people for the faithful execution of that law.[45]

If the agreement did not represent a complete victory for the proprietor, it sanctioned many of his goals. Baltimore won the charter/boundary dispute: Maryland was not going to be subsumed into Virginia. He prevailed on the matter of who would govern in the colony. He succeeded in keeping his oath of fidelity, although in a somewhat altered form. He received a stamp of approval for his religious policy. His triumph as proprietor ensured Maryland's continued existence as a Catholic colony. For the rest, he could afford to be magnanimous. Agreeing to the adjudication of offenses resulting from the recent turmoil removed an impediment to establishing a more stable society. Allowing his opponents to keep their land left him where he wanted to be in 1648 when he invited the Virginia dissenters into their colony. Now he had the agreement that stipulated they had to comply with conditions they had cavalierly refused in the early

1650s: patent their lands, remit past fees, pay the quitrent, and swear their allegiance.[46]

Fendall returned to the province in February 1658 with the treaty between the proprietor and the Virginians, his new instructions, and an understanding of proprietary expectations. The proprietor believed he had the means to secure the loyalty of those whom he appointed. First and foremost, he appealed to their material interests by using the vast domain at his disposal. The new governor received two thousand acres, while new councillors John Langford and Luke Barber received grants of fifteen hundred and one thousand acres, respectively. Three other loyalists received grants of one thousand acres. The usual conditions, that the land must not have been previously assigned and that the recipients must pay a yearly rent of two shillings per one hundred acres, applied. In the wake of Philip Calvert's appointment as a councillor and secretary, Baltimore assigned him six thousand acres for one or more manors. He instructed his council to reward those widows who "lost their husbands by occasion of the late troubles there" out of his own revenues and to give preference in employment to those who proved faithful to him. He authorized a grant of ten thousand acres to Edward Eltonhead. The land and loyalty concept even extended to the lower end of society. He affirmed his 1648 commitment that every servant who served his time was entitled to fifty acres of land.[47]

In addition to using the land to secure loyalty, Baltimore sought loyalty from his colonists through his guarantee of freedom of conscience to all Christians. He wanted his officers to assure Marylanders that religion would no longer be used to deprive them of their political and economic rights and that the government would not interfere with their private religious practices.

He also sought assurances of loyalty through the administration of oaths, returning to the controversial oath of fealty. Indeed, he required these oaths as if the difficulties between him and the Virginia émigrés had never happened. Anyone receiving patents for land had to take them in the form altered to comply with the September 16, 1656, report of the Committee of Trade. The proprietor needed to have loyalty assured and persisted in his belief that testimonies in open court would bind his officers to him. He exempted no one who served him. He required his half brother to take the oath of a councillor and the oath of the secretary in open court. He further required Philip to administer an oath to Fendall in open court. As Fendall would soon demonstrate, however, interests, not oaths, determined loyalty.[48]

Finally, he sought loyalty through a limited amnesty. His instructions included the form of submission for those who had opposed his government. Inhabitants taking the oath promised to submit to Lord Baltimore's authority according to his patent and to the officers he appointed. They swore not to obey or assist anyone in opposition to his officers. The need for rent-paying colonists overcame whatever animosity the proprietor felt toward those who opposed him.[49]

The proprietor expected Fendall and the new council, in return for land and the perquisites of office, to reestablish his authority by ousting Fuller and his cohorts without completely forfeiting support for the Restoration. At a council meeting in late February 1658, Fendall made public the November 30, 1657, agreement. With the long-awaited final resolution in hand, the council sent letters to Fuller and his council convening a meeting in March between representatives of the two Maryland governments. When the two parties met in March at St. Leonard's, Fendall read the articles of agreement and then demanded the colony's records, the Great Seal, and the resignation of Fuller's government. On March 24, 1658, representatives from both sides signed articles of agreement. On the next day, the beginning of the new year under the old-style calendar and the twenty-fourth anniversary of taking possession of the land in the proprietor's name, a councillor publicly read Fendall's commission and proclaimed the end of more than six years of civil strife. Lord Baltimore's persistence and the support of a few loyal planters had led to complete triumph for the proprietary interest.[50]

The proprietor looked forward to achieving the stability and success that had been so elusive. He knew that his multifaceted "Maryland designe" had not developed as he had envisioned and that it had fallen short of the mark in a number of key areas. He had made the privatization of religion a primary means for accomplishing his objectives, but the tolerant spirit Baltimore sought never took hold. Many of the English men and women who came to Maryland obviously had trouble putting religious differences aside. In the name of civil peace, the Act concerning Religion significantly altered the "Maryland designe" and opened the door to greater government involvement in religious affairs than Baltimore originally intended. Further, his plan had depended on Catholic leadership and a successful transplant of the manorial system. After 1647 Protestants dominated political leadership. The manorial system had failed to mature as a means of securing social stability and keeping religious matters private. Rather than a land dominated by large manors and loyal lords of the manors, Maryland was fast becoming a colony of small tobacco farms and independent farmer-capitalists who were not necessarily predisposed to support the proprietary cause. Robert Cole, who emigrated in 1652, was a Catholic who prospered not as a manor lord but as a tobacco farmer. His great enemy was not his Protestant neighbors but disease.

Through all the setbacks, the proprietor held fast to his vision that Catholics and Protestants could live and work together under Catholic leadership. Conditions after 1660 boded well for success. Some of the issues that had loomed so large before 1660, such as the controversy with the Jesuits or the dispute with Bennett, had diminished or disappeared. Baltimore calculated that the new king's accession would result in a more relaxed attitude toward Catholics in England and, by implication, in the colonies. At the least, he could look forward to less scrutiny from England. Other problems, such as the assembly's quest for a greater role in decision making, had not dissipated. Still, the withdrawal of the parliamentary commissioners, the Restoration of Charles II, and the appointment of new, seemingly loyal subordinates, afforded Baltimore an excellent opportunity to make his religious and economic policies work.[51]

Beginning in 1659 and until his death in 1675, the proprietor reiterated his commitment to the Act concerning Religion. When Governor Fendall read his instructions to the council on March 3, 1660, he noted that the proprietor was making enforcement of the 1649 act a priority. Baltimore had copies of the act printed in England, and he urged Fendall to display them in all provincial and inferior courts in the province. Fendall was to maintain the act and to proceed "in all your courts exactly according to it." In 1666 Baltimore referred to the act when he authorized the governor to summon assemblies of the freemen as needed. He placed four restrictions on the legislative process. The laws should be reasonable and should not contradict the laws and customs of England. They should not infringe on his proprietary rights. And he stressed that no law should be passed that contradicted the 1649 Act concerning Religion. He further instructed the governor to observe, keep, and execute the act in a strict and careful manner.[52]

The proprietor recommitted to oaths as a means to secure the religious freedom of the inhabitants. He required his governor and councillors to swear that they would not directly or indirectly trouble, molest, or discountenance any person "professing to believe in Jesus Christ for or in respect of his or her Religion" or in "his or her free Exercise" as long as the person remained faithful to the proprietor and did not conspire against the civil government. He further required the governor to swear not to discriminate "in respect of their said Religion" when appointing officers or conferring rewards in the proprietor's name. Justices in St. Mary's County, where most of the remaining Catholics lived, took oaths similar to the councillors' oaths. When he became the principal secretary on March 16, 1673/74, William Calvert took an oath to keep all articles of "One certaine act of Assembly," the Act concerning Religion.[53]

Baltimore's commitment and his officers' willingness to swear to uphold the law aside, one essential question remained. Could the religiously diverse population put aside their differences and keep religion out of the political arena in order to enjoy the bounty that the proprietor's colony offered? The challenge was whether this act, which was a compromise bill and a less generous policy than the original informal policy, could function effectively under the more promising conditions of the Restoration. The issue for the restored proprietary government once more centered on when and under what circumstances the government should intervene in religious matters to preserve the peace or to respond to imperial issues. Actions taken by Marylanders and the responses of proprietary officials in the period between 1657 and 1660 determined the meaning of the act. Three cases, one involving Quakers, another a Catholic priest, and a third a non-Christian, quickly emerged. Did the Quakers' refusal to assert their loyalty violate the principles of the 1649 act, or were their actions protected? Did Jesuit priest Francis Fitzherbert exceed the limits of the act in his pursuit of his priestly functions? Did the protection of this law extend to Jews? These cases helped to define what the new proprietary religious policy meant in practice.

Members of the Society of Friends, a radical Protestant sect, were the first to question the new religious policy. The English at home and in the colonies scorned the Quakers. Civil authorities in most colonies did everything they could to drive the disruptive dissenters from their midst. After some initial problems, Marylanders adjusted to the Quaker presence in the colony and demonstrated that the Calverts did indeed pursue a coherent and consistent policy when it came to religious freedom. The second Lord Baltimore wanted—in some ways desperately needed—to place people on the land. In return for loyalty to him and his proprietary government, he allowed them to create whatever Christian forms of worship they pleased.

A small number of Quakers, led by Elizabeth Harris, entered Maryland more than a year before Baltimore's restoration. Relations between this troublesome sect and the restored proprietary government started badly, because the Quakers refused to leave their tender consciences at home and swear an oath of fidelity. Anne Arundel County, where the Virginian Independents had settled, provided a fertile recruiting area for the early missionaries of this faith, and Quakerism spread rapidly in 1656–58. The success of three Quakers, Thomas Thurston, Josiah Coale, and Thomas Chapman, in converting Independents led to a rapid increase in the number of people who subscribed to Quaker tenets. These decidedly "Zealous, great pretenders to Holiness" quickly came to the attention of the government.[54]

Implementation of Baltimore's objectives fell to Fendall, his new and untried governor. The proprietor charged him with building a coalition that included those who had remained loyal to him but also incorporated those who had been disloyal. The governor worked successfully with some of the leaders of the former Fuller regime in the Anne Arundel area. Many of the Independents accommodated to the newly restored government and subscribed to the revised oath of fidelity. Members of the emerging Quaker element, however, refused to comply with this engagement and other regulations, thereby putting the government in a delicate position. Some members of the council, but especially Catholic Thomas Gerard, led the charge to crack down on the Quakers. Gerard alleged that Fendall seemed willing to give in to demands of "people at Annarundell," no matter how prejudicial such actions were to those who had recently "asserted his lordships Just Rights" in the colony. Edward Lloyd and Nathaniel Utie, leading residents of the areas where the most conversions took place, told Fendall that the Quakers were obstructing all government in their areas.[55]

Thurston's refusal to take the oath of fidelity to the proprietor and Josiah Coale or Cole's "seducing the People & diswadeing the people from takeing the engagement according to the Articles of the Surrender" blurred the line that Baltimore wanted to draw between religion and politics. Did the government's hard line with the Quakers violate one of the principles of the "Maryland designe"? Was the government persecuting the Quakers on account of their religious beliefs? Only to the extent that the Quakers' belief that they "were to be governed by Gods lawe and the light within them & not by mans lawe" had political implications. If Baltimore held freedom of conscience dearly, he held loyalty and the creation of a stable society even higher. In a very unsettled time, the Quakers refused to take the requisite oaths designed to ensure loyalty and produce a stable society. Their failure to subscribe to the revised oath brought religion into the public sector in the very manner Baltimore wanted to avoid.

Quaker "disobedience to the Proclamation could not but tend to the embroiling of this Province in further troubles." The insolent behavior of the Quakers led to a council debate that concluded that their refusal and their principles "tended to the destruction of all Government." The council ordered that they subscribe to the engagement or depart the colony by March 25, 1659. The numerous conversions, the refusal to comply with mandates of the restored government, and tensions with the government gave rise to the brief but vigorous persecution of that sect under Fendall. His government fined, jailed, and in a few instances, banished colonists for refusing to swear oaths, for entertaining Quaker missionaries, and for refusing to participate in the militia.[56]

The Catholic situation also started on an acrimonious note. This controversy centered on Father Francis Fitzherbert, a Jesuit who immigrated in 1653 but fled to Virginia during Fuller's tenure as governor. He returned to Maryland in 1658 and remained until his departure in 1662 as the only priest in the Maryland mission. He combined a zealous spirit with an aggressive style that "offended everybody with whom he dealt." This Jesuit, unlike his predecessor Father Copley, did not claim all of the rights the church exercised in Catholic countries. Rather, in the course of carrying out his office, he called attention to two issues, proselytizing and church discipline, that should have been beyond the interest of Baltimore's government. In more settled times, his attempts to gain converts and his effort to chastise a church member whom he considered errant might not have come to the attention of government authorities.[57]

Restoration of the 1649 act did not end the tensions that existed between Protestants and Catholics. Another case, which came before the court in 1658, indicated the difficulties involved in maintaining a separation between religious matters and the government interest in them. The incident forced Fendall and the other officials to consider when and under what circumstances the government should intervene in religious affairs. The case in question involved a reprobate named Robert Holt, who with the (apparent) blessing of William Wilkinson, the Church of England priest for St. George's Church at Popular Hill, divorced (illegally) his wife and married another in contravention of Maryland law. The court inquired whether Holt, who contemporaries thought did not have the fear of God before his eyes, acted against the peace of his lordship by marrying Christian Bonnefeild. The attorney general, who also brought charges against Fitzherbert, charged both Holt and Wilkinson with felonies. After their presentment, both prisoners challenged the jury-selection process, observing that those present at court were Catholics. They questioned whether

Catholics could act impartially. The governor recognized their request for a Protestant jury as legitimate. Religious rancor still abounded.[58]

Fitzherbert's conspicuous proselytizing exacerbated the tensions between Catholics and Protestants. As the new government struggled to plant itself on a firm basis, he used a series of military musters to bring Marylanders into the Catholic fold. In addition to his uninvited preaching, he distributed books and a catechism that resulted in at least one conversion. These activities did not sit well with some residents, and especially with the newly appointed attorney general, Henry Coursey. More significant, the Jesuit confronted one prominent longtime resident who was now a member of the new government. He threatened Catholic councilor Thomas Gerard with excommunication if he did not bring his Protestant wife and children to church. The priest told Gerard's Protestant son-in-law, Robert Slye, that although Gerard professed to be a Catholic, his actions did not agree with that profession. Slye quoted the angry priest as saying that if Gerard did not educate his children in "the principles of the Romish Religion," he would undertake their education in Gerard's own house. Did these zealous but also heavy-handed tactics violate the intent of the 1649 Act concerning Religion?[59]

Coursey, a Protestant gentleman and a protégé of Philip Calvert, who had appointed him attorney general, thought so, and in 1658 he charged the priest with four counts of "practising of Treason & Sedition & gyving out Rebellious & mutinous speeches" and endeavoring to cause distractions and raise disturbances within the colony. Two of the counts charged him with attempting to seduce and draw certain inhabitants from "their Religion." A third claimed that his treacherous and seditious behaviors had caused several colonists to refuse to appear at musters, thereby threatening the security of the colony. The fourth count asserted that, contrary to "a known Act of Assembly" in the province, he had tried to force Gerard's Protestant wife and children to attend his church. Father Fitzherbert offered no apology, but he did write to his superiors in England for advice. When the attorney general attempted to deal with the matter in private, the priest responded that he must be directed by his conscience and not by "the Law of any Country," namely, the 1649 act.[60]

Jacob Lumbrozo, a Jewish doctor, brought attention to the 1649 act in another way. As written, the law limited its protection to those who professed a belief in Jesus Christ. Coursey charged Lumbrozo with blasphemy for words he uttered against "Our Blessed Savior Jesus Christ." Testimony indicated that Lumbrozo had been baited and that his explanations of the Resurrection (Jesus' disciples stole him away) and Jesus' miracles (he attributed them to necromancy or sorcery) left him vulnerable. Based on this testimony, the councillors remanded him to the custody of the sheriff. A general pardon issued by Governor Fendall in the proprietor's name to honor the accession of Richard Cromwell as lord protector spared Lumbrozo a trial and the government the possible embarrassment of convicting him for his beliefs. Although Jews were not protected by the Act concerning Religion, the disposition of the case reflected the generally open religious climate that marked Calvert's Maryland. In spite of his abrasive personality, Lumbrozo gained acceptance from his Christian contemporaries and enjoyed limited prosperity.[61]

Before the government resolved these issues, Baltimore's proprietary authority underwent still another severe test. Once again, political turmoil in England affected affairs in Maryland. Richard Cromwell, who succeeded his father on September 3, 1658, lacked the skills needed to keep the protectorate going. His dismissal from office in May led to talk of a restored Stuart monarchy. All that was certain was uncertainty. Baltimore's efforts to achieve political stability in Maryland proved equally elusive. The final challenge to the restoration of proprietary authority came in March 1660, when the long-standing tensions between the proprietor and his assembly erupted and led to a desperate effort to reestablish the commonwealth government. Governor Fendall's inability or unwillingness to defend proprietary prerogatives in the face of the legislative demands threatened Baltimore's role as proprietor. Renewed turmoil in the troubled province resulted when Fendall joined the assembly against the proprietor and fostered still another change in the government leadership. As George Alsop aptly phrased it, "here sprang up in this Province of Mary-Land a kind of pigmie Rebellion: A company of weak-witted men, which thought to have traced the steps of Oliver in Rebellion."[62]

The olive branch extended by Baltimore did not include allowing the restive Virginia émigrés to retain their former offices. They tested proprietary authority in the assembly election in the winter of 1659–60. The returns indicated that not all Marylanders were able to put the turmoil of the past decade behind them. Freemen in the areas where the Virginia émigrés and supporters of the commissioners dominated returned delegates who wanted to limit the charter rights of their absentee landlord and curb the renewed Catholic political presence in the colony. The presence of the former commissioner governor, William Fuller, did not bode well for a congenial atmosphere.

The antiproprietary forces in the assembly tried a new tactic this time. They gambled that they could seize control from the proprietor by eliminating the upper house, the members of which Baltimore chose and who served at his pleasure. The showdown came on March 14, 1660. After considerable debate between the two houses, Fendall gained assurances that he would be president of the assembly and agreed to sit with the lower house on its terms. He forfeited his commission from the proprietor and accepted a new one from the assembly. Philip Calvert and two other councillors refused and offered reasons for their belief that a single house with the governor sitting as a member violated proprietary rights and jurisdictions. The governor refused Calvert's request to have his comments recorded in the journal of the lower house. Fendall did not attempt to stop Calvert and another councillor from leaving; he told them, "you may if you please, wee shall not force you to goe or stay." The majority of representatives in the lower house then declared that the assembly, "without dependence on any other Power in the Province," constituted "the highest court of Judicature."[63]

The assembly's action, which occurred in the context of the recent struggle between the Catholic proprietor and the Protestant commissioners and immigrants from Virginia, had a larger setting as well, namely, the constant clashes between the proprietor and the freemen in the assembly. The freemen, regardless of their religion, wanted a greater influence in the decision-making process within the colony than Baltimore had ever intended. The legislators' assertion of their right to initiate legislation irked the proprietor, and that group and Baltimore sparred over this critical issue for many years. His actions in defense of his legislative prerogatives at times seemed obsessive, but they were not those of a megalomaniac. The proprietary response arose from two sources, his lordship of the Maryland manor and the fact that he was a Catholic proprietor trying to survive and prosper in a Protestant world. To be certain, his approach was paternalistic. He was too invested to yield control gracefully.

The assembly coup took place in March, but word did not get back to England until late June. Two ship captains trading in Maryland testified about the events of late March and April. Both reported that the governor had raised a faction against Baltimore's jurisdiction by endeavoring to impose a commonwealth form of government. Both asserted that the assembly's action greatly prejudiced proprietary rights and brought "a great deale of trouble and confusion among the people there."[64]

Baltimore's response to the news of the assembly coup can only be surmised. He understood that the revolt not only tarnished his triumph over the parliamentary commissioners but also dashed his hopes for a speedy restoration. Of greater importance, it emphasized the difficulties he faced in managing the enterprise from afar and the tenuous nature of his support. The assembly-led revolt again called attention to an inherent weakness in his "Maryland designe." The people he most depended on to implement his will had failed him. Land did not bind Fendall to his cause. Sharing in the exercise of political power did not bind councillor Nathaniel Utie. A shared faith and the freedom to worship as a Catholic did not bind councillor Thomas Gerard.

Before the discouraging account of the coup reached Baltimore, he learned that on May 8, 1660, members of a new parliament had requested that Charles Stuart return to England. That same day it proclaimed him king. His arrival at Dover a few weeks later effectively ended twenty years of internecine warfare. Baltimore wasted no time contemplating the implications of Parliament's move. Charles II's return proved propitious for the proprietor of Avalon and Maryland. In June, in a display of Baltimore's remarkable ability to elicit support from the English government, the new king ordered the governor and council of Virginia, captains and masters of ships trading to Maryland, and all magistrates and officers and others of the king's subjects in those parts to aid and assist Baltimore's officers to restore order and settle his jurisdiction. As a further indication of Baltimore's growing influence, the restored king came down squarely on the proprietor's side in Avalon. After years of controversy over that colony, a report confirmed that Sir George Calvert's grant remained in force. Charles issued a warrant ordering the Kirkes to return any houses or land they possessed to Baltimore.

The king's Restoration allowed Baltimore to move quickly to reestablish proprietary authority. Within a month, he wrote instructions for still another overhaul of his government. He revoked his commission to the mutinous and seditious Fendall, who had violated his oath and trust when he surrendered his commission to a "pretended Assembly there," and he nullified all council appointments. He appointed his half brother, Secretary Philip Calvert, whose courage and loyalty impressed him, to serve as his lieutenant and chief governor. To confront the leadership crisis, Baltimore reverted to his initial intention to governor through family members. For the first time since Leonard died in 1647, he had a family member to take the helm of government. He entrusted to Philip the naming of a new council and the restoration of peace.[65]

Fendall's coup, however, dulled Baltimore's conciliatory instincts, and he offered less generous terms than he had three years earlier. His August 24, 1660, letter to Philip instructed him to proceed against Fendall and his accomplices. Baltimore raged against the perfidious and treacherous former governor, who furthered his "own ambitious design" by betraying the proprietary trust. Having vented his spleen, the proprietor gave Philip flexibility in dealing with those who "engaged against me in this Second Rebellion" and ended his letter on a somewhat conciliatory note. Except for the people he singled out, Baltimore counseled that Philip would do well to "proclaim a general pardon to all of them that shall submit to my jurisdiction and not to act any thing afterwards against it, or my right there." Governor Calvert described Fendall to the sheriff of St. Mary's as a "dangerous person not fitt to be at liberty in these distracted tymes."[66]

By November Governor Calvert had regained control of the government. He took a number of steps designed to restore order. He initiated the healing process with a general pardon on November 27, 1660. With a few notable exceptions, he pardoned all who had engaged in the late mutiny and sedition. The new council, consisting of Catholics and Protestants who had displayed loyalty to the proprietor, was in place. He issued a proclamation recognizing Charles II as king. Thus, by the end of the month, both proprietor and king had been restored.[67]

The final step in reconstituting the proprietary government came on September 14, 1661, when Baltimore replaced his brother with his son Charles. Philip Calvert no doubt understood that the proprietor had little choice but to appoint his son and the future proprietor to the office. However, he never fully accepted his demotion. Philip, now the deputy lieutenant and chancellor, also relinquished his position as the colony's secretary. Despite the strained relations between uncle and nephew and other members of the Calvert clan, they managed to function effectively when it came to administering the government, and especially the Act concerning Religion.[68]

The penultimate chapter for the "Maryland designe" followed the assembly's abortive revolt and the return to full Calvert control. Baltimore once more charged his officers to implement a religious policy fashioned to foster the stability and prosperity he desired. To the extent possible, he wanted to dissociate matters related to individual worship from the public arena. When the government did intervene in issues that might be considered religious, it did so to enforce the Act concerning Religion. For example, when Governor Philip Calvert issued licenses for ordinaries, he did so with the stipulation that the innkeeper would not permit evil rule or disorder, especially on the Lord's Day by gaming or excessive drinking during the time of divine services. He clearly understood the importance the proprietor placed on the 1649 act.[69]

Under the "Maryland designe," church development lagged. Civil authorities in Maryland—in contrast to those in England and most of the other English colonies—took no responsibility for generating religious institutions. Baltimore offered Marylanders an equal opportunity to establish and maintain their own churches free of government interference or support. Three closely related issues, the development of viable religious communities, the intensity of religious controversy, and the intervention of the restored government in matters pertaining to religion, demonstrate the degree to which the revised religious policies succeeded.

Quakers, Catholics, and Episcopal Protestants had the opportunity to prosper under the restored government. Baltimore's policies succeeded best among two denominations that enjoyed the least benefits from the traditional state establishment of religion. Upstart Quakers and weathered Catholics had this much in common: the English ranked them among the most despised and distrusted religious people, and both prospered under the "Maryland designe." Indeed, colonists of these two persuasions provided much of the leadership of the colony after 1660. Adherents to the Church of England, long accustomed to the privileges of their state-sponsored status, responded poorly to the freedom offered by the proprietor.

With the Calverts now in control, the persecution of the Quakers quickly abated as both sides looked for ways to reconcile their differences. After 1661 Baltimore and his officers viewed the Quakers as less of a political threat, especially after they made concessions regarding attestations of their fealty to him as lord proprietor. As the Society of Friends rapidly increased in numbers and gained adherents among influential settlers, the proprietor and his officers in Maryland saw their potential. In keeping with past practices, Baltimore extended the offer of religious liberty with the proviso that the beneficiaries support him and his government. Ever the practical visionary, he gave the Quakers something they dearly wanted and in return he secured something he needed. And the exchange worked (at least for a time). No longer harassed on account of religion, these zealous missionaries recruited new members and organized more effectively than other Protestants. By the time the first Maryland General Meeting took place in 1672, the Society of Friends enjoyed widespread support in the majority of counties. In return, the Quakers provided much-needed political leadership in the colony, serving through the end of Cecil Calvert's proprietorship (in 1675) in all levels of government. Quakers conspicuously served on the governor's council.[70]

The growth of the Quaker community after 1661 demonstrated a high level of satisfaction with the government's religious policies. Two decades after his father's restoration, Charles Calvert, now the third Lord Baltimore, estimated that the "greatest part of the Inhabitants of that Province (three of four at least)" were Presbyterians, Independents, Anabaptists, and Quakers. Of all the Protestant groups named, the Quakers were the most numerous, although their participation in the government diminished rapidly after the death of Cecil Calvert in November 1675. Quaker success in Maryland in the period between 1661 and 1681 demonstrated that the "Maryland designe," despite its uneven course, was not whimsical.[71]

Maryland was a Catholic enterprise, however, and the success of the effort has to be measured by the experiences of the Catholics who ventured to the colony. The resolution of Father Fitzherbert's case also demonstrated the impact of Calvert leadership after 1661. When the case came before the provincial court in 1662, Father Fitzherbert demurred, neither denying nor admitting to the charges. Rather than resisting the 1649 Act concerning Religion, he now juxtaposed it with the earlier 1639 Act for Church Liberties and used them to his advantage. He argued that by the first enactment the "Holy Church within this Province shall have & Enjoy all her Rights libertyes and Franchise wholy and with out blemish." Preaching and teaching were not the least of these rights. Furthermore, the law did not make explicit "what Church is there meant," since by the second act "every Church professing to believe in God the father Sonne and holy Ghoste is accounted Holy Church here." Father Fitzherbert's historical accuracy aside, he was preaching to the choir.

For his second point, he wrapped himself in the protection of the 1649 act. That act prohibited the molestation of Christians on account of their religion. No doubt existed in the priest's mind that preaching and teaching were "the free Exercise of every Churchmans Religion." On that lofty thought, he rested his case. The court ruled that the language used by the priest constituted neither rebellion nor mutiny. By endorsing the priest's position, the court ratified the proprietary position. Catholics, and by implication all Christians, had regained the freedom of conscience the proprietor had promised from the beginning.[72]

In the twenty years or so between the restoration of Cecilius Calvert and the period immediately following his death, the restored 1649 act worked remarkably well as an instrument for keeping the peace between members of Maryland's diverse population. Religious concerns dissipated dramatically. By the mid-1660s the absentee proprietor had a government administered by people whom he trusted to carry out his mandates. The "Maryland designe," with its emphasis on keeping religion out of the public realm, seemed to be working the way Baltimore envisioned. George Alsop liked what he saw in the mid-1660s. "He that desires to see the real Platform of a quiet and sober Government extant, Superiority with the meek and yet commanding power sitting at the Helme, steering the actions of State quietly, through the multitude and diversity of Opinionous waves of diversity meet, let him look to Mary-Land with eyes admiring, and then he'le judge her, The Miracle of this Age." Alsop, in a fit of hyperbole, proclaimed that in Maryland Roman Catholics and Episcopal Protestants, seemingly implacable enemies, "concur in a unanimous parallel of friendship, and inseparable love intayled unto one another." More important, he noted that the "several Opinions and Sects" within Maryland "meet not together in mutinous contempts to the disquiet" of proprietary rule, but with "a reverend quietness [obey] the legal commands of Authority."[73]

If Alsop exaggerated, he did not err when it came to Quakers and Catholics. More than any other religious group, Catholics benefited from the diminution of religious tensions. After 1661 they enjoyed security of conscience, access to priests, and increasing prosperity. Despite this, they remained only a small portion of the population. Charles Calvert in 1678 estimated that they had the fewest numbers of all denominations in the colony. Richard Shepherd, an English captain who traded in Maryland, probably overstated the actual numbers when he declared in 1681 that "there are thirty Protestants to one Papist."[74]

However small their numbers, Catholics dominated Maryland life after 1660. By removing state support for a particular church, the proprietor had leveled the playing field. Individual Catholics, freed from the restraint of the English penal laws, thrived on their own initiative. In keeping with past practices, Cecil Lord Baltimore did little after 1660 to provide for the individual spiritual needs of his fellow Catholics. He maintained contact with representatives from Rome. He expected that the Church hierarchy would support the mission and was irritated by the weak effort put forth on behalf of Maryland. When Claudius Agretti, who was on a special mission to examine the condition of ecclesiastical affairs in England, visited Baltimore "at his villa near London" in 1669, the proprietor angrily repudiated the impression that he opposed the presence of religious orders in his colony. He criticized the Holy See, which, influenced by this false impression, had consigned no missionaries to Maryland in the course of twenty-four years. Baltimore lamented that there were but two ecclesiastics for about two thousand Catholics and that efforts to secure diocesan priests had been stymied because Maryland had been reserved for the Jesuits. After this meeting, Propaganda Fide sought to reach an accord with Baltimore in order to send "pious ecclesiastics" who met with his approval. The two Franciscans who arrived in 1672 may have come as a result of Baltimore's complaint.[75]

In addition, the proprietor and his relatives provided some funds and material aid to sustain the priests in Maryland. In 1663 Governor Calvert thanked his father for covering the money (presumably a portion of his salary) promised to Mr. Fitzherbert. He informed his father of the arrival of Fitzherbert's replacement and noted that he would pay him six barrels of corn and give him all the encouragement fitting. When the two Franciscans arrived in 1672, Governor Calvert and Chancellor Calvert housed them. The governor provided a horse for one of the priests and "will allow him ten pounds and more if I find him able." Subsidizing the salaries of Maryland clergy led to some hard feelings on the part of the Jesuits. In 1673 they complained that Baltimore extended his favor to other orders who had not served as long in Maryland mission. Charles offered them encouragement of the "same favour upon them," which seemed to satisfy them. In providing this small support for the Catholic clergy, the proprietor and members of his family did not violate their policy. They supported the priests as individual Catholics, not as the chief civil officers in Maryland. But not all Marylanders recognized the subtle distinction the Calverts tried to maintain.[76]

The proprietor continued to keep as close a watch over the religious life of the Catholic community as could be expected from his remote post in England. Not wanting a notorious incident involving the clergy, Baltimore monitored the priests who served in his Chesapeake domain. Governor Calvert dutifully kept his father informed. Father Fitzwilliams, Fitzherbert's successor, whether by accident or by design, committed a grievous error. The Jesuit abruptly departed London without calling upon Baltimore. The snubbed proprietor dispatched an angry letter to his son, who in turn informed the priest of his faux pas. The governor reported that the Jesuit acknowledged that he had left without seeing the proprietor and asked for Baltimore's pardon. In wanting to examine the priests going to Maryland, Baltimore remained consistent with his views on the priesthood and his role as lord of the manor.[77]

Despite the occasional rub and the presence of the two Franciscans, Maryland remained a Jesuit province. On board from the beginning, the Jesuits had persevered through the various disruptions and maintained their mission. In their annual letters, they continued to claim converts among the Protestants; and in spite of their small number, they served the needs of Maryland's Catholics. Roman Catholics, in accordance with the governing principles, were expected to maintain their own clergy without support of the government.[78]

The Jesuit-Catholic revival paralleled an initiative from the proprietor that led to the incorporation of St. Mary's as a city in 1667. The proprietor, the chancellor, and the governor had grandiose plans for their little colony. Lord Baltimore wanted to transform his capital into a city based on the principles of baroque design. Planning included a brick Catholic chapel that was to be located at one end of the city opposite the intended state house. The brick church, which began the transformation of the landscape at St. Mary's, symbolized the new Maryland that followed Baltimore's restoration and epitomized Catholic and Calvert triumphs and tribulations. That building boldly stated that the "Maryland designe" had worked. It was a visual expression of the success of English Catholics, who without government support and without a church hierarchy, demonstrated their vitality as a religious community. Built on the highest plot of land in St. Mary's, the chapel stood as a testimonial to the first Lord Baltimore's conviction that he and his family could worship as Catholics and prosper as Englishmen.[79]

For Catholics church building meant more than just having a place to worship. It marked a sharp divergence from Baltimore's 1633 injunction to keep all acts of the Roman Catholic religion as private as possible. For the first time since the Reformation, English Catholics (albeit only in Maryland) could worship in churches of their own construction. With a spirit of optimism, and with brick and stone, some Maryland Catholics built a church for the ages. The chapel also reminded Protestants of their failure to succeed under the existing rules.

The idea of the chapel coincided with the renewal of the Jesuit mission in the early 1660s and the implementation of a plan for a city. Jesuit missionary priest Father Henry Warren arrived in 1661. He brought a contagious enthusiasm that helped to revitalize a demoralized Catholic community. He was a stranger to the troubles between the proprietor and the Jesuits of two decades earlier. Neither the Jesuits nor the proprietor showed any inclination to resume the acrimonious relationship. The aversion some Protestants harbored toward Catholics, especially their Jesuit priests, never disappeared, but it no longer had a public platform. The new Protestant king favored Catholics in many ways and created an attitude of benign neglect toward his Catholic subjects that lasted at least for a decade. These conditions encouraged and invigorated English Catholics in Maryland. The Jesuits moved quickly to exploit the new opportunities. A year after Warren arrived, Maryland Catholics constructed new wooden chapels north of St. Mary's City.

The chapel at St. Mary's City differed conspicuously from the other rough, wooden structures built in the early 1660s. Those buildings reflected the fleeting condition of the immigrants. Life was harsh and it was short, especially for male immigrants. A significant native population had not yet established itself. The design of the chapel, a massive and ornate brick building with a flat ceramic tile roof, ran counter to the prevailing standards of impermanent architecture. Catholics in the capital area built a brick building on a scale that was uncommon for seventeenth-century America. To support a substantial building, they built a foundation that was three feet wide and extended about five feet below the surface. They constructed their building in the shape of a Latin cross, with a shallow chancel and small transepts. The chapel was fifty-four feet along its main axis and almost fifty-seven feet across the arms of the cross. The main body of the church consisted of the nave and the chancel. The Catholics constructed their chapel, which contained about 1,405 square feet of floor space, for between £365 and £650, a sum three to six times greater than the average estate value during this period. Who among them, prosperous as they might be by Maryland standards, had the resources to build such a substantial structure?[80]

The evidence provides few details regarding proprietary–Jesuit–lay Catholic cooperation in laying out and constructing the chapel. Most likely the chapel was a community affair. The Society of Jesus could not have built the chapel with its limited resources. The mission was always in financial trouble. In 1672 the priests applied to Lord Baltimore for a subsidy of twenty pounds per year to help meet their obligations. The role of the proprietor remains equally elusive. Whether the idea of a baroque city in the wilderness came from him or originated with Philip Calvert, whose education in Lisbon may have given him the idea, is unknown. Philip's acquaintance with Father Thomas White in that cosmopolitan city undoubtedly led him to welcome the priest's nephew, Jerome White, who served as the proprietor's first surveyor general from 1661 to 1670. The Catholic White, who was born and educated in Rome and was the grandson of George Calvert's longtime associate Sir Richard Weston, may have carried tentative plans for the new city. Little was done, however, until the

proprietor ordered the incorporation of St. Mary's as a city in 1667. He appointed an eight-person city council to oversee the project. To be sure, he expected to be fully informed. His most likely conduit was his chancellor. As a
member of the church and a prominent resident of the city, Philip Calvert was
well positioned to influence the construction of the new brick chapel and to acquaint his half brother with the progress of the city and the chapel. The creation
of a memorial of some sort at the time of his death and the location of his bur-
ial implies that he served as a patron of the St. Mary's church.[81]

The construction of the chapel and its intimate relation to the baroque plan
raises a question about proprietary involvement and whether or not the church
violated the basic principles of the Act concerning Religion. For Baltimore to
have financed a Catholic church using public funds would have violated his
charter. Even with the lax enforcement of the penal laws in England after 1660,
Baltimore could not risk opening any discussion of his charter rights. The
chapel was not a public building. By differentiating public and private behavior,
Baltimore and his relatives avoided any possible transgressions against the act.
To Maryland Protestant immigrants in the 1660s or 1670s, however, accultur-
ated to a state-supported church, such an argument might have sounded disingenuous or even incredible.

Lord Baltimore maintained his distance from the project. The chapel did not
receive any significant financial support from the proprietor or from public
funds. However, it could not have been built without his approval and, more important, without the support of Governor Calvert and Chancellor Calvert. But
they acted as individual Catholics, not in their public capacity. Charles Calvert
and Father Warren arrived in the colony on the same ship. It was significant that
Governor Calvert and Chancellor Calvert had the financial resources to make
substantial contributions. While a paper trail leading back to the Calverts does
not exist, "it is unlikely that such a building could have been constructed in such
a prominent location in St. Mary's City without the cooperation and approval of
these two men." Public money supported the chapel only in the most indirect
way. Neither the governor nor the chancellor enjoyed wealth outside of their
appointed positions. In 1662 the assembly awarded the new governor a hand-
some annual subsidy of £450. Indeed, the acrimonious relationship between
the nephew and the uncle stemmed from their jostling for rewards of government office. As Catholics, however, they had no reason to extend their hard feelings to the chapel project, which both men would have supported with their
salaries.[82]

The Calverts acted as members of the Catholic community in St. Mary's City, not as proprietary authorities. Most likely, the prospering members of this community provided the requisite funds to build the chapel. Wills written during this period provided the means. Catholic testators throughout Maryland frequently left bequests to the Catholic Church. Robert Cole of Newtown bequeathed to "my honored friend Mr. Francis Fitzherbert or his Successor" the best hogshead of his tobacco crop and his best steer, in testimony that he died a Roman Catholic. In the decade 1660–70, perhaps as many as 60 percent of Catholic testators left legacies in their wills to support the Church. Bequests came from all social and economic levels, indicating that this kind of support "was generally viewed as an obligation incumbent on all Catholics." For example, a bequest from Walter Hall in 1678 provided five thousand pounds of tobacco to purchase ornaments for the chapel. St. Mary's Catholics, given the numerous bequests in their wills, also donated similar sums while they were alive. Catholics also provided sweat equity, which may explain why this large and expensive building generated no recorded lawsuits. Construction done by enthusiastic volunteers lessened the likelihood of acrimonious legal actions.[83]

Whatever the financial arrangements, the Jesuits owned the chapel, which had been built on their land at a time when they were the only priests in Maryland. The Franciscans who officiated at St. Mary's in the 1670s did so only with the cooperation and approval of the Jesuits. They assisted the Society in ministering to the widely spread Catholic population. Governor Francis Nicholson identified the structure as a Jesuit chapel in 1697, and a Jesuit celebrated the last mass in the chapel in 1704.[84]

One outcome, perhaps unintended, of Baltimore's policy to remove religion from public life was the absence of educational institutions. Not until 1671 did the assembly consider public support for a school or college for the "education of youth in learning and virtue." The act failed when the two houses disagreed on its provisions. Baltimore had some interest in the education of his colonists but did not extend himself on the matter. He wrote on behalf of Mr. Robert Douglas, who arrived in the colony in November of 1672. Charles responded that he intended to employ him to teach his children and that he would encourage the organization of a school with Douglas as its master. The governor despaired of developing a school along the lines Baltimore wished and further noted his fear that the educator would not find "the people here so desirous of Educating their Children" as he might anticipate. It was not the proprietor but the Jesuits who finally established a school. The Jesuits' annual letter for 1681 noted that four years earlier they had founded, "in the midst of barbarism, a school of humane letters." They proclaimed that the "new-born school" had already sent two students to St. Omer for further education. A new school started privately and without government support or intervention conformed nicely to the original principles of the "Maryland designe." It also demonstrated the remarkable vitality of the Catholic community. No other religious group was prepared to follow suit.[85]

Although Catholics were a small minority of the population, they had considerable importance. As in England, Catholics in Maryland tended to be found in the upper social stratum. After 1660 they assumed a political role far beyond what their numbers would have suggested, although never to the extent of the 1630s. His experiences of the 1640s notwithstanding, the proprietor expected that Catholics would remain loyal to him. But just as in the earlier decade, religion as a method of determining loyalty was far from foolproof. In 1672 Governor Calvert wrote of his determination to keep the present membership of the assembly for the foreseeable future. But he lamented the behavior of some of the Catholics in the assembly, who did not vote as expected. They would, he hopefully predicted, endeavor "to understand themselves Better and their own interests." The freedom of conscience and the right to worship as Catholics competed with other interests, and Catholics did not always recognize the proprietary priorities as the best means to protect their interests.[86]

The independence they reflected in the political realm perhaps reflected the freedom they enjoyed in the spiritual realm. In the absence of the traditional religious hierarchy and without support from civil authorities, Maryland Catholics looked like kindred spirits to the congregationalists. The priests obviously depended on the voluntary support of their churches. Governor Calvert thought the Catholics of St. Mary's church were "very cold in their Contribution" to a Mr. Carew, who he thought was so modest a gentleman that he never demanded anything of them. Charles Calvert offered to intervene on his behalf, but the priest refused. In the same letter, he intimated that Maryland priests moved about at their will. Father Carew told the governor of his intention to move to Anne Arundel, where he had reconciled some to the Church. Certainly the presence of the priests was crucial; but of greater importance, lay Catholics and their priests willingly moved beyond their traditional organizational lines and created new ones. As one observer proclaimed, Maryland Catholics "have great, indeed, all freedom."[87]

As lord of the Maryland manor, Baltimore saw himself as a bulwark against those who tried to take his colony in directions he did not want it to go. On November 30, 1675, the second Lord Baltimore relinquished control of his colony. Acting on the certain advice and information that his father had died, Governor Calvert by a proclamation of March 4, 1675/76, informed the people of Maryland that he was the new proprietor and the third Lord Baltimore. If Marylanders mourned his father's passing or toasted his accomplishments, they left no record of such feelings or actions. He had been singularly important in their lives yet far removed from them. With remarkable persistence, he had kept the enterprise going. Catholic Maryland had been his Maryland.[88]

The more than four decades of his proprietorship can only be described as tumultuous. To a considerable measure, his troubles resulted from his steadfast adherence to the Roman Catholic faith. For Baltimore religious freedom was the means to two significant ends. First, he desired peace and stability within his domain. This was the sine qua non of his prosperity and the prosperity and well-being of those who ventured to Maryland. Second, freedom of conscience was the only way he could assure English Catholics that they could worship with relative freedom in Maryland. These ends squared with his liberal personality. In an age that demanded uniformity, he seemed indifferent to the religious commitments of others. Soon after Charles became governor, Baltimore seemingly scandalized his son by recommending a surgeon whom he had dispatched to the colony. Charles dutifully received the surgeon into his home, only to find him lacking in those things Baltimore had recommended. He was "an Indifferent good Chirurgeon & as indifferent in his religion." Charles believed that he was little better than an atheist and noted that some called him the "Heathen doctor."[89]

A devout Catholic in his own way, Cecilius Calvert did not seem unduly concerned with converting others to his faith. His only extant comment regarding conversion in the Restoration period came during his conversation with Agretti. The precise language the proprietor used remains unknown. The papal representative reported that the proprietor said it would be easy to convert the others since there were no heretical preachers in that country. A privately made charge in 1673 indicated that Charles believed his father was very sensitive about meddling in others' religion. The former attorney general, Henry Coursey, wrote the proprietor that the governor had tried to convert one of his servant boys to Catholicism. Charles angrily responded that he did not appreciate the accusation and protested that he had never troubled any of his servants, nor indeed any other person, about religion. He called the accusation a lie. The religious affiliations of his colonists concerned Cecil less than their secular loyalties. As long as they affirmed their loyalty to him, he willingly accepted all comers regardless of their religion.[90]

This relative indifference regarding the religious commitments of those who went to Maryland served him well. The period that followed Baltimore's restoration was one of remarkable accomplishment. The bold enterprise that George Calvert envisioned and that Cecil Calvert implemented came to fruition. For fifteen years, maybe twenty, the Calverts—English Catholics—made religious freedom a reality. The fact that religiously diverse English Christians enjoyed the freedom to worship as they pleased startled a Presbyterian minister. Reverend Matthew Hill, who through "divine goodness" came to Maryland in 1669, reported that he and other Presbyterians enjoyed a great deal of liberty, particularly in matters of religion. He did not find it unusual that many, including the governor, "give obedience" to the church of Rome but still enjoyed their public liberty. Hill noted the presence of many of the reformed religion who had lived without pastoral assistance for many years. He delighted that "devine providence" had placed him among a loving and a willing people where they enjoyed their public opportunities "with a greate deale of freedome." Hill's assessment confirms that Marylanders in the 1660s worshiped according to the dictates of their consciences. They conformed neither to a state-established uniformity in worship nor to the demands of Christian magistrates who protected the "true" religion.[91]

CHAPTER NINE

"Scandalous and offensive to the Government"

The "Popish Chappel" at St. Mary's City and the End of Religious Freedom (1676–1705)

Charles Calvert, the third Lord Baltimore, inherited a prospering and relatively stable colony, or so it seemed. The economy was healthier in the early 1660s than contemporary reports suggested, and a strong recovery began in 1668. The Chesapeake economy experienced a genuine boom in the late 1670s. No one knew the colony better in 1676 than the colony's first resident proprietor. Cecil Lord Baltimore had appointed his twenty-three-year-old son and heir to govern the colony in 1661. Over the next fourteen years, Charles directed the council, met the assembly, brought in tobacco crops, entertained at his home, and worshiped at the Catholic chapels in St. Mary's City. Letter after letter from his ever-inquisitive father pressed him for details on all aspects of the ebbs and flows of life in the colony, which he dutifully answered, if not in a timely fashion, at least through 1673. By the time he became the proprietor, Governor Calvert knew the inhabitants and, for better or worse, they knew him.[1]

Three events in the first year of his proprietorship indicated what lay ahead. First, fear of Indian reprisals in Maryland that coincided with Bacon's Rebellion in Virginia brought higher taxes, which in turn led to a revolt centered in Calvert County. Disputes centering on assembly representation and taxation demanded, but did not always command, Charles's attention throughout his proprietary rule. Second, in June 1676 he departed for England to secure his inheritance. Leaving the province in the charge of others, as Charles would learn, entailed some risk. Third, workers completed construction of an imposing brick statehouse that formed one of the focal points in the planned city that the Calvert family initiated in the mid-1660s. Built at opposite ends of the St. Mary's City's town center, the brick chapel and the statehouse, the most impressive buildings in the city, signified both the possibilities for a prosperous capital town and a commitment to the separation of church and state.[2]

That successful separation of church and state allowed Charles to be sanguine about religious controversies that had inflamed the province in earlier decades. In 1678 a triumphant but credulous third Lord Baltimore wrote to the English government that his province was "in great peace and Quiett." He reasoned that all people were "secured to their content for a quiett enjoyment Of every Thing that they can Reasonably desyre." This he attributed to the general toleration, which the assembly had legislated in 1649, that allowed all Christians the liberty to worship "God in such Manner" as was most agreeable to their judgments and consciences without any penalty. The proprietor's optimistic pronouncement aside, he failed to maintain the colonial enterprise that his family had labored so diligently to establish. About ten years after he wrote, the Protestant Associators toppled the Calvert coalition, ended his proprietary rule, and set the Calverts' broad-based religious toleration on the road to extinction.[3]

Why did the Calverts' bold experiment end so ignobly? A number of forces, among them the innovative nature of the enterprise, a revival of anti-Catholicism in England, a severe depression in the tobacco economy, a growing and increasingly restive number of unchurched Episcopal Protestants, and the absence of proprietary leadership at critical junctures, converged in the mid-1680s. The emerging crisis surpassed in gravity the challenges presented by Richard Ingle in the mid-1640s and by Richard Bennett and others in the mid-1650s. Unlike the earlier troubles, which outsiders had perpetrated, this one arose within the small community.

Was the Calverts' goal of a society where Protestants and Catholics lived side by side on terms of religious and political equality too radical to succeed on a long-term basis? Without doubt, the "Maryland designe" that Charles inherited ran contrary to the prevailing tenets of his era. When the Protestant Associators overthrew the Catholic proprietor and moved toward the establishment of the Church of England, no major Christian denomination had embraced, let alone practiced, doctrines such as freedom of conscience and liberty of worship for all Christians. Indeed no major European state allowed Christians to worship as they pleased without any restraints on their secular activities. The English, despite occasional flirtations with such ideas, demonstrated repeatedly that they still clung to traditional ideas of uniformity, conformity, and the belief that the state should protect the "true religion." The liberty permitted to Catholics in England still scandalized learned English Protestants. The dreaded penal laws, most of which survived into the next century, remained a threat to English and Maryland Catholics. The fear of international Catholicism, as the toppling of James II demonstrated in 1688, still incited the English. The Act of Toleration passed by Parliament in 1689 proved more restrictive than the informal toleration practiced by Charles II and James II and did nothing to remove the civil disabilities of those who worshiped in chapels other than those of the Church of England. But these factors, though necessary preconditions, neither make the rebellion against Catholic rule inevitable nor explain adequately why the Calverts ultimately failed.[4]

The continued success of the enterprise depended on the political and social skills of the third Lord Baltimore and the support he could muster from the colony's inhabitants. Like his father, he came to his position of authority at a young age and without any administrative or political experience. Unlike his father, Charles did not prove to be an astute learner in the political arena. His aloof personality, his authoritarian political demeanor, and the actions he and those most closely associated with him took, especially after 1684, became the triggering events that provoked rebellion. He neglected to respond imaginatively to the changes taking place in his colony. His words and his deeds indicated that he only partially grasped the remarkable accomplishments of his father. Most important, he ignored the likelihood that Catholic success would almost certainly exacerbate Protestant fears and jealousy. As a result, the third Lord Baltimore squandered his inheritance.

Charles faced a series of political, economic, and religious crises. In the political sphere, members of the assembly remained his chief nemesis. Charles evidenced the same disdain for grasping legislators as his father had. He, too, found curbing the aspirations of the freemen in the assembly a daunting task. The proprietor's continued assertion of his charter prerogatives, his lack of patience, and his inability to accommodate the assembly on key issues prolonged disputes. Acrimony over fundamental issues such as the number of delegates that were to be elected only served to alienate a significant portion of the population. Uneven economic prosperity caused further disaffection. The proprietor's policies did little to alleviate the plight of small planters and freed servants. Finally, religious tensions within the small community remained as a divisive element that would have required the greatest management skills to keep in check.[5]

The proprietor received ample warning that elements of his religiously diverse population needed urgent attention. John Yeo, a Church of England minister in Maryland, wrote to the archbishop of Canterbury shortly after Charles became the proprietor to inform him of the "Deplorable estate & condition of the Province of Maryland for want of an established ministry." He claimed that there were only three ministers who were conformable to the doctrine and discipline of the Church of England to serve the approximately twenty thousand souls scattered throughout Maryland. The result was that Episcopal Protestants "fell away" either to "Popery, Quakerism or Phanatiscisme." In addition, he maintained that in the absence of an established Church, inhabitants profaned the Lord's Day, despised religion, and committed all sorts of notorious vices. Maryland had "become a Sodom of uncleanness" and a pest-house of iniquity. He compared his church's situation with that of its professed enemies, the popish priests and Jesuits, who were encouraged and provided for, and the Quakers, who provided for their speakers in their conventicles. Jasper Danckaerts, on a visit to the Chesapeake three years later, echoed Yeo's assessment about the social and religious life of the Protestants. He noted that the lives of the planters "are very godless and profane. They listen neither to God nor his commandments." He attributed the deplorable condition to the dearth of ministers and the poor quality of the few who were ministering to those affiliated with the Church of England. Their complaints inadvertently highlighted one of the unintended consequences of the implementation of the Calverts' radical religious policies.

For better or worse, the colony was becoming more secular. Civil government in Maryland took no responsibility for the religious or educational needs of the inhabitants. It downplayed clerical influence by assigning duties having to do with marriage and probate to the secular authority. The secularization fostered a growing sense of individualism, which did not always work to the proprietor's advantage. When it came to religion and education, Marylanders had to take responsibility for their own institutions and their commitment to abide by them. Only one school, a brick one built for the Jesuits, stood in 1677. When Yeo and Danckaerts surveyed this society, they saw a Sodom filled with "godless and profane" people, and they implicitly blamed the religious policies pursued by the third Lord Baltimore. Yeo concluded that Maryland's salvation lay in establishing a church that conformed to the English model.[6]

When Yeo sent his diatribe the archbishop, he implored him to use his influence with the English government to secure the establishment of a Protestant ministry in Maryland. Anonymous inhabitants from Maryland and Virginia made a similar plea but directed their "Complaint From Heaven With a Hue and a crye" to the king. The composers of that letter (many of whom came to Maryland as servants) bared their suppressed emotions and revealed their unremitting hostility toward the proprietor. They couched their arguments in particularly virulent anti-Catholic terms and sent the denunciation to England at about the same time the Jesuits opened their second school in Maryland. In a tone reminiscent of the attacks on the second Lord Baltimore made by Bennett and others two decades earlier, they attacked the Catholic connection and the nature of proprietary government. The authors based their frenetic letter on two false assumptions: papal determination to conquer England by force of arms and the intention of Maryland Papists, with the help of French clerics, to drive "us Protestants to Purgatory."[7]

After the authors recounted the recent Indian troubles that preceded Bacon's Rebellion in Virginia, they lambasted Governor Calvert for his reckless behavior. In a gesture reminiscent of how the English dealt with Charles I in 1649, they called for the proprietor to be held accountable by the king for, among other things, murders in Virginia and Maryland and the ruin of the entire province. They attacked Baltimore's dominance of a pliant assembly that he controlled through a crude manipulation of the electoral process. They found the high taxes imposed by what they considered a corrupt proprietary government even more onerous, and they sought amelioration by appealing to the king.[8]

The authors saved their most spirited language for an attack on Baltimore and his Catholic connections specifically and the threat Catholicism posed in general. They wondered why English bishops did not send Protestant pastors as the pope sent priests to his American Papists. Ridiculing Baltimore as "an inferior Irish lord," they characterized the proprietor, who then was in England, as one of the "Popes privy Agents in England." The facile connection between Catholicism and absolutism reinforced their anxieties. The proprietor had assumed more royal power to himself over his subjects than the king did in England. The authors demanded to know why Episcopal Protestants must

submit to Maryland's "arbitrary government" and thereby entangle "our innocent posterity" under the tyrannical yoke of papacy. They claimed that the (assumed) vast conspiracy to set Protestants against each other to secure papal
supremacy and to overthrow Protestants would lead to Lord Baltimore's canon-
ization at Rome. The letter writers, having vented their collective spleen, concluded by urging the king to intervene in extraordinary ways. They wanted him
to seize the government, appoint a Protestant governor, and establish regular
salaries based on the present tax on tobacco. The dissidents implored the king
to send six or seven hundred "resolute Scotts Highlanders" to protect the colony
from the Indians and "French robbers." They called for the establishment of
Protestant ministers, free schools, and glebe lands in every county, "liberty of
conscience" notwithstanding. They wanted the king and Parliament to interpret
the charter justly and in favor of the "good people inhabiting the province," and
further to allow the freemen to appeal decisions made in Maryland to the king.[9]

The authors' casual reference to liberty of conscience signified a deep dissatisfaction with both the charter and the religious freedom that resulted from its
implementation. They argued that nothing in the charter warranted turning the
province into "the Pope's devotion." Nor did liberty of conscience justify that
result. The dissidents saw liberty of conscience as nothing more than a device to
protect and enhance Catholics and their priests. Concentrating only on
Catholic success overlooked the opportunities other Christians had in both spiritual and material realms. Their attack on liberty of conscience, albeit in a veiled
form, should have alerted the proprietor that one of the pillars of the "Maryland
designe" was in jeopardy.[10]

If Baltimore responded to the charges advanced by these critics and their call
to restructure the colony through imperial intervention, his reply has not survived. He did, however, have an opportunity to address some of the issues when
he responded to a set of questions sent by the Committee of Trade and Plantations. Baltimore's answers reveal some of the thinking that lurked behind his
actions, or lack thereof, relating to religious matters. He understood the utili-
tarian value of the "Maryland designe" for fending off the growing English
colonial bureaucracy. His answers also show, however, that he failed to recognize the threatening implications of these inquiries from the government. Two
of the questions specifically addressed religious demographics. The committee
wanted to know the religious persuasion of Marylanders and the number of
churches and ministers within the province. The Roman Catholic proprietor
muted Catholic success by noting the great variety of religious commitments

in the colony. He emphasized that Marylanders supported their spiritual leaders through the free-will offerings "of their own persuasion." They built churches and meeting houses through "free and voluntary" contributions. The Jesuits in 1681 corroborated the proprietor's statement by noting that they maintained the mission from the agricultural labors of their tenants and the charity of their faithful parishioners. The proprietor emphasized that the religiously diverse nature of the population would make gaining consent for a law that compelled Marylanders to maintain ministers of the Church of England "a most difficult task." In addition, the Act concerning Religion gave the people religious freedom without any payments imposed on them for maintaining a particular denomination.[11]

His responses provide additional insight into his understanding of the origins of his father's religious policies. Charles, who was born about four years after his father dispatched the *Ark* and the *Dove*, did not have firsthand knowledge of the events of that period. His responses indicate that he came to see "toleration" as something the first colonists forced on his father. His tone suggests that he begrudged the presence of non-Catholics in his colony. He was the first proprietor who had lived his entire life as a Catholic. He had every reason to resent the attacks on his religion. The authors of "a Hue and a crye" clearly slandered Maryland Catholics and reported rumors designed to inflict maximum damage in England. For example, they compared priests in England who traveled disguised as tradesmen with those in Maryland who traveled openly as priests to propagate the "Pope's interest and supremacy in America." They reported that priests received five pounds sterling for every turncoat they converted. Whatever the reasons, Charles appeared to be a less tolerant man than his father, and this attitude helps to explain another point he made in the letter.[12]

The proprietor did not grasp the implications of the growing unchurched population. One outcome of the restoration of the 1649 Act concerning Religion, perhaps unintended, was the lack of development of a Protestant Episcopal faith community. These Protestants, for the most part unchurched, gained the least from the Calvert religious policies. Charles Calvert, content with the peace and quiet he saw, paid little heed to their situation. After all, these Episcopal Protestants enjoyed the same freedom as the Catholics did. But unlike their hierarchical Catholic counterparts, the hierarchical Protestants lacked the will or the ability to create viable religious communities through voluntary associations and seemed incapable of organizing without government support.[13]

The Episcopal Protestants presented a dilemma for the proprietor. He knew that he could not acquiesce to their clamors for a tax-supported clergy without abandoning the basic principles that his father had established. Rather than seeking an alternative solution, he ignored the problem. He persisted in his beliefs that no significant religious strife existed and that the colony would continue to prosper in its absence. Shipmaster Richard Shepherd reinforced the notion of religious tranquility when he testified a few years later that he knew of "no quarrel between the Protestants and Papists." The absence of open conflict only concealed the deep discontent that existed in the Protestant community.[14]

The number of Episcopal Protestants rapidly increased in the late seventeenth century. The immigrants of the 1670s and 1680s tended to be adherents of the Church of England, and, finding little in the way of institutionalized religion in Maryland, they became increasingly iconoclastic. Some, as we have seen, showed no reticence in making their complaints directly to English authorities.[15]

Not all Church of England supporters were so disgruntled. In an attempt to answer the charges that his government showed partiality "on all occasions towards those of the Popish Religion to the discouragement of his Majesties Protestant Subjects," Baltimore produced a statement in 1682 signed by twenty-five influential Episcopal Protestants. The signatories acknowledged "the general freedom & privilege which we and all persons whatsoever" enjoy in Maryland. They touted the Act concerning Religion, which assured the free and public exercise and enjoyment of religion for them and any other inhabitants "professing the name of Jesus." From their own observations, these Protestants knew that Baltimore distributed positions of honor and profit impartially without any respect to religious persuasion and that Protestants were well represented in the government. However, perhaps because so many of the signatories were related to the proprietor by marriage, their protestation had little effect with English authorities. At any rate, Charles's defense came too late to stem the course of events.[16]

The unchurched Episcopal Protestants seemed unwilling to accept the basic rules laid down by the Catholic Lords Baltimore. Given the church-state relationship to which they were accustomed in England, they were quite uncomfortable having their ministers "maintained by a voluntary contribution of those of their own persuasion," even though, as Charles Lord Baltimore pointed out, the situation was the same for Presbyterians, Independents, Anabaptists, Quakers, and Roman Catholics. They lacked the missionary zeal of the Quakers and the affluence of the Catholics and saw their only hope in a tax-supported institution. Dissatisfied on so many counts, these unchurched Marylanders were a continuing source of political unrest.[17]

The proprietor never lacked malcontents willing to register protests in Virginia, England, or Maryland. He received another warning in 1681. That year his government charged former governor Josias Fendall with mutinous and seditious speeches, practices, and attempts against the proprietor. Numerous witnesses testified that the Protestant gentleman had publicly declared the Catholic proprietor a traitor, had ridiculed as fools those who paid their taxes, and had claimed that a Catholic-Indian conspiracy intended to destroy all the Protestants. After hearing the evidence, a jury found Fendall guilty of speaking "severall seditious words" but heard no evidence that he had acted upon his words. The court stopped short of imposing the extreme sentences of "boaring of the Tongue" or "cropping of one or both ears." Rather, in a spirit of moderation, the justices imposed a fine of forty thousand pounds of tobacco to be paid to the proprietor and banished Fendall from the province forever. Baltimore took this threat from Fendall and his supporters seriously. Had they not been apprehended in a timely manner, he informed colonial officials in London, "you would soon have heard of anther Bacon." Rather than looking at the root causes, however, the proprietor seemed more concerned with the potential impact that Protestant complaints might have with the emerging imperial bureaucracy. Reassuring the Privy Council that his government constituted no threat to Protestants did not have the effect that taking steps to reduce the tension would have had.[18]

By the 1680s, unrest among the Episcopal Protestants, combined with endemic anti-Catholicism in England and in the colony and a lack of effective leadership threatened the experiment in religious freedom for all Christians. The third Lord Baltimore, by depreciating the threat posed by the Episcopal Protestants, demonstrated that he lacked the political acumen necessary to keep the experiment going. His father had understood well the reliability of governing through family members. At the same time, he had remained sensitive to shifting conditions within the colony and had taken the necessary steps to try to co-opt those who threatened his rule. Charles embraced the first principle but ignored the second. With the exception of a temporary liaison with Quaker leaders, he consolidated power within a narrowing coalition of family and coreligionists. Under his leadership, the composition of the council changed from one having a significant Protestant representation to one dominated by Catholics and a few Protestant relatives of the Calverts. Of the ten appointments made by Charles between 1677 and 1684, only one went to an unrelated Protestant. By confining his appointments to a relatively small portion of Maryland's population, namely, Catholics and those Protestants who had married into the family, Baltimore made Maryland vulnerable to attacks from England. This was increasingly true in the wake of the popish plot (1678) and the anti-Catholic Exclusion Crisis (1679–81) in England, which attempted to eliminate James, duke of York, who was by then an avowed Catholic, as heir to Charles II. Immigrants arriving in the late 1670s and 1680s reflected the increasing anti-Catholicism that swept England. To have a chance to continue, Baltimore had to remain true to the vision. This meant he should have educated the newcomers about the "Maryland designe" and integrated these nominal members of the Church of England into his circle. His failure to accommodate them in the 1680s indicates that he did not grasp, or at least did not fully comprehend, what his father and his grandfather wanted for their colony.[19]

The success and visibility of Maryland Catholics in the late 1680s, and the increasing anti-Catholicism of this period in England and America, boded ill for a continuation of the Calvert enterprise. The behavior of Catholics undoubtedly contributed to the crisis. The success of the priests and their "Tribe," as a later governor characterized them, bred contempt and envy among the many Marylanders who were left out. Here was the paradox of the "Maryland designe." Could Maryland Catholics survive their own success? Cecil Lord Baltimore initially sought unity and peace by requiring his coreligionists to practice their religion as privately as possible, to remain silent upon all occasions of religious discourse, and to treat Protestants with as much mildness and favor as justice would permit. Above all, he feared complaints entered in London or Virginia. Catholic success, paradoxically, rendered the rules less relevant. The struggles of the past seemed remote in the 1680s. Catholic amnesia led to complacency on the one hand and a closing of ranks in the face of growing hostility on the other.

The Jesuits exemplified a Catholic success story that accelerated during Charles's proprietorship. Still guilty of treason by their very presence in England, the priests reported in 1681 that their mission was flourishing and recounted their success in sending young Marylanders overseas for additional education. They noted that enemies of the Society spread reports of the Society's immense wealth. The priests thought this mocked their generosity in sharing their modest resources and decried the vigilante violence used against them.

Ironically, the success of their endeavors undermined the colony's continued existence under Catholic leadership.[20]

Catholics, always a minority of the population, represented a success story while the Episcopal Protestants faced an uncertain future. When two groups compete for scarce resources such as access to public office, the success of one group becomes the other group's failure and creates a breeding ground for conflict. When such groups live within a relatively small community, as Maryland was, two important developments may be more prominent than in a larger community. The first is increased hostility between the opposing groups, and the second is an intensification of loyalty within the groups. In the face of an alienated group (unchurched Episcopal Protestants who saw only continued exclusion from political appointments and diminished chances to prosper) and their increased hostility, the successful group (proprietary Catholics and their associates) closed their ranks. As proprietor, Charles alone had the opportunity to stem the tide. Instead of reaching out, he retrenched. He left those in opposition little choice but to take up arms against a government closed to all but a few proprietary cronies.[21]

Two external threats to the Maryland charter in the 1680s may in part explain the proprietor's failure to address the deteriorating situation in his colony. First, a charter granted to William Penn in 1681 conflicted with the Maryland charter and imperiled Lord Baltimore's claim to present-day Delaware. The dispute that ensued elicited little sympathy from the vast majority of inhabitants. Second, a growing commitment by the English colonial bureaucracy to vacate proprietary charters and replace them with royal control also endangered proprietary interests. Baltimore's departure from the province in 1684 accelerated the progressive decline in religious harmony. The situation demanded more than assurances or declarations. One weakness that became increasingly evident was Charles's lack of discernment when it came to choosing his subordinates. He entrusted his government to a group of deputy governors who were either relatives or Catholics (or both). With the death or departure of a number of Protestants by 1688, his government seemed to fit the Catholic image long projected by unhappy Protestants. Charles's absence and the resultant appointments provided the opening scenario for a series of events that would provoke one final rebellion against the rule of the Catholic Lords Baltimore.[22]

For most unchurched Episcopal Protestants, Maryland had become a closed society that could only be opened by force of arms. Catholic success bred resentment, especially among recent immigrants. Their deeply seated anti-Catholic sentiments, fears of popish plots, and the inept leadership of the proprietary family converged in 1689. That summer another band of discontented Marylanders under the pretense of religion rebelled. This uprising, led by the Protestant sons-in-law of that irascible Catholic Thomas Gerard, toppled the Calvert enterprise. The overthrow of the Calverts was the work of a small group "primarily intent on increasing its own power." These men effectively exploited "real anxieties and grievances" in a period of economic hard times. Confronted by an armed band of rebels and without any means to repel them, the governor's council surrendered. The new English government of William and Mary, both stalwart Protestants, eventually ratified the 1689 armed victory of the rebels and brought Maryland under their control. The appointment of a Protestant royal governor closed the book on religious freedom in Maryland.[23]

An English Catholic family held some of the fundamental beliefs of its culture at bay for close to sixty years. More important, in the absence of government support, the Maryland Catholics developed a faith community capable of sustaining its own institutions and clerics. Church of England Protestants, in contrast, proved incapable of throwing off the shackles of the past. As a religious community, these Protestants floundered. Developing and sustaining religious institutions without the heavy hand of the state was beyond their grasp. They looked to the government to provide sustenance. With the overthrow of the Calverts' propriety rule, these Protestants had their opportunity. After nearly six decades, religious uniformity finally triumphed. In 1692 Maryland Protestants turned their backs on the future and embraced an established church. In their march to the statehouse, they trampled the 1649 Act concerning Religion, which had served as the basis for freedom of worship without interference or support from the secular government. Within a short time, the assembly responded by passing legislation that established the Church of England as the religion of the colony. A few years later the assembly moved the capital to Annapolis, the seat of much of the earlier dissatisfaction with the Catholic Lords Baltimore and their coreligionists. The new Protestant government excluded from full membership in Maryland society Catholics and Quakers, the two most feared or despised religious minorities in England and America.

Having stuck their collective knife into the proprietary side, the newly elected Protestant assemblymen twisted it. With cruel mockery, they paraphrased the preamble of the 1649 Act concerning Religion in the preamble of their repressive act of 1692. The 1649 act began with these words: "Forasmuch as in a well governed and Christian Commonwealth matters concerning Religion and the honor of God ought in the first place to bee taken into serious consideration and endeavoured to bee settled." This act, passed in the proprietor's name, assured freedom of conscience to Christians living in Maryland. Its 1692 successor began with these words: "Forasmuch as in a well Governed Commonwealth Matters of Religion and Honour of God ought in the first place be taken in serious consideration, and nothing being more acceptable to Almighty God, then the true and Sincere worship and Service of him according to his Holy Word." This act, passed under the authority of the newly established Protestant monarchs, ended freedom of worship, the concept on which George and Cecil Calvert acted. It established the Church of England as the official religion for Marylanders and provided the steps by which the tax-supported church would come into existence.[24]

The Jesuits' "good brick Chappell," as Governor Francis Nicholson characterized the church in St. Mary's City in 1697, symbolized the success of a few English Catholics who took advantage of the Maryland enterprise. It had graced the landscape for perhaps three decades and epitomized the Calvert experiment with liberty of conscience. Now, however, the brick chapel stood in defiance of the new order. Catholic fortunes had taken a downturn. No longer would they enjoy "any Custom of Toleration" that had existed from the beginning. Over the next few years, the Protestant governor, council, and assembly had the opportunity to express their views on religious freedom in Maryland as it related to Catholics.[25]

In 1704 the new governor, John Seymour, summoned "two Popish Priests" before his council. Jesuit William Hunter denied consecrating the chapel but acknowledged that he had been there "in his common Priests vestments." His colleague Father Robert Brooke admitted that "he did say mass in the Court Time at the Chappel of St. Maries." The governor, informed that this was "the first Complaint" against the two, severely reprimanded them, warning them to expect "the utmost Severity of the Law" upon any future "Exercise of your Superstitious Vanities."[26]

On September 11, 1704, the council took note of this "use of the Popish Chappel" at St. Mary's City, where "there is a protestant Church" and where the county court met. This the council found "both Scandalous and offensive to the Government" and advised the governor that he should immediately close the "Popish Chappel and that no Person [should] presume to make use thereof under the pretence whatsoever." An order quickly went forth to the sheriff of St.

Mary's County to lock up the chapel and keep the key. In an unprecedented act in Maryland history, the government prevented some of its inhabitants from using their own church.[27]

Within weeks the assembly followed this order with its own legislation. It acted to protect the king's Protestant subjects in Maryland against the insolence and growth of popery. This act, which passed on September 30, marked a significant departure from the policies implemented by the Catholic proprietors and bore a striking, if somewhat subdued, resemblance to the penal legislation that the Catholics thought they had left behind. Civil authorities now intervened to keep the unthinking "Multitude" from the beguiling but superstitious vanities of Roman Catholic teachings. The assembly moved to restrict the activities of priests. It allowed priests to baptize (only) the children who had "Popish Parents" but prohibited them from saying Mass or exercising their functions as popish bishops or priests. It criminalized any attempts to proselytize among loyal English subjects in Maryland. The assembly authorized a hefty fine of fifty pounds sterling for each violation of the law. The act struck a blow against Catholic education by prohibiting priests or anyone making profession of the "Popish Religion" from maintaining schools. Those convicted faced deportation to England. Finally, the act empowered the governor to intervene when Catholic parents tried to compel their Protestant children to change religion by refusing to allow the children maintenance suitable to the degree and ability of the parents and the age and education of the children. This completed the revolution that began with the ousting of the third Lord Baltimore. Civil authorities claimed jurisdiction over the religion and the education of Marylanders.[28]

Later Jesuits dismantled the locked chapel, reclaiming the bricks for another building some distance from the former capital city. They used the bricks to construct a brick manor house at St. Inigoes, the 1637 plantation that remained in their possession until just before World War II. Eventually, sometime between 1705 and 1753, the Jesuits lost control of the Chapel Land, the twenty-five-acre site on which so much of Maryland's history unfolded. The destruction of the chapel symbolized the demise of the Calvert vision that the second Lord Baltimore had implemented in 1633.

It is perhaps fitting that the tale of English Catholics who migrated to Maryland should end where it began. In the early seventeenth century, many English Catholics looked to Spain for an amelioration of their condition. Sir George Calvert, as the King James's principal secretary of state, expended considerable time and energy attempting to negotiate the Spanish match on behalf of his monarch. The effort, which would have improved conditions for Catholics in England, came to naught. Soon after the rebels unseated his grandson, the third Lord Baltimore, a group of Maryland Catholics, fearful of the changes taking place in their colony, petitioned the Spanish ambassador on behalf of their fellow Catholics. Maryland Catholics now looked beyond English borders for protection. This effort also came to naught, and it illustrates that English and Catholic seemed no less compatible in 1690 than they had been in 1632.[29]

The "Maryland designe" was an aberration. With their innovative attempts to forge a new understanding for church-state relations, the Catholic Lords Baltimore had dared to rise above their age. Their effort to implement freedom of conscience for Christians must not be diminished by its ultimate failure, for it pointed to the future. The 1649 Act concerning Religion, a hybrid of proprietary and legislative ideas, freed the human spirit from the shackles of tradition. It allowed Christians to practice their religion on a voluntary basis without any impositions by civil authorities. For a brief period, from about 1661 to 1688, it helped to preserve civil peace. The act demonstrated the limitations of legislated religious freedom. One group, the Catholics, succeeded too well. The proprietary element could not sustain the act in the face of increased discontent from the Episcopal Protestants, who felt that the act disadvantaged them. By 1688 too many Marylanders no longer saw the value of the act.

Marylanders, and for that matter, English men and women, were not ready for broad religious freedom based on voluntary associations. English history provides comparable examples in the efforts of both James I and James II, who merely attempted to extend toleration to Catholics and other dissenters through executive power. But neither of these Stuart kings, popularly identified with absolutism, could establish toleration, a concept that was so contrary to public opinion. That the Catholic second Lord Baltimore established and maintained religious liberty for as long as he did attests to his skills as a proprietor. This daring experiment with religious freedom failed because the third Lord Baltimore could not find ways to maintain it.

George Calvert wrote a charter that placed the proprietor at the head of the colonial society. The charter invested great powers and responsibilities in that office. First and foremost, the proprietor had to provide effective leadership. To have deflected the crisis of the mid-1680s would have taken some bold initiatives by the third Lord Baltimore. His father, when faced with a similar crisis in the late 1640s, made such a move when he fostered a revolution in his own government. He appointed a Protestant governor and council and required them to take oaths not to abuse the Catholics. These moves in turn led to the 1649 Act concerning Religion. They did not prevent the crisis, but the actions made it possible for him to regain his colony from the government of Oliver Cromwell. The second Lord Baltimore sought ways to co-opt his enemies by offering them freedom of conscience and the opportunity to prosper. Charles made no such effort. The 1692 act establishing the Church of England and the subsequent dismantling of the chapel visibly marked an end to the Calverts' attempt to found a colony that radically reordered the relationship between civil and religious institutions. The 1692 act and the destruction of the chapel also represented a failure of leadership on the part of the third Lord Baltimore, who was exiled in England until his death in 1715. In overthrowing proprietary rule, the Maryland rebels moved to satisfy their political, economic, and religious interests. Ironically, however, they rejected the future and opted for a traditional established church. The only method for regaining his colony open to the fourth Lord Baltimore was to convert to the Church of England. As one priest so quaintly phrased it, Charles's son, Benedict Leonard Calvert, turned Protestant, and his colony "was restored to him, instead of heaven, in 1715."[30]

Concepts such as religious uniformity and conformity and the magistrates' duty to protect the "true religion," so fundamental to sixteenth- and seventeenth-century thinking, increasingly garnered suspicion in the eighteenth century. By the time of the American Revolution, state-established churches financed by taxes authorized by civil authorities came under attack on a variety of fronts. Revolutionary Americans wanted not only greater political and economical freedom. They wanted to prevent state interference in religious matters and end religion's control over political or secular concerns. George Calvert's vision, which his son implemented against great odds, had triumphed. When it came to their religious policies, these Catholic Lords Baltimore fit the image of artists an age ahead of their time. To prosper as proprietors, however, they had to succeed as politicians who maneuvered within the sometimes narrow confines of the values and interests of their times. Events demonstrated once again that even the greatest politicians cannot move too far ahead of their times.[31]

By attempting to separate Marylanders' religious concerns from the political sphere, the Calverts pointed to the future. Whether they intended it or not, the Catholic Lords Baltimore moved toward the creation of a more secular society, one in which religious practices were to be kept as private as possible. Secularization was an extremely complex process, and the Calvert involvement in it was a by-product, not an objective. Their circumstances as English Catholics led the Calverts to challenge two accepted theological tenets of their world, uniformity and the state's responsibility to protect the "true" religion. The corollary, however, was a society that was too secular for many of its inhabitants.

Contrary to the traditional view, which portrayed the colony with its manors and feudal trappings as a throwback to an older era, when it came to political and religious loyalties, the Calverts' vision transcended traditional thinking. Their model for a new relationship between religious and political institutions ranged too far ahead of their contemporaries. That they eventually lost their enterprise is perhaps not surprising. That they held it for almost sixty years is remarkable. Their failure must not sully their effort. The first and second Lords Baltimore, neither priests nor theologians, embraced the concept of freedom of conscience for practical reasons. They rightly understood that a publicly supported religion in the seventeenth century would corrupt the body politic. The new relationship between church and state, the new thinking on freedom of conscience and political allegiance, and the move to a more secular society that the Catholic Lords Baltimore envisioned—and struggled diligently to implement—was not for their times. In attempting to protect civil society by removing religion from the public realm, they stood closer to Thomas Jefferson than to their contemporaries. The unfortunate result was that Marylanders and other Americans had dumped the 1649 Act concerning Religion into the dustbin of history. Only a handful of Maryland Catholics, now legally restricted in the practice of their religion and the exercise of their political rights, kept the memory of the 1649 Act concerning Religion alive.

The Catholic Calverts ranged too far ahead of their contemporaries in their effort to prosper as English colonists. Long after they passed from the scene, their innovative ideas triumphed. After the American Revolution and after the writing of the Constitution, one contemporary recognized the visionary nature of the Calvert enterprise. James Wilson, a prominent patriot during the American Revolution and a jurist, decried the "ungracious silence" that denied recognition to the second Lord Baltimore for his part in fostering American understanding of religious toleration. His call, however, did not excite the imagination of his contemporaries.[32]

The Calvert family may have lost its place in the history of religious liberty, but the first amendment of the Constitution affirmed the radical concepts advanced by George and Cecil Calvert. The establishment clause of that amendment ("Congress shall make no law respecting the establishment of religion . . . ") does more than buttress freedom of religion, which the same amendment separately protects. Its authors sought to defuse potentially explosive situations by uncoupling religion and politics. For contemporary Americans, the "establishment clause separates government and religion so that we can maintain civility between believers and unbelievers as well as among the several hundred denominations, sects, and cults that thrive in our nation, all sharing the commitment to liberty and equality that cements us together." George and Cecil Calvert could have resonated with a statement that prohibited the legislature from passing any laws abridging freedom of religion or establishing an exclusive form of worship.[33]

Abbreviations and Frequently Cited Works

APC	*Acts of the Privy Council of England*, ed. John Roche Dasent et al., 44 vols. (London, 1890–).
Babylon's Fall	Leonard Strong, *Babylon's Fall in Maryland: a Fair Warning to Lord Baltamore; or a Relation of an Assault made by divers Papests, and Popish Officers of the Lord Baltamore's against the Protestants in Maryland* (1655), in *Narratives*, ed. Hall, 235–46.
Baltemore's Case	*The Lord Baltemore's Case, Concerning the Province of Maryland, adjoyning to Virginia in America, With full and clear Answers to all material Objections, touching his Rights, Jurisdiction, and Proceedings there, And certain Reasons of State, why the Parliament should not impeach the same* (London, 1653), in *Narratives*, ed. Hall, 167–80.
BL	British Library, London
Calvert Papers	*The Calvert Papers*, 3 vols. (Baltimore, 1889–99).
Calvert Papers, ed. Cox	Maryland Historical Society, *Calvert Papers* (microfilm edition, ed. Richard J. Cox).
CD1621	*Commons Debates, 1621*, ed. Wallace Notestein, Francis Helen Relf, and Hartley Simpson, 7 vols. (New Haven, CT, 1935).
Chamberlain, ed. McClure	*The Letters of John Chamberlain*, ed. Norman Egbert McClure, 2 vols. (Philadelphia, 1939).
Charles, ed. Birch	*The Court and Times of Charles the First Illustrated by Authentic and Confidential Letters, From Various Public and Private Collections Including Memoirs of the Mission in the England of the Capuchin Friars in the Service of Queen Henrietta Maria*, ed. Thomas Birch, 2 vols. (London, 1848).
CJ	*The Journals of the House of Commons*, 220 vols. (n.p., 1803–).
Clarendon, ed. Ogle and Bliss	*Calendar of the Clarendon State Papers preserved in the Bodleian Library*, ed., O. Ogle and W. H. Bliss, 3 vols. (Oxford, 1872–76).
Codignola, *Stock*	Luca Codignola, *The Coldest Harbour of the Land: Simon Stock and Lord Baltimore's Colony in Newfoundland, 1621–1649*, trans. Anita Weston (Kingston, [ON], 1988).
CSP, Charles I	*Calendar of State Papers, Domestic Series of the Reign of Charles I*, ed. John Bruce et al., 22 vols. (London, 1858–93).
CSP, Charles I, Addenda	*Calendar of State Papers, Domestic Series of the Reign of Charles I:*

	Addenda: March 1625 to January 1649, ed. William Douglas Hamilton and Sophie Crawford Lomas (London, 1897).
CSP, Colonial, America	*Calendar of State Papers, Colonial Series, America and West Indies*, ed. W. Noel Sainsbury et al., 37 vols. (London, 1860–).
CSP, Colonial, East Indies	*Calendar of State Papers, Colonial Series, East Indies, China, and Japan*, ed. W. Noel Sainsbury, 5 vols. (London 1862–).
CSP, James I	*Calendar of State Papers, Domestic Series, of the Reign of James I. Preserved in the State Paper Department of Her Majesty's Public Record Office*, ed. Mary Anne Everett Green, 4 vols. (London, 1858–59).
CSP, Venice	*Calendar of State Papers and Manuscripts Relating to English Affairs, Existing in the Archives and Collections of Venice, and in Other Libraries of Northern Italy, 1206–[1675]*, ed. Rawdon Lubbock Brown et al., 38 vols. (London, 1864–1947).
Danckaerts, *Journal*	*Journal of Jasper Danckaerts, 1679–1680*, ed. Bartlett Burleigh James and J. Franklin Jameson (New York, 1913).
English SJ, ed. Foley	*Records of the English Province of the Society of Jesus; historic facts illustrative of the labours and sufferings of its members in the sixteenth and seventeenth centuries*, ed., Henry Foley. 7 vols. (London, 1877–83).
Fortescue	*The Fortescue Papers; Consisting—Chiefly of Letters Relating to State Affairs, Collected by John Packer, Secretary to George Villiers Duke of Buckingham*, ed. Samuel Rawson Gardiner (Westminster, 1871).
Goodman, *James*	Godfrey Goodman, *The Court of King James the First, by Dr. Godfrey Goodman, Bishop of Glouchester, to Which are Added, Letters Illustrative of the Personal History of the Most Distinguished Characters in the Court of That Monarch and His Predecesors. Now First Published from the Original Manuscripts*, ed. John Sherren Brewer, 2 vols. in one (London, 1839).
Hammond versus Heamonds	John Hammond, *Hammond versus Heamonds or an Answer to an audacious Pamphlet, published by an impudent and ridiculous Fellow, named Roger Heamans* (London, 1656), in *MdHM* 4 (September 1909): 236–51.
HMC	Historical Manuscripts Commission.
HMC, *Downshire*	HMC, *Report on the Manuscripts of the Marquess of Downshire, Preserved at Easthampstead Park, Berks*, ed. Edward Kelly Purnell and Allen Banks Hinds, 4 vols. (London, 1924).
HMC, *Salisbury*	HMC, *Calendar of the Manuscripts of the Most Honorable the Marquess of Salisbury Preserved at Hatfield House Hertfordshire*, ed. M. S. Giuseppi and G. D. Owen, 22 parts (London, 1883–).
HMC, *Salvetti*	HMC, *The Manuscripts of Henry Duncan Skine, Esq: Salvetti Correspondence* (London, 1887).
Hughes, *SJ, Text, SJ, Documents*	Thomas Aloysius Hughes, *History of the Society of Jesus in North America: Colonial and Federal*, 2 vols. (Cleveland, 1907–17).

James, ed. Birch	*The Court and Times of James the First: Containing a Series of Historical and Confidential Letters, In Which Will Be Found a Detail of Public Transactions and Events in Great Britain during That Period, With a Variety of Particulars Not Mentioned by Our Historians*, ed. Thomas Birch, 2 vols. (London, 1849).
Just and Cleere Refutation	John Langford, *A Just and Cleere Refutation of a False and Scandalous Pamphlet Entitled Babylons Fall in Maryland &c and a true discovery of certaine strange and inhumane proceedings of some ungratefull people in Maryland, towards those who formerly preserved them in time of their greatest distresse* (London, 1655), in *Narratives*, ed. Hall, 254–75.
Laud, *Works*	*The Works of the Most Reverend Father in God, William Laud*, ed. James Bliss, 7 vols. (Oxford, 1847–60).
Letters, ed. Ellis	*Original Letters, illustrative of English History; Including Numerous Royal Letters from Autographs in the British Museum, and One or Two Other Collections*, ed. Sir Henry Ellis, 3rd ser., 4 vols. (London, 1846).
LJ	*Journals of the House of Lords*, 395 vols., n.p., n.d.
Magee, *Recusants*	Brian Magee, *The English Recusants: A Study in the Post-Reformation Catholic Survival and the Operation of the Recusancy Laws* (London, 1938).
MdArch	*Archives of Maryland*, ed. William Hand Browne et al., 72 vols. (Baltimore, 1883–).
MdHM	*Maryland Historical Magazine.*
Narratives, ed. Hall	*Narratives of Early Maryland, 1634–1684*, ed. Clayton Coleman Hall (New York, 1910).
Newfoundland, ed. Cell	*Newfoundland Discovered: English Attempts at Colonisation, 1610–1630*, ed. Gillian T. Cell (London, 1982).
Nicholas, *Debates*	Edward Nicholas, *Proceedings and Debates of the House of Commons in 1620 and 1621: Collected by a member of That House and Now Published from His Original Manuscripts, In the Library of Queen's College, Oxford*, ed. Thomas Tywhitt, 2 vols. (Oxford, 1766).
Nichols, *The Progresses*	J. B. Nichols, *The Progresses, Processions, and Magnificent Festivities, of King James the First his Royal Consort, Family, and Court; Collected from Original Manuscripts, Scarce Pamphlets, Corporation records, Parochial registers, &c.*, 4 vols. (London, 1828).
Nicklin, "Notes"	John Bailey Calvert Nicklin, "Some Notes concerning Sir George Calvert (1579–1632), First Lord Baltimore, and His Family from the English Records," *MdHM* 27 (December 1932).
PRO	Public Record Office, London.
Register, ed. Mason	*A Register of Baptisms, Marriages, and Burials in the Parish of St. Martin in the Fields, in the County of Middlesex*, ed. Thomas Mason (London, 1898).

Roe,
Negotiations
The Negotiations of Sir Thomas Roe, in His Embassy to the Ottoman Porte, From the Year 1621 to 1628 Inclusive: Containing a Great Variety of Curious and Important Matters . . . , Relating to the Other States of Europe, In That Period His Correspondences With the Most Illustrious Persons . . . and Many Useful and Instructive Particulars Now First Published from the Originals, ed. S. Richardson (London, 1740).

"*Short Treatise*"
To Live Like Princes: "A Short Treatise Sett Downe in a Letter Written by R.W. to His Worthy Freind C.J.R. Concerning the New Plantation Now Erecting Under the Right Ho[nora]ble the Lord Baltemore in Maryland," ed. John D. Krugler (Baltimore, 1976).

Strafforde's Letters, ed. Knowler
The Earl of Strafforde's Letters and Dispatches, With an Essay Towards His Life, by Sir George Radcliffe, From the Originals in the Possession of His Great Grandson . . . Thomas, Earl of Malton, Knight of the Bath. ed. William Knowler, 2 vols. (London, 1739).

Three Charters
The Three Charters of the Virginia Company of London with Seven Related Documents; 1606–1621 (Williamsburg, VA, 1957).

"Tobacco or Codfish," ed. Wroth
"Tobacco or Codfish: Lord Baltimore Makes His Choice," ed. Lawrence C. Wroth, *Bulletin of the New York Public Library* 58 (November 1954).

Virginia and Maryland
Virginia and Maryland, or The Lord Baltamore's printed CASE, uncased and answered. Shewing, the illegality of his Patent, and Usurpation of Royal Jurisdiction and Dominion there (London, 1655), in *Narratives,* ed. Hall, 181–230.

Wentworth Papers, ed. Cooper
Wentworth Papers, 1597–1628, ed. J. P. Cooper (London, 1973).

Wilson, *History*
Arthur Wilson, *The History of Great Britain, Being the Life and Reign of King James the First, Relating to What Passed from His First Access to the Crown, Till His Death* (London, 1653).

Yonge, *Diary*
Diary of Walter Yonge, Esq. Justice of the Peace, and M.P. for Huniton, Written . . . From 1604 to 1628, ed. George Roberts (London, 1848).

Notes

Introduction: "A man is not English who gives first allegiance elsewhere"

Title is from Catherine Drinker Bowen, *The Lion and the Throne: The Life and Times of Sir Edward Coke (1552–1634)* (London, 1957), 254. After 1571 it was "impossible for any one to be at once a good Roman Catholic and a good subject." *Select Statutes and other Constitutional Documents*, ed. G. W. Prothero, 3rd ed. (Oxford, 1906), xlviii.

1. *Letters of Hooper to Bullinger*, Old South Leaflets, vol. 3, no. 58 (Boston, 1890), 3.

2. *English SJ*, ed. Foley, 3:362.

3. *Puritanism and Liberty: Being the Army Debates (1647–9) from the Clarke Manuscripts with Supplementary Documents*, ed. A. P. S. Woodhouse, 2nd ed. (Chicago, 1951), 81.

4. Blair Worden noted the emergence of religious laissez-faire during the Puritan Revolution. "Toleration and the Cromwellian Protectorate," in *Persecution and Toleration*, Studies in Church History, 21 (London, 1984), 205.

5. John Chamberlain to Sir Dudley Carleton, October 25, 1623, in *Chamberlain*, ed. McClure, 1:519. Goodman, *James*, 1:379–80.

6. Quoted in Sally Schwartz, *"A Mixed Multitude": The Struggle for Toleration in Colonial Pennsylvania* (New York, 1987), 22.

7. Robert Wintour used "Maryland designe" to summarize the essence of the recently launched enterprise and to note that the Calverts had a carefully structured purpose for their overseas adventures. *"Short Treatise,"* 36, 38.

8. One member of Parliament recognized the uneven enforcement of the penal law when he observed that "there was no prosecution against rich papists but only the poor." Sir Edward Giles, February 7, 1620/21, *CD1621*, 2:38.

ONE: "There should be a correspondence betwixt the Church and the State"

Title is from Joseph Hall, *The Works of the Most Reverend Father in God, Joseph Hall Now First Collected*, ed. Josiah Pratt, 10 vols. (London, 1808), 9:520.

1. *Documents of English Church History*, ed. Henry Gee and William John Hardy (London, 1896), 244.

2. Ibid., 390, 449. Edward Cardwell, *Synodalia: A Collection of Articles of Religion, Canons, and Proceedings of Convocations in the Province of Canterbury*, 2 vols. (Oxford, 1852), 1:71.

3. John Hooper, *A briefe and clear confession*, art. 79, in *Later Writings of Bishop Hooper Together with his Letters and Other Pieces*, ed. Charles Newman (Cambridge, 1852), 54. *Epistola D. Sciponem*, in *The Works of John Jewel, Bishop of Salisbury*, ed. John Ayer, 4 vols.

(Cambridge, 1854–50), 4:1125–26. *The Decades of Henry Bullinger,* ed. Thomas Harding, 4 vols., Parker Society Publications, 7–10 (Cambridge, 1849–52), 1:324, 329.

4. Richard Hooker, *Of the Laws of Ecclesiastical Polity: Preface, Book I, Book VIII,* ed. Arthur Stephen McGrade (Cambridge, 1989), 130. Allen, *An Apologie and True Declaration of the Institution and Endeavours of the two English Colleges* (Rheims, 1581), fol. 102, quoted in Michael C. Questier, *Politics and Religion in England, 1580–1685* (Cambridge, 1996), 99. *CD1621,* 5:404; and *CJ,* 1:645–46, November 26, 1621.

5. *Tudor Constitutional Documents, A.D. 1485–1603, with an Historical Commentary,* ed. J. R. Tanner, 2nd ed. (Cambridge, 1940), 142–43. Punishment for violating the statute regarding praemunire (appealing to papal authority) included loss of property as well as possible imprisonment.

6. Ibid., 146, 149. Sir Robert Naunton, *Fragmenta Regalila: Memoirs of Elizabeth, her Court and Favorites* (London, 1824), 55.

7. *Tudor Constitutional Documents,* ed. Tanner, 150–59. Thomas Fuller, *The Church History of Britain from the Birth of Jesus Christ Until the Year MDCXLVIII,* 3rd. ed., 3 vols. (London, 1868), 3:22 (quote), 20.

8. *Tudor Constitutional Documents,* ed. Tanner, 159–63.

9. J. R. Tanner, *Constitutional Documents of the Reign of James I, A.D. 1603–1625, with an Historical Commentary* (Cambridge, 1930), 27. Wright, *The Disposition or Garnishments of the Soule* (Antwerp, 1596), sig. A3v, quoted in Alexandria Walsham, *Church Papist: Conformity and Confessional Polemic in Early Modern England* (Suffolk, 1993), 9. Bargrave quoted in Robert Ruigh, *The Parliament of 1624: Politics and Foreign Policy* (Cambridge, 1971), 5.

10. Willet, *Synopsis papismi,* quoted in Anthony Milton, *Catholic and Reformed: The Roman and Protestant Churches in English Protestant Thought, 1600–1640* (Cambridge, 1995), 44, 54.

11. Quoted in Magee, *Recusants,* 2, 106.

12. John Colleton, *A Supplication to the kings most excellent Majestie, wherein severalll reasons of State and Religion are briefly touched* (1604), 4–5, quoted in Kenneth L. Campbell, *The Intellectual Struggle of the English Papists in the Seventeenth Century: The Catholic Dilemma* (Lewiston, NY, 1986), 165. Persons to Father Anthony Rivers, July 6, 1603, in "The Memoirs of Father Robert Persons," ed. J. H. Pollen, *Miscellanea II,* Catholic Record Society (London, 1906), 214–18 (quote).

13. William Barlow, *The Summe and Substance of the Conference, which it pleased his Excellent Majestie to have . . . at Hampton Court. January 14, 1603* (London, 1604), 71. *Diary of John Manningham of the Middle Temple, and of Bradbourne, Kent, Barrister-at-Law, 1602–1603,* ed. John Bruce (Westminster, 1868), 162. *The Political Works of James I,* ed. C. H. McIlwain (Cambridge, 1918), 55.

14. *Diary of Manningham,* 170. *CSP, Venice, 1603–1607,* 10 (April 24, 1603) (quote), 20, 21 (May 8, 1603).

15. King James to Sir Robert Cecil, undated, in *Correspondence of King James VI of Scotland with Sir Robert Cecil and Others in England,* ed. John Bruce (London, 1861), 36–38. *Works of James I,* ed. McIlwain, 276 (quote). Nicol Molin reported Cecil's conversation. *CSP, Venice, 1603–1607,* 230 (1605 [month and day obliterated]).

16. *Works of James I,* ed. McIlwain, xvii. Pym as recorded in the Parliament of 1621, quoted in Conrad Russell, "The Parliamentary Career of John Pym, 1621–1629," in

Conrad Russell, *Unrevolutionary England, 1603–1642* (London, 1990), 216. *CSP, Venice, 1603–1607*, 68 (July 23, 1603).

17. James's first parliament passed "An Act for the due execution of statutes against Jesuits, Seminary Priests, Recusants, etc." This act put in force all the penal laws passed during Elizabeth's reign. Tanner, *Constitutional Documents James I*, 83–84. *Works of James I*, ed. McIlwain, 274–75.

18. Cecil to Sheffield, February 20, 1605, in HMC, *Salisbury*, 17:61. *CSP, Venice, 1603–1607*, 224 (March 2, 1605). Nicol Molin reported Cecil's conversation. Ibid., 227 (1605 [month and day obliterated]).

19. Tanner, *Constitutional Documents James I*, 86–104.

20. *Works of James I*, ed. McIlwain, 274–75.

21. Tanner, *Constitutional Documents James I*, 90–91.

22. *CSP, Venice, 1603–1607*, 68, 81, 86, 227.

23. *Works of James I*, ed. McIlwain, 97 (quotes). *Recusant Documents from the Ellesmere Manuscripts*, ed. Anthony G. Petti, Catholic Record Society publications, Records series, 60 (London, 1968), 162 n.

24. Papal representatives' quotes in Father Robert Persons to Father Henry Garnet, August 26, 1606, quoted in Thomas H. Clancy, *Papist Pamphleteers: The Allen Persons Party and the Political Thought of the Counter-Reformation in England, 1572–1615* (Chicago, 1964), 91, 216. "Papal brief prohibiting taking the oath, 22 September 1606" and "Reasons for refuzall," in *Ellesmere Manuscripts*, ed. Petti, 157–61. *Works of James I*, ed. McIlwain, 85, 322 (quote).

25. *Works of James I*, ed. McIlwain, 341.

26. Yonge, *Diary*, 22 (June 13, 1610). "Parliamentary Petition for Proclamation Against the Recusants," May 26, 1610; A "summary of legislation against recusants, 1570–1610," in *Ellesmere Manuscripts*, ed. Petti, 201–2, 241–43. The government promulgated expulsions of priests in 1604, 1606, and 1625.

27. Parliament added "An Act for Administering the Oath of Allegiance, and reformation of Married Women Recusants" in 1610. Tanner, *Constitutional Documents James I*, 105–9. *Documents of English Church History*, ed. Gee and Hardy, 485. "Spanish Correspondence," September 22, 1613, *CSP, James I, 1611–1618*, 199.

28. George Calvert to George Gage, January 5, 1622/23, in *Clarendon*, ed. Ogle and Bliss, 1:26–27. William McElwee, *The Wisest Fool in Christendom: The Reign of King James I and VI* (New York, 1966), 245–46, 263–64.

29. The total collected for 1623–24 was £3141. Magee, *Recusants*, 72–74. James to Lord Keeper Lincoln, September 9, 1623, in *CSP, James I, 1623–1625*, 76–77. Minute, Conway's Letter Book, 84 (September 12, 1623), ibid., 78.

30. As recorded by William Pym in *CD1621*, 4:4.

31. *CSP, James I, 1619–1623*, 448 (August 1622).

32. Sir Dudley Digges, November 26, 1621, in *CJ*, 1:644. Francis Lord Verulum, *Considerations Touching a War* (1629), in *The Harleian Miscellany; or, A Collection of Scarce, Curious, and Entertaining Pamphlets and Tracts*, 12 vols. (London, 1810), 4:141. Sir Robert Philips, April 1, 1624, in *CJ*, 1:752. Goodman, *James*, 1:379–80.

33. Rev. Joseph Mead to Sir Martin Stuteville, April 19, 1623; unsigned letter to Mead, April 25, 1623, in *James*, ed. Birch, 2:390. May 4, 1621, *CD1621*, 4:302. April 29, 1624, and June 22, 1625, in *CJ*, 1:779, 800.

34. J. R. Green, *A Short History of the English People*, 3 vols., rev. ed. (New York, 1900), 2:159.

35. *CSP, Charles I, 1633–1634*, 22 (September 19, 1633). Edward Cardwell, *Documentary Annals of the Reformed Church of England: Being a Collection of Injunctions, Declarations, Orders, Articles of Inquiry, &c. From the year 1546 to the year 1716*, 2 vols. (Oxford, 1839), 2:169–70 (October 14, 1633). Laud, *Works*, 5, pt. 1, p. 325, October 14, 1633.

36. *CSP, Charles I, 1633–1634*, 204 (September 8, 1633). Laud, *Works*, 1:157, 5, pt. 2, p. 613.

37. P. Heylyn, *Cyprianus Anglicus: or, the History of the Life and Death of the Most Reverend and Renowned Prelate William by Divine Province, Lord Archbishop of Canterbury* (London, 1671), 154. Cardwell, *Synodalia*, 2:159. Laud, *Works*, 1:22–23.

38. C[alybute] D[owninge], *A Discourse of the State Ecclesiasticall of this Kingdom in relation to the Civil* (Oxford, 1634).

T W O : "Conformitie to the form of service of God now established"

Title is from a proclamation of James I, July 1604, quoted in Pauline Croft, "The Religion of Robert Cecil," *Historical Journal* 34 (1991): 776.

1. Gargrave to William Cecil, February 4, 1570, in SP15/17/69, PRO.

2. James W. Foster, *George Calvert: The Early Years* (Baltimore, 1983), 27. "The orders of the Yorkshire High Commission relating to Leonard Calvert and his family, as abstracted by Father Aveling from the Act Books," ibid., 37–39. Edward Peacock, *List of Roman Catholics in the County of York in 1604* (London, 1872), 69. Mead to Stuteville, March 20, 1629/30, in *Charles*, ed. Birch, 2:68–69.

3. Foster, *Calvert*, 53.

4. *The Records of the Honourable Society of Lincoln's Inn*, vol. 1, *Admissions from A.D. 1420 to A.D. 1799* (London, 1896), 127. Wilfred R. Prest, *The Inns of Court under Elizabeth I and the Early Stuarts, 1590–1640* (Titowa, NJ, 1972), 180. "Dispensation for George Calvart [*sic*], to enable him to propose a grace in the House of Congregation," in Foster, *Calvert*, 52. "To the King's Most Excellent Majesty the humble petition of George Calvert your Majesty's servant," December 3, 1614, in SP63/232/273, PRO. Richard Percivall to Cecil, April 19, 1603, in HMC, *Salisbury*, 21:15, 54.

5. HMC, *Salisbury*, 22:vi.

6. Foster, *Calvert*, 69. Ralph Ewens's will, September 26, 1611, in *Descendants of Virginia Calverts*, compiled by Ella Foy O'Gorman (privately printed in Los Angeles, 1947), 2–3.

7. John More to Ralph Winwood, October 5, 1604, in HMC, *Report on the Manuscripts of the Duke of Buccleuch and Queensbury, K.G., K.T., Preserved at Montague House Whitehall*, 3 vols. (London, 1899–1926), 1:50. Foster, *Calvert*, 69. Dudley Carleton to Calvert, May 29, 1609, quoted in ibid., 74.

8. SP 14/48/384, PRO, quoted in Foster, *Calvert*, 75.

9. *A Register of all the Christninges, Burialls & Weddings within the Parish of Saint Peeters upon Cornhill, Beginning at the Raigne of our Most Soveraigne Ladie Queen Elizabeth*, ed. Granville William Gresham Leveson Gower (London, 1877), 244. Nicklin, "Notes," 334–36. *A Record of All the Christenings, Burials and Weddings Within the Parish of St. Peters Upon Cornwall*, Publications of the Harleian Society (London, 1877), 244.

10. Samuel Calvert to Sir Ralph Winwood, April 5, 1606, in HMC, *Buccleuch and*

Queensbury, 1:63, 68. Foster, *Calvert,* 83. Substitutes stood in for both Cecil and Clifford. *Register,* ed. Mason, 25:38. Samuel Calvert to William Trumbull, July 1607, in HMC, *Downshire,* 2:29.

11. *Register, Parish of Saint Peeters upon Cornhill,* 244. Nicklin, "Notes," 334–36. J. T. Cliffe, *The Yorkshire Gentry from the Reformation to the Civil War* (London, 1969), 204.

12. Resentment of priests noted in Cecil to King James, undated, in *Correspondence,* ed. Bruce, 33–34. Anonymous information enclosed with letters from Robert Bishop of London to Cecil, April 27, 1602, in SP12/283A/no 86 II, PRO. Cecil quoted in *The Autobiography of an Elizabethan,* ed. Philip Caraman (London, 1954), 245–46. Nicol Molin to Doge and Senate, 1605, *in CSP, Venice, 1603–1607,* 230. HMC, *Salisbury,* 17:293.

13. Samuel Calvert to Ralph Winwood, April 6, 1605, in *Memorials of Affairs of State in the Reigns of Q. Elizabeth and K. James I, Collected (Chiefly) from the Original Papers of . . . Sir R[alph] Winwood,* ed. Edmund Sawyer, 3 vols. (London, 1725), 2:58. Nichols, *The Progresses,* 1:556. HMC, *Salisbury,* 17:584. *Calendar of the State Papers, Relating to Ireland, of the Reign of James I,* ed. C. W. Russell and John P. Prendergast, 5 vols. (London, 1872–80), *1603–1605,* 515. Foster, *Calvert,* 70.

14. Rowland Whyte to the earl of Shrewsbury, January 26, 1607/8, in Edmund Lodge, *Illustrations of British History, Biography, and Manners,* 2nd ed., 3 vols. (London, 1838), 3:226. Few Calvert letters survive from this period. The *Eighth Report of the Royal Commission on Historical Manuscripts,* 3 parts (London, 1881), pt. 1, p. 380, noted two letters from 1607 to the mayor of Chester written on Cecil's behalf. Samuel Calvert to Trumbull, October 25, 1609, summarized in HMC, *Downshire,* 2:171, and transcribed in Foster MSS 2002, Maryland Historical Society, Baltimore. The phrase "auricular minister" most likely signified Calvert's role as an unofficial adviser, one who could speak directly to the king and ministers while still not holding an office of major responsibility. Foster, *Calvert,* 72–73.

15. William P. Courtney, *Parliamentary Representation of Cornwall to 1832* (London, 1899), 322–23. *CSP, James I, 1603–1610,* 438. Foster, *Calvert,* 73.

16. *Three Charters,* 54. *The Records of the Virginia Company of London,* ed. Susan Myra Kingsbury, 4 vols. (Washington, DC, 1906–35), 3:81.

17. The East India Company admitted him at the meeting of September 5–6, 1609. *CSP, Colonial, East Indies, 1513–1616,* 192, 273; *1617–1621,* 274. Foster, *Calvert,* 103, 72.

18. Samuel Calvert to Trumbull, November 13, 1609, in HMC, *Downshire,* 2:185. Foster MSS 2002. Foster, *Calvert,* 77. Anne did die in childbirth, but not until 1622.

19. Sanford to Sir Thomas Edmondes, March 6, 1609/10, in *James,* ed. Birch, 1:108. Samuel Calvert to Trumbull, July 25, 1610, in HMC, *Downshire,* 2:328. John Gore to Winwood, July 28, 1610, in HMC, *Buccleuch and Queensbury,* 1:91.

20. Samuel Calvert to Sir Ralph Winwood, in *Memorials of Affairs of State,* 2:58. Samuel Calvert to William Trumbull, November 13, 1609; July 25, August 10, 1610, in HMC, *Downshire,* 2:185, 328, 353, See also Sir Dudley Carleton to Edmondes, June 17, 1610, in *James,* ed. Birch, 1:116–17.

21. Sanford to Edmondes, March 6, 1609/10, in *James,* ed. Birch, 1:108. Samuel Calvert to Trumbull, August 24, 1610, in HMC, *Downshire,* 2:353. John More to Trumbull, August 16, 1610, ibid., 2:348. Sanford to Trumbull, November 2, 1610, ibid., 2:391. On January 31, 1610/11, one of Trumbull's correspondents wrote that Salisbury recalled Calvert from his trip. Ibid., 3:16. Beaulieu to Trumbull, ibid., 3:24 (February 14, 1610/11).

22. Calvert to Edmondes, March 7, 1610/11, transcription in Foster MSS 2002. John More to Trumbull, February 8, 1610/11, in HMC, *Downshire*, 3:21. Edmondes to Trumbull, March 9, 1610/11, ibid., 3:34.

23. Beaulieu to Trumbull, March 28, 1611; More to Trumbull, September 10, 25, December 13, 1611, in HMC, *Downshire*, 3:46, 139, 146, 201. Foster, *Calvert*, 90, 92. Calvert to Edmondes, May 6, 1611, in Stowe MSS, BL, transcribed in Foster MSS 2002.

24. *Chamberlain*, ed. McClure, 1:331. Calvert to Salisbury, January 15, 1611/12, in SP14/68/17, PRO. John More to Trumbull, in HMC, *Downshire*, 3:234. *CSP, James I, 1611–1618*, 111. More to Trumbull, January 1, February 17, 1611/12, in *Memorials of Affairs of State*, 3:319, 337–38.

25. April 23, 1612, HMC, *Downshire*, 3:283. The editors attributed the letter to George, but Foster identified the author as Samuel. Foster MSS 2002. Foster, *Calvert*, 91. HMC, *Salisbury*, 22:xii. Calvert was party to a suit to recover expenses. Stephen Higgins, apothecary, plaintiff *vs.* William, earl of Salisbury, Sir Walter Cope, George Calvert, Roger Houghton, John Dackombe, executors of Robert, earl of Salisbury, defendants, ibid., 22:8.

26. Henry Clifford described Calvert to Salisbury in 1611 as devoted to his service. SP14/61/105, PRO. Abbot to Trumbull, April 20, 1614, in HMC, *Downshire*, 4:379.

27. Samuel Calvert to Trumbull, March 20, 1610/11, in HMC, *Downshire*, 3:272. *CSP, James I, 1611–1618*, 199 (September 22, 1613).

28. Calvert to Edmondes, August 1, 1612, in *James*, ed. Birch, 1:191. Foster MSS 2002. John Parker to Trumbull, June 12, 1612, in HMC, *Downshire*, 3:315. Chamberlain to Carleton, June 17, 1612, in *Chamberlain*, ed. McClure, 1:359. *APC, 1613–1614* (May 9, 14, 1613; July 14, 1614), 25, 27, 496–97.

29. John More to Trumbull, July 24, 1613, in HMC, *Downshire*, 4:170.

30. Calvert submitted a claim for £230 for his allowance and another £40 for "transportation, land carriage, post horses, &c going and returning." *Issues of the Exchequer; Being Payments Made out of His Majesty's Revenue during the Reign of James I. Extracted from the Original Records Belonging to the Ancient Pell Office, in the Custody of the Right Honorable Sir John Newport*, ed. Frederick Devon (London, 1836), 315. John Lodge reprinted the report in *Desiderate Curiosa Hibernica; or, A Select Collection of State Papers and Historical Tracts, . . . Illustrating the Political Systems of the Government of Ireland during the Reigns of Elizabeth, James I. and Charles I., Comprehending Likewise the Negotiations of Sir H. Neville, Sir C. Cornwallis, Sir D. Carleton, Sir T. Edmondes, Mr. Trumbull, Mr. Cottington, and Others, at the Courts of France and Spain, and in Holland, Venice, etc. [including their dispatches]*, 2 vols. (Dublin, 1772), 1:359–62.

31. William Devick to Trumbull, March 7, 1610/11; John More to Trumbull, September 10, 25, 1611; John Sanford to Trumbull, December 25, 1613; Sanford to Sir John Throckmorton, April 23, 1614, in HMC, *Downshire*, 3:31, 139, 146; 4:274, 389. Chamberlain to Carleton, March 3, 1613/14; May 12, 1614, in *Chamberlain*, ed. McClure, 1:514, 529.

32. John Sanford to Trumbull, December 25, 1613; Samuel Calvert to Trumbull, June 4, 1613, in HMC, *Downshire*, 4:125, 274. Chamberlain to Carleton, February 3, March 3, 1614, in *Chamberlain*, ed. McClure, 1:503, 514. *James*, ed. Birch, 1:134, 176. *APC, 1613–1614*, 188. *CSP, Ireland, 1611–1614*, 436–38. *APC, 1615–1616*, 141; *1616–1617*, 56. *Chamberlain*, ed. McClure, 1:503, 514; 2:25.

33. *CSP, Colonial, East Indies, 1513–1616*, 273. Alexander Brown, *The Genesis of the United States: A Narrative of the Movement in England, 1605–1616, Which Resulted in the Plantation of North America*, 2 vols. (reprint, New York, 1964), 2:841–42. Foster, *Calvert*, 104.

34. Pass for George Calvert, May 3, 1615, in *APC, 1615–1616*, 141. Elizabeth to James, May 28, 1615, in L. H. Baker, *The Letters of Elizabeth Queen of Bohemia* (London, 1953), 40–42. Foster, *Calvert*, 96–98.

35. Calvert to Carleton, April 10, 1619, in SP84/19/125, PRO. Sir Thomas Wynne to Carleton, February 14, 1619, in SP14/105/104, PRO. Chamberlain to Carleton, February 20, 1619, in *Chamberlain*, ed. McClure, 2:216.

36. Wilson, *History*, 97.

37. Ibid., 144, 171. William Sanderson, a more credible historian, whose refutation of Wilson has been ignored until recently, wrote that "A. W." had "some regret of what he had malitiously writ" and intended to destroy the manuscript. *A Compleat History of the Lives and Reigns of Mary Queen of Scotland, and of Her Son and Successor, James the Sixth, King of Scotland; and (After Queen Elizabeth) King of Great Britain, France, and Ireland, the First . . . Reconciling Several Opinions, in Testimony of Her, and Confuting Others, in Vindication of Him, Against Two Slanderous Authors*, 2 vols. (London, 1656), the "Proeme" to the second volume. *Correspondencia official de do Diego Sarmiento de Acuna, Conde de Gondomar*, ed. Antonio-Ballesteros y Berretta, Documentos Inéditos para la Historia de España, 4 vols. (Madrid, 1936–45), 3:221. Wynne to Carleton, February 14, 1618/19, in SP14/105/104, PRO. *James*, ed. Birch, 2:136.

38. Chamberlain to Carleton, February 20, 1619, in *Chamberlain*, ed. McClure, 2:216.

39. Thomas Fuller, *The History of Worthies of England*, ed. J. Fuller (London, 1662), "Yorkshire," 202. Lord Burghley defined protocol for his son Robert Cecil, Calvert's mentor: "Be sure to keep some great man thy friend, but trouble him not for trifles. Complement him often with many, yet small gifts, & of little charge. And if thou hast cause to bestow any great gratuity, let it be something which may be daily in sight," quoted in Perez Zagorin, *The Court and Country: The Beginnings of the English Revolution* (New York, 1971), 45.

40. *James*, ed. Birch, 2:136. Fuller, *Worthies*, "Yorkshire," 202. *CSP, Venice, 1618–1619*, 480. *Letters*, ed. Ellis, 3:120. Harwood to Carleton, February 16, 1618/19, in SP14/105/112, PRO. Chamberlain to Carleton, February 20, 1619, in *Chamberlain*, ed. McClure, 2:216. George Conn, *De Duplici Statu Religionis apud Scotos* (Rome, 1628), 148–49, quoted in Albert J. Loomie, "King James I's Catholic Consort," *Huntington Library Quarterly* 34 (August 1971): 313–14. Nichols, *The Progresses*, 3:529.

41. Lando to Doge and Senate, February 18/28, 1619/20, in *CSP, Venice, 1617–1619*, 480; January 2/12, 1619/20, in *CSP, Venice, 1619–1621*, 117–18. Trumbull to Carleton, March 1/10, 1618/19, in SP84/89/3, PRO. In 1614 Spanish ambassador Gondomar claimed that "Lac era católico." *Correspondencia official de Don Diego Sarmiento de Acuña Conde de Gondomar*, 3:211. *APC, 1618–1619*, 373. Harwood to Carleton, February 16, 1619, in SP14/105/112, PRO. Fuller, *Worthies*, "Yorkshire," 202.

42. Naunton to Buckingham, November 27, 1619, in *Fortescue*, 95–96 (quote). Roland Woodward to Francis Windebank, May 22, 1620; Thomas Locke to Carleton, January 20, February 5, 1620/21, in *CSP, James I, 1619–1623*, 147, 215, 220. Chamber-

lain to Carleton, May 27, October 14, 1620, in *Chamberlain*, ed. McClure, 2:303, 322. Some viewed Naunton's suspension in February 1621 as the first move toward Lake's restoration. Ibid., 2:336.

43. Cottington to Sir John Finet, April 7, 1628, in Sloane MS 3827, fols. 124–25v, BL, reprinted in *Newfoundland*, ed. Cell, 277–79. Professor Cell collected the relevant documents relating to Calvert's involvement in Newfoundland. In subsequent notes, I cite both the manuscript references and Cell's printed version of these documents. Codignola, *Stock*, 12–13.

44. December 13/23, 1621, in *CSP, Venice, 1621–1625*, 185. As secretary of state, Calvert often defended the honor of the Spanish king. When Sir Edward Francis's wife was "traduced to be a Recusant," he defended his family by saying that he "cared not a figge (or somewhat worse) for the Pope nor the King of Spaine." Calvert taxed him for his "unreverent speach." April 30, 1621, *CJ*, 1:598; May 2, 1621, *CD1621*, 2:369. Conversely, he defended the established Church's clergy when necessary. We give "our adversaries" the greatest advantage when we "abase our ministers." May 1, 1621, ibid., 2:333.

45. Chamberlain to Carleton, February 10, 1621, in *Chamberlain*, ed. McClure, 2:341. Wentworth to Calvert, August 14, 1624, in *Strafforde's Letters*, ed. Knowler, 1:23. Calvert to Buckingham, November 29, 1619, in *Fortescue*, 98 (quote). For an example of the king's curt attitude toward his secretary, see James to Calvert (draft), November 1622, ibid., 187–88.

46. Calvert to Nethersole, August 26, 1621, in Add. MS 5950, fol. 123, BL. Calvert to Trumbull, August 11, 1621, in Trumbull MS, 14/76. Calvert to Carleton, October 28, 1621, in SP 84/103/147, PRO. Conway to Buckingham, September 3, 1623, in HMC, "The Manuscripts of the Rev. Francis Hopkinson, LLD, Malvern Wells, Co. Worchester," in *The Third Report of the Royal Commission on Historical Manuscripts, Appendix* (London, 1872), 265.

47. Wynne to Carleton, February 14, 1619, in *CSP, James I, 1619–1623*, 14. Calvert to Lord Doncaster, August 11, 1621, in Egerton MSS, 2594, fol. 67, BL. Lando to Doge and Senate, September 7/17, 1621, in *CSP, Venice, 1621–1623*, 133. Comte de Tillieres to Puysieulse, November 15/25, 1621, in SP31/3/55, PRO. Dudley Carleton to Sir Dudley Carleton, February 27, 1622/23, in SP84/111/152, PRO. Calvert to [?], February 11, 1622/23, ibid., 86b.

48. Calvert to Wentworth, September 12, 1630, in *Wentworth Papers*, 12/136, Sheffield City Library (SCL).

49. *Calvert Papers*, ed. Cox, roll 5, nos. 25, 28. *Wentworth Papers*, ed. Cooper, 126–27. Clifford to earl of Salisbury, March 6, 1611, N.S., in SP14/61/105, PRO.

50. Wentworth was in London in October 1617, February 1618, February 1619, and January and May 1620. Wentworth to Calvert, July 22, October 4, 1619, in *Wentworth Papers*, ed. Cooper, 104, 109, 120–27, 129, 132. Quotations in Wentworth to Sir Thomas Fairfax, December 3, 1620; and Wentworth to Henry Bellassys, November 25, 1620, in *Strafforde's Letters*, ed. Knowler, 1:10, 8. Wentworth to Sir Robert Askwith, December 7, 1620, in *Wentworth Papers*, ed. Cooper, 142.

51. Sir Henry Savile to Sir Richard Beaumont, December 4, 1620, in *Chapters in the History of Yorkshire: Being a Collection of Original Letters, Papers, and Public Documents, Illustrating the State of That Country in the Reigns of Elizabeth, James I., and Charles I*, ed. James Joel Cartwright (Wakefield, Eng., 1872), 203. Buckingham to Wentworth, Sep-

tember 5, 23, 1617, in *Strafforde's Letters*, ed. Knowler, 1:4. Wentworth to Buckingham, September 15, 1617, in *Fortescue*, 23–27.

52. Wentworth to Calvert, December 5, 1620, in *Strafforde's Letters*, ed. Knowler, 1:10–11.

53. The correspondence published in *Chapters in the History of Yorkshire*, 199–204, 207–9, indicated the tactics used by Wentworth to gain victory. *Strafforde's Letters*, ed. Knowler, 1:8–13. *Papers Relating to Thomas Wentworth, First Earl of Strafforde: From the Mss. of Dr. William Knowler*, ed. C. H. Firth, The Camden Miscellany, vol. 9 (Westminster, 1895), 2. Wentworth to Sir Henry Savile of Methley (a Wentworth ally not related to Sir John Savile of Hawley), November 28, 1620; Wentworth to Sir Arthur Ingram, December 6, 1620; Wentworth to Sir Henry Slingsby, December 8, 1620, ibid., 11–13. Wentworth to George Weatheridde, December 8, 1620; Wentworth to Lord Scrope, December 8, 1620; Wentworth to Askwith, December 7, 1620, in *Wentworth Papers*, ed. Cooper, 142–44. Calvert to Carleton, August 9, 1621, in SP84/102/9, PRO.

54. Samuel Casson to Wentworth, December 12, 1620, in *Strafforde's Letters*, ed. Knowler, 1:13.

55. Calvert to Buckingham, February 7, 1621, in *Fortescue*, 150–51. *CJ*, 1:54, 556–57, 572. Nicholas, *Debates*, 1:38–39, 60–61, 175, 216–17. *CD1621*, 2:45, 259–60; 4:187; 5:45; 6:82. *Chamberlain*, ed. McClure, 2:341–42.

56. "A Speache spoken by Sir Thomas Wentworth upon taxing of the subsidy 1621." The bill was read for the third time on March 19, 1621. *CD1621*, 2:153–55, 244.

THREE: "But by God's help many have been lifted out of the mire of corruption"

Title is from *English SJ*, ed. Foley, vol. 7, pt. 2, p. 1057.

1. The records do not reveal the names of individual oath-takers. Calvert's absence would have been conspicuous. *CJ*, 1:508, 756. HMC, *Salvetti*, 26. Buckingham's wife on February 11, 1620/21, received the sacrament in Westminster Church as "an assured testimony of her conversion from Popery to the true religion." *The Autobiography and Correspondence of Sir Simonds D'Ewes, bart, during the Reigns of James I, and Charles I*, ed. James Orchard Halliwell, 2 vols. (London, 1845), 1:175–76.

2. In the absence of contrary evidence, I assume that Calvert participated in the service that took place on Sunday, February 18. CD1621, 2:16–17 n, 56; 5:432. The leadership expelled some members for recusancy. Thomas Locke to Carleton, February 16, 1621, in *CSP, James I, 1619–1623*, 224. Nicholas, *Debates*, 1:13–14, 30. *CJ*, 1:510, 514–17, 529. John Chamberlain to Dudley Carleton, February 10, 27, 1620/21, in *Chamberlain*, ed. McClure, 2:341, 347. Girolamo Lando to Doge and Senate, February 16/26, 1621, in *CSP, Venice, 1619–1621*, 577. Letter to Rev. Joseph Mead, February 10, 1621, in *James*, ed. Birch, 2:220. Mead to Stuteville, May 6, 1625, in *Charles*, ed. Birch, 1:20.

3. *CD1621*, 2:2–13, 4:4, 5:424–29. Lando to Doge and Senate, February 2/12, 1621, in *CSP, Venice, 1619–1621*, 562.

4. Chamberlain to Carleton, February 10, 1620/21, in *Chamberlain*, ed. McClure, 2:341.

5. Ibid., January 20, 1620/21, 2:336. Gondomar to Philip III, February 10, 1621, N.S., in SP31/12/2, PRO. *Autobiography of D'Ewes*, 1:168. Comte de Tillieres to M. d Puysieux, January 27, 1621, N.S., in SP31/3/54, PRO. Lando to Doge and Senate, Feb-

ruary 5, 1621, N.S., in *CSP, Venice, 1619–1621*, 552. Locke to Carleton, February 2, 1621; John Woodford to [Sir Francis Nethersole], February 2, 1621, in SP14/119/60, 61, PRO. Sir George Moore, February 5, 1620/21, in *CJ*, 1:509 (quote).

6. *CD1621*, 2:16–17 n, 19–20; 4:13–14; 5:432, 435. *CJ*, 1:508–9. Joseph Mead to Sir Martin Stuteville, February 10, 1620/21, in *James*, ed. Birch, 2:224. Chamberlain to Carleton, February 10, 1620/21, in *Chamberlain*, ed. McClure, 2:341–42. Locke to Carleton, February 16, 1620/21, in *CSP, James I, 1619–1621*, 224.

7. *CD1621*, 2:37, 87; 5:462–63; 7:576–77.

8. *LJ*, 3:117. *CD1621*, 2:37, 179. Calvert to Carleton, February 17, 1620/21, in SP84/99/178–79, PRO. Chamberlain to Carleton, February 17, 1620/21, in *Chamberlain*, ed. McClure, 2:345.

9. *CD1621*, 2:39; 4:28. Lando to Doge and Senate, February 16/26, 1621, in *CSP, Venice, 1619–1621*, 577. Chamberlain to Carleton, February 17, 1621, in *Chamberlain*, ed. McClure, 2:343, 345. Calvert to Buckingham, February 7, 1620/21, in *Fortescue*, 150–51.

10. Calvert to Aston, February 10, 1620/21, in Additional MSS, 36445, fol. 36, BL. Calvert to Carleton, March 1, 16, 23, 1620/21; March 28, 1621, in SP84/100/1, 66, 89, 112, PRO. Of the privy councillors, only Sir Edward Coke spoke more frequently. *CD1621*, 1:154, 156, 167–68, 183, 193. Lando to the Doge and Senate, March 16/23, March 23/April 2, 1620/21, in *CSP, Venice, 1619–1621*, 617; *1621–1623*, 2.

11. Calvert to Aston, April 21, 1621, in Add. MSS, 36445, fol. 94–95, BL. Chamberlain to Carleton, April 7, 1621, in *Chamberlain*, ed. McClure, 2:361–62. *CSP, James I, 1619–1623*, 245. Mead to Stuteville, April 9, 1621, in *James*, ed. Birch, 2:247–49. Lando to Doge and Senate, April 13/23, 1621, in *CSP, Venice, 1621–1623*, 31.

12. Nicholas, *Debates*, 2:211. *CD1621*, 2:298, 6:112. Locke to Carleton, April 23, 1621, in *CSP, James I, 1619–1623*, 246, 249. Chamberlain to Carleton, April 23, 1621, in *Chamberlain*, ed. McClure, 2:366–67.

13. *CD1621*, 2:359, 365, 386, 398, 407–8 (quotes); 4:331, 368, 382–83. Calvert to Carleton, June 7, 1621, in SP84/101/140, PRO.

14. Chamberlain to Carleton, February 3, June 9, 1621, in *Chamberlain*, ed. McClure, 2:339, 382. Lando to Doge and Senate, April 28/May 7, 1621, in *CSP, Venice, 1621–1623*, 40. Calvert to Aston, June 26, 1621, in Add. MSS, 36445, fol. 151, BL. Calvert to Salisbury, September 24, 1621, in HMC, *Salisbury*, 22:152. Endymion Porter to his wife, October 9, 1621, in *The Knyvett Letters (1620–1644)*, ed. Bertram Schofield (London, 1949), 56. Calvert to Aston, October 19, 1621, in Add. MSS, 36445, fol. 261, BL. *CSP, James I, 1619–1623*, 296.

15. Calvert to Trumbull, October 19, 1621, in HMC, *Downshire*, 4:80. Calvert to Doncaster, October 20, 1621, in Egerton MSS, 2594, fol. 143, BL. Locke to Carleton, November 3, 1621, in *CSP, James I, 1619–1623*, 306. Calvert to Carleton, November 5, 1621, in SP84/102/211, PRO.

16. *CD1621*, 2:432–39, 4:423–29. Locke to Carleton, November 24, 1621, in *CSP, James I, 1619–1623*, 313. Calvert to Doncaster, December 27, 1621, in Egerton MSS, 2595, fols. 7–9, BL.

17. Nicholas, *Debates*, 2:197–200. *CD1621*, 2:441, 484 n, 486 n; 5:411. James I to Council, June 15, 1621; James I to Calvert, August 30, 1621, in *CSP, James I, 1619–1623*, 265, 286, 202, 278. Chamberlain to Carleton, June 23, November 24, 1621, in *Chamberlain*, ed. McClure, 2:384, 411.

18. *CJ*, 1:645–46, 648, 650. *CD1621*, 2:449–50; 5:213–14, 225 (quotes on 2:449–50 and 5:225). Nicholas, *Debates*, 2:213–14, 216, 241–42.

19. Goring to Buckingham, November 29, 1621, in *CD1621*, 7:620–21. *CJ*, 1:652, 654. Nicholas, *Debates*, 2:58, 261–67, 276. *CD1621*, 5:5, 232. *CSP, James I, 1619–1623*, 316.

20. *CJ*, 1:658. King to Speaker, December 3, 1621, in Nicholas, *Debates*, 2:277–78. Calvert to Doncaster, December 4, 1621, in Egerton MSS, 2595, fols. 7–9, BL. Calvert to Carleton, December 8, 1621, in SP84/104/38, PRO. Locke to Carleton, December 8, 1621, in *CSP, James I, 1619–1623*, 318. Calvert to Buckingham, December 4, 1621, in *CD1621*, 7:621–22. In February an unidentified official confided to the Venetian ambassador that the king's men "can no longer be sure of his Majesty's wishes, not even after he expressed them." Lando to Doge and Senate, February 24/March 5, 1621, in *CSP, Venice, 1619–1621*, 586.

21. Calvert to Doncaster, December 27, 1621, in Egerton MSS, 2595, fols. 7–9, BL.

22. Lando to Doge and Senate, December 13/23, 1621, in *CSP, Venice, 1619–1621*, 185. *CJ*, 1:658–61. Nichols, *Debates*, 2:287. *CD1621*, 2:233–34. Calvert to Buckingham, December 7, 1621, ibid., 7:624–625. Carleton to Carleton, December 8, 1621, in SP84/104/38, PRO.

23. Nicholas, *Debates*, 2:305–6. *CD1621*, 2:509–10, 513–14, 518. *CJ*, 1:661–63.

24. James I to Calvert, December 17, 1621; Calvert to Buckingham, December 17, 1621, in *CD1621*, 2:528–30 (quote), 7:626–27, 5:240. Nicholas, *Debates*, 2:341. *CJ*, 1:668–69. Calvert to Doncaster, December 27, 1621, in Egerton MSS, 2595, fols. 7–9, BL. Calvert to Salisbury, January 3, 1621/22, in Salisbury MSS, Hatfield House Library, Hatfield, Herts., UK, 130/30. Calvert to earl of Salisbury, January 3, 1621/22, in HMC, *Salisbury*, 22:159.

25. Wentworth to Lord Darcy, January 9, 1621/22, in *Strafforde's Letters*, ed. Knowler, 1:15.

26. Alvise Valaresso, the Venetian ambassador, wrote of how difficult it was to interpret events because the king's mind was hidden and "the negotiations secret and open to very few." Letter of August 16/26, 1622, in *CSP, Venice, 1621–1623*, 398. Buckingham detailed how English Catholics were benefiting from the negotiations in a letter to Gondomar, September 9, 1622, in Hugh Ross Williamson, *George Villiers, First Duke of Buckingham: Study for Biography [with Extracts from His Correspondence and with Portraits]* (London, 1940), 274–79. Lord Keeper Williams attempted to justify the king's policy toward the Catholics. Letter of September 17, 1622, in *Cabala: Sive Scrinia Sacra: Mysteries of State & Government: In Letters of Illustrious Persons, and Great Agents; in the Reigns of Henry the Eighth, Queen Elizabeth, K: James, and the Late King Charles. In Two Parts, In Which the Secrets of Empire, and Publique Monage of Affairs Are Contained* (London, 1654), 109–13. W. Ashton to Christopher Keighley, January 4, 1622/23, in HMC, *Salisbury*, 22:167. Gondomar to Philip III, February 10, 1621/22, in SP 31/12/21, PRO. March 22, 1621/22, *APC*, *1621–1623*, 169. Calvert to Carleton, July 1, 1622, in SP84/107/95r, PRO. *Chamberlain*, ed. McClure, 2:443. *CSP, Colonial, East Indies, 1574–1660*, 31. Chamberlain to Carleton, October 5, November 16, 1622, in *Chamberlain*, ed. McClure, 2:455, 462–63.

27. Williams to Buckingham, July 22, 1621, in *Cabala*, 61–62. Calvert to Buckingham, July 31, 1621, in Hartley Russell MSS, D/Etty 01, 91, in Foster MSS 2002.

28. Calvert to marquis of Buckingham, January 17, 1621/22, in *Fortescue*, 194. Calvert to Buckingham, November 8, 1622, in Hartley-Russell MSS, D/EHyol, fols. 93, 94, transcribed in Foster MSS 2002. Calvert to Conway, March 28, 1623, in *CSP, James I, 1619–1623*, 541. "Certain reasons delivered by the Earl of Danbye whye the discipline ecclesiastical in the Isle of Guernsey should not be made comfortable to the Church of England," April 23, 1637, in *CSP, Charles I, Addenda*, 536.

29. Calvert to Carleton, July 29, 1622, in SP 84/107/208–9, PRO. Calvert to Bristol, October 21, 1622, in SP94/25/257, PRO. Calvert to Roe, December 6, 1622, in Roe, *Negotiations*, 104.

30. Thomas Locke to Trumbull, January 10, 1622/23, in Trumbull MS, 29/146. Sir John Hipsley to Buckingham, September 1, 1623, in *Cabala*, 316.

31. Between May and September, the Privy Council met thirty-five times, usually at Whitehall. Although the number of members attending fluctuated, Calvert missed only four meetings. *APC, 1621–1623*, 478–512; *1623–1625*, 5–82.

32. Minutes of the Council of New England, July 5, 1622, in *CSP, Colonial, America, 1574–1660*, 31.

33. Wentworth to Wandesford, July 30, 1623; Wentworth to Leonard Calvert, June 2, 1623; Wentworth to Mrs. Danby, June 2, 1623, in *Wentworth Papers*, ed. Cooper, 172–74.

34. Conway to Calvert, July 5, 1623; Calvert to Conway, August 27, 1623, in *CSP, James I, 1623–1625*, 7, 68. *APC, 1621–1623*, 466. Wentworth to Wandesford, July 30, 1623, in *Wentworth Papers*, ed. Cooper, 191. Wentworth to Wandesford, October 2, 1623, in *Strafforde's Letters*, ed. Knowler, 1:17–18.

35. Wentworth to Calvert, June 16, 1623, in *Wentworth Papers*, ed. Cooper, 188.

36. Rumors that the Prince of Wales would shortly leave for Spain, where he was "to be instructed in the Catholic religion," journey to Rome "to be reconciled with the Pope," and then return to Spain to marry the Infanta, surfaced as early as April. Mead to Stuteville, April 19, 1623, in *James I*, ed. Birch, 2:390. A letter to the king attributed to the archbishop of Canterbury questioned the wisdom of sending the prince without the consent of the council or the people. August 8, 1623 [?], *CSP, James I, 1623–1625*, 48. Buckingham told a member of Parliament that the prince went to Spain because he saw his father deluded by delays and his sister robbed of her inheritance. *The Hollis Account of Proceedings in the House of Commons in 1624*, trans. Christopher Thompson (Orsett, Essex, 1985), 3. Calvert to Carleton, February 27, 1623, in SP84/111/148, PRO. Thomas, earl of Kellie, to John, earl of Mar, March 14, 18, 1622/23; March 31, July 11, 1623, in HMC, *Supplementary Report on the Manuscripts of the Earl of Mar & Kellie, Preserved at Alloa House, Clackmannanshire*, ed. Henry Paton, 2 vols. (London, 1930), 2:136–57, 161, 174. *Knyvett Letters*, 58. Buckingham to Conway, c. July 1623, in Williamson, *George Villiers*, 320. *CSP, Venice, 1621–1623*, 106.

38. Alvise Valaresso to Doge and Senate, September 27/October 6, 1623, in *CSP, Venice, 1623–1625*, 127.

39. Calvert to Conway, September 12, 1623; Lord Keeper Williams to Conway, September 18, 1623; Conway to Calvert, October 9, 1623; Dudley Carleton to Sir Dudley Carleton, October 10, 25; November 1, 10, 1623; Sir Richard Weston to Lord Edward Zouche, October 20, 1623, in *CSP, James I, 1623–1625*, 4, 78, 80, 91, 100, 103, 106, 109.

HMC, *Manuscripts of Mar & Kellie*, 2:182–83. Chamberlain to Carleton, October 11, 25; November 8, 1623, in *Chamberlain*, ed. McClure, 2:516, 519.

40. Letters of November 11, 29, 1623, in *Manuscripts of Mar & Kellie*, 2:183, 184. Chamberlain to Carleton, November 8, 21; December 20, 1623, in *Chamberlain*, ed. McClure, 2:522, 527–28, 534.

41. Chamberlain to Carleton, November 21, 1623; January 31, 1624, in *Chamberlain*, ed. McClure, 2:527, 542. Kellie to Mar, November 29, 1623, in *Manuscripts of Mar & Kellie*, 2:184. Calvert noted the king's resolution to call Parliament in his letter to Sir Walter Aston, December 31, 1623, in Additional MSS, 36446, fol. 267.

42. Castle to Trumbull, November 17, 1623, in Trumbull MS, 17/109, quoted in Thomas Cogswell, *The Blessed Revolution: English Politics and the Coming of War, 1621–1624* (Cambridge, 1984), 89. Chamberlain to Carleton, November 8, 1623, in *Chamberlain*, ed. McClure, 2:522.

43. Wentworth to Lord Clifford, January 23, 1623/24, in *Strafforde's Letters*, ed. Knowler, 1:19. Chamberlain to Carleton, January 31, 1624, in *Chamberlain*, ed. McClure, 2:542–43. HMC, *Manuscripts of Mar & Kellie*, 2:193. CSP, *James I, 1623–1625*, 172.

44. *CJ*, 1:670–71, 675. Yonge, *Diary*, 73.

45. Chamberlain to Carleton, February 21, March 20, 1624, in *Chamberlain*, ed. McClure, 2:546, 548. Conway to Carleton, February 24, 1624; Locke to Carleton, April 3, 1624; Calvert to Conway, May 21, 1624, in CSP, *James I, 1623–1625*, 169, 205, 251. Erskine to earl of Mar, March 1, 1624; Kellie to Mar, April 5, 1624, in HMC, *Mar and Kellie Manuscripts*, 1:123, 2:197.

46. *CJ*, 1:675. Chamberlain to Carleton, February 21, 1624, in *Chamberlain*, ed. McClure, 2:546. Conway to Carleton, February 23, 26, 1624; earl of Kellie to Conway, March 2, 4, 1624; Conway to Calvert, March 2, 1624; Calvert and Conway to Kellie, March 3, 1624; Dudley Carleton to Sir Dudley Carleton, March 5, 1624, in CSP, *James I, 1623–1625*, 169, 170, 175–77, 179. Henry Erskine to Mar, March 1, 1624, in HMC, *Manuscripts of Mar & Kellie*, 1:123. *LJ*, 3:210, 220–32, 234, 238.

47. Dudley Carleton to Sir Dudley Carleton, April 24, 1624, in SP14/163/47, PRO; and Kellie to Mar, April 5, 1624, in HMC, *Manuscripts of Mar & Kellie*, 2:197.

48. Dudley Carleton to Sir Dudley Carleton, April 4, 1624, in SP14/162/13, PRO. Sir Francis Nethersole to Sir Dudley Carleton, March 29, 1624; Thomas Locke to Sir Dudley Carleton, April 3, 1624; Sir Richard Young to Lord Edward Zouche, April 7, 1624; Dudley Carleton to Sir Dudley Carleton, April 11, 1624, in CSP, *James I, 1623–1625*, 201, 205, 209, 213.

49. CSP, *James I, 1623–1625*, 208–9, 223, 231, 263. Dudley Carleton to Sir Dudley Carleton, April 4, 24, 1624; May 6, 17, 1624, in SP14/162/13, SP14/163/47, SP14/164/44, SP14/162/91, PRO. Locke to Sir Dudley Carleton, May 12, 1624, in CSP, *James I, 1623–1625*, 242.

50. Dudley Carleton to Sir Dudley Carleton, May 3, 13; June 26, 1624, in SP14/164/7, 72, 14/168/47, PRO (Conway quotes). Calvert to Sir Dudley Carleton, May 21, 1624, in SP14/165/11, PRO. Calvert's hope might have been buoyed by the king's efforts to reconcile Buckingham and Bristol. Chamberlain to Sir Dudley Carleton, May 13, 1624, in *Chamberlain*, ed. McClure, 2:558. Wentworth to Wandesford, June 17, 1624, in *Strafforde's Letters*, ed. Knowler, 1:21.

51. SP14/167/37, 38, PRO. Goodman, *James*, 2:400. Chamberlain to Carleton, Au-

gust 21, 1624, in Chamberlain, ed. McClure, 2:577–78. For Bristol, see *The Earl of Bristol's Defence of his Negotiations in Spain*, ed. Samuel R. Gardiner, The Camden Miscellany, vol. 6 (Westminster, 1871).

52. Kellie to Mar, July 6, August 8, 1624, in HMC, *Manuscripts of Mar & Kellie*, 2:207, 209. Archbishop Abbot to Sir Dudley Carleton, August 13, 1624, in SP14/171/59, PRO. Calvert to Carleton, July 26, 1624, in SP84/118/262, PRO. Thomas Locke to Carleton, July 24, 1624, in SP14/170/53, PRO. Chamberlain to Carleton, August 7, 1624, in *Chamberlain*, ed. McClure, 2:575, 585.

53. Thomas Middleton, *A Game at Chess*, ed. T. H. Howard-Hill (Manchester, 1993), act 1, line 56, and Appendix I: "Documents Relating to *A Game at Chess*," 192–213 (including the ambassador's comments). Henry Gibb to Lord Mayor of London and the Court of Aldermen, October 1, 1624, in *Analytical Indexes to Volumes 11 and VIII of the Series of Records Known as the Remembrancia: Preserved among the Archives of the City of London, A.D. 1580–1664*, ed. W. H. Overall and H. C. Overall (London, 1870), 8, "Water," no. 52.

54. Conway to Calvert, August 6, 1624, in SP14/171/23, PRO. On September 2, Conway sent Calvert information on state business and asked him to assemble the council. *CSP, James I, 1623–1625*, 333. Conway to Calvert, September 20, 1624, in SP14/167/44, PRO. Williamson dated this letter late September 1622, in *George Villiers*, 244. An earlier edition, which reprinted the letter in a collection of twenty-one letters, all hastily written, "some of them blotted rather than written on slips of dirty paper," did not arrange them in chronological order. *Letters of the Kings of England, Now First Collected from the Royal Archives, and Other Authentic Sources, Private as well as Public*, ed. James Orchard Halliwell, 2 vols. (London, 1848), 2:252–53, 237. The internal evidence of the letters suggests that Buckingham wrote them after he returned from Spain. Conway's letter of September 20 hints that what the duke described took place after September 20. Calvert's return to London on October 7 indicates that the incident took place shortly after that date.

55. On September 26 young Carleton reported that Buckingham patronized Sir John Coke as Calvert's successor. SP14/172/57, PRO. Chamberlain to Carleton, October 23, 1624, in *Chamberlain*, ed. McClure, 2:585. Wentworth to Calvert, October 12, 1624, in *Strafforde's Letters*, ed. Knowler, 1:24. Calvert to Conway, October 24, 1624, in *CSP, James I, 1623–1625*, 372. Calvert to Buckingham, 1624, in Stowe MSS, 743, fol. 58, BL. Dudley Carleton to Sir Dudley Carleton, November 23, 1624, in SP84/121/116–17, PRO. *CSP, James I, 1623–1625*, 390. Young Carleton noted that the duke never did anything post-haste and that the prince referred everything to him. He had his head and hands full with matters more important than the secretary's position. Dudley Carleton to Sir Dudley Carleton, December 18, 1624, in *CSP, James I, 1623–1625*, 413.

56. Wentworth to Calvert, October 12, 1624, in *Strafforde's Letters*, ed. Knowler, 1:24. Chamberlain to Carleton, October 23, 1624, in *Chamberlain*, ed. McClure, 2:585. Chamberlain noted that Calvert was "to have as much more somewhere" that is, another £3000, "besides an Irish baronie for himself, or where he list to bestow it for his benefit." *Chamberlain*, ed. McClure, 600. The summary in *CSP, James I, 1623–1625*, 472, incorrectly gives the sum of £6000. Roe, *Negotiations*, 369. *APC, 1623–1625*, 453. Whether Calvert received the additional £3000 is not known.

57. William Laud may have suspected that something was amiss, but he did not pur-

sue the matter in his diary. Laud, who would be named by Charles to succeed to the archbishopric of Canterbury in 1633, visited Buckingham on January 5, 1625. As he waited to speak with the duke, "Secretary Calvert fell in speech with me about some differences between the Greek and Ro. Ch. Then also, and there, a young man, that took on him to be a Frenchman, fell into discourse about the Church of England. He grew at earnest for the Ro. Ch. . . . I believe he was a priest; but he wore a lock down to his shoulders. I heard after, that he was a French gentleman." Laud, *Works*, 3:156.*CJ*, 1:776.

58. *CSP, Venice, 1623–1625*, 568; *1626–1628*, 147. Roe, *Negotiations*, 372. Dudley Carleton to Sir Dudley Carleton, November 24, 1624, in SP84/121/116b–117, PRO.

59. Archbishop of Canterbury to Sir Thomas Roe, March 30, 1625, in Roe, *Negotiations*, 372.

60. Locke to Carleton, August 10, 1622, in *James*, ed. Birch, 2:328. Chamberlain to Carleton, August 10, 1622, in *Chamberlain*, ed. McClure, 2:449. HMC, *Salisbury*, 22:165. Calvert to Carleton, September 16, 1622, in SP84/109/64, PRO. One other discrepancy exists that cannot be explained from the existing evidence. The published register for St. Martin's in the Field does not list a baptism for his son Leonard, who was born sometime in 1610. *Register*, ed. Mason. At about the same time, Cecil sent Calvert on a diplomatic mission, the purpose of which confounded court gossips. Did Cecil temporarily banish him for a religious faux pas? The records stand mute.

61. Calvert to Salisbury, August 12, 1622, in HMC, *Salisbury*, 22:328. Locke to Carleton, August 10, 1622, in *James*, ed. Birch, 2:165. Locke to Trumbull, August 9, 16, 1622, in Trumbull MSS, 29/136, 137, British Manuscripts Project, Library of Congress, Washington, DC. Yonge, *Diary*, 64. Chamberlain to Carleton, September 25, 1622, in *Chamberlain*, ed. McClure, 2:451. Mary F. S. Hervey, *The Life, Correspondence, and Collections of Thomas Howard, Earl of Arundel* (Cambridge, 1932), 220.

62. Goodman, *James*, 2:376 (emphasis added). The bishop acknowledged his commitment to the Roman Catholic Church, the only Church that had "salvation in it," in a letter dated January 17, 1655. John E. B. Mayor, "Original Letter of Godfrey Goodman, Together with Materials For his Life," in Communications Made to the Cambridge Antiquarian Society, 11 Being No. 2 of the Second Volume (Cambridge, 1861), 121.

63. Locke to Carleton, November 11, 1620, in SP114/117/11, PRO. Calvert to Conway, August 12, 1623, in *CSP, James I, 1623–1625*, 53. In his will, Arundell referred to Peasley, who succeeded Calvert as clerk of the Privy Council and later married one of his daughters, as his (Arundell's) friend. Will of Thomas Lord Arundell, November 5, 1639, *MdHM* 22 (1927): 315. Locke thought the king appointed Calvert and Arundell to the commission to balance the influence of the archbishop of Canterbury and Secretary Naunton. Locke to Carleton, November 11, 1620, in SP14/117/11, PRO. The English tended to blame their woes on Gondomar and decried his "potency." *Autobiography of D'Ewes*, 2:187, 168.

64. Chamberlain to Carleton, October 18, 1617; September 25, 1622, in *Chamberlain*, ed. McClure, 2:105–6, 451. Yonge, *Diary*, August 19, 1622.

65. Dr. Meddus to Rev. Joseph Mead, April 13, 1625, in *Charles*, ed. Birch, 1:120. Chamberlain to Carleton, February 26, 1624, in *Chamberlain*, ed. McClure, 2:603, 518. Calvert to Buckingham, April 28, 1623, in Harleian MSS, BL, 1580/184.

66. Cottington to Sir John Finet, April 7, 1628, in *Newfoundland*, ed. Cell, 278. Wilson, *History*. At this point, Calvert might legitimately be labeled a crypto-Catholic, for he

had surely in his own mind made a leap of faith. Bishop Goodman's commentary may apply to these few months. Still, Calvert hung back from any open or public commitment until January 1625.

67. Simon Stock to [Cardinal Ottavio Bandini, member of Propaganda in Rome] London, November 15, 1624, in Codignola, *Stock*, 76. For Codignola's identification of the two councillors, see 11–13.

68. *APC, 1623–1625*, 402–3; *CSP, Ireland, 1615–1625*, 550. *Calendar of Patent and Close Rolls*, membrane 2, PRO.

69. In welcoming Calvert back, Wentworth wrote, "I am right glad for your Ague recovered." Letter of October 12, 1624, in *Strafforde's Letters*, ed. Knowler, 1:24.

70. Additional MSS, 27962C. Translated by John Patrick Donnelly, S.J.

71. Chamberlain to Carleton, January 8, 1624/25, in *Chamberlain*, ed. McClure, 2:595. Cottington reported on February 6 that Calvert had delivered his seals and was to be made an Irish baron. To Sir Dudley Carleton, in SP 84/122/115b, PRO. February 9, 1624/25, *APC, 1623–1625*, 453–54.

72. Carew to Roe, March 25, 1624/25, in Roe, *Negotiations*, 369 (emphasis added). A later family account remembered that Calvert had obtained his dismissal with some difficulty, his majesty having had a particular "Affection to him by reason of his great abilities & integrety." Sloane MS 3662, excerpt printed in *Newfoundland*, ed. Cell, 252. *Calvert Papers*, ed. Cox. The February report is in Hughes, *SJ, Text*, 1:178–79. HMC, *Salvetti*, 3. Dr. Meddus to Rev. Joseph Meade, April 13, 1625, in *Charles*, ed. Birch, 1:120.

73. Hughes, *SJ, Text*, 53, 179.

74. Wilson, *History*, 151.

FOUR: "Upon this new shuffle of the packe"

Title is from Sir Thomas Wentworth to Christopher Wandesford, April 4, 1625, in *Wentworth Papers*, ed. Cooper, 229.

1. His East India Company investments did well. During 1624 Wentworth reported the arrival of 150 bales of silk. Wentworth to Calvert, August 14, 1624, *Strafforde's Letters*, ed. Knowler, 1:23. K. N. Chaudhuri valued Persian silk in London in September 1624 at twenty-six shillings a pound. K. N. Chaudhuri, *The East India Company: The Study of an Early Joint-Stock Company, 1600–1640* (London, 1965), 205. Using the latter figure, Ronald Edward Zupko used data in his *British Weight and Measures: A History from Antiquity to the Seventeenth Century* (Madison, WI, 1977) to calculate that Calvert's silk was worth £21,840. *Newfoundland*, ed. Cell, 15, 16, 26.

2. *CD1621*, 2:314–15, 258, 320–21, 332; 4:256; 5:5, 232; 6:112. Nicholas, *Debates*, 1:318–19 (quote), 2:276. Captain Daniel Powell to Calvert, July 28, 1622, in Richard Whitbourne, *A Discourse and Discovery of New-Found-Land* (1622), in *Newfoundland*, ed. Cell, 199. Richard A. Preston, "Fishing and Plantation: New England in the Parliament of 1621," *American Historical Review* 45 (October 1939): 35 (quote).

3. Wynne to Calvert, August 21, 1621, in *Newfoundland*, ed. Cell, 253, 255–56.

4. Wynne to Calvert, July 1622, in Whitbourne, *Discourse*, 196. Wynne referred to letters written on February 19, March 14, May 4, and May 10, 1622. Unfortunately, the letters have not survived.

5. Ibid., 196–98. Wynne to Calvert, August 17, 1622, ibid., 202. NH [Nicholas

Hoskins] to William Peasley, August 18, 1622, ibid., 205, 204 n. Baltimore to Wentworth, August 29, 1629, *Wentworth Papers*, 12/75, SCL.

6. Powell to Calvert, July 28, 1622, in Whitbourne, *Discourse*, 200.

7. Ibid., 100, 101, 167.

8. Ibid., 204, 203. Wynne cautioned against sending any more boys and girls, or "anyone else who has not been brought up to labor, for they are unfit for these affairs."

9. Rev. Joseph Mead to Sir Martin Stuteville, January 23, 1629/30, in *Charles*, ed. Birch, 2:53. Simon Stock, a discalced Carmelite, to [Propaganda de Fide, in Rome], February 3, 1625, in Codignola, *Stock*, 77.

10. Calvert's attempt to spread the risk cannot be documented. In 1622 Powell referred to the rest of the investors but did not elaborate. Powell to Calvert, July 28, 1622, in *Newfoundland*, ed. Cell, 220. A year later, Calvert referred to unidentified "associates" in his infant plantation. Calvert to Conway, August 11, 1623, SP14/150/82, , PRO, in *CSP, James I, 1623–1625*, 52–53. Later, George Cottington sued Calvert to recoup the amount due to him "upon our fishing adventure, at Newfoundland." He specifically noted "seeing others satisfied to the full" while Calvert neglected his satisfaction. Cottington to Sir John Finet, April 7, 1628, in *Newfoundland*, ed. Cell, 278.

11. *Newfoundland*, ed. Cell, 258–69. Cell collated CO1/2/23, PRO; and Sloane MS170, fols. 7–14, BL.

12. Calvert to Buckingham, April 3, 1621, in Harleian MS 1580, 182, quoted in Alice Mildred Shipley, "Why George Calvert Favored Religious Toleration" (master's thesis, University of Maryland, 1966), 99. *APC, 1621–1623*, 466. Chamberlain to Carleton, May 3, 1623, in Nichols, *The Progresses*, 4:852. Calvert to Conway, August 11, 1623, in SP14/150/82, PRO. *CSP, James I, 1623–1625*, 52–53.

13. Eliot to [Conway], June 10, 1623 (quote); Conway to Eliot, Conway to Navy Commissioners, June 12, 1623; Eliot to Conway, June 16, 1623; Conway to Eliot, June 20, 1623; Eliot to Conway June 25, 1623, in *CSP, James I, 1619–1623*, 603, 605, 611, 614, 619. Calvert to Conway, August 11, 1623, in SP14/150/82, PRO.

14. Baltimore to Wentworth, August 12, 1630, in *Strafforde's Letters*, ed. Knowler, 1:53.

15. Parsons to Mr. Winslade, March 18, 1605, in Hughes, *SJ, Documents*, 1:3–5.

16. Stock to [Propaganda], February 8, 1625, in Codignola, *Stock*, 77. Calvert used the name Avalon in the 1623 charter, well before any contact with Stock can be documented.

17. Baltimore to Wentworth, August 12, 1630, in *Strafforde's Letters*, ed. Knowler, 1:53. Wentworth's father had advised him to be in "conversation" with Catholics rather than speaking earnestly against them. Catholics, he urged, were very learned and wise and could say much for their cause. "They hold the same fundamental points as we do." Only ambition, pride, covetousness, and a want of charity caused the hateful contentions between Protestant and Catholic. *Wentworth Papers*, ed. Cooper, 18.

18. Sloane MS 3662, BL. *APC, 1625–1626*, March 27, 1625, 5. Baltimore to Sir John Coke, March 15, 1625, in HMC, *The Manuscripts of the Earl of Cowper, K. G., Preserved at Melbourne House, Derbyshire*, 3 vols. (London, 1888–89), 1:187.

19. *Calendar of Patent and Close Rolls*, 37, PRO. Calvert to Coke, March 15, 1624/25; Buckingham to Coke, March 17, 1624/25, in HMC, *Cowper*, 1:187.

20. *APC, 1625–1626*, 5. Stock to [Propaganda], December 5, 1625; March 7, 1626, in

Codignola, *Stock*, 91, 96. Pesaro to Doge and Senate, December 5, 1625, in *CSP, Venice, 1625–1626*, 237. King Charles to [Archbishop Abbot], December 15, 1625, in *CSP, Charles I, Addenda*, 75. Bede to Silvester Pardo of Yres, December 25, 1625, in *CSP, Charles I, 1625–1626*, 187. Tuscan Resident Amerigo Salvetti to Grand Duke of Florence, April 1/11, 1625, in HMC, *Salvetti*, 4.

21. HMC, *Salvetti*, 3. A later family commentary reflected the family's view of George Calvert's withdrawal: The king wanted Baltimore to stay on the council and re-solved not to require him to take the oath of supremacy. At Baltimore's request, the king gave him leave to retire from court. Sloane MSS 3662, BL; and *Newfoundland*, ed. Cell, 252. Chamberlain to Carleton, April 9, 1625, in *Chamberlain*, ed. McClure, 2:609.

22. *APC, 1625–1626*, 5, 33. Charles dismissed six other council members. Salvetti to Grand Duke, April 1/11, 1625, in HMC, *Salvetti*, 3. Chamberlain to Carleton, April 9, 1625, in *Chamberlain*, ed. McClure, 2:609. Mr. Mead to Sir Martin Stuteville, April 13, 1625, in *Letters*, ed. Ellis, 3:187. David Rothe to Peter Lombard, September 25, 1625, in Irish Manuscripts Commission, *Wadding Papers, 1614–1638*, ed. Brendan Jennings (Dublin, 1953), 101–2.

23. Abbot to Roe, March 30, 1625, in Roe, *Negotiations*, 372. [?] to Rev. Joseph Mead, April 13, 1625, in Harleian MS, 389/422. *Charles*, ed. Birch, 1:10.

24. Charles to Lord Falkland, May 6, 1625, in *Calendar of Patent and Close Rolls*, 37, PRO. Stock to [Cardinal Ottavio Bandini], May 10, 1625, in Codignola, *Stock*, 81.

25. Rothe to Lombard, September 17, 1625, in Irish Manuscripts Commission, *Wadding Papers*, 101–2.

26. *APC, 1625–1626*, April 26, 1625, 33.

27. Ibid., April 5, 1625, 20. Stock to [Cardinal Ottavio Bandini], May 10, 1625, in Codignola, *Stock*, 81.

28. Irish Manuscripts Commission, *Wadding Papers*, 101–2. As clerk of the council, Calvert gained knowledge of both Wexford and the manorial system. He copied and sent "A Project for the Division and Plantation of the serval small territories in the county of Wexford" into manors to English authorities in Ireland. February 28, 1616, in *Calendar of the Carew manuscripts, [1515–1624], preserved in the archi-episcopal library at Lambeth . . .*, ed. J. S. Brewer and William Bullen, 6 vols. (London, 1867–73), 6:321–24.

29. Irish Manuscripts Commission, *Wadding Papers*, 101–2. Joan's religion at the time she became a servant in Calvert's household cannot be determined. Wroth dated the marriage between August 8, 1622, and September 17, 1625. One child, Philip, born before March 20, 1628, resulted from this union. "Tobacco or Codfish," ed. Wroth, 530.

30. Irish Manuscripts Commission, *Wadding Papers*, 101–2.

31. Codignola, *Stock*, 3, 9. 15.

32. Stock to [Propaganda], March 2, May 31, 1625, ibid., 79, 84. Stock lobbied Pro-paganda to send discalced Carmelites, for "no priests are better suited to convert nations than ours." Stock to [Cardinal Bandini], May 10, 1625, ibid., 81.

33. Stock to [Propaganda], February 8, March 2, May 10, 1625, ibid., 77, 79, 81.

34. Stock to [Propaganda], February 8, May 31, 1625, ibid., 77, 84. Propaganda's re-sponse to his letter of May 10, 1625, ibid., 82. "The Note-Book of John Southcote D. D. From 1623 to 1637," in *Miscellanea I*, Publications of the Catholic Record Society (London, 1905), 103.

35. Stock to [Propaganda], September 13, October 20, December 5, 1625; Stock to Paolo Simone de Gesú, April 22, 1626, in Codignola, *Stock*, 86, 89, 91, 101–2.

36. Stock to [Propaganda], December 5, 1625, March 7, April 22, June 30, 1626, ibid., 91, 95, 100, 103.

37. Copy of certificate by the earl of Westmeath et al., November 30, 1626; Baltimore to Buckingham, November 30, 1626, in SP63/243/266–67, PRO. *A Guide to Manuscripts Relating to America in Great Britain and Ireland*, ed. B. R. Crick and Miriam Alman (Oxford, 1961), 34. In July of the next year, a list of commissioners of the counties, presumably for raising money for the army, included Baltimore as representing County Wexford. *Calendar of the State Papers, Relating to Ireland, of the Reign of Charles I. Preserved in the Public Record Office, 1625–[1659]*, ed. Robert Pentland Mahaffy, 4 vols. (London, 1900–1903), *1625–1632*, 251.

38. [?] to Rev. Joseph Meade, February 9, 1626/27, in *Charles*, ed. Birch, 1:92–93. Cantarine to Doge and Senate, March 12, 1627, in *CSP, Venice, 1626–1628*, 147.

39. *Calvert Papers*, roll 5, no. 107, April 23, 1627.

40. Baltimore to Edward Nicholas, Buckingham's secretary, April 7, 1627, CO1/4/19, PRO. *CSP, Colonial, America, 1574–1660*, 83.

41. Baltimore to Wentworth, May 21, 1627, in *Strafforde's Letters*, ed. Knowler, 1:39.

42. Ingram to Wentworth, November 7, 1625; Wentworth to Wandesford, December 5, 1625, ibid., 1:28, 33.

43. Calvert to Edward Nicholas, April 7, 1627; Wentworth to Sir Richard Weston, undated; Baltimore to Wentworth, May 1, 27, 1627; and Clifford to Wentworth, May 20, 1627, ibid., 34–35, 37, 38. *CSP, Colonial, America, 1574–1660*, 83. *APC, 1627–1628*, 216.

44. Stock to [Propaganda], October 10, 1627, in Codignola, *Stock*, 107. "Note-Book of Southcote," 103.

45. "Note-Book of Southcote," 103. Father Lagonissa, bishop of Conza, apostolic nuncio to Propaganda, September 21, 1630, in *Propaganda Fide Archives*, 5:205, translated by John M. Lenhart, "An Important Chapter in American Church History (1625–1650)," *Catholic Historical Review* 8 (January 1929): 504–5.

46. Sloane MS 3662. *Newfoundland*, ed. Cell, 252. Hayman to Buckingham, 1628, and "A Proposition of Profitt and Honor Proposed to My Dread, and Gratious Soveraigne Lord, King Charles, By his humble subject Robert Hayman," in G. G. Moore Smith, "Robert Hayman and the Plantation of Newfoundland," *English Historical Review* 129 (January 1928): 30, 32.

47. Lagonissa to Propaganda, September 21, 1630, in Lenhart, "An Important Chapter," 504–5.

48. Ibid. [?] to Rev. Joseph Meade, June 16, 1627, in *Charles*, ed. Birch, 1:242. December 31, 1627, *APC, 1627–1628*, 216.

49. Charles to Falkland, January 19, 1627/28, in SP63/246/16–17v, PRO (Ireland), in *Newfoundland*, ed. Cell, 276. Charles's letter paraphrased information provided by Baltimore.

50. Pesaro to Doge and Senate, January 21/31, 1625, in *CSP, Venice, 1623–1625*, 568. Cottington to lord treasurer, December 12, 1628, CO1/4/60, PRO. Baltimore to Cottington, August 18, 1629, in "Tobacco or Codfish," ed. Wroth, 523–33.

51. Chamberlain called his deathbed conversion a "relapse." He noted that Cottington further alienated Buckingham and speculated that Cottington would be discarded

from the prince's service. Chamberlain to Carleton, October 11, 1623, in *Chamberlain*, ed. McClure, 2:516–17.

52. Baltimore to Cottington, August 18, 1629, in "Tobacco or Codfish," ed. Wroth, 527.

53. Baltimore to John Harrison, February 5, 1627, in Stowe MS 743, 16, BL. *Calvert Papers*, ed. Cox, March 30, 1628, roll 5, no. 39. Baltimore to Wentworth, April 17, 1628, in *Wentworth Papers*, ed. Cooper, 291–92.

54. Quotations in Baltimore to Wentworth, April 17, 1628, in *Wentworth Papers*, ed. Cooper, 291. Baltimore to Wentworth, August 29, 1629, in *Wentworth Papers*, 12/75, SCL. John Treshur to Sir Robert Killgrew, April 10, 1628, in *CSP, Charles I, 1628–1629*, 71.

55. Stock to [Propaganda], June 28, July 28, 1628, in Codignola, *Stock*, 108, 39, 112. "Examination of Erasmus Stourton," October 9, 1628, in CO1/4/59, PRO.

56. Baltimore to Charles I, August 25, 1628 (quote); Baltimore to Buckingham, August 25, 1628, in CO1/4/56, 57, PRO. *Newfoundland*, ed. Cell, 279–82.

57. Baltimore to Charles I, August 25, 1628; Baltimore to Buckingham, August 25, 1628, in CO1/4/56, 57, PRO. *Newfoundland*, ed. Cell, 279–82. "The Second Lord Baltimore Describes his Father's Involvement in Newfoundland," in CO 1/9/43, extract, PRO. *Newfoundland*, ed. Cell, 297–98.

58. Baltimore to Buckingham, August 25, 1628; Baltimore to Charles I, August 25, 1628; petition of William Peasley, December [?], 1628), in CO1/4/57, CO1/4/56, CO1/4/61, PRO. *Newfoundland*, ed. Cell, 285–86.

59. "Examination of Erasmus Stourton," October 9, 1628. *CSP, Colonial, America, 1579–1660*, 100. Baltimore to Charles I, August 19, 1629, in CO1/5/27, PRO. *Newfoundland*, ed. Cell, 295.

60. Lagonissa to Propaganda, September 21, 1630, in Lenhart, "An Important Chapter," 504–5.

61. *CSP, Colonial, America, 1579–1660*, 95. Baltimore to Charles I, August 25, 1628, in CO1/4/56, PRO. He also used the term in his letter to Cottington, August 18, 1629, in "Tobacco or Codfish," ed. Wroth, 527.

62. Lord Percy to earl of Carlisle, September 3, 1628, in *CSP, Charles I, Addenda*, 293. Martin J. Havran, *Caroline Courtier: The Life of Lord Cottington* (Columbia, SC, 1973), 89, 111.

63. Havran, *Caroline Courtier*, 112. *Strafforde's Letters*, ed. Knowler, 2:430. C. V. Wedgwood, *Thomas Wentworth, First Earl of Strafford, 1593–1641: A Revaluation* (New York, 1962), 68.

64. Wandesford to Wentworth, December 29, 1628, in *Strafforde's Letters*, ed. Knowler, 1:49–50. Cecil Calvert to Wentworth, December 14, 1628, in *Wentworth Papers*, 12/42, SCL.

65. Cottington to lord treasurer, December 13, 1628, in CO1/4/60, PRO. "State of Lord Baltimore's Cause," [December 1628 (?)], in CO1/4/63, 64, , PRO, in *Newfoundland*, ed. Cell, 288–89. Christopher Levett to Sir John Coke, November 29, 1626; September 10, November 17, 1627, in *Guide to Manuscripts Relating to America*, ed. Crick and Alman, 34. Baltimore to Coke, January 16, 1628, in *CSP, Colonial, America, 1574–1660*, 69.

66. Baltimore to Charles I, August 19, 1629, in CO1/4/56, PRO.

67. Champlain quoted in Samuel Eliot Morrison, *Samuel de Chaplain: Father of New*

France (Boston, 1972), 54–55. Baltimore saved his poignant assessment of the Newfoundland winter for the king. Baltimore to Charles, August 25, 1628, in CO1/4/56, PRO.

68. Hayman, "Qvodlibets," in Smith, "Robert Hayman," 27.

69. Baltimore to Cottington, August 18, 1629, in "Tobacco or Codfish," ed. Wroth, 523–33. Baltimore to King Charles, August 19, 1629, in CO1/4/56, 57, PRO.

70. Stock to [Propaganda], July 2, 1629; January 1, 1631, in Codignola, *Stock*, 114, 122, 186 n.

71. Baltimore to Cottington, August 18, 1629, in "Tobacco or Codfish," ed. Wroth, 523–33. Baltimore to King Charles, August 19, 1629, in CO1/4/56, 57, PRO.

72. Baltimore to Wentworth, August 29, 1629, in *Wentworth Papers*, 12/75, SCL.

73. Ibid.

74. Kirke to Laud, October 2, 1639, in *CSP, Colonial, America, 1574–1660*, 304.

75. CO1/9/43, PRO, in *Newfoundland*, ed. Cell, 298. Baltimore to Wentworth, August 29, 1629, in *Wentworth Papers*, 12/75, SCL.

76. Baltimore to Wentworth, August 29, 1629, in *Wentworth Papers*, 12/75, SCL. Stock to [Propaganda], January 1, 1631, in Codignola, *Stock*, 122.

FIVE: "If yo*ur* M*ajesty* will please to grant me a precinct of land with such priviledges as the k*ing* your father my gracious M*aster* was pleased to graunt me"

Title is from Baltimore to Charles I, August 19, 1629, in CO1/5/27, PRO, *Newfoundland*, ed. Cell, 296.

1. Baltimore to Wentworth, August 29, 1629, in *Wentworth Papers*, 12/75, SCL. Mead to Stuteville, January 23, 1629/30, in *Charles*, ed. Birch, 2:53.

2. *Three Charters*, 54, 81. The controversy ended only with the deaths of the second Lord Baltimore and his principal antagonist William Claiborne in the 1670s.

3. Governor John Pott et al. to Privy Council, November 30, 1629, in CO1/5/40, PRO, *MdArch*, 3:16–17. Mead stated that Baltimore took the oath of allegiance but refused the oath of supremacy. Mead to Stuteville, January 23, 1629/30; Mr. Pory to Mead, February 12, 1629/30, in *Charles*, ed. Birch, 2:53–54. William Waller Hening, *The Statutes at Large: Being a Collection of All the Laws of Virginia*, 13 vols. (Richmond, 1809–23), 1:522.

4. Pott et al. to Privy Council, November 30, 1629, *MdArch*, 3:16–17. Letters patent for managing the business of the Virginia colony, July 15, 1624, in *CSP, Colonial, America, 1675–1676, Addenda, 1574–1674*, 65. Earlier, in May, on the king's orders Calvert had canceled the scheduled election of company officers, and then in June 1623 the king instructed the Privy Council, which Calvert directed, to attend diligently and daily to the business of Virginia. Calvert to the earl of Southampton, May 14, 1623, in CO1/2/29, PRO. Conway to Calvert, June 30, 1623, in *CSP, Colonial, America, 1574–1660*, 47. Sir Francis Nethersole to Dudley Carleton, May 6, 1624, in SP14/164/46, PRO.

5. Baltimore to Middlesex, March 28, 1632, in "Unpublished Letter of the First Lord Baltimore," ed. Matthew Page Andrews, *MdHM* 60 (June 1945): 90–91.

6. King Charles to Baltimore, November 22, 1629, in *CSP, Colonial, America, 1574–1660*, 101, CO1/5/39, PRO. *Newfoundland*, ed. Cell, 295–97. Pory to Mead, February 12, 1629/30, in *Charles*, ed. Birch, 2:53–54.

7. CO1/4/62, PRO. Summarized in *CSP, Colonial, America, 1574–1660*, 95. The editor incorrectly assigned the date of December 1628 to the document, and Cell, who reprinted the document, followed the Calendar. *Newfoundland*, ed. Cell, 287–88. Internal evidence dates the memorial between December 1629 and February 1630. Pory to Mead, February 12, 1629/30, in *Charles*, ed. Birch, 2:54. Stock to [Propaganda], January 1, 1631, in Codignola, *Stock*, 123.

8. "Tobacco or Codfish," ed. Wroth, 529–30. A mid-July missive from the Privy Council to the lords justice of Ireland, intervening on Baltimore's behalf, may indicate that he returned to London in early July. *APC, 1630 June–1631 June*, 53.

9. *MdArch*, 5:15.

10. March 18, 1629, in *CSP, Colonial, East Indies, 1625–1629*, 359. W. Robinson to Wentworth, August 27, 1630, in *Wentworth Papers*, 12/129, SCL, transcribed in Foster MSS 2002. Baltimore to Wentworth, September 12, 1630, in *Wentworth Papers*, 12/136, SCL.

11. July 15, 1630, *APC, 1630 June–1631 June*, 53. Baltimore to Wentworth, August 12, 1630, in *Strafforde's Letters*, ed. Knowler, 1:53. Cottington returned on March 31. *CSP, Venice, 1629–1632*, 490.

12. Baltimore to Wentworth, August 12, 1630, in *Strafforde's Letters*, ed. Knowler, 1:53. Baltimore to Wentworth, September 12, 1630, in *Wentworth Papers*, 12/136, SCL.

13. Baltimore to Wentworth, September 12, 1630, in *Wentworth Papers*, 12/136, SCL.

14. Baltimore did not know that infected fleas hosted by rats carried plague. "No rats, no plague, at least no urban plague." The epidemiology of plague was not fully grasped until the end of the nineteenth century, when the bacillus responsible was scientifically described in 1894. Londoners, who saw no relationship between dying rats and the onslaught of plague, grew accustomed to the sight of dead rats. J. F. D. Shrewsbury, *A History of Bubonic Plague in the British Isles* (Cambridge, 1971), 2–4.

15. Baltimore's fears about his servant's death were well founded, since 60 to 80 percent of those infected died. What he noted as a frenzy was probably the delirium that usually preceded a final coma. One of the sores was undoubtedly the blister that formed at the site of the original fleabite. The blister would develop into a gangrenous black carbuncle, and other carbuncles would appear, along with blisters and large subcutaneous spots that could change color between orange and black, blue and purple. The lymph nodes would swell and suppurate, forming the buboes that gave the disease its name. Paul Slack, *The Impact of Plague in Tudor and Stuart England* (London, 1985); and "Metropolitan Government in Crisis: The Response to Plague," in *London, 1500–1700: The Making of a Metropolis*, ed. A. L. Beier and Roger Finlay (New York, 1986), 60–81.

16. Baltimore mentioned his servant in his will. "Item I doe give unto my servant Bridgett Draycoate the some of Twenty pounds" *Calvert Papers*, 1:7.

17. Baltimore to Wandesford, September 27, 1630, in *Wentworth Papers*, 12/141, SCL. Giovanni Soranzo to Doge and Senate, March 16/26, 1630, in *CSP, Venice, 1629–1632*, 304. March 10, 1629/30, *APC, 1629–1630*, 303–4. Mead stated that the king did not allow pursuivants to violate the ambassador's houses. Mead to Stuteville, March 20, 1629/30, in *Charles*, ed. Birch, 2:68–69. The Venetian ambassador reported a number of violent encounters that resulted from Charles's policy. Giovanni Soranzo to Doge and Senate, March 29/April 5, 1630, in *CSP, Venice, 1629–1632*, 308, 315.

18. Baltimore reported in December that Charles I and Philip IV were to proclaim the peace that month. Baltimore to Wentworth, December 9, 1630; September 17, 1631, in *Wentworth Papers*, 12/249, SCL.

19. Baltimore to Wentworth and Baltimore to Christopher Wandesford, September 27, 1630, ibid., 12/140, 12/141.

20. Richard Montagu lumped the Jesuits and the Puritans together. Montagu to Cosin, January 3, 1624/25, in *The Correspondence of John Cosin, D.D. Lord Bishop of Durham: Together with Other Papers Illustrative of his Life and Times*, Publications of the Surtees Society (London, 1869), 52, 40. On February 22, 1632, one Henry Alleyn presented the king with a book that unfavorably compared Jesuits and Puritans. *CSP, Charles I, 1631–1633*, 276. Stock to Propaganda Fide, March 2, May 24, May 31, September 13, October 20, December 5, 1625, Codignola, *Stock*, 79–91.

21. Hughes, *SJ, Text*, 1:156–57, 168–74. *English SJ*, ed. Foley, vol. 7, pt. 2, pp. 834–35.

22. Cecil, Lord Baltimore to Governor Calvert, November 21, 23, 1642, in *Calvert Papers*, 1:217–19.

23. Stock to Propaganda, June 27, July 2, 1629; April 6, June 25, 1631; January 28, 1632, in Codignola, *Stock*, 108, 114, 124, 126, 129.

24. Lay Catholics of England to Richard Smith, bishop of Chalcedon, 1627, in Hughes, *SJ, Text*, 1:204–6. Sir Edwin Sandys, May 4, 1621, in *CD1621*, 5:141.

25. *The Answer to Tom-Tell-Truth, The Practice of Princes and the Lamentations of the Kirke*, 1, 6, 31. The tract was published without attribution in London in 1642.

26. Ibid., 31.

27. Baltimore to Wentworth, December 9, 1630, in *Wentworth Papers*, 12/176, SCL. Warrant to pay George Lord Baltimore two thousand pounds, to be deducted from the increase of subsidy on raw silk imported, March 2, 1630/31, in *CSP, Charles I, 1629–1631*, 524.

28. Baltimore summarized the request he made to Cottington in his letter to Wentworth, September 7, 1631, in *Wentworth Papers*, 12/249, SCL. Baltimore referred to his bequest from the king as an "ayuda de costa," a help for sharing expenses or a contribution. Grant to George Lord Baltimore, October 31, 1631, *CSP, Charles I, 1631–1633*, 175.

29. Baltimore to Wentworth, October 11, 1631, in *Strafforde's Letters*, ed. Knowler, 1:59–60.

30. Grant to George Lord Baltimore, October 31, 1631, in *CSP, Charles I, 1631–1632*, 175. *Calvert Papers*, ed. Cox, roll 5, no. 107. C66/2579, PRO, copy and transcript in Foster MSS 2002.

31. First "Warrant to Mr. William Noye Esqr. His Majesties Atturney Generall" and "Second Warrant to Mr. William Noye Esqur. His Majesties Atturney Generall," February 1631/32), Young MSS, Enoch Pratt Free Library, Baltimore. "The Lo: Baltemores Declaration to the Lords," *Calvert Papers*, 1:222.

32. "The Lo: Baltemores Declaration to the Lords," ibid., 1:222.

33. *Calvert Papers*, 1:223. Baltimore to Middlesex, March 28, 1632, in "Unpublished Letter," 91. (Second) "Warrant to Mr. William Noyes Esqr. His Majesties Atturney Generall," March 1632, in Young MSS.

34. He dated the will April 14 and it was proved a week later. *Calvert Papers*, 1:48.

35. Ibid., 1:49. Cecil, Lord Baltimore, to Wentworth, January 10, 1633/34, in *Strafforde's Letters*, ed. Knowler, 1:178–79. Baltimore acknowledged the continuance of Wentworth's favor, July 9, 1635, in *Wentworth Papers*, 15/141, SCL.

36. Cecil, Lord Baltimore, to Wentworth, January 10, 1633/34, in *Strafforde's Letters*, ed. Knowler, 1:178. Cecil, Lord Baltimore, to the Privy Council, "The humble Declaration of the Lord Baltemores proceedings in the procuring & passing of his Pattent of the Province of Maryland adjoyning to Virginea, and of severall unjust molestations which some of the old dissolved Company of Virginea have given him both before & since, to his great prejudice," *Calvert Papers*, 1:224–25.

37. The "Objections" as reprinted in Bradley T. Johnson, *The Foundation of Maryland and the Origins of the Act Concerning Religion* (Baltimore, 1883), 24–30. "Considerations upon the Patent to Lord Baltimore," June 20, 1632, *MdArch*, 3:17–19. *Objections Answered Touching Maryland*, in Hughes, *SJ, Documents*, 1:14–15.

38. *Objections Answered*, in Hughes, *SJ, Documents*, 1:14–15.

39. Ibid. Admiralty register, in SP16/228/72a, 73, PRO (July 31, 1633), transcribed in Foster MSS 2002.

40. Baltimore to Wentworth, January 10, 1633/34, in *Strafforde's Letters*, ed. Knowler, 1:178. Cecil, Lord Baltimore, to the Privy Council, "The humble Declaration of the Lord Baltemores proceedings," *Calvert Papers*, 1:221–29. Star Chamber, June 28, July 3, 1633, in *Acts of the Privy Council of England: Colonial Series* (London, 1908–12), *1618–1680*, 1:188–90. *MdArch*, 3:21–22. Edward Watkins, searcher for London, to Privy Council, October 29, 1633, in *MdHM* 1 (December 1906): 352–54. Sir John Harvey to Lords Commissioners for foreign plantations, 1635, in *Virginia Magazine of History and Biography* 1 (April 1894): 425–30.

41. Andrew White, S.J., *A Briefe Relation of the Voyage unto Maryland* (London, 1634), in *Narratives*, ed. Hall, 29. Baltimore to Wentworth, January 10, 1633/34, in *Strafforde's Letters*, ed. Knowler, 1:178.

42. Panzani to Barberini, August 15, 1635, in Hughes, *SJ, Documents*, 1:150. Cecil, Lord Baltimore, to the Privy Council, "The humble Declaration of the Lord Baltemores proceedings," in *Calvert Papers*, 1:221–29. Baltimore to Wentworth, January 10, 1633/34, in *Strafforde's Letters*, ed. Knowler, 1:178. For the litigation against Baltimore over the additional expenses incurred, see High Court of Admiralty, Instance and Prize, Libels etc., HCA 24/91/I 14, 134, 154, PRO.

43. Baltimore to Wentworth, January 10, 1633/34, in *Strafforde's Letters*, ed. Knowler, 1:177–78. "Instructions 13 Novem: 1633 directed by the Right Honourable Cecilius Lo: Baltimore and Lord of the Provinces of Mary Land and Avalon who his beloved Brother Leo: Calvert Esqr his Lops Deputy Governor of his Province of Mary Land and unto Jerom Hawley and Thomas Cornwaleys Esqrs. his Lordshipps Commissioners for the government of the said Province," in *Narratives*, ed. Hall, 16–23.

44. For the Newfoundland charter, see *Newfoundland*, ed. Cell, 258–69. For the Maryland Charter, see *A Relation of Maryland; together with a Map of the Countrey, the Conditions of Plantation, with His Majesties Charter to the Lord Baltemore* (London, 1635), in *Narratives*, ed. Hall, 101–12. Hughes, *SJ, Text*, 1:236.

45. *Narratives*, ed. Hall, 103, 103 n. George, Lord Baltimore to Charles I, August 25, 1628; August 19, 1629, in CO1/4/56, CO1/5/27, PRO; Charles I to Baltimore, November 22, 1629, in CO1/5/39, , PRO, all in *Newfoundland*, ed. Cell, 281–82, 296–97.

46. *Narratives*, ed. Hall, 101.

47. Ibid., 107.

48. Ibid, 103.

49. Ibid., 104

50. Ibid.

51. Ibid., 106. Calvert's charter did not require colonists to take the oath of supremacy.

52. Ibid., 110–11. The statute Quia emptores terrarum, 18 Edward I, chapter 1, 1290, is referred to in a note on 110.

53. *Narratives*, ed. Hall, 111–12.

s I x : "Such a designe when rightly understood will not want undertakers"

Title is from *"Short Treatise,"* 38.

1. Nicklin, "Notes," 335. Most likely, Cecil was born in late January or early February 1606. Foster, *Calvert*, 83 n.

2. Goodman, *James*, 1:376. Hughes, *SJ, Text*, 1:206.

3. Acts of the Privy Council, PC2/32/235, PRO. The council issued the pass on January 31, 1623/24. General Mutius Vitelleschi to the English provincial Edward Knott, October 31, 1643, Hughes, *SJ, Text*, 1:558.

4. Baltimore to Wentworth, January 10, 1633/34, May 16, 1634, in *Strafforde's Letters*, ed. Knowler, 1:178–79, 257. Wentworth to Coke, May 13, 1634, ibid., 1:246. Baltimore to Wentworth, July 1, 1634; Wentworth to Cecil, Lord Baltimore, February 6, 1638/39, in *Wentworth Papers*, 10a/255, 14/117, SCL.

5. Cecil, Lord Baltimore, to Wentworth, May 16, 1634, in *Strafforde's Letters*, ed. Knowler, 1:257. Cecil, Lord Baltimore, to Wentworth, July 1, December 1, 1634; Wentworth to Cecil, Lord Baltimore, February 17, 1638/39, in *Wentworth Papers*, 14/177, 14/236, 10a/255, SCL. Thomas, Lord Arundel, to Secretary of State Windebank, February 17, 1638/39, in *CSP, Charles I, 1638–1639*, 476.

6. *"Short Treatise,"* 38.

7. Ibid., 27, 37, 38. Baltimore most likely consulted the revised and expanded version of Captain John Smith's *The General History of Virginia, New England, and the Summer Isles*, published in 1624. *A Declaration of Lord Baltemore's Plantation in Mary-land, nigh upon Virginia: manifesting the Nature, Quality, Condition, and rich Utilities it Contayneth* (London, 1633), reprinted as *A Declaration of The Lord Baltemore's Plantation in Mary-land. February 10, 1633* ([Annapolis, MD], 1983), 2.

8. Baltimore to Governor William Stone, August 26, 1649; August 26, 1651, *MdArch*, 1:272, 328.

9. White, *A Declaration of The Lord Baltemore's Plantation in Mary-land*. In his letter of February 20, 1638/39, White noted Baltimore's corrections of "the written Copie which I made" of the *Declaration*. *Calvert Papers*, 1:20. Hughes reprinted *Objections Answered* in Hughes, *SJ, Documents*, 1:10–15; and Bradley T. Johnson reprinted it in *Foundation of Maryland*, 24–30.

10. *Calvert Papers*, 3:26–45; and with notes in *Narratives*, ed. Hall, 29–45. *Narratives*, ed. Hall, 27–28. Barbara Lawatsch-Boomgaarden (with Josef Ijsewijn) published a modern translation as *Voyage to Maryland: Relatio Itineris in Marilandiam* (Wauconda, IL,

1995). White may have also written the 1633 "An Account of the Colony of the Lord Baron of Baltimore, in Maryland, near Virginia," which accompanied Father Richard Blount's effort to secure permission for the Society to establish a mission in Maryland. *Narratives*, ed. Hall, 5–10. *A Relation of the Successful beginnings of the Lord Baltimore's Plantation in Mary-Land. Being an extract of certaine Letters written from thence, by some of the Adventurers, to their friends in England. To which is added, the conditions of plantation propounded by his Lordship for the second voyage intended this present yeere, 1634* (London, 1634).

11. *Narratives*, ed. Hall, 76–77.

12. At one time Baltimore had possession of Wintour's letter. The Enoch Pratt Free Library, Baltimore, owns the only known copy of the letter. *Descriptive catalog of the exhibition of documents relating to the early days of the colony of Maryland, shown in the central Hall of the library, January 5 to February 15, 1935* [Baltimore, 1935].

13. The name is spelled variously in the records as Winter, Wintour, and Wynter. Maryland records consistently spelled Robert's name as Wintour. A document dated February 14, 1633, represented Robert Winter as brother to Sir John Winter. *CSP, Charles I, 1631–1633*, 537–38. Robert Wintour was probably related to the Wintours who were executed for their role in the Gunpowder Plot of 1605. See the political libel circulated in 1640 entitled "Reasons why ship and conduct-money ought to be had and also money [lent] by the City of London," ibid., *1640–1641*, 126.

14. "Short Treatise," 33, 28. *CSP, Charles I, 1631–1633*, 537–38, 549.

15. Coke to Pennington, in *MdArch*, 3:123. Wintour's name was not on any of the extant lists naming the gentlemen adventurers. White made no reference to Wintour in his three accounts of the voyage. In addition, Baltimore's "Instructions" gave Leonard clear authority over the colonists once the ships were at sea. "The Ark and the Dove," *MdHM* 1 (December 1906): 353–54. Suit of Richard Orchard against Cecilius Lord Baltimore et al., February 1635, PRO. High Court of Admiralty Papers, Instance and Prize. Libels, etc. HCA 91/114. *Calvert Papers*, 1:132–36.

16. "Short Treatise," 26.

17. "A Modell of Christian Charity," in *Winthrop Papers*, 5 vols. (Boston, 1929–), 2:295.

18. "Short Treatise," 33. *Objections Answered*, in Hughes, *SJ, Documents*, 1:12.

19. White, *Declaration*, 1.

20. "Short Treatise," 36, 37, 28. As Wintour thought of Maryland, so John Winthrop thought of Massachusetts: that it was of a far different and nobler nature than the other English colonization attempts. "General Observations for the Plantation of New England," in *Winthrop Papers*, 2:111–21.

21. "Short Treatise," 27, 31. Wintour postulated his idyllic concepts on peaceful relations with the natives.

22. Vicenzo Gussoni to Doge and Senate, October 14, 1633, in *CSP, Venice, 1632–1636*, 154. White, "A Briefe Relation," in *Narratives*, ed. Hall, 39. "Charter of Maryland," ibid., 101.

23. "Short Treatise," 28, 29. Wintour described England as "the garden of the earth for plenty and pleasure, the flower of kingdomes for power and ma[jes]tie, the envy of countries for freeborne nurslings, the terror of nations untamed spirits, the magazine of the world of trade and commerce. Queene of I[s]lands, Empresse of the Sea." In a way, Baltimore followed an argument employed by Richard Hakluyt in his 1584 treatise, "A

Discourse of Western Planting." The author of *Objections Answered* implied that Maryland was a Catholic version of the safety value theory.

24. "Lord Baltimore's Instructions," in *Narratives*, ed. Hall, 16–23. "*Short Treatise*," 30.

25. *Declaration*, 2–3.

26. "*Short Treatise*," 30, 31, 34, 35.

27. Ibid., 31. *Declaration*, 2. *1635 Relation*, in *Narratives*, ed. Hall, 91–92.

28. "*Short Treatise*," 31, 34–36. *1635 Relation*, in *Narratives*, ed. Hall, 81–83. Wintour missed the mark on crop diversification.

29. "*Short Treatise*," 31.

30. White dated his pamphlet "February, 10. anno 1633." He may have used the new style Gregorian calendar, which was used by the Roman Church and Catholic countries, to suggest a Catholic connection.

31. "*Short Treatise*," 38.

32. John Lewger's diary, quoted in Hughes, *SJ, Text*, 1:501. "The Charter of Mary Land," in *Narratives*, ed. Hall, 107.

33. "*Short Treatise*," 38, 39.

34. Baltimore to Wentworth, January 10, 1634, in *Strafforde's Letters*, ed. Knowler, 1:178–79. *CSP, Venice, 1632–1636*, 158.

35. *The Popes Nuntioes or, The Negiotiations of Seignior Panzani, Seignior Con, &c. Resident here in England with the Queen, and the treating about the Alternatives of Religion with the Archbishop of Canterbury, and his Adherents, in the yeares of our Lord, 1634, 1635, 1636, & . . . (London, 1643), 4–5.*

36. *In Durham, for example, Catholicism survived mainly among "gentry households with their dependent bodies of servants." Mervyn James*, Family, Lineage and Civil Society: A Study of Society, Politics, and Mentality in the Durham Region, 1500–1640 (Oxford, 1974), 140–42.

37. SP16/349/228, PRO. *James*, ed. Birch, 2:277.

38. Panzani, *Relatione dello Stato della religione Catholica in Inghilterra*, quoted in Magee, *Recusants*, 104–5.

39. *CSP, Charles I, 1636–1637*, 499 (March 15, 1636/37). A document in the Public Record Office detailing the arrests of London Catholics indicates that Catholics pursued a rich variety of occupations. SP16/495, PRO.

40. "Analytical Catalogue, 1621–1645," in *English SJ*, ed. Foley, vol. 7, pt. 1, p. clxviii. Francis Edwards, *The Jesuits in England from 1580 to the Present Day* (London, 1985), 58, 62.

41. Cornwallis to Baltimore, April 6, 1638, in *Calvert Papers*, 1:172–73.

42. "*Short Treatise*," 38, 39.

43. Ibid., 12, 38, 39.

44. Ibid., 37, 39. In Massachusetts Bay Colony, a higher authority screened potential colonists: "God sifted a whole nation that he might send choice grain into the Wilderness." William Stoughton, "Election Sermon" (1668), quoted in Julius Herbert Tuttle, *Massachusetts and Her Royal Charter* (Boston, 1924), 16.

45. "*Short Treatise*," 39. *MdArch*, 5:267–68.

46. "*Short Treatise*," 40.

47. Ibid., 39. Hall of Records, Annapolis. Land Office Records, Liber 1, fol. 18. Phebe Jacobsen, "Land Notes, 1634–1655," *MdHM* 5 (June 1910): 167. "The Inventory

of the goods of Capt: Robt Wintour late of St. Maries Esq. deceased; as they were appraised by James Baldridge, and Thomas Hebden: 4 Sept:1638," *MdArch* 4:85–89.

SEVEN: "With free liberty of religion"

Title is from John Winthrop, *The History of New England From 1630 to 1649*, ed. James Savage, 2nd ed., 2 vols. (Boston, 1853), 2:72, 149.

   1. "A Relation of Maryland" and "A Briefe Relation of the Voyage unto Maryland," in *Narratives*, ed. Hall, 74, 42.

   2. "A Relation of Maryland," in *Narratives*, ed. Hall, 42, 73–74.

   3. We "call it a feudal tenure." Papal representative Geogorio Panzani frequently used the term *feudal* in describing Baltimore's holdings. Hughes, SJ, Text, 1:355.

   4. *Narratives*, ed. Hall, 20, 118. Baltimore to Wentworth, January 10, 1633/34, in *Strafforde's Letters*, ed. Knowler, 1:178. "The Lord Baltemores Declaration to the Lords," in *Calvert Papers*, 1:232–25. "*Short Treatise,*" 36.

   5. *MdArch*, 5:267–68.

   6. Cornwallis to Baltimore, April 6, 1638, in *Calvert Papers*, 1:172–73. *Narratives*, ed. Hall, 5.

   7. *CSP, Venice, 1632–1636*, 158. *Narratives*, ed. Hall, 70, 118.

   8. *MdArch*, 5:267–68.

   9. Records exist only for the court-leet held at St. Clement's Manor (1659–72). *MdArch*, 43:627–37. *Calvert Papers*, 1:172–73. "A Relation of Maryland," 91–92.

   10. *Calvert Papers*, 1:132–36. *Narratives*, ed. Hall, 16, 70.

   11. *MdArch*, 1:158, 4:35–39. White, *A Brief Relation*, in *Narratives*, ed. Hall, 40 (quote). Smith dated his will September 22, 1635. *MdArch*, 4:16–17. Thomas Copley to Baltimore, April 3, 1638, in *Calvert Papers*, 1:163.

   12. *Records of the Governor and Company of the Massachusetts Bay*, ed. Nathaniel B. Shurtleff, 5 vols. in 6 (Boston, 1853–54), 1:79, 82. *The Works of John Jewel, Bishop of Salisbury*, ed. John Ayre, 4 vols. (Cambridge, 1845–50), 4:1125–26. John Norton, *The Answer to the Whole Set of Questions of the Celebrated Mr. William Apollonius, Pastor of the Church of Middelburg*, trans. Douglas Horton (Cambridge, 1958), 161. *Narratives*, ed. Hall, 103.

   13. On April 4, 1638, the lords commissioners for plantations ruled that the disputed Kent Island was within the bounds of Baltimore's grant. *MdArch*, 1:71–73.

   14. "Lord Baltimore's Instructions," in *Narratives*, ed. Hall, 20–21. *MdArch*, 1:40–41. The papal envoy, who sometimes erred as an intelligence gatherer, provided confusing and contradictory information about Baltimore's effort to write an oath. Panzani to Barberini, August 22, September 19, December 5, 1635; March 12, 1636, in Hughes, *SJ, Text*, 1:355–59; *SJ, Documents*, 1:151, 152, 154.

   15. In spite of his own financial situation, on January 1, 1635/36, Baltimore gave the king a small gift, a sconce valued at £169. "The Aspinwall Papers," *Collections of the Massachusetts Historical Society*, 4th ser., 9 (1871): 131–52. Harvey to Windebank, December 16, 1634, in *MdArch*, 3:30. "Lord Baltimore's Memorial," December 22, 1635, CO1/8/84, PRO, in MdArch, 3:40.

   16. "Notes by Nicholas of a meeting of the Privy Council at which the King

Presided," in *CSP, Colonial, America, 1574–1660*, 216. Mathews to Sir John Wolsten-holme, May 25, 1635, in *MdArch*, 3:37.

17. Baltimore to Windebank, February 25, 1636/37, CO1/9/42, PRO, in *MdArch*, 3:41–42. Memorial of Baltimore to Windebank, [March 1637], ibid., 3:42–43.

18. Windebank notified Governor Harvey that Hawley had been appointed treasurer and was to be admitted to the council upon taking the oath of allegiance. On May 8, 1638, however, Hawley confessed his inability to give as good account of the king's revenues as he desired. Letter of January 10, 1636/37, CO1/9/34, PRO. *Documents relative to the colonial history of the State of New-York, procured in Holland, England, and France, by John Romeyn Brodhead*, ed. E. B. O'Callaghan, 15 vols. (Albany, NY, 1853–87), 3:20. "Sir Edmund Plowden's Advice to Cecilius Calvert, Second Lord Baltimore: A Letter of 1639," ed. Edward C. Carter II, *MdHM* 56 (June 1961): 123.

19. Baltimore to Windebank, January 27, 1638/39; Arundel to Windebank, February 17, 1638/39, in *CSP, Charles I, 1638–1639*, 374, 476.

20. Bernard C. Steiner, "More Fragments from the English Archives," *MdHM* 5 (September 1910): 245–49.

21. "Briefe pro Baltimore con Reynell," in Additional MSS, 25302, fols. 97, 99, 101, 103, 105, BL; "Cecill Lord Baltimore plt," ibid., 107, 109, 111, 113, 117, 117; fragment of a document dated August 19, 1639, ibid., 118. The heirs went before the Court of Wards to have the deed voided in law. Both sides prepared for a hearing, but the matter came to an end with the outbreak of hostilities between king and Parliament. The coheirs hoped to have their case heard by the House of Lords in 1648, but again national events intervened and led to a postponement. "The Wiltshire Compounders," comp. James Waylen, *The Wiltshire Archaeological and Natural History Magazine*, n.d., 23:324.

22. *English SJ*, ed. Foley, 3:370–71.

23. *MdArch*, 4:35–39 (July 1–3, 1638).

24. *MdArch*, 4:35.

25. "Silver Tongued" according to Thomas Fuller, who published Smith's collected sermons. *The Sermons of Master Henry Smith . . . Whereunto is added, Gods Arrow against Atheists* (London, 1657). *MdArch*, 4:36.

26. *MdArch*, 4:35–39.

27. Ibid.

28. *MdArch*, 1:119 (quotes). Hughes, *SJ*, *Text*, 1:540.

29. *MdArch*, 1:72–73, 82–83.

30. *1635 Relation*, in *Narratives*, ed. Hall, 71.

31. Knott to either the cardinal secretary of state or the cardinal secretary of the Holy Office, undated, 1641 or 1642, in Hughes, *SJ*, *Text*, 1:248–49; *SJ*, *Documents*, 1:178–79. *English SJ*, ed. Foley, 3:363. Baltimore's letter no longer exists.

32. Hughes, *SJ*, *Text*, 1:249, 496; *SJ*, *Documents*, 1:183–84.

33. Father Edward Knott, provincial, to papal nuncio in Belgium, in Hughes, *SJ*, *Text*, 1:255–56. Thomas M. McCoog, "'Laid Up Treasure': The Finances of the English Jesuits in the Seventeenth Century," in *The Church and Wealth*, ed. W. J. Sheils and Diana Wood (Oxford, 1987), 260, 261.

34. *English SJ*, ed. Foley, 3:363.

35. Ibid., 3:363–64. *Narratives*, ed. Hall, 118. Thomas Copley to Lord Baltimore, April 3, 1638, in *Calvert Papers*, 1:165–66, 217–18.

36. Henrietta Maria to Brett, October 28, 1635, in *Clarendon*, ed. Ogle and Bliss, 1:355–56. Hughes, *SJ, Text*, 1:355, 518 n; *SJ, Documents*, 1:168–72. Panzani to Barberini, August 15, 1635, in Hughes, *SJ, Documents*, 1:150; translated in *SJ, Text*, 1:355.

37. Panzani to Barberini, September 5, October 24, 1635, in Hughes, *SJ, Documents*, 1:152; *SJ, Text*, 1:357.

38. Hughes, *SJ, Text*, 1:366, 422. Edwin W. Beitzell, "Thomas Copley, Gentleman," *MdHM 47* (September 1952): 215–16, 218.

39. *English SJ*, ed. Foley, 3:363–66. Panzani to Barberini, July 11, 1635, in Hughes, *SJ, Text*, 1:359.

40. *Calvert Papers*, 1:159.

41. *MdArch*, 1:2, 5. Copley told Baltimore that their proxies would not be admitted and maintained that they were excluded. *Calvert Papers*, 1:158.

42. *Calvert Papers*, 1:158, 162–68. The assembly rejected the proprietary draft on January 29. *MdArch*, 1:5, 9. It passed a number of laws, some of which retained the proprietor's text and many more that the assemblymen altered. The new laws, having been "faire ingrossed," were read in the House and signed by the governor and the members. *MdArch*, 1:23.

43. Thomas Copley to Cecil, Lord Baltimore, April 3, 1638, in *Calvert Papers*, 1:163.

44. Ibid., 1:164.

45. Ibid., 1:166.

46. *English SJ*, ed. Foley, 3:363–66 (quote). *Calvert Papers*, 1:165. Hughes published the "cases" in Hughes, *SJ Documents*, 1:158–61 (quote). Johnson, *Foundation of Maryland*, published a slightly different version.

47. *MdArch*, 1:96. Thomas, Lord Arundell, to Secretary of State Windebank, February 17, 1638/39, in SP16/413/17, PRO. Copley to Baltimore, April 3, 1638; Cornwallis to Baltimore, April 16, 1638, in *Calvert Papers*, 1:168–71.

48. Calvert to Baltimore, April 25, 1638; Lewger to Baltimore, January 5, 1638/39, in *Calvert Papers*, 1:191, 194.

49. *MdArch*, 1:83, 40. Hughes, *SJ, Text*, 1:446. *Calvert Papers*, 1:217.

50. *MdArch*, 1:40, 96.

51. *MdArch*, 1:97. Hughes, *SJ, Documents*, 1:160.

52. *MdArch*, 1:41, 42, 3, 100. The fifth and sixth articles were in the papers relating to the Society of Jesus in Stoneyhurst College. A translated version of the Latin articles is in Johnson, *Foundation of Maryland*, 67.

53. *Calvert Papers*, 1:166. The bull *Pastoralis Romani Pontificis* or *Bulla in Coena Domini*, published by Pope Urban VIII in April 1627, provided excommunication for specific transgressions against the Church. The fifteenth, eighteenth, and nineteenth were most relevant to the Maryland situation. Hughes, *SJ, Text*, 1:436–37; *SJ, Documents*, 1:166–68.

54. Knott to the nuncio Monsignore Rosetti, November 17, 1641, in Hughes, *SJ, Text*, 1:417. Lord Baltimore to William Peasley, September 30, 1642; William Peasley to Mr. Gervits, S.J., September 30, October 1, 1642; Ann Calvert Peasley to Gervits, October 5, 1642, in "Applications for the Maryland Mission—1640," *Woodstock Letters* 9 (1880): 91–93. Baltimore to Governor Calvert, November 21, 23, 1642, in *Calvert Papers*, 1:221.

55. Baltimore to Governor Calvert, November 21–23, 1642, in *Calvert Papers*, 1:217. The proprietor sent some of his dispatches to his brother on a ship captained by Richard

Ingle. The Jesuit who sailed in defiance of Baltimore's prohibition sailed on the same ship. Ibid., 1:212, 217.

56. Baltimore to Governor Calvert, November 21, 23, 1642, in *Calvert Papers*, 1:217–19. Knott to the nuncio Rosetti, November 17, 1641, in Hughes, *SJ, Text*, 1:505–6. George Gage to Richard Smith, bishop of Chalcedon, July 21, 1642, in "Catholic Clergy in Maryland," ed. Henry F. Thompson, *MdHM* 4 (September 1909): 263.

57. Baltimore to Governor Calvert, November 21, 23, 1642, in *Calvert Papers*, 1:217–19.

58. Ibid., 1:212, 216–17. *English SJ*, ed. Foley, 3:385. George Gage to bishop of Chalcedon, July 21, 1642, in "Catholic Clergy," ed. Thompson, 263–64.

59. The general Vitelleschi to Knott, October 31, 1643, in Hughes, *SJ, Documents*, 1:28–29; *SJ, Text*, 1:558.

60. Petition of Thomas, Lord Arundell, of Wardour, to the king, [September?] 1639, in *CSP, Charles I, 1638–1639*, 543.

61. Petition of William Arundell, March 26, 1642, in HMC, *Fifth Report of the Royal Commission on Historical Manuscripts*, "The Manuscripts of the House of Lords," 2 parts (London, 1876), 1:14.

62. January 23, 1643/44, *MdArch*, 3:130.

63. *MdArch*, 4:237–39, 241, 245–48, 251–52, 258.

64. *Proceedings and Debates of the British Parliaments respecting North America*, ed. Leo Francis Stock, 5 vols. (Washington, DC, 1924), 1:155. *MdArch*, 1:270, 3:165, 4:262. Henry More, S.J., *Anglia Historia* (1645), in Hughes, *SJ, Documents*, 1:125–26.

65. *MdArch*, 3:166; 4:231, 262.

66. *MdArch*, 1:270, 3:165. Copley property claim as quoted in Timothy B. Riordan, *The Plundering Time: Maryland in the English Civil War, 1642–1650* (Baltimore, 2004), 209.

67. *MdArch*, 3:164. 165. "The humble peticon of Mary Foorde," Ibid., 3:171. Widow Ford accused Thomas Cornwallis of kidnapping her children and carrying them to Maryland to plant the colony with Catholics.

68. "Ordinance for Maryland," November 24, 1646, in *MdArch*, 3:173–75. If the ordinance was sent to Commons, as ordered, that body did not act on it. *Proceedings and Debates*, ed. Stock, 1:179, 183.

69. *Proceedings and Debates*, ed. Stock, 1:187, 194–95. *MdArch*, 3:180–81.

70. Baltimore's letter to Governor Calvert, November 21, 23, 1642, contained a number of sharp rebukes. His strongest rebuke came as a result of the governor's willingness to grant more land to the Jesuits "against my will." He called it an usurpation of authority. *Calvert Papers*, 1:219–20. *Virginia and Maryland, or the Lord Baltamore's printed CASE, uncased and unmasked* (London, 1655), in *Narratives*, ed. Hall, 200.

71. *MdArch*, 3:201. "A Baltimore draft of a unilateral Concordat," in Hughes, *SJ, Documents*, 1:191–96.

72. *English SJ*, ed. Foley, 3:381. Winthrop, *History of New England*, ed. Savage, 1:172; 2:72, 149. *MdArch*, 4:103, 204. Gibbons eventually relocated in Maryland. On January 20, 1650/51, Baltimore appointed him to the council and named him "Admiral of our Province." Ibid., 3:261–62.

73. *The Statutes at Large . . . of Virginia from the First Session of the Legislature in the Year 1649*, ed. William W. Hening, 13 vols. (Richmond, 1809–23), 1:277, 341, 359. Winthrop, *History of New England*, ed. Savage, 2:93–94, 407. Emigrant quote in Leonard Strong,

Babylons Fall in Maryland: A Fair Warning to Lord Baltamore or a Relation of an Assault made by divers Papists and Popish Officers of the Lord Baltamore's against the Protestants in Maryland (London, 1655), in *MdHM* 3 (September 1908): 229. Governor Berkeley, "to prevent the infection from reaching that Country, made severe laws against the Puritans." Robert Beverley, *The History and Present State of Virginia*, ed. Louis B. Wright (Charlottesville, VA, 1968), 63.

74. Thomas H. Clancy, "The Jesuits and the Independents, 1647," *Archivium Historicum Societatis Jesu* 40 (1971): 70, 73, 77, 78, 82, 85, 86.

75. *MdArch*, 1:40 (quote), 44–45.

76. *MdArch*, 3:85 (quote), 105, 117, 145, 174.

77. *MdArch*, 3:209–11 (quotes), 213–14, 218.

78. "A Letter sent to his Lordship from the Assembly," *MdArch*, 1:238–43.

79. Baltimore to Gov. Stone, August 26, 1649, *MdArch*, 1:272.

80. *MdArch*, 1:262–63.

81. *MdArch*, 4:234, 404, 431.

82. *MdArch*, 1:244. This part of the act should be compared to Baltimore's "An Act for Felonies," presented to the assembly in 1639. Ibid., 1:71–72.

83. *MdArch*, 1:245–46. "The persecution of the Tongue is more fierce and terrible than that of the hand." John Davenport to My Lady Vere (c. 1633), in *Letters of John Davenport: Puritan Devine*, ed. Isabel MacBeath Calder (New Haven, CT, 1937), 38–39.

84. *MdArch*, 3:237–41.

85. *MdArch*, 1:246–47.

86. *MdArch*, 1:244–46; 3:108–116, 187, 201–14.

87. The document was signed on April 17, 1650. Printed in *Just and Cleere Refutation*, 63. *MdArch*, 1:318–19, 3:257, 10:354–55 (April 3, 1654).

88. *Baltemore's Case*, 171–72. *MdArch*, 3:264, 271, 276, 311–12. "A Surrender of Virginia to the Parliamentary Commissioners, March 1651–52," *Virginia Magazine of History and Biography* 2 (July 1903): 34.

89. *MdArch*, 1:340–41. The number of Catholics in Maryland cannot be accurately stated. John Hammond maintained, "they are but few." *Hammon versus Heamonds*, 239. The Independents, the Virginians who accepted Baltimore's invitation, defy simple labeling. They generally adhered to congregational principles, and many of them later converted to Quakerism. The contemporary reference, "those of Putuxent and Severn," although clumsy, seems to describe them accurately. *Virginia and Maryland*, 203.

EIGHT: "The People there cannot subsist & continue in peace and safety without som good Government"

Title is from Cecil, Lord Baltimore, to inhabitants of Maryland, July 10, 1656, in *MdArch*, 3:323–24.

1. Agreement between Baltimore, Humphrey Weld, Clare Weld, and Catherine Eure, March 1, 1654/55. Baltimore, who possessed the manors of Christ Church and Westover, agreed to pay others (Clare Weld and Catherine Eure), as heirs to Lady Anne Arundell, three hundred pounds. *Calvert Papers*, ed. Cox, roll 5, no. 61. "Baltimore vs Kirke, 1651: Newfoundland Evidence in an Interregnum Lawsuit," ed. Peter E. Pope, *Avalon Chronicles* 3 (1998): 1–18. John Hammond, a former Virginian and a Baltimore partisan, described Claiborne as "a pestilent enemie to the wel-faire" of Maryland and the

proprietor. *Leah and Rachel, or, the Two Fruitfull Sisters Virginia and Mary-land; Their Present Condition, Impartially stated and related* (London, 1656), in *Narratives,* ed. Hall, 303.

2. *Baltemore's Case,* 167–80.

3. Cromwell to Taaffe, October 19, 1649, in *The Writings and Speeches of Oliver Cromwell,* with an introduction, notes, and a sketch of his life by Wilbur Cortez Abbott, with the assistance of Catherine D. Crane, 4 vols. (New York, 1970), 2:146.

4. R[oger] W[illiams] to the truly Christian Reader, in *The Forth Paper, Presented by Major Butler, To the Honourable Committee of Parliament, for the Propagating of the Gospel of Christ Jesus. . . . (London, 1652), preface. Cromwell to Mazarin, December 26, 1658, in Abbott,* Writings and Speeches, 4:368. "An Act for Relief of religious and peaceable Persons from the Rigours of former Acts of Parliament, in matters of Religion," September 27, 1650, *CJ,* 6:474.

5. *Virginia and Maryland,* 191, 199–200, 216. The fine was ten shillings, not ten pounds, as Hall transcribed it. *Narratives,* ed. Hall, 216 n. *Babylon's Fall,* 235–36. Roger Heamans, *An Additional Brief Narrative of a late bloody design against the Protestants in Anne Arundel County* (London, 1655), in *MdHM* 4 (June 1909): 141. William Bennett and Samuel Mathews, "Objections," in *A Collection of the State Papers of John Thurloe, Esq: Secretary, First, to the Council of State, and afterwards to the Two Protectors, Oliver and Richard Cromwell,* ed. Thomas Birch, 7 vols. (London, 1742), 5:482.

6. "A breviat of the proceedings of the lord Baltimore and his officers and compliers in Maryland against the authority of the Parliament," in Bennett and Mathews, "Objections," in *State Papers of Thurloe,* 5:486.

7. *Baltemore's Case,* 167–80. In another document Baltimore gave the figure he and his friends disbursed for settling a colony of his majesty's subjects as above ten thousand pounds. "Cecil, The Lo: Baltemores Declaration to the Lords" commissioners for foreign plantations, in *Calvert Papers,* 1:228.

8. *Just and Cleere Refutation,* 256, 258. Bennett and Mathews, "Objections" (number 4), in *State Papers of Thurloe,* 5:482.

9. The papers included with Mathews and Bennett's letter to Cromwell of October 10, 1656, summarized the arguments they had made over the years. *State Paper of Thurloe,* 5:482–87.

10. *Baltemore's Case,* 170–71.

11. Ibid, 173–74. The Instrument of Government, article 32, in *The Constitutional Documents of the Puritan Revolution,* ed. Samuel Rawson Gardiner, 3d ed., rev. (Oxford, 1906), 415.

12. *Baltemore's Case,* 174. Baltimore's letter to Stone of September 29, 1659, demonstrated familiarity with the legalities of the manorial system. *MdArch,* 3:383–84. Michael James Graham, "Lord Baltimore's Pious Enterprise: Toleration and Community in Colonial Maryland, 1634–1724" (Ph. D. diss., University of Michigan, 1983), 62.

13. *Baltemore's Case,* 174. Bennett and Mathews, "Objections" (number 2), in *State Paper of Thurloe,* 5:482.

14. Hammond, *Leah and Rachel,* 302.

15. *Baltemore's Case,* 175. Bennett and Mathews, "Objections" (number 4), in *State Paper of Thurloe,* 5:482. *CD1621,* 2:314–15, 320–21, 332; 4:256; 6:112. Nicholas, *Debates,* 1:318–19.

16. *Baltemore's Case,* 175. Bennett and Mathews, "Objections" (number 4), in *State Paper of Thurloe,* 5:482.

17. *Baltemore's Case*, 177. Bennett and Mathews summarized their arguments for bringing Maryland under the control of Virginia in their "Objections" of October 1656, in *State Paper of Thurloe*, 5:483.

18. *Virginia and Maryland*, 187–230. The Instrument of Government, article 33, in *Constitutional Documents*, ed. Gardiner, 416. *MdArch*, 3:296. *CSP, Colonial, America, 1574–1660*, 412.

19. *Just and Cleere Refutation*, 260. Barber to Cromwell, April 13, 1655, ibid., 263. *Narratives*, ed. Hall, 186.

20. February 7, 1653/54, *MdArch*, 10:298–99. The author of *Virginia and Maryland* cast this decision in religious terms (202).

21. March 2, 1653/54, *MdArch*, 3:300.

22. Stone's instructions were dated September 28, 1653, but not acted on until July 3, 1654. Ibid., 3:308. *Just and Cleere Refutation*, 260, 255. *MdArch*, 3:304–5.

23. *Virginia and Maryland*, 202–3. Hammond, *Leah and Rachel*, 304, 302.

24. *MdArch*, 3:311–12. See also *Virginia and Maryland*, 203, 225. *Hammond versus Heamonds*, 239

25. July 22, 1654, *MdArch*, 3:312–13. Governor Stone tried unsuccessfully to bring Fuller into the proprietary coalition, November 29, 1652, ibid., 3:287–88; December 13, 18, 1652, 3:289–90. Heamans, *Additional Narrative*, 140. *Hammond versus Heamonds*, 238. *Babylon's Fall*, 238. The 1654 Act concerning Religion paralleled article 37 of the Instrument of Government.

26. *MdArch*, 1:340–41.

27. *Babylon's Fall*, 239. *Virginia and Maryland*, 204. Hammond, *Leah and Rachel*, 304–6. Bennett and Mathews, "Objections" (number 6), in *State Paper of Thurloe*, 5:483. Heamans, *Additional Narrative*, 150. *Hammond versus Heamonds*, 240, 246.

28. Virlinda Stone to Lord Baltimore, c. late March or early April 1655, reprinted in *Just and Cleere Refutation*, 265–67. *MdArch*, 3:333. Hammond, *Leah and Rachel*, 306. *Just and Cleere Refutation*, 262.

29. Cromwell to Bennett, January 12, 1654/55, in Abbott, *Writings and Speeches*, 3:570–71. Hammond reprinted this letter in his pamphlet *Hammond versus Heamonds*, 248–49.

30. April 24, 1655, *MdArch*, 3:315–16. "Northampton County Records," *Virginia Magazine of History and Biography* 5 (1897–98): 40. Digges to Cromwell, June 29, 1655, in *State Paper of Thurloe*, 3:596.

31. Abbott, *Writings and Speeches*, 3:833 (September 26, October 8, 1655).

32. *MdArch*, 3:324.

33. *MdArch*, 3:324. *State Paper of Thurloe*, 3:596. *Journals of the House of Burgesses of Virginia*, vol. 1, *1616–1658/59*, ed. H. R. McIlwaine (Richmond, VA, 1915), 105. *CSP, Colonial, America, 1574–1660*, 435–36.

34. July 31, 1656, *MdArch*, 3:320, 324–25.

35. Mathews and Bennett to Thurloe, October 10, 1656, in *State Paper of Thurloe*, 5:482. Perhaps this explains why Cromwell allowed the case to be argued before the Council of State at such great length on December 17, 1656. Instructions to Fendall, October 23, 1656, *MdArch*, 3:325.

36. December 17, 1656 *MdArch*, 3:330. *CSP, Colonial, America, 1574–1660*, 435. *MdArch*, 3:331.

37. *MdArch*, 3:323–24. The proprietor gave Fendall the right to nominate three others to the council and appoint the secretary and the receiver general.

38. *MdArch*, 3:325.

39. "Commissioners from Catholics in Maryland Seek in 1661 Toleration in the New Netherland Territory on the South River," *American Catholic Historical Researches* 9 (October 1892): 147.

40. *Report on the Franciscan Manuscripts Preserved in the Convent, Merchants' Quay, Dublin*, comp. G. D. Burtchaell and J. M. Rigg (Dublin, 1906), 80–81.

41. Timothy B. Riordan, "Philip Calvert: Patron of St. Mary's City," paper presented at the Council of Northeast Historical Archaeology annual meeting, St. Mary's City, MD, October 1999. Lois Green Carr, "Report on Philip Calvert," Historic St. Mary's City Commission, December 1992–93, unpublished paper, 1.

42. October 5, 1655, *MdArch*, 10:427–28. September 25, 1656, ibid., 10:463.

43. *MdArch*, 3:348. June 8, 1657, ibid., 3:331.

44. [Agreement between the Proprietary and Commissioners], *MdArch*, 3:332–34.

45. Baltimore, for political reasons, noted that this stipulation came from the report of the Committee for Trade. *MdArch*, 3:333–34.

46. Fendall's proclamation of July 23, 1658, contained the modified oath of fidelity, now called an engagement. *MdArch*, 3:352–53.

47. Instructions to Fendall, October 23, 1656, *MdArch*, 3:325, 326. Instructions to his "Lordships Lieutenant & the rest of his Lordships Councell," ibid., 3:329–30. Instructions to Fendall and Council, November 20, 1657, ibid., 3:337. A declaration of September 22, 1658, was directed to the governor concerning grants of manors for persons transported thither after June 20, 1659. Fendall noted this matter in his declaration of October 4, 1660. Ibid., 3:458–59.

48. Commission to Philip Calvert, November 7, 1656, *MdArch*, 3:327–29. Instructions to his "Lordships Lieutenant & the rest of his Lops Councell," November 12, 1656, ibid., 3:329–30.

49. Instructions, November 20, 1657, *MdArch*, 3:337, 339. Baltimore's letter empowered the governor and the secretary to appoint an attorney general until they received further orders. Council meeting, October 5, 1658, ibid., 3:354.

50. February 27, 1657/58, *MdArch*, 3:331–41. March 25, 1658, ibid., 3:340.

51. Statement by Benjamin Denham, chaplain to the Earl of Winchelsea, January 27, 1662, in *Calendar of State Papers, Domestic Series, of the reign of Charles II*, ed. Mary Anne Everett Green et al., 28 vols. (London, 1893–1947), *1661–1662*, 255–56.

52. *MdArch*, 3:383–84, 424. February 16, 1665/66, ibid., 3:544. February 16, 1665/66, ibid., 15:13. *Calvert Papers*, ed. Cox, roll 5, no. 213.

53. *MdArch*, 15:35. 1668, ibid., 15:40, 42.

54. George Alsop, *A Character of the Province of Mary-Land. Together with a Collection of Historical Letters* (London, 1666), in *Narratives*, ed. Hall, 353.

55. *MdArch*, 3:354–55.

56. July 16, 1658, *MdArch*, 3:349–50. The council issued the warrant for their arrest on July 8. Ibid., 3:348. Thurston indicated his desire to depart Maryland on July 25, and the council issued orders that he was not to be bothered "during the limited time of his stay." Ibid., 3:352. The council ordered Quakers to take the engagement on July 23. Ibid., 3:352–53, 362.

57. Hughes, *SJ, Text*, 2:57–59. Hughes quoted the rector of St. Omer's College, who wrote a sketch of Father Fitzherbert. Ibid., 2:64–65.

58. *MdArch*, 41:150–51, 229, 243, 244. Christian Bonnefeild testified that she would not have married Holt but for Wilkinson's assurance that she could marry lawfully. Ibid., 41:230. Nelson Waite Rightmyer, *Maryland's Established Church* (Baltimore, 1956), 219.

59. Hughes, *SJ, Text*, 2:61–62. Fitzherbert had clashed with Slye over Slye's harsh treatment of his Irish servants who refused to convert to Protestantism. *MdArch*, 41:145–46.

60. *MdArch*, 41:132–33, 144–46.

61. February 23, 1658/59, *MdArch*, 41:203, 258–59.

62. Alsop, *Character of the Province*, 381.

63. *MdArch*, 1:391, 388. An assembly was held at Gerard's and Robert Slye's home, February 28–March 14, 1659/60, ibid., 1:381–91.

64. Affidavit of Miles Cooke of London, master of a ship trading to Maryland, June 20, 1660, in *MdArch*, 3:387, and CO1/14/no12, PRO. Sworn testimony of Samuel Tilghman of London, mariner, June 29, 1660, in *MdArch*, 3:387, and CO1/14/no12-I, PRO.

65. *MdArch*, 3:387–88 (after June 29). Philip Calvert noted this instruction from King Charles II, who wrote to Virginia governor Berkeley on December 14, 1660. June 24, 1660, ibid., 3:397–98, 391. Petition of Sir Lewis Kirke on behalf of himself and the sons of Sir David Kirke, deceased, late governor of NFL to king, in CO1/14/no8, PRO. *CSP, Colonial, America, 1574–1660*, 481. Sir Orlando Bridgeman and Sir Heneage Finch reported to the king that the patent granted to Sir George Calvert was valid (February 28, 1661). In June, Charles II ordered Sir Lewis Kirke, John Kirke, and others to give up possession of any houses or land belonging to Baltimore. Colonial Entry Book, 65:31–38, in *CSP, Colonial, America, 1574–1660*, 482. CO1/14/no9-I, PRO (February 28, 1661). *CSP, Colonial, America, 1574–1660*, 481–82.

66. *MdArch*, 3:396–97. The governor shared his brother's letter with the council on November 29. After some debate, the council voted to commit Fendall to the custody of the sheriff. Philip Calvert to sheriff, ibid., 3:396–97. September 14, 1661, ibid., 1:420–21.

67. *MdArch*, 3:394. Appointment of Baker Brooke, John Bateman, and Henry Coursey to the council. Ibid., 3:393–94 (November 23, 1660). After he felt in control, Philip Calvert pardoned both Fendall and Gerard on February 28, 1660/61, and restored their estates to them. He prohibited Fendall from holding public office and required security for his good behavior. Ibid., 3:406–9.

68. Commission to Charles Calvert, November 28, 1661, *MdArch*, 3:439, 441. For Philip's subsequent problems with provincial secretary Henry Sewall, see *Calvert Papers*, 1:241, 276. Charles vented his anger and evidenced his distrust of his uncle in a letter to the proprietor on April 27, 1664. Ibid., 1:252.

69. See the licenses issued on January 30 and March 4, 1660/61. *MdArch*, 41:399, 412. These licenses further attest to the proprietary desire to placate former Virginians.

70. David W. Jordan, "'Gods Candle' within Government: Quakers and Politics in Early Maryland," *William and Mary Quarterly*, 3rd. ser., 39 (October 1982): 632.

71. *MdArch*, 5:133.

72. *MdArch*, 41:566–67.

73. Alsop, *Character of the Province*, 349.

74. *MdArch*, 5:133, 301.

75. Agretti's report, December 14, 1669, in *United States Documents in the Propaganda Fide Archives: A Calendar,* ed. Finbar Kinneally, 1st ser., 8 vols. (Washington, DC, 1966–), 3:109, 203. *English SJ,* ed. Foley, 3:392.

76. August 3, 1663, *Calvert Papers,* 1:237. April 27, 1664, ibid., 1:247. April 24, 1672, ibid., 1:273. June 3, 1673, ibid., 1:297–98. The governor had to wait for his father to confirm his promise.

77. Only the letters Charles Calvert sent to his father exist. While economic matters dominated, religious issues were frequently present. April 27, 1664, ibid., 1:249.

78. Calvert to Lord Baltimore, June 2, 1673, ibid., 1:281–82. For the years 1671, 1672, 1673, and 1674, the Jesuits claimed 184 converts and 299 infant baptisms. *English SJ,* ed. Foley, 3:392.

79. *MdArch,* 51:64.

80. Timothy B. Riordan estimated the cost based on the construction data for the state house. John D. Krugler and Riordan, "'Scandalous and offensive to the Government': The 'Popish Chappel' at St. Mary's City, Maryland and the Society of Jesus, 1634 to 1705," *Mid-America: An Historical Review* 73 (October 1991): 202. *MdArch,* 2:407, 23:81.

81. *MdArch,* 51:64. Timothy B. Riordan, Silas D. Hurry, and Henry M. Miller, "'A Good Brick Chappell': The Archaeology of the c. 1667 Catholic Chapel at St. Mary's City, Maryland," draft, Historic St. Mary's City Archaeology Series, no. 3 (St. Mary's City, 1995), 1–11. Henry M. Miller, "Baroque Cities in the Wilderness: Archaeology and Urban Development in the Colonial Chesapeake," *Historic Archaeology* 22 (1988): 57, 66, 67, 70. Henry M. Miller, "Mystery of the Lead Coffins," *American History* 30 (1995): 65.

82. *MdArch,* 1:452, 491; 2:149, 217. Riordan, Hurry, and Miller, "A Good Brick Chappell," 4–23 (quote).

83. Cole's will (1662), in Lois Green Carr, Russell R. Menard, and Lorena S. Walsh, *Robert Cole's World: Agriculture and Society in Early Maryland* (Chapel Hill, NC, 1991), 170–73. Graham, "Lord Baltimore's Pious Enterprise," 123. *MdArch,* 64:95, 97, 206, 229.

84. Nicholson's report, in *MdArch,* 22:81. Ibid., 26:44–46.

85. April 13, 1671, *MdArch,* 2:262–64. June 3, 1673, *Calvert Papers,* 1:286. "Extracts from the Annual Letters of the English Province of the Society of Jesus, 1634, 1638, 1639, 1640, 1642, 1654, 1656, 1681," in *Narratives,* ed. Hall, 143.

86. Charles Calvert to Lord Baltimore, April 26, 1672, in *Calvert Papers,* 1:265–66.

87. June 2, 1673, ibid., 1:281–82. Danckaerts, *Journal,* 137. He thought the freedom Catholics enjoyed was because "the governor professed that faith, and consequently there are priests and other ecclesiastics who travel and disperse themselves everywhere."

88. *MdArch,* 15:65.

89. July 26, 1663, *Calvert Papers,* 1:236. Charles stated that he was civil to him out of regard to his father's "pleasure and Commands to me."

90. June 2, 1673, ibid., 1:283.

91. "Rev. Matthew Hill to Richard Baxter," *MdHM* 25 (March 1930): 50–51.

NINE: "Scandalous and offensive to the Government"

Title is from Privy Council, September 11, 1704, *MdArch,* 26:46.

1. *Calvert Papers,* vol. 1.

2. *MdArch,* 51:64, 567–70.

3. "Answer of the Lord Baltimore to the Queryes about Maryland," March 26, 1678, in *MdArch*, 5:267–68.

4. John Evelyn, *Diary and Correspondence of John Evelyn, FRS, to which is Subjoined the Private Correspondence between Charles I and Sir Edward Nicholas and between Sir Edward Hyde, afterward Earl of Clarendon and Sir Richard Brown*, ed. William Bray, 4 vols. (London 1895–1900), 2:72, 77–78.

5. David W. Jordan, *Foundations of Representative Government in Maryland, 1632–1715* (Cambridge, 1987), 80–82, 235. Lois Green Carr and David William Jordan, *Maryland's Revolution of Government, 1689–1692* (Ithaca, NY, 1974), 224–25.

6. *MdArch*, 1:404, 406; 2:86; 5:133, 139–41, 143. Danckaerts, *Journal*, 135.

7. "Complaint," in *MdArch*, 5:134 (quotes), 138, 139, 140, 143, 147. "From the Annual Letter of 1681," in *Narratives*, ed. Hall, 143. Governor Nicholson on March 27, 1697, noted few schools in the province and described them as "very mean ones." *MdArch*, 23:81.

8. *MdArch*, 5:137.

9. *MdArch*, 5:139, 140, 147, 148, 149.

10. *MdArch*, 5:147.

11. "Whereupon the Lord Baltemore presents a Paper setting forth the Present State of Religion in Maryland," in *MdArch*, 5:133. "From the Annual Letter of 1681," in *Narratives*, ed. Hall, 142.

12. *MdArch*, 5:147.

13. *MdArch*, 5:133, 267–68.

14. April 10, 1676; October 31, 1681, *MdArch*, 5:130, 301.

15. *MdArch*, 5:267.

16. "Letter from the Councill to the Lord Baltemore about partiality to Papists in Maryland," October 12, 1681; and "Lord Baltemore's Declaration," May 13, 1682, in *MdArch*, 5:300, 353–55.

17. *MdArch*, 5:133.

18. *MdArch*, 5:311–28.

19. Carr and Jordan, *Maryland's Revolution*, 221.

20. "From the Annual Letter of 1681," in *Narratives*, ed. Hall, 143–44. Governor John Seymour used the term "Tribe" in 1704. *MdArch*, 26:45. *Narratives*, ed. Hall, 16. Carr and Jordan, *Maryland's Revolution*, 163–78, 203, 212–13.

21. Stephen L. Franzoi, *Social Psychology*, 2nd ed. (Boston, 2000), 236. Realistic group conflict theory assumes that "group conflicts are rational in the sense that groups do have incompatible goals and are in competition for scarce resources." The proposition that a real threat causes in-group solidarity helps to explain why the third Lord Baltimore specifically and the Catholics and proprietary adherents responded as they did. Robert A Levine and Donald T. Campbell, *Ethnocentrism: Theories of Conflict, Ethnic Attitudes, and Group Behavior* (New York, 1972), 29, 31.

22. "Letter to the Lord Baltemore about Mr. Penn," April 2, 1681; Lord Baltimore to Secretary Sir Lionel Jenkins, April 6, 1684, in *MdArch*, 5:273–74, 403. Baltimore appointed the deputy governors on May 9. He attended his first meeting of the Committee for Foreign Plantations on July 23, 1684. Ibid., 5:407, 418. Carr and Jordan, *Maryland's Revolution*, 221–22.

23. Carr and Jordan, *Maryland's Revolution*, 43–45, 149–57, 222 (quotes), 226–27.

24. "An Act for the Service of Almighty God and the Establishment of the Protestant Religion within this Province, 1692," in *MdArch*, 13:425–30.

25. *MdArch*, 23:81, 26:44.

26. *MdArch*, 26:45.

27. *MdArch*, 26:46

28. September 19, 1704, *MdArch*, 61. Governor Hunter to "some Romish priests," September 18, 1704, ibid., 26:159. "An Act to prevent the Growth of Popery within this Province," September 30, 1704, ibid., 26:340–41.

29. "A Plea for Maryland Catholics," ed. David W. Jordan, *MdHM* 67 (winter 1972): 429–35. Tricia T. Pyne questioned the validity of some of the charges made in the petition. "A Plea for Maryland Catholics Reconsidered," *MdHM* 92 (spring 1997): 163–81. For the petitions of eighteenth-century Maryland Catholics for equal participation with all other subjects "in All the rights and Privileges" of government, see "Popery in Maryland," *American Catholic Historical Researcher*, n.s., 4 (April 1908): 258–76; and the anonymous statement, "Liberty and Property or the Beauty of Maryland Displayed," *United States Catholic Historical Magazine* 3 (1890): 237–63.

30. Father Grival, March 10, 1835, quoted in *English SJ*, ed. Foley, 3:378.

31. "Hence politics cannot be understood or analyzed apart from the wider society which gives it coloration and direction." Richard N. Goodwin, "The Shape of American Politics," *Commentary* 43 (June 1967): 25.

32. *The Works of James Wilson*, ed. James DeWitt Anderson, 4 vols. (Chicago, 1896), 1:4–5.

33. Leonard W. Levy, *The Establishment Clause: Religion and the First Amendment*, 2nd ed. (Chapel Hill, NC, 1994), xiii–xiv.

Essay on Sources

With all due respect to John Donne, George Calvert's contemporary, no scholar is an island. Scholarship is a collaborative effort. This study traverses more than a century of history, spans two continents, and considers issues critically important to the expansion of human liberty. The questions that drew my attention have long interested historians of early modern England and America. Thus, there is a vast and rich historical literature relating to religious uniformity and toleration; the Calverts and their contemporaries; colonization in Virginia, Newfoundland, and Maryland; Catholicism; religious conversions; English politics and religion; and imperial connections. The labors of untold numbers of scholars informed the conclusions I reached from reading the primary source materials. This essay is neither a list of all sources consulted nor a comprehensive bibliography; it merely acknowledges, in the absence of fuller citations in the notes, the scholars who have contributed to this study. For additional documentation, refer to my publications noted elsewhere in the essay.

PREFACE

Tobie Mathew's unsigned and undated petition is in *Miscellanea: Recusant Records*, ed. Clare Talbot, Publications of the Catholic Record Society, 53 (London, 1961), 183–84. His correspondence with the earl of Salisbury, conveniently reprinted in Arnold Harris Mathew, *The Life of Sir Tobie Matthew: Bacon's Alter Ego* (London, 1907), demonstrates the synergy among personal relations, status, religious commitment, and uniformity.

INTRODUCTION

Most historians respond to anomalies they perceive to exist between the historical literature and the primary sources. My original interest in questions about uniformity and conformity began not in Maryland but in Massachusetts. There, recognizably radical, dissatisfied English Protestants expended considerable ink justifying the system they had devised to secure their religious freedom. To better understand that experience, I compared the Bay colony to an English colony that seemed to differ in so many particulars. Research for my dissertation, "Puritan and Papist: Politics and Religion in Massachusetts and Maryland before the Restoration of Charles II" (University of Illinois at Urbana-Champaign, 1971), led me to believe that the Maryland story regarding issues of church and state had been misrepresented or understated. Specifically, I concentrated on the process and meaning of George Calvert's conversion to Catholicism and resignation from government service and his family's ability to manipulate the government for its benefit, along with its motivations (religious, economic, nationalistic, and personal-status) for colonization and the implementation of their vision, the "Maryland designe."

TEXT

General studies of toleration include Joseph Lecler, *Toleration and the Reformation*, trans. T. L. Westow, 2 vols. (London, 1960); Wilbur K. Jordan, *The Development of Religious Toleration in England*, 4 vols. (Cambridge, 1932–40); and John Coffey, *Persecution and Toleration in Protestant England, 1558–1689* (Harlow, UK, 2000). Conrad Russell, "Arguments for Religious Uniformity in England, 1530–1650," in *Unrevolutionary England* (London, 1990), 91–116; Herbert Butterfield, "Toleration in Early Modern Times," *Journal of the History of Ideas* 38 (October–December 1977): 573–84; and Avihu Zakai, "Religious Toleration and Its Enemies: The Independent Divines and the Issue of Toleration during the English Civil War," *Albion* 21 (spring 1989): 1–33, provided useful information and perspective, especially on the negative connotations of toleration.

Making sense of the Catholic Lords Baltimore necessitates melding British and American historiography. The past generation or so has seen an eruption of scholarship that has altered thinking about the complex relation between politics (secular) and religion (spiritual) in England and what it meant to be Catholic in England under Queen Elizabeth and her successors. This scholarship provides a new and exciting context for revisiting the Calverts.

The long-standing Whig interpretation that portrayed the Stuarts and their sympathizers as tyrants who sought absolute power and Parliament and the radical Protestants who opposed them as champions of liberty has been laid to rest. Even though no consensus exists, the new "revisionist" scholarship, and the responses it evoked, has given a richer and fuller understanding of the dynamics of the political and religious landscapes. Synthesizing this work defies easy summary, but see the editors' essay "Revisionism and Its Legacies: The Work of Conrad Russell," in *Politics, Religion, and Popularity in Early Stuart Britain: Essay in Honour of Conrad Russell*, ed. Thomas Cogswell, Richard Cust, and Peter Lake (Cambridge, 2002), 1–20; and Peter Lake, "Retrospective: Wentworth's Political World in Revisionist and Post-Revisionist Perspective," in *The Political World of Thomas Wentworth, Earl of Strafford, 1621–1641*, ed. J. F. Merritt (Cambridge, 1996), 252–83.

The continuing reformation in Catholic studies brings new insights to Catholic responses to uniformity. Caroline Hibbard, "Early Stuart Catholicism: Revisions and Re-Revisions," *Journal of Modern History* 52 (May 1980): 1–34, provides an excellent starting point for assessing Catholic historiography. Of the many important overviews on Catholics, I found John Bossy's *English Catholic Community, 1570–1850* (New York, 1976) the most persuasive.

Elizabethan Catholicism and apologists for the state church have been much studied. Still useful analyses include Peter Guilday, *The English Catholic Refugees on the Continent, 1558–1795* (London, 1914); David Mathew, *Catholicism in England 1535–1935* (London,

1936); William Raleigh Trimble, *The Catholic Laity in Elizabethan England* (Cambridge, 1964); Thomas H. Clancy, "English Catholics and the Papal Deposing Power, 1570–1640," *Recusant History* 4 (October 1961): 114–40; 4 (April 1962): 205–27; 5 (January 1963): 2–10; *Papist Pamphleteers: The Allen-Persons Party and the Political Thought of the Counter-Reformation in England, 1572–1615* (Chicago, 1964); Patrick McGrath, *Papists and Puritans under Elizabeth I* (New York, 1967); "Elizabethan Catholicism: A Reconsideration," *Journal of Ecclesiastical History* 35 (July 1984): 414–28; and Arnold Oskar Meyer, *England and the Catholic Church under Queen Elizabeth*, trans. J. R. McKee (New York, 1967). Newer works include Allen Pritchard, *Catholic Loyalism in Elizabethan England* (Chapel Hill, NC, 1979); Christopher Haigh, "The Continuity of Catholicism in the English Reformation," *Past and Present* 93 (November 1981): 37–69; and "From Monopoly to Minority: Catholicism in Early Modern England," *Transactions of the Royal Historical Society*, 5th ser., 31 (1981): 129–47. J. C. H. Aveling's studies, *Northern Catholics: The Catholic Recusants of the North Riding of Yorkshire, 1558–1790* (London, 1966) and *The Handle and the Axe: The Catholic Recusants in England from Reformation to Emancipation* (London, 1976), are critical for understanding Catholic survival.

For the penal laws and their impact, I relied primarily on A. B. Forbes, "'Faith and true allegiance,' The Law and the Internal Security of England, 1559–1714: A Study of the Evolution of the Parliamentary Legislation and the Problem of Its Local Administration and Enforcement" (Ph.D. diss., University of California at Los Angles, 1960); Brian Magee, *The English Recusants: A Study in the Post-Reformation Catholic Survival and the Operation of the Recusancy Laws* (London, 1938); and Francis Xavier Walker, "The Implementation of the Elizabethan Statutes against Recusants, 1581–1603" (Ph.D. diss., University of London, 1961). For the Restoration, J. Anthony Williams, "English Catholicism under Charles II: The Legal Position," *Recusant History* 7 (October 1963): 123–43; and *Catholic Recusancy in Wiltshire, 1660–1791*, Catholic Record Society Publications, Monograph Series, vol. 1 (London, 1968) remain indispensable.

On Catholics' responses under the early Stuarts, I found Martin J. Havran, *The Catholics of Caroline England* (Stanford, CA, 1962), especially useful for his analysis of the penal laws and Catholic survival among the gentry. Also helpful were Keith Lindley, "The Lay Catholics of the Reign of Charles I," *Journal of Ecclesiastical History* 8 (July 1971): 199–221; "The Part Played by the Catholics," in *Politics, Religion and the English Civil War*, ed. Brian Manning (London, 1973), 127–76; Kenneth L. Campbell, *The Intellectual Struggle of the English Papists in the Seventeenth Century: The Catholic Dilemma* (Lewiston, NY, 1986); and Anthony Milton, *Catholic and Reformed: The Roman and Protestant Churches in English Protestant Thought, 1600–1640* (Cambridge, 1995).

The controversial Gunpowder Plot, a defining element of Stuart Catholicism, occurred while Calvert served in Cecil's household. To what extent he knew of his master's involvement remains problematic. Francis Edwards, *Guy Fawkes: The Real Story of the Gunpowder Plot?* (London, 1969); and Mark Nicholls, *Investigating Gunpowder Plot* (Manchester, UK, 1991), provide contrasting views of Cecil's involvement, while Jenny Wormald, "Gunpowder, Treason, and Scots," *Journal of British Studies* 24 (April 1985): 141–68, argues that the plotters found the new king's promises insufficient. Clarence J.

Ryan, "The Jacobean Oath of Allegiance and English Lay Catholics," *Catholic Historical Review* 48 (July 1942): 159–83; and Maurus Lunn, "English Benedictines and the Oath of Allegiance, 1606–1647," *Recusant History* 10 (October 1969): 146–63, are important for understanding the Catholic response.

Activities such as the Gunpowder Plot fostered anti-Catholicism: for this effect of the event, I relied on Carol Z. Weiner, "Popular Anti-Catholicism in England, 1559–1618" (Ph.D. diss., Harvard University, 1968); "The Beleaguered Isle: A Study of Elizabethan and Early Jacobean Anti-Catholicism," *Past and Present* 51 (May 1971): 27–62; Peter Lake, "Anti-Popery: The Structure of a Prejudice," in *Conflict in Early Stuart England: Studies in Religion and Politics, 1603–1642*, ed. Richard Cust and Ann Hughes (London, 1989), 72–106; Robin Clifton, "Fear of Popery," in *The Origins of the English Civil War*, ed. Conrad Russell (London, 1973), 144–67, 271–74; and "The Popular Fears of Catholics during the English Revolution," *Past and Present* 52 (August 1971): 23–55.

No Stuart monarch has undergone a greater historical metamorphosis than the much-maligned King James I. For biographical details I used David Harris Willson, *King James VI and I* (New York 1956); G. P. V. Akrigg, *Jacobean Pageant; or, The Court of King James I* (Cambridge, MA, 1962); and William McElwee, *The Wisest Fool in Christendom: The Reign of King James I and VI* (New York, 1966). Reassessments of the king's ecclesiastical policies and his actions toward his papist subjects abound. Especially helpful were John LaRocca, "Who Can't Pray with Me, Can't Love Me: Toleration and the Early Jacobean Recusancy Policy," *Journal of British Studies* (spring 1984): 22–36; "James I and his Catholic Subjects, 1606–1612: Some Financial Considerations," *Recusant History* 18 (May 1987): 251–62; K. Fincham and P. Lake, "The Ecclesiastical Policy of James I," *Journal of British Studies* 24 (April 1995): 169–201; and Michael B. Young, *James VI and I and the History of Homosexuality* (Basingstoke, 2000).

Historians have not neglected the Catholic Lords Baltimore, but they have never demonstrated the same interest accorded other seventeenth-century reformers, such as Roger Williams and William Penn. Of the nineteenth- and early-twentieth-century studies on the Calverts, only Lewis W. Wilhelm, *Sir George Calvert: Baron of Baltimore* (Baltimore, 1884); and William Hand Browne, *George Calvert and Cecilius Calvert: Barons Baltimore of Baltimore* (New York, 1890), remain useful. James W. Foster, whose death in 1962 prevented completion of his biography of George Calvert, collected and painstakingly transcribed most of Calvert's letters. Anyone who has tried to read Calvert's scrawl must acknowledge an indebtedness to his meticulous transcriptions. The Foster Manuscripts 2002 are at the Maryland Historical Society, Baltimore. The society published the first four chapters of Foster's intended biography as *George Calvert: The Early Years* (Baltimore, 1983). For an overview of Calvert's life, see John D. Krugler, "George Calvert: Courtier, Colonizer, Capitalist, Catholic," *Avalon Chronicles* 6 (2001): 1–18. For his schooling, Bromley Smith, "George Calvert at Oxford," *Maryland Historical Magazine* (*MdHM*) 26 (June 1931): 109–30; Herbert E. D. Blakiston, *Trinity College* (London, 1898); and Mark Curtis, *Oxford and Cambridge in Transition, 1558–1642: An Essay on Changing Relations between the English Universities and English Society* (Oxford, 1959).

A number of important studies provide a context for Calvert's relations with Sir Robert Cecil: Thomas Malcolm Coakley, "The Political Position and Domestic Policy of Robert Cecil, First Earl of Salisbury, 1603–1612" (Ph.D. diss., University of Minnesota, 1959); "Robert Cecil in Power: Elizabethan Politics in Two Reigns," in *Early Stuart Studies: Essays in Honor of David Harris Wilson*, ed. Howard S. Reinmuth Jr. (Minneapolis, 1970), 64–94; Eric N. Lindquist, "The Last Years of the First Earl of Salisbury, 1610–1612," *Albion* 18 (spring 1986): 23–41; Lawrence Stone, "The Fruits of Office: The Case of Sir Robert Cecil, First Earl of Salisbury," in *Essays in the Economic and Social History of Tudor and Stuart England*, ed. F. J. Fisher (Cambridge, 1961), 89–116; and Alan G. R. Smith, "The Secretariats of the Cecils, circa 1580–1612," *English Historical Review* 83 (July 1968): 481–504. For the earl of Salisbury's religion, Joel Hurstfield, "Church and State, 1558–1612: The Task of the Cecils," in *Freedom, Corruption, and Government in Elizabethan England* (Cambridge, MA, 1973), 79–103; and Pauline Croft, "The Religion of Robert Cecil," *Historical Journal* 34 (1991): 773–96, are useful.

For Calvert's involvement in the Vorstius Affair, see Frederick Shriver, "Orthodoxy and Diplomacy: James I and the Vorstius Affairs," *English Historical Review* 85 (July 1970): 449–74. For Calvert's land acquisitions in Yorkshire, "A History of Yorkshire North Riding: Danby Wiske," in *The Victorian History of the County of York: North Riding*, ed. William Page (London, 1914); G. Bernard Wood, "Kiplin," *Yorkshire Illustrated* (July 1950): 14–16; and Constance B. Schulz, *Kiplin Hall and Its Families: A History* (Cleveland, UK, 1994).

Recent studies reveal that the Catholic response to the penal legislation or the destruction of the Catholic hierarchy in England was not uniform. Family-by-family and county-by-county investigations provide an appreciation of what it meant to be Catholic at this time and demonstrate the complexity of the responses. These studies put Calvert's religious life in perspective. Determining the number of Catholics in England is a function of definition, as P. R. Newman, "Roman Catholics in Pre-Civil War England: The Problem of Definition," *Recusant History* 15 (October 1979): 148–52, points out. For example, Edward Terrar's expansive definition leads him to overstate the number of English Catholics who survived. See his *Social, Economic, and Religious Beliefs among Maryland Catholic People during the Period of the English War, 1639–1660* (San Francisco, 1996). Two historians shed light on conflicted commitments of the English: Alexandra Walsham, *Church Papist: Catholicism, Conformity, and Confessional Polemic in Early Modern England* (Suffolk, 1993); and Michael C. Questier, *Conversion, Politics, and Religion in England, 1580–1625* (Cambridge, 1996); "'Like Locusts over all the World': Conversion, Indoctrination, and the Society of Jesus in Late Elizabethan and Jacobean England," in *The Reckoned Expense: Edmund Campion and the Early English Jesuits*, ed. Thomas M. McCoag (Suffolk, 1996), 265–84. Others who consider the confusing nature of religious commitments and provide a context for Calvert include Lawrence Stone, *The Crisis of the Aristocracy, 1558–1641* (Oxford, 1967); and J. T. Cliffe, *The Yorkshire Gentry from the Reformation to the Civil War* (London, 1969). For godparents and women, see Judith Diane Maltby, "Approaches to the Study of Religious Conformity in late Elizabethan and

Early Stuart England: With Special Reference to Cheshire and the Diocese of Lincoln" (Ph.D. diss., University of Cambridge, 1991); and Marie B. Rowlands, "Recusant Women, 1560–1640," in *Women in English Society, 1500–1800* (London, 1985), 149–80.

An established church that demanded uniformity confused the relationship between state and church. I found John E. Booty, *John Jewel as Apologist of the Church of England* (London, 1963); R. Buick Knox, *James Ussher: Archbishop of Armagh* (Cardiff, Wales, 1976); and Peter E. McCullough, *Sermons at Court: Politics and Religion in Elizabethan and Jacobean Preaching* (Cambridge, 1998), helpful.

Assessing George Calvert's career in government profited not only from the "revisionists" and their critics, but from some "classics" as well. Still useful treatments include Florence M. Greir Evans, *The Principal Secretary of State: A Survey of the Office from 1558 to 1680* (Manchester, 1923); Wallace Notestein, *The Winning of the Initiative by the House of Commons* (London, 1924); David Harris Willson, *Privy Councillors in the House of Commons, 1604–1629* (Minneapolis, 1940); and Perez Zagorin, *The Court and Country: The Beginnings of the English Revolution* (New York, 1971). More recent studies demonstrate the complexity of the relationship between king and Parliament and the intensity that certain foreign policy issues generated. For James's aversion to Parliament, see Anthony Thrush, "The Personal Rule of James I, 1614–1620," in *Politics, Religion, and Popularity*, ed. Cogswell, Cust, and Lake, 84–102. Excellent studies for the critical years 1621–24 include Robert Zaller, *The Parliament of 1621: A Study in Constitutional Conflict* (Berkeley, CA, 1971); Robert Ruigh, *The Parliament of 1624: Politics and Foreign Policy* (Cambridge, 1971); Arthur Wilson White Jr., "Suspension of Arms: Anglo-Spanish Mediation in the Thirty Years War, 1621–1625" (Ph.D. diss., Tulane University, 1978); and Thomas Cogswell, *The Blessed Revolution: English Politics and the Coming of War, 1621–1624* (Cambridge, 1984). Other valuable studies of Parliament and its procedures are Derek Hirst, *The Representative of the People? Voters and Voting in England under the Early Stuarts* (Cambridge, 1975); and Mark A. Kishlansky, *Parliamentary Selection: Social and Political Choices in Early Modern England* (Cambridge, 1986). Studies analyzing specific issues include Robert Zaller, "'Interest of State': James I and the Palatinate," *Albion* (summer 1974): 144–75; Derek Hirst, "Court, Country, and Politics before 1629," in *Faction and Parliament: Essays on Early Stuart History*, ed. Kevin Sharpe (Oxford, 1978), 105–37; Conrad Russell, "The Foreign Policy Debate in the House of Commons in 1621," in *Unrevolutionary England*, 59–79; W. B. Patterson, "King James I and the Protestant Cause in the Crisis of 1618–22," in *Religion and National Identity*, ed. Stuart Mews (Oxford, 1982), 319–34; S. L. Adams, "Foreign Policy and the Parliaments of 1621 and 1624," in *Faction and Parliament*, ed. Kevin Sharp, 139–71; "Spain and the Netherlands: The Dilemma of Early Stuart Foreign Policy," in *Before the English Civil War: Essays on Early Stuart Politics and Government*, ed. Howard Tomlinson (New York, 1983), 79–101, 196–200; Thomas Cogswell, "England and the Spanish Match," in *Conflict in Early Stuart England: Studies in Religion and Politics, 1603–1642*, ed. Richard Cust and Ann Hughes (London, 1989), 107–33. For Calvert's political-administrative-diplomatic roles and his family's ability to manipulate the bureaucracy for its own benefit, see John D. Krugler, "'Our Trusty and Wellbeloved Councillor': The Parliamentary Career of Sir George Calvert, 1609–1624,"

MdHM 72 (winter 1977): 470–91; and "The Calvert Family, Catholicism, and Court Politics in Early Seventeenth-Century England," *Historian* 43 (May 1981): 378–92.

For Wentworth, see C. V. Wedgwood, *Thomas Wentworth, First Earl of Strafford, 1593–1641: A Revaluation* (New York, 1962); Hugh F. Kearney, *Strafford in Ireland* (Manchester, 1959); Terrence Ranger, "Strafford in Ireland: A Revaluation," in *Crisis in Europe, 1560–1660,* ed. Trevor Aston (New York, 1967), 285–308; John K. Gruenfelder, "The Election to the Short Parliament, 1640," in *Early Stuart Studies,* ed. Reinmuth, 180–230; "The Electoral Patronage of Sir Thomas Wentworth, Earl of Strafford, 1613–1640," *Journal of Modern History* 49 (December 1977): 567–74; S. P. Salt, "Sir Thomas Wentworth and the Parliamentary Representation of Yorkshire, 1614–1628," *Northern History* 16 (1980): 130–68; and J. P. Cooper, "The Fortunes of Thomas Wentworth, Earl of Strafford," *Economic History Review,* 2nd ser., 11 (December 1958): 227–48.

No other member of James's government caused Calvert as much grief as the royal favorite. Roger Lockyer, *Buckingham, the Life and Political Career of George Villiers, First Duke of Buckingham, 1592–1628* (New York, 1981), provides useful details, while Victor Treadwell, *Buckingham and Ireland, 1616–1628: A Study in Anglo–Irish Politics* (Dublin, 1998), sorts through the complicated web of court politics relating to Ireland and Buckingham's tight control of patronage. Also see John H. Bancroft, "Carleton and Buckingham: The Quest for Office," in *Early Stuart Studies,* ed. Reinmuth, 122–36; James Fulton MacClear, "Puritan Relations with Buckingham," *Huntington Library Quarterly* 21 (February 1958): 111–32. For other colleagues, helpful studies include Menna Prestwich, *Cranfield: Politics and Profit under the Early Stuart: The Career of Lionel Cranfield* (Oxford, 1966); Linda Levy Peck, *Court Patronage and Corruption in Early Stuart England* (Boston, 1990); Harold Hulme, *The Life of Sir John Eliot, 1592–1632: Struggle for Parliamentary Freedom* (London, 1957); Michael Van Cleave Alexander, *Charles I's Lord Treasurer: Sir Richard Weston, Earl of Portland (1577–1635)* (Chapel Hill, NC, 1975); and Ann L. Gohl, "English Power Struggle, 1628–1635: Laud and Wentworth vs. Weston and Cottington" (Ph.D. diss., University of Missouri—Columbia, 1976). Robert Elliot Bonner's "Administration and Public Service under the Early Stuarts: Edward Viscount Conway as Secretary of State, 1623–1628" (Ph.D. diss., University of Minnesota, 1963) exemplifies how to write an administrative biography. It contains an excellent analysis of the acrimonious relations between Calvert and Conway. It also models the kind of study that needs to be written about Calvert's secretariat. For the Spanish and their supporters at court, see Albert J. Loomie, "The Spanish Faction at the Court of Charles I, 1630–8," *Historical Research: Bulletin of the Institute for Historical Research* 59 (1986): 37–49; and Charles Howard Carter, "Gondomar: Ambassador to James I," *Historical Journal* 7 (1964): 199–208.

Understanding George Calvert's convoluted journey to Catholicism is an essential ingredient for telling the story. The internal steps that led individuals to convert generally are not known. Perhaps this explains why the historical analysis regarding his religious commitments from 1592 to 1625 runs the gamut: he was a Protestant; he converted to Catholicism in 1622; he was a Catholic sympathizer; he was a crypto-Catholic, a notorious closet Catholic. His resignation and his conversion are discussed in John D. Krugler, "Sir George Calvert's Resignation as Secretary of State and the Founding of Maryland,"

MdHM 68 (fall 1973): 239–54; and "'The Face of a Protestant, and the Heart of a Papist': A Reexamination of Sir George Calvert's Conversion to Roman Catholicism," *Journal of Church and State* 20 (autumn 1978): 507–31. Luca Codignola's publication of Father Simon Stock's letters established closer parameters for dating Calvert's conversion.

A number of case studies of individuals who faced the same dilemma as Calvert proved invaluable: for example, Martin J. Havran, *Caroline Courtier: The Life of Lord Cottington* (Columbia, SC, 1973), who provided essential details on Cottington's life, questioned Cottington's deathbed conversion to Roman Catholicism in 1623. Michael Foster, "Sir Richard Forster (?1585–1661)," *Recusant History* 14 (May 1978): 163–74, found a Catholic connection that came through Sir Richard Forster, a Catholic who had close ties to both Cottington and Calvert. Goodman was the only bishop of an English see since the Reformation to have died "in the Roman obedience," according to Geoffrey Ingle Soden, *Godfrey Goodman: Bishop of Gloucester, 1583–1656* (London, 1953). Studies that demonstrate that many willingly subordinated their religion to political demands include David L. Smith, "Catholic, Anglican, or Puritan? Edward Sackville, the Fourth Earl of Dorset and the Ambiguities of Religion in Early Stuart England," in *Religion, Literature, and Politics in Post-Reformation England, 1540–1688*, ed. Donna B. Hamilton and Richard Strier (Cambridge, 1996), 105–24; David Mathew, *Sir Tobie Mathew* (London, 1950); Robert Torsten Petersson, *Sir Kenelm Digby, the Ornament of England, 1603–1665* (Cambridge, 1956); the previously noted biography of Richard Weston; and Howard S. Reinmuth, "Lord William Howard (1563–1640) and His Catholic Associations," *Recusant History* 12 (April 1974): 226–34. Other studies demonstrate the difficulties of analyzing individual religious commitments: Albert J. Loomie, "A Jacobean Crypto-Catholic: Lord Wotton," *Catholic Historical Review* 53 (October 1967): 328–45; "King James I's Catholic Consort," *Huntington Library Quarterly* 34 (August 1971): 303–16; and "Appendix: Anna of Denmark and Catholicism," in *Anna of Denmark, Queen of England: A Cultural Biography*, by Leeds Barroll (Philadelphia, 2001), 162–72. Michael C. Questier noted that illness frequently occupied a central place in explanations of evangelical conversion, that the "sufferer was compelled to think seriously about grace and about which Church offered salvation," and that Carrier's "change of religion demonstrates that it was not a simple matter of transference of loyalty, like a politician's change of parties," in "Crypto-Catholicism, Anti-Calvinism, and Conversion at the Jacobean Court: The Enigma of Benjamin Carier," *Journal of Ecclesiastical History* 47 (January 1996): 45–64, quotations on 57 and 64.

Calvert's involvement in Ireland needs exploration beyond the helpful essays in *Wexford: History and Society*, ed. Kevin Whalen (Dublin, 1989). A number of studies facilitate understanding George Calvert's Newfoundland experiences: R. J. Lahey, "The Role of Religion in Lord Baltimore's Colonial Enterprise," *MdHM* 72 (winter 1972): 492–511; "Avalon: Lord Baltimore's Colony in Newfoundland," in *Early European Settlement and Exploitation in Atlantic Canada: Selected Papers* (St. John's, NF, 1982), 115–37; and Thomas Malcolm Coakley, "George Calvert and Newfoundland: 'The Sad Face of Winter,'" *MdHM* 71 (spring, 1976): 1–18. For Catholic colonization before Newfoundland, see David B. Quinn, *England and the Discovery of America, 1481–1620, from the Bristol Voyages of the Fifteenth Century to the Pilgrim Settlement at Plymouth: The Exploration, and Trial-and-Error Colonization of North America by the English* (New York, 1974). For the limited Catholic response to the Calverts, John Bossy, "Reluctant Colonists: The English Catholics Confront the Atlantic," in *Early Maryland in a Wider World*, ed., David B. Quinn (Detroit, 1982), 149–64.

The Calvert experience in Maryland cannot be studied without an eye on the Virginians, who profoundly affected what they could do. Most helpful were Bernard Bailyn, "Politics and Social Structure in Virginia," in *Seventeenth-Century America: Essays in Colonial America*, ed. James Morton Smith (Chapel Hill, NC, 1959), 91–115; J. Frederick Fausz, "Merging and Emerging Worlds: Anglo-Indian Interest Groups and the Development of the Seventeenth-Century Chesapeake," in *Colonial Chesapeake Society*, ed. Lois Green Carr, Philip D. Morgan, and Jean B. Russo (Chapel Hill, NC, 1988), 47–98; "Present at the 'Creation': The Chesapeake World That Greeted the Maryland Colonists," *MdHM* 79 (spring 1984): 7–20; Edmund S. Morgan, *American Slavery, American Freedom: The Ordeal of Colonial Virginia* (New York, 1975); Nathaniel C. Hale, *Virginia Venturer: A Historical Biography of William Claiborne, 1600–1677* (Richmond, VA, 1951); Nicholas Varga, "The English Parliament's Authority over Virginia before the Restoration," *Virginia Magazine of History and Biography* 62 (July 1954): 280–88; J. Mills Thornton III, "The Thrusting Out of Governor Harvey: A Seventeenth Century Rebellion," *Virginia Magazine of History and Biography* 76 (January 1968): 11–26; and Kevin Butterfield, "Puritans and Religious Strife in the Early Chesapeake," *Virginia Magazine of History and Biography* 109 (2002): 5–36. Douglas Steven Crow, "'Left at Libertie:' The Effects of the English Civil War and Interregnum on the American Colonies, 1640–1660" (Ph.D. diss., University of Wisconsin, 1974), thoroughly examines the actions of Cromwell and the parliamentary commissioners.

For the details of Father Andrew White's life, see Leo J. A. LeMay's essay in *Men of Letters in Colonial Maryland* (Knoxville, TN, 1972), 8–27. For the archpriest controversy, Havran, *Catholics of Caroline England*; A. F. Allison, "Richard Smith, Richelieu, and the French Marriage: The Political Context of Smith's Appointment as Bishop for England in 1624," *Recusant History* 7 (January 1964): 148–211; Bossy, *English Catholic Community*; and Aveling, *Northern Catholics* and *Handle and Axe*.

For the colonization tracts, I used Lawrence C. Wroth, "Maryland Colonization Tracts," in *Essays Offered to Herbert Putnam* (1929; reprint, Freeport, NY, 1967), 539–52; Lathrop Colgate Harper, "A Maryland Tract of 1646," in *Bibliographical Essays: A Tribute to Wilberforce Eames* (1924; reprint, Freeport, NY, 1967), 143–48; L. Leon Bernard, "Some New Light on the Early Years of the Baltimore Plantation," *MdHM* 44 (June 1949): 93–100; Howard Mumford Jones, "The Colonial Impulse: An Analysis of 'Promotional' Literature of Colonization," *Proceedings of the American Philosophical Society* 90 (1946): 131–61; and Hugh T. Lefler, "Promotional Literature of the Southern Colonies," *Journal of Southern History* 33 (February 1967): 3–25. Lois Green Carr, "The Founding of St. Mary's City," *Smithsonian Journal of History* 3 (winter 1968–69): 77–100, has an annotated bibliography of Maryland promotional literature.

For the Maryland land system, Robert Bruce Harley, "The Land System of Colonial

Maryland" (Ph.D. diss., University of Iowa, 1948), remains valuable. On the extension of English law to America: Carr persuasively argued that Calvert had the 1608 Calvin case in mind when he wrote his colonial charters. She makes this point in "Extension of Empire: English Law in Colonial Maryland," paper presented at the conference "Maryland, A Product of Two Worlds," May 1984.

Anyone studying the Calvert political and religious experience in Maryland must depend on a cluster of historians: Lois Green Carr and David William Jordan, *Maryland's Revolution of Government, 1689–1692* (Ithaca, NY, 1974); Susan R Falb, *Advice and Ascent: The Development of the Maryland Assembly, 1635–1689* (New York, 1986); David W. Jordan, "Maryland's Privy Council, 1637–1715," in *Law, Society, and Politics in Early Maryland: Proceedings of the First Conference on Maryland History*, ed. Aubrey C. Land, Lois Green Carr, and Edward C. Papenfuse (Baltimore, 1977), 65–87; "Political Stability and the Emergence of a Native Elite in Maryland," in *The Chesapeake in the Seventeenth Century: Essays on Anglo-American Society and Politics*, ed. Thad W. Tate and David L. Ammerman (New York, 1979), 243–73; *Foundations of Representative Government in Maryland, 1632–1715* (Cambridge, 1987); Michael James Graham, "Lord Baltimore's Pious Enterprise: Toleration and Community in Colonial Maryland, 1634–1724" (Ph.D. diss., University of Michigan, 1983); John D. Krugler, "Lord Baltimore, Roman Catholics, and Toleration: Religious Policy in Maryland during the Early Catholic Years, 1634–1649," *Catholic Historical Review* 65 (January 1979): 49–75; "'With promise of Liberty in Religion': The Catholic Lords Baltimore and Toleration in Seventeenth-Century Maryland, 1634–1692," *MdHM* 79 (spring 1984): 21–43; Lois Green Carr, "Toleration in Maryland: Why It Ended," in *Lectures in the History of Religious Toleration in Maryland* (Baltimore, 1984), 61–62; and David W. Jordan, "'The Miracle of this Age': Maryland's Experiment in Religious Toleration," *Historian* 47 (May 1985): 338–59.

For social and economic developments, see Gloria L. Main, *Tobacco Colony: Life in Early Maryland, 1650–1720* (Princeton, NJ, 1982); Russell R. Menard, *Economy and Society in Early Maryland* (New York, 1985); "Population, Economy, and Society in Seventeenth-Century Maryland," *MdHM* 79 (spring 1984): 71–92; Lois Green Carr, Russell R. Menard, and Lorena S. Walsh, *Robert Cole's World: Agriculture and Society in Early Maryland* (Chapel Hill, NC, 1991); Lorena S. Walsh and Russell R. Menard, "Death in the Chesapeake: Two Life Tables for Men in Early Colonial Maryland," *MdHM* 69 (fall 1974): 211–27; Lorena S. Walsh, "'Till Death Us Do Part': Marriage and Family in Seventeenth Century Maryland"; and Lois Green Carr and Russell R. Menard, "Immigration and Opportunity: The Freemen of Early Colonial Maryland," both in *Chesapeake in the Seventeenth Century*, ed. Tate and Ammerman, 126–52, 206–42. Architecture reflected life expectancy: Cary Carson, Norman F. Barka, William M. Kelso, Garry Wheeler Stone, and Dell Upton, "Impermanent Architecture in the Southern American Colonies," *Winterthur Portfolio* 16 (summer-autumn 1981): 135–96. Debra A. Meyers, "Religion, Women, and the Family in Maryland, 1634–1713" (Ph.D. diss., University of Rochester, 1997), made a very interesting point about the Calverts' use of inclusive language. For the development of educational institutions, see Robert Ebeling, "Education and Religious Toleration in Seventeenth-Century Maryland" (Ph.D. diss., University of

Maryland, 1991). For manors and religious policy, Gary Wheeler Stone, "Manorial Maryland," *MdHM* 82 (spring 1987): 3–36.

For the civil wars and the interregnum, see J. S. Morrill, *The Revolt of the Provinces: Conservatives and Radicals in the English Civil War, 1630–1650* (London, 1976); J. M. Green, "'England's Wars of Religion'? Religious Conflict and the English Civil Wars," in *Church, Change, and Revolution: Transactions of the Fourth Anglo-Dutch Church History Colloquium* (Leiden, 1991), 100–121; and Claire Cross, "The Church of England 1646–1660," in *The Interregnum: The Quest for Settlement, 1646–1660*, ed. G. E. Aylmer (London, 1972), 99–120.

For the complexities of the English imperial bureaucracy and the complicated personal relationships in the 1650s, I relied on Alison Gilbert Olson, *Anglo-American Politics, 1660–1775: The Relationship between Parties in England and Colonial America* (London, 1973); James W. Vardaman, "Lord Baltimore, Parliament, and Cromwell: A Problem of Church and State in Seventeenth-Century England," *Journal of Church and State* 4 (May 1962): 31–46; and Robert P. Brenner, "Commercial Change and Political Conflict: The Merchant Community in Civil War London" (Ph.D. diss., Princeton University, 1970).

For the controversial lord protector, useful works include J. C. Davis, "Cromwell's Religion," in *Oliver Cromwell and the English Revolution* (London, 1990), 181–208; Blair Worden (who provided the phrase religious *laissez-faire*), "Toleration and the Cromwellian Protectorate," in *Persecution and Toleration*, Studies in Church History, vol. 21 (London, 1984), 190–231; Thomas H. Clancy, "The Jesuits and the Independents, 1647," *Archivium Historicum Societatis Jesu* 40 (1971): 73–85; Roger Howell Jr., "Cromwell and English Liberty," in *Images of Oliver Cromwell: Essays for and by Roger Howell, Jr*, ed. R. C. Richardson (Manchester, 1993), 158–79; and Tom Reilly, *Cromwell: An Honourable Enemy: The Untold Story of the Cromwellian Invasion of Ireland* (Dingle, Co. Kerry, Ireland, 1999).

For the people involved in the Lewis case, I referred to R. B. Jenkins, *Henry Smith: England's Silver-Tongued Preacher* (Macon, GA, 1983); Garry Wheeler Stone, "Society, Housing, and Architecture in Early Maryland: John Lewger's St. John's" (Ph.D. diss., University of Pennsylvania, 1982); and Edwin W. Beitzell, "Thomas Copley, Gentleman," *MdHM* 47 (September 1952): 209–23.

Timothy B. Riordan's meticulous reconstruction of Maryland society before and after Ingle's raid in *The Plundering Time: Maryland in the English Civil War, 1642– 1650* (Baltimore, 2004) renders obsolete older studies. Recent treatments by Russell R. Menard, "Maryland's 'Time of Troubles': Sources of Political Disorder in Early St. Mary's," *MdHM* 76 (June 1981): 124–40; and Lois Green Carr, "Sources of Political Stability and Upheaval in Seventeenth-Century Maryland," *MdHM* 79 (spring 1984): 44–70, remain valuable.

For Catholics, I used James Axtell, "White Legend: The Jesuit Missions in Maryland," in *After Columbus: Essays in the Ethnohistory of Colonial North America* (New York, 1988), 73–85; Edwin W. Beitzell, *The Jesuit Missions of St. Mary's County, Maryland County, Maryland* (privately printed, 1959); "The Maryland Assembly of 1638/1639," *Chronicles of St. Mary's* 7 (1959): 396–401; Gerald P. Fogarty, "Property and Religious

Liberty in Colonial Maryland Catholic Thought," *Catholic Historical Review* 72 (October 1986): 573–600; James Hennessy, "Roman Catholicism: The Maryland Tradition," *Thought: A Review of Culture and Ideas* 51 (September 1976): 282–95; Michael L. Carrafiello, "Runnymeade or Rome? Thomas Copley, Magna Carta, and *In Coena Domini*," *Maryland Historian* 16 (1985): 59–69; Thomas O'Brien Hanley, "Church and State in the Maryland Ordinance of 1639," *Church History* 26 (December 1957): 325–41; and *Their Rights and Liberties* (Westminster, 1959).

For Protestants, Lawrence C. Wroth, "The First Sixty Years of the Church of England in Maryland, 1632–1692," *MdHM* 11 (March 1916): 1–41; and Babette May Levy, "Puritanism in the Southern and Island Colonies," in *Proceedings of the American Antiquarian Society* 70, pt. 1 (April 1960): 69–348; Dennis M. Moran, "Anti-Catholicism in Early Maryland Politics: The Puritan Influence," American Catholic Historical Society of Philadelphia, *Records* 61 (September 1950): 139–54; Michael James Graham, "Popish Plots: Protestant Fears in Early Colonial Maryland, 1676–1689," *Catholic Historical Review* 79 (April 1993): 197–216; and Eric John Maloney, "Papists and Puritans in Early Maryland: Religion in the Forming of Provincial Society, 1632–1665" (Ph.D. diss., State University of New York at Stony Brook, 1996). For Lumbrozo, Carr's unpublished paper "Jacob, Alias, John Lumbrozo (?between Nov. 17, 1665 and May 1666)," Historic St. Mary's City Research Report, July 1, 1989, collected the limited material on the Jewish doctor. Raphael Semmes, *Crime and Punishment in Early Maryland* (Baltimore, 1938), summarized his legal difficulties.

For Quakers, Kenneth L. Carroll's studies provide the broadest analysis: "Maryland Quakers in the Seventeenth Century," *MdHM* 47 (December 1952): 297–313; "Persecution of Quakers in Early Maryland (1658–1661)," *Quaker History* 53 (autumn 1964): 67–80; "Thomas Thurston, Renegade Maryland Quaker," *MdHM* 62 (1967): 170–92; "Quaker Opposition to the Establishment of a State Church in Maryland," *MdHM* 65 (summer 1970): 149–70; and "Elizabeth Harris, the Founder of American Quakerism," *Quaker History* 58 (autumn 1968): 96–111. Studies by J. Reaney Kelly, *Quakers in the Founding of Anne Arundel County, Maryland* (Baltimore, 1963); David W. Jordan, "'Gods Candle' within Government: Quakers and Politics in Early Maryland," *William and Mary Quarterly*, 3rd. ser., 39 (October 1982): 628–53; Michael James Graham, "'The Collapse of Equity': Catholic and Quaker Dissenters in Maryland, 1692–1720," *MdHM* 88 (spring 1993): 4–25; and "Meetinghouse and Chapel: Religion and Community in Seventeenth-Century Maryland," in *Colonial Chesapeake Society*, ed. Carr, Morgan, and Russo, 242–74, provided valuable information on Quaker interaction with the Calverts. For English Quakers, I consulted Barry Reay, *The Quakers and the English Revolution* (New York, 1985).

Historical archaeologists at Historic St. Mary's City have made significant contributions by uncovering and analyzing the remains of the city. Henry M. Miller broke new ground with his "Baroque Cities in the Wilderness: Archaeology and Urban Development in the Colonial Chesapeake," *Historic Archaeology* 22 (1988): 57–73; and "Archaeology and Town Planning in Early British America," in *Old Worlds and New Worlds: Historical/Post Medieval Archaeology Papers*, ed. Geoff Egan and R. L. Michael (Oxford,

1999), 72–83. For the chapel, I referred to Timothy B. Riordan, Silas D. Hurry, and Henry M. Miller, "'A Good Brick Chappell': The Archaeology of the c. 1667 Catholic Chapel at St. Mary's City, Maryland," draft, Historic St. Mary's City Archaeology Series, no. 3 (St. Mary's City, 1995).

The Calvert vision created a secular state. For secularization, I relied on Peter Burke, "Religion and Secularisation," in *The New Cambridge Modern History*, vol. 13, *Companion Volume* (Cambridge, 1979); and C. John Sommerville, *The Secularization of Early Modern England: From Religious Culture to Religious Faith* (New York, 1992), 293–317. For issues relating to toleration in England, I consulted John Miller, *Popery and Politics in England, 1660–1688* (Cambridge, 1973), 204. Thomas J. Curry, *The First Freedoms: Church and State in America to the Passage of the First Amendment* (New York, 1986), gives another perspective on Calvert achievements.

Maryland Catholics lost most heavily with the Protestant ascendancy. For their fortunes in the eighteenth century, see Beatriz Betancourt Hardy, "Papists in a Protestant Age: The Catholic Gentry and Community in Colonial Maryland, 1689–1776" (Ph.D. diss., University of Maryland, 1993); "Roman Catholics, Not Papists: Catholic Identity in Maryland, 1689–1776," *MdHM* 92 (summer 1997): 139–81; and Tricia Terese Pyne, "The Maryland Catholic Community, 1690–1775: A Study in Culture, Region, and Church" (Ph.D. diss., Catholic University of America, 1995). For English Catholics, A. B. Forbes, "The Struggle for Roman Catholic Civil Rights in Eighteenth-Century England," *Michigan Academician* 1 (spring 1969): 81–91.

Index